Citizenship, Gender and Diversity

Series Editors
Beatrice Halsaa
Centre for Gender Research
University of Oslo
Oslo, Norway

Sasha Roseneil
Faculty of Social and Historical Sciences
University College London
London, UK

Sevil Sümer
Department of Sociology
University of Bergen
Bergen, Norway

Aims of the Series
Developed out of FEMCIT, a research project funded under the Sixth Framework of the European Commission examining gendered citizenship, multiculturalism and the impact of contemporary women's movements in Europe, the series also welcomes submissions from scholars around the globe working in this area on projects with either a European or international focus.

More information about this series at
http://www.palgrave.com/gp/series/14900

Trine Rogg Korsvik

Politicizing Rape and Pornography

1970s Feminist Movements in France and Norway

Translated by Elisabet Rogg, with Trine Rogg Korsvik

Trine Rogg Korsvik
Kilden Gender Research.no
Oslo, Norway

Translated by
Elisabet Rogg
Nesodden, Norway

Citizenship, Gender and Diversity
ISBN 978-3-030-55638-9   ISBN 978-3-030-55639-6   (eBook)
https://doi.org/10.1007/978-3-030-55639-6

Preface

Today, sexuality and abuse are discussed intensively in online spaces. Through organized internet campaigns, women and girls speak openly about the sexual abuse they have endured. In addition, complicated questions have arisen around these topics: is it appropriate to publicize names of the abusers? Is the extent of the sexualized violence exaggerated, or is it just the tip of the iceberg? Does pornography work as a positive means of sexual liberation, or is it commercial exploitation and a form of prostitution in front of cameras? The answers to such questions are far from unanimous, even among feminists.

However, public debates about sex, violence and feminism are not new. For hundreds of years, sexuality and rape have been the subjects of legislative regulations. When the modern women's emancipation movement arose in the second half of the nineteenth century, suffragettes not only promoted equal rights for women, but they also put rape and the sexual exploitation of women through prostitution on the agenda. In the context of the women's liberation movement of the 1970s, feminist activists made the fight against the sexual oppression of women one of their main political issues.

Sex and violence do not become political issues by themselves— someone has to take action. This book is precisely about the politicization of such phenomena, that is, how sex and violence have been discussed in public; how such phenomena have been understood and explained; and how they have become subject to legal regulations. A lot has been written about law regulations and public debates about sex and violence; however, it has been less common to direct attention to how grassroots activists have dealt with such issues. To get attention, feminist grassroots activists have had to shout louder than politicians, religious leaders, journalists, lawyers, sexologists, and other academics. Often, grassroots activists' views have been caricatured or oversimplified.

In this book, feminist grassroots activists play the lead role. Attention is directed to how French and Norwegian feminist activists have constructed sex and violence as specific feminist political issues; how they have mobilized and campaigned, argued with opponents and with each other; how they have performed in the media and how they have made new alliances.

Even if feminist grassroots activists are playing the lead role in this book, there are no winners in this book. The politicization of rape and pornography has aroused controversy also among feminists, who have agreed neither on political ideologies nor on strategies. However, knowing the history of the politicization of rape and pornography gives a better understanding of present-days debates about sexual exploitation and violence against women.

This book is based on material from the doctoral thesis *"Pornografi er teori, voldtekt er praksis": Kvinnekamp mot voldtekt og pornografi i Frankrike og Norge ca. 1970–1985* [*"Pornography is the theory, and rape is the practice": Women's struggle against rape and pornography in France and Norway ca. 1970–1985*], funded by the research project FEMCIT— Gendered Citizenship in Multicultural Europe: The Impact of Contemporary Women's Movements, and defended for the Ph.D. degree at the Faculty of Humanities, University of Oslo, in 2014. The thesis is based on comprehensive source material, including newspapers, radio and television programs, feminist publications, archival material by organizations and interviews with former activists. As the title of the thesis indicates, the account concludes in the 1980s, while this book continues into recent times. To explore how French and Norwegian feminist activists of the 2010s politicized sexual violence and exploitation, a handful of them were interviewed in the summer of 2017.

Nesodden, Norway   Trine Rogg Korsvik

Acknowledgments

I wish to thank a number of people for the realization of this book: my former colleagues at the Centre of Gender Research at the University of Oslo, and my former supervisors Knut Kjeldstadli and Beatrice Halsaa, for their advice and enthusiasm. Thanks also to Editor of Cappelen Damm Akademisk, Elisabeth Holmberg, for supporting the book project, and to external reviewer Tone Hellesund who critically commented on a previous version of the manuscript. I am deeply grateful to the women who benevolently shared their activist experiences with me or who have lent me archival material: Ellen Aanesen, Liv Alming, Inge Ås, Birgit Bjerck, Alison Boyer, Liv Finstad, Liv Jakobsen, Cathrine Linn Kristiansen, Claudine Legardinier, Sissa Lindqvist, Gro Nylander, Eléonore Stévenin-Morguet, Ane Stø, Vigdis Vollset, and the two anonymous former activists "Anne" and "Kari."

As for the English version of the book, I wish to thank Palgrave Macmillan and the editors of the *Citizenship, Gender, and Diversity* series for inviting me to publish an English translation of the book. I would also like to thank former Palgrave Editor Amelia Derkatsch and current Palgrave Editor Nina Guttapalle for providing practical support.

I owe profound thanks to my mother Elisabet Rogg for helping me with the translation from Norwegian to English, and to Tom Bechtle, a hardworking American proofreader, who patiently and carefully helped me with every single sentence of the manuscript. Also, I am grateful to the Centre of Gender Research at the University of Oslo for having funded Mr. Bechtle's thorough proofreading work. Last, but not least, I thank my husband and children for their patience with me.

CONTENTS

LIST OF FIGURES

CHAPTER 1

The Sexual Revolution and the Women's Liberation Movement

INTRODUCTION

How did sexual exploitation, abuse, and violence against women become gender-political issues? This book relates how feminist movements in Norway and France have politicized rape, pornography, and the sexual exploitation of women from the 1970s to the present. It is a compelling tale of sex and violence, brutal political disputes, hazardous actions, and blunt confrontations between feminist activists and their opponents. It is also a story about consciousness-raising, laborious political work, strategy development, and the formation of new alliances. The narrative is set in the recent past and describes how collective mobilization succeeded in bringing previously undiscussed matters into the public arena. Sexuality, gender, and power were now debated in a way that had been unthinkable, and to such an extent that legislative changes ultimately resulted.

The struggle against sexual exploitation and abuse of women that characterized the 1970s women's liberation movement was transnational. However, there were national variations as to how the women's liberation movements engaged politically: how they mobilized, what their main targets were, the types of action they carried out, the alliances they made, and the outcomes of their mobilizations. The focus of this book will be on the women's liberation movements' politicization of sexual exploitation, abuse, and violence against women in France and Norway. The rather different political, social, and cultural contexts of these countries had an

© The Author(s) 2021
T. R. Korsvik, *Politicizing Rape and Pornography*,
Citizenship, Gender and Diversity,
https://doi.org/10.1007/978-3-030-55639-6_1

impact on the character of the women's movements and on their political opportunities therein. Further, contact between the women's movements in France and Norway was, and still is, scarce. As a consequence, the politicizations of sexual exploitation and abuse of women were articulated differently. In France, fighting rape became one of the most important issues for the women's liberation movement after abortion on demand was sanctioned in 1974. In Norway, on the other hand, battling pornography became the top priority of the women's liberation movement in the late 1970s.

Despite their differences, the two movements—the mobilization against rape in France and against pornography in Norway—had much in common. On the one hand, they aimed to change structural gendered power relations; on the other, they sought to transform intimate relations, including individual men's sexual and violent behaviors. In both countries, the politicization of sexual exploitation and abuse of women gave rise to increased feminist activity and mobilization in the second half of the 1970s, as well as the formation of new alliances, including with actors outside the radical women's movement. In both countries, women's liberation activists engaged in militant actions to draw attention to the sexual exploitation of women as a social problem in need of a political solution. These often controversial actions attracted media attention, and, as a result, politicians, intellectuals, and other groups outside the women's movement, such as labor unions, became engaged in the matter. As a response to the feminist mobilizations, legislative reforms were made in the 1980s. In France, a new law against rape was adopted in 1980; in Norway, legislation regarding pornography was updated in 1985. In the parliamentary debates in both France and Norway, the MPs referred specifically to the mobilization of the women's movements as instrumental in precipitating change, and argued that the sexual exploitation of women was inconsistent with the ideals of a gender-equal society.

Yet this account is not an unqualified success story. Rape is still a problem, and the pornography industry has expanded considerably since the 1980s. In the 2010s there remains no general consensus on where to set the boundaries between sexual liberty and abuse, or between freedom of expression and offensive actions. As in the 1970s, these continue to be contentious issues, even among feminists. Political efforts aimed at combatting pornography and rape continue to be interpreted as attacks on sexual freedom, expressions of prudishness or hatred of men, or a perception of women as passive victims. To understand the dilemmas and controversies surrounding the issue of sexual exploitation and violence against women as gender-political matters, one must revisit the 1960s and the sexual revolution.

ANTIAUTHORITARIAN REVOLT AND THE SEXUAL REVOLUTION OF THE 1960S

The 1960s were characterized by economic growth and modernization as well as by political and cultural upheaval. Never before in history had so many young people possessed the economic means to seek higher education and to buy goods that were specifically targeted to them as a new group of consumers. The baby-boom generation used its newfound freedom to question and challenge the authority and morality of parents, teachers, governments, and other representatives of the established order. The 1960s were also characterized by the Cold War, anti-colonial liberation wars in the "Third World," the civil rights movement and rise of the Black Panthers in the United States, and student protests all over the world. A "New Left" radicalism arose, one that promoted participatory democracy and autonomy, freedom of speech and civil rights, while opposing capitalism, imperialism, and militarism, but distancing itself from Soviet-style communism.[1] The radicalization of this "New Left" was triggered by the U.S. war in Vietnam from 1964 onward—a war broadcast on television in a detailed way never before seen, shocking the viewers. The student and workers' revolts that erupted in many countries in 1968 led to further radicalization. In France, seven million people took part in the general strike of May–June 1968, the highest-ever turnout in France.

In the late 1960s, many young people in the West became fascinated by Chairman Mao and the Cultural Revolution he had initiated

---

[1] The radicalization in the 1960s is a major international research field. Here I confine myself to referencing a small selection of research into 1960s radicalism in France and Norway: Artières, Philippe, and Michelle Zancarini-Fournel (eds.) (2008): *68. Une histoire collective (1962–81)* [68: A Collective History (1962–81)]. Paris: Éditions La Découverte; Førland, Tor Egil, and Trine Rogg Korsvik (eds.) (2006): *1968. Opprør og motkultur på norsk* [1968: Rebellion and Counterculture in Norway]. Oslo: Pax Forlag; Førland, Tor Egil, and Trine Rogg Korsvik (2008): *Ekte sekstiåttere* [Real Sixty-Eighters]. Oslo: Gyldendal Akademisk; Godbolt, James (2008): *Den norske vietnambevegelsen 1967–1973* [The Norwegian Vietnam Movement 1967–1973]. DPhil thesis, Faculty of Humanities, University of Oslo.

in China in 1966, which they interpreted as a revolt by youth against adult authority. At the same time, anarchist ideals gained popularity. Anti-conformist politics and lifestyles merged, and young people, as well as some adults, sought new and more "authentic" ways of being together, free of what they perceived to be oppressive power relations. The anti-conformist lifestyles were displayed through experimental rock music, long hair, psychedelic drugs, and sexual experimentation. The sexual revolution, which brought with it easier access to birth control such as "the pill," undermined conventional norms of sexual behavior. Marriage as the "natural" institution for regulating heterosexual intercourse was no longer considered the prototype. On the contrary, sexual activity outside monogamy was part of the antiauthoritarian revolt.

The Women's Liberation Movement

Many women participated enthusiastically in the new social movements that emerged in the 1960s, including the student movement, the Vietnam War protests, and the civil rights movement. However, some female activists began to question women's positions in these antiauthoritarian movements. They pointed to the fact that men had all the leading roles in the movements, that men spoke the most at meetings, and that women generally had subordinate roles, being assigned to boring, menial tasks such as making coffee. In addition, they complained that women were expected to be sexually available to male activists so as not to be perceived as "prudes." In response to what some women experienced as persistent male dominance in the movements of the New Left, a new sort of women's movement emerged in the United States in the late 1960s. Rude and provocative in style, these women fought for their own liberation.[2] They believed that in order to liberate women from oppression, it was necessary for women to organize themselves into groups that offered no access to men. The idea was that women, like other oppressed groups, had to fight for their own liberation without interference from their

---

[2] On the U.S. women's liberation movement in the 1960s and 1970s, see, for example, Rosen, Ruth (2000): *The World Split Open: How the Modern Women's Movement Changed America*. New York: Viking.

oppressors.[3] The separatist strategy could seem provocative both to men who felt excluded and to women who were used to seeing themselves

[3] On the women's liberation movement of the 1970s, especially the one that took place in France and Norway, see, for example, Bard, Christine (2012): *Le féminisme au-delà des idées reçues* [Feminism Beyond Preconceived Ideas]. Paris: Editions Le Cavalier Bleu; Bergen Kvinnesaksforening [Bergen Association for Women's Rights] (2007): *Vi var med ... Kvinnekamp i Bergen på 1970-tallet* [We Participated ... Women's Struggle in Bergen in the 1970s]. Bergen: Bodoni Forlag; Bergman, Solveig (2002): *The Politics of Feminism: Autonomous Feminist Movements in Finland and West Germany from the 1960s to the 1980s*. Turku: Åbo Akademi University Press; Bernheim, Cathy, Liliane Kandel, Françoise Picq, and Nadia Ringart (eds.) (2009): *Mouvement de Libération des Femmes. Textes premiers* [The Feminist Movement: First Texts]. Paris: Stock; Blom, Ida (2005): "Brudd og kontinuitet. Fra 1950 mot årtusenskiftet" [Rupture and Continuity: From 1950 to the Turn of the Millennium], in I. Blom and S. Sogner (eds.): *Med kjønnsperspektiv på norsk historie* [Gender Perspective on Norwegian History]. Oslo: Cappelen Akademisk Forlag; Bonnet, Marie-Josèphe (2012): *Histoire de l'émancipation des femmes* [History of Women's Emancipation]. Editions Ouest-France; Chaperon, Sylvie (2000): *Les années Beauvoir (1945–1970)* [The Years of Beauvoir (1945–1970)]. Paris: Fayard; Dahlerup, Drude (1998): *Rødstrømperne. Den danske Rødstrømpebevægelses udvikling, nytænkning og gennemslag 1970–1985* [Red Stockings: The Danish Red-Stockings Movement's Development, Innovation and Impact, 1970–1985]. Copenhagen: Gyldendal; Danielsen, Hilde (ed.) (2013): *Da det personlige ble politisk. Den nye kvinne- og mannsbevegelsen på 1970-tallet* [When the Personal Became Political: The New Women's and Men's Movement in the 1970s]. Oslo: Scandinavian Academic Press/Spartacus Forlag; Duchen, Claire (1986): *Feminism in France: From May '68 to Mitterand*. London, Boston, and Henley: Routledge & Kegan Paul; Ezekiel, Judith (2002): "Le Women's Lib: Made in France," *European Journal of Women's Studies*, vol. 9, no. 3, pp. 345–361; Fouque, Antoinette et al. (eds.) (2008): *Génération MLF 1968–2008* [The MLF Generation 1968–2008]. Paris: Des femmes—Antoinette Fouque; Greenwald, Lisa (2019): *Daughters of 1968: Redefining French Feminism and the Women's Liberation Movement*. Lincoln, NE: University of Nebraska Press;Gulli, Brita M. (1979): "Flat organisering" [Flat Organization], *Pax Leksikon*. Oslo: Pax Forlag, pp. 352–356; Hagemann, Gro (2004): "Norsk nyfeminisme—amerikansk import?" [Norwegian New Feminism—American Import?], *Nytt Norsk Tidsskrift*, nos. 3–4; Haukaa, Runa (1982): *Bak slagordene. Den nye kvinnebevegelsen i Norge* [Behind the Slogans: The New Women's Movement in Norway]. Oslo: Pax Forlag; Isaksson, Emma (2007): *Kvinnokamp. Synen på underordning och motstånd i den nya kvinnorörelsen* [Women's Struggle; The View of Subordination and Resistance in the New Women's Movement]. Stockholm: Atlas; Jaggar, Alison M. (1983): *Feminist Politics and Human Nature*. Totowa, NJ: Rowman & Allanheld; Jenson, Jane (1996): "Representations of Difference: The Varieties of French Feminism," in M. Threlfall (ed.): *Mapping the Women's Movement: Feminist Politics and Social Transformation in the North*. London: Verso; Korsvik, Trine Rogg (2010): "Kvinnekamp! Politiske spenninger i kvinnefrigjøringsbevegelsene i Norge og Frankrike i 1970-åra" [Women's Struggle! Political Tensions in the Women's Liberation Movements in Norway and France in the 1970s], in I. Helle, K. Kjeldstadli, and J. Sørvoll (eds.): *Historier om motstand* [Histories About Resistance]. Oslo: Abstrakt forlag; Korsvik, Trine Rogg (2013): *"Pornografi er teori, voldtekt er praksis": Kvinnekamp mot voldtekt og pornografi i Frankrike og Norge ca. 1970–1985*

"as activists like everyone else."[4] Nevertheless, the women's liberation movement spread rapidly from the United States to other countries. The number of women participating in this transnational movement is not known. Nonetheless, in a few frenetic years they succeeded in changing cultural ideas about what women should say and do, and in expanding the notion of what was considered political.

Breaking down the boundaries between what was considered private and public, and between the individual and the collective, was typical of the 1970s women's liberation movement. What had been considered personal problems in the individual woman's everyday life were placed in a political and collective context, as formulated in the internationally famous feminist slogan "the personal is political."[5] Unintended

["Pornography Is the Theory, and Rape Is the Practice": Woman's Struggle Against Rape and Pornography in France and Norway approx. 1970–1985]. PhD thesis in history. Department of Archeology, Conservation and History, Faculty of Humanities, University of Oslo; Lønnå, Elisabeth (1996): *Stolthet og kvinnekamp. Norsk Kvinnesaksforenings historie fra 1913* [Pride and Women's Struggle: History of the Norwegian Association for Women's Rights 1913]. Oslo: Gyldendal Norsk Forlag; Nørve, Siri (1978): "Bevisstgjøring" [Consciousness Raising], *Pax Leksikon*. Oslo: Pax Forlag, pp. 366–369; Picq, Françoise (1993): *Libération des femmes. Les années mouvement* [Liberation of Women: The Movement Years]. Paris: Éditions du Seuil; Remy, Monique (1990): *De l'utopie à l'intégration. Histoire des mouvements des femmes* [From Utopia to Integration: History of Women's Movements]. Paris: L'Harmattan; Riot-Sarcey, Michèle (2002): *Histoire du féminisme* [The History of Feminism]. Paris: La Découverte; Rowbotham, Sheila (1990): *The Past Is Before Us: Feminism in Action since the 1960s*. Harmondsworth: Penguin Books; Rowbotham, Sheila (1996): "Introduction: Mapping the Women's Movement," in M. Threlfall (ed.): *Mapping the Women's Movement: Feminist Politics and Social Transformation in the North*. London: Verso; Sineau, Mariette (2003 [1991]): "The MLF's Contribution to the Political Scene: An Unacknowledged Debt," in D. Haase-Dubosc et al. (eds.): *French Feminism: An Indian Anthology*. New Delhi: Sage Publications; Storti, Martine (2010): *Je suis une femme, pourquoi pas vous? 1974–1979. Quand je racontais le mouvement des femmes dans Libération* [I Am a Woman, Why Not You? 1974–1979: When I Told About the Women's Liberation Movement]. Paris: Éditions Michel de Maule; Wiig, Birgit (1984): *Kvinner selv* [Women Themselves]. Oslo: Cappelen; Zancarini-Fournel, Michelle (2004): *Le siècle des féminismes* [The Century of Feminisms]. Paris: L'Atelier; Zancarini-Fournel, Michelle (2005): *Histoire des femmes en France: XIXe–XXe siècles* [The History of Women in France: XIXth–XXth Centuries]. Rennes: Presses Universitaires de Rennes.

[4] Picq 1993, p. 16.

[5] According to Rosen, it was Carol Hanisch, an activist in the civil rights movement and a member of the New York Radical Women, who launched this slogan in 1968. Rosen 2000, p. 196.

pregnancies, lack of career opportunities, low wages, burdensome house-work chores, the threat of rape, invisibility, commodification of the female body, and sexist jokes—in short, all kinds of phenomena that women experienced as limiting their freedom to flourish as autonomous human beings—were politicized. The struggle for women's liberation took place in most areas, and by the 1970s there was hardly a single phenomenon, from social structures to the very intimate, that was not politicized and analyzed according to a woman's perspective. Events that occurred in the family, at work and in school, on the streets and in bed, were explained as manifestations of a power relationship wherein men as a group wielded the dominant power. The women's liberation struggle was about revealing and challenging such power relations—or women's oppression, as it was typically named—through consciousness-raising groups, political action, text production, arts and music, and other means. The aim was not gender equality with men, but the liberation of women.

In the 1970s, women's liberation was a revolutionary project. However, the utopian visions were not regarded as a distant goal; the revolution was already underway, and the goal of political organizing was to point to a completely different future in which the subjuga-tion of women was entirely absent. Accordingly, the activists wanted to include all women in the making of a new politics based on their personal situation. Also, they aimed at avoiding all sorts of hierarchies in the feminist groups, through participatory democracy or "flat" structure without formal leaders. Rather than dealing with established institutions or abstract theories, the politics of liberation was to be based on the direct personal experiences of activists. The philosophy was that "only the wearer knows where the shoe pinches." Engaging in charity work and fighting on behalf of others was now rejected; women were to take up the fight on their own behalf.

The participants in the women's liberation movement strongly believed that it was possible to change the world and that "sisterhood is powerful," as a famous American feminist slogan went. Instead of women competing with each other, they were to find out what they had in common and support each other. Since women's liberation was a struggle for freedom and autonomy, the call for abortion on demand was undoubtedly the major issue that united the women's liberation movements across the West (Fig. 1.1). Whereas most countries of the communist Soviet bloc had already liberalized their policies on abortion, it was not until the

Fig. 1.1 Abortion on demand was the single most important demand of the 1970s women's liberation movement of the West, including at this rally in Oslo on the International Women's Day 8th of March, 1974 (Photo: Unknown © The Norwegian Labour Movement Archives and Library (Arbark) [Reprinted with permission])

1970s that Western countries liberalized their abortion laws. In the same decade, reforms that granted formal gender equality were enacted.

The Feminist Mobilization for Abortion Rights and Against Sexual Exploitation and Abuse of Women

The feminist mobilization for abortion on demand was framed as women's right to control their own bodies, an idea that was also applied when feminists in many countries from the mid-1970s on began to mobilize against the sexual exploitation and abuse of women and girls. This rising up to combat what was eventually framed as sexual violence against women also included fighting pornography and prostitution. Until then, these phenomena had taken a back seat to feminist demands for abortion rights, workplace equality, equal pay, and free childcare, as gender-political issues.[6] In the early 1970s, sexual exploitation and abuse of women was generally regarded as politically irrelevant and thus rarely spoken of. According to American historian Ruth Rosen, one of the most important contributions of the women's liberation movement to society was its making public of previously "hidden crimes" such as rape, wife battering, incest, and sexual harassment.[7] By the 1980s, the "sex crimes" identified by the women's liberation movement in the 1970s were recognized as societal problems by the authorities. Hence, bringing an end to sexual abuse became a matter of public gender equality policies.

Research on women's movements in many countries shows that campaigns against sexual exploitation and violence against women had a mobilizing effect on the women's liberation movements of the mid-1970s, which had experienced a certain downward cycle once the first euphoric years of the early 1970s had passed.[8] Key to this revitalization was the organizing of large international feminist conferences in which sexual violence against women was placed on the agenda. The women's conference in Mexico in 1975 (organized as an alternative to the official United Nations' International Women's Year, which many grassroots

---

[6] But see Hagemann, Gro (2003): "Seksualmoral eller samfunnsmoral: stridende dirskurser i sedelighetsdebatten" [Sexual Morality or Social Morality: Conflicting Discourses in the Moral Debate], in G. Hagemann, *Feminisme og historieskriving. Inntrykk fra en reise* [Feminism and Historiography: Impressions from a Journey]. Oslo: Universitetsforlaget; Kingsley Kent, Susan (1987): *Sex and Suffrage in Britain 1860–1914*. Princeton, NJ: Princeton University Press; Korsvik, Trine Rogg (2014): "Fra offentlig skjøgevæsen til horekunder. Hundre års kollektiv mobilisering mot prostitusjon" [From Public Prostitution to Sex Buyers: One Hundred Years of Collective Mobilization Against Prostitution]. *Materialisten. Tidsskrift for forskning, fagkritikk og teoretisk debatt*, nos. 1–2 (2014), pp. 11–43; Riot-Sarcey, Michèle (2008): *Histoire du féminisme* [History of Feminism]. Paris: Éditions La Découverte.

[7] Rosen 2000, p. 184.

[8] See, e.g., Bronstein, Carolyn (2011): *Battling Pornography: The American Feminist Anti-pornography Movement, 1976–1986*. Cambridge: Cambridge University Press; Long, Julia (2012): *Anti-porn: The Resurgence of Anti-pornography Feminism*. London: Zed Books; Hellesund, Tone (2013): "Intimiteter i forandring—om hvordan den nye norske kvinnebevegelsen satte intimitet på dagsordenen" [Intimacy in Change—On How the New Norwegian Women's Movement Put Intimacy on the Agenda], in H. Danielsen (ed.): *Da det personlige ble politisk. Den nye kvinne- og manns-bevegelsen på 1970-tallet* [When the Personal Became Political: The New Women's and Men's Movement in the 1970s]. Oslo: Scandinavian Academic Press/Spartacus Forlag. Also see Bergman 2002; Haukaa 1982; Isaksson 2007; Korsvik 2013; Lønnå 1996; Picq 1993; Remy 1990; Rosen 2000; Rowbotham 1990 and 1996.

feminists perceived as too top-down and bureaucratic), as well as the International Tribunal on Crimes against Women in Brussels in 1976, offered opportunities for thousands of women activists from all parts of the world to come together.[9] These conferences contributed to the transnational exchange of ideas and experiences. For example, in Norway, the first shelter for battered and raped women was created by members of the New Feminists who had attended the Brussels Tribunal in 1976, where they had learned about the British feminist crisis center movement. Inspired by that initiative's model of women helping other women in feminist sister solidarity, the Camilla Crisis Centre was opened in Oslo in 1978, the first such facility in the Nordic countries. Feminist activists, not least from the United States, published a series of books and articles on rape and other forms of sexual violence against women that received international attention. By the 1970s, their belief that there was a connection between rape and pornography, as powerfully stated in U.S. radical feminist Robin Morgan's slogan "Pornography is the theory, and rape is the practice," was adopted by feminist movements in several countries.[10]

However, there were local variations in regard to political praxis. In France, fighting rape became a major issue for the *Mouvement de libération des femmes* (Women's liberation movement), while in Norway the struggle against sexual exploitation and the abuse of women was primarily manifested as a forceful, uncompromising mobilization against pornography. In order to explain these differences in political priorities, this book compares the women's movements in France and Norway and their interactions with other actors, including social movements, intellectuals, institutions, and the media. The study employs a wide selection of primary sources, ranging from various organizations' archival material,

[9] Russell, Diana E.H., and Nicole Van de Ven (1976): *Crimes Against Women: Proceedings of the International Tribunal.* Milbrae, CA: Les Femmes; Halsaa, Beatrice (2007): "Det internasjonale kvinneåret 1975" [The International Women's Year 1975], Kvinnehistorie.no.

[10] Morgan, Robin (1977): "Theory and Practice: Pornography and Rape," *Going Too Far: The Personal Chronicle of a Feminist.* New York: Random House.

women's movement publications, and interviews with activists, to newspaper articles and radio and television broadcasts. The research literature in the field is relatively sparse, but is considerably more extensive in France than in Norway.[11]

CROSS-NATIONAL COMPARISON OF WOMEN'S MOVEMENTS

Since the nineteenth century, women's movements have been transnational and have shared many political demands across countries. Nevertheless, in historical research, cross-national comparisons have been rare.[12] Most often, such studies are restricted to the women's movement in a single country. There are valid reasons for taking this national approach, but it may facilitate oversimplified explanations, such as describing a phenomenon as "typical" of the country in question. Take as an illustration the way in which the standard reference work on Norwegian history of ideas represents the feminist mobilization against pornography in Norway as a "particular Norwegian" phenomenon. Here, the author claims that the Norwegian women's liberation movement turned its attention to fighting pornography because it "presented itself in a more puritan

---

[11] In addition to the general literature on the French women's movement referenced above, there is also research on the development of sexual politics in France, for example: Welzer-Lang, Daniel (1988): *Le viol au masculin* [Masculine Rape]. Paris: Éditions L'Harmattan; Mossuz-Lavau, Janine (1991): *Les lois de l'amour. Les politiques de la sexualité en France (1970–1990)* [The Laws of Love: The Politics of Sexuality in France (1970–1990)]. Paris: Éditions Payot; Vigarello, Georges (1998): *Histoire du viol. XVI–XXI siècle* [History of Rape: XVI–XXI Century]. Paris: Éditions du Seuil; Corbin, Alain, Jean-Jacques Courtine, and Georges Vigarello (eds.) (2006): *Histoire du corps* [History of the Body], vol. 2, *Les mutations du regard. Le XXe siècle* [The Mutations of the Gaze: The Twentieth Century]. Paris: Éditions du Seuil. On the details of the primary sources used for this book, see the list of references.

[12] See, e.g., Delamotte, Eugenia, Natania Meeker, and Jean O'Barr (1997): *A Global Anthology of Women's Resistance: From 600 B.C.E. to Present*. New York: Routledge; McFadden, Margaret H. (1999): *Golden Cables of Sympathy: The Transatlantic Sources of Nineteenth-Century Feminism*. Lexington: University Press of Kentucky; Ferree, Myra Marx, and Carol McClurg Mueller (2004): "Feminism and the Women's Movement: A Global Perspective," in D.A. Snow, S.A. Soule, and H. Kriesi (eds.): *The Blackwell Companion to Social Movements*. Malden, MA: Blackwell; Ferree, Myra Marx, and Aili Mari Tripp (eds.) (2006): *Global Feminism: Transnational Women's Activism, Organizing, and Human Rights*. New York: New York University Press; Rupp, Leila J. (1997): *Worlds of Women: The Making of an International Women's Liberation Movement*. Princeton, NJ: Princeton University Press.

version" than in other countries, such as Denmark.[13] Admittedly, feminist anti-pornography campaigns were rarely carried out in Denmark. The reason was, according to political scientist Drude Dahlerup, that the Danish Red-Stocking Movement (*Rødstrømpebevægelsen*) was part of a libertarian, left-wing movement that considered pornography to embody rebellion against the prudish morale of the bourgeoisie. In Denmark, the left was pushing for the complete legalization of all sorts of pornography, which in fact was enacted into law in 1969.[14] However, in regard to the framing of pornography as a gender-political issue, it was the Danish women's liberation movement, and not the Norwegian, that differed from similar movements in other countries. For example, feminist activists in Sweden, the United Kingdom, the United States, West Germany, and France campaigned against pornography in the 1970s. Their arguments against it were similar: Pornography was framed as a manifestation of how a patriarchal, capitalist society utilized the female body as a commodity, and feminists protested against men's power to define and judge women's value as sex objects.[15] In several countries, feminist activists engaged in spectacular acts of resistance against sexist commercials, porn shops, and sex clubs in the early 1970s, and the campaign against pornography gained importance from the mid-1970s into the 1980s. But contrary to the Norwegian case, the anti-pornography campaigns in the United Kingdom and particularly in the United States caused wrenching divisions in the feminist movements, as some intellectual feminists disagreed that pornography was necessarily oppressive to women. In the United States, the conflict over pornography culminated in the so-called "feminist sex wars" of the early 1980s that left deep divisions in the movement and a weakened feminist anti-pornography campaign.[16] This example illustrates the value of cross-national comparisons: on the one hand, there were transnational similarities in terms of how women's liberation movements framed pornography as a gender-political issue; on the other, there were

[13] Hompland, Andreas (2003): "Det feminiserte Norge" [The Feminized Norway], in T. Berg-Eriksen, A. Hompland, and E. Tjønneland (eds.): *Et lite land i verden. Norsk idéhistorie* [A Small Country in the World: Norwegian History of Ideas], vol. VI. Oslo: Aschehoug, p. 284.

[14] Dahlerup 1998, vol. 1, p. 529.

[15] See Isaksson 2007; Long 2012; Rowbotham 1990 and 1996; Bronstein 2011; Rosen 2000; Bergman 2002.

[16] Rosen 2000; Bronstein 2011.

national and local variations in terms of the prominence of this issue and how the mobilization took place. Hence, the comparison helps to distinguish between national and local characteristics and the shared features of the transnational feminist movement.[17]

The basic principle of the comparative method is to systematically study similarities and differences between two or several phenomena. Comparison can be applied as a "strict" scientific method whose aim is to develop general theoretical insights that can eventually be tested. Comparative methods can also be carried out through a more open and pragmatic approach. In this book the goal is to explain how and why the mobilization against sexual exploitation and abuse of women became a major issue for the transnational women's liberation movements in the 1970s, though it was carried out in different ways. In the service of achieving this goal, the methodological approach is to identify similarities and differences between the various women's movements, as well as the societies and political cultures in which they worked. It concentrates on the interaction between the women's movements and other societal actors, such as institutions, the media, and intellectuals, as well as other social movements, such as the labor movement. This comparative approach calls into play another perspective and sheds light on more phenomena than the study of a single country's movement would.[18] Moreover, explanations may acquire more validity when one society is compared to another. As the above example illustrates, feminist campaigns against pornography were not a "Norwegian peculiarity" but part of an international

---

[17] Bergman 2002; Beckwith, Karen (2005): "The Comparative Politics of Women's Movements," *Perspectives on Politics*, vol. 3, no. 3.

[18] Regarding comparative methods in historical research, see, e.g., Kjeldstadli, Knut (1988): "Nytten av å sammenlikne" [The Benefits of Comparing], *Tidsskrift for samfunnsforskning*, no. 5; Ågotnes, Knut (1989): *Kvar i sin dal—?: komparasjon som metode i lokalhistoriske studiar: rapport frå HIFO-seminar 14–16 oktober 1988* [Everyone His Valley—? Comparison as Method in Local History: Report from HIFO Seminar 14–16 October 1988]. Trondheim: Tapir forlag; Kocka, Jürgen (1996): "The Uses of Comparative History," in R. Björk and K. Molin (eds.): *Societies Made Up of History: Essays in Historiography, Intellectual History, Professionalisation, Historical Social Theory & Proto-Industrialisation*. Edsbank: Akademitryck; Rucht, Dieter (1996): "The Impact of National Contexts on Social Movement Structures: A Cross-Movement and Cross-National Comparison," in D. McAdam, J. McCarthy, and M.N. Zald (eds.): *Comparative Perspectives on Social Movements: Political Opportunities, Mobilizing Structures, and Cultural Framings*. Cambridge: Cambridge University Press.

trend. There indeed existed local peculiarities—for example, the anti-pornography campaign in Norway did not lead to the deep splits that a similar campaign caused within the U.S. feminist movement in the 1980s. In the words of historian Jürgen Kocka, the comparison helps to avoid simple "local pseudo-explanations."[19]

Comparing the Mobilization Against Rape in France with the Anti-pornography Campaigns in Norway

A comparison between the women's liberation movement's mobilization against rape and pornography in France and Norway, respectively, proves fascinating for several reasons. In both countries, these campaigns received great media attention; they mobilized widely and recruited new activists; and they led to increased cooperation and new alliances—as well as to new adversaries. The campaigns also set in motion important learning processes that led to the development of theory and to the introduction of new methods of protest and political action. In the cases of both France and Norway, the response from the outside world to the campaigns was strikingly similar and yet paradoxical. The women's liberation movements succeeded in obtaining widespread recognition of sexual exploitation and violence against women as societal problems that called for political solutions. The issues of rape and pornography made their way onto the mainstream political agenda, and legislative changes that incorporated some of the women's liberation movements' demands were adopted. In France, an archaic 1832 law on rape was replaced in 1980 by a law that provided a clearer, extended definition of rape: "Any act of sexual penetration, of any nature whatsoever, committed on the person by another, by violence, coercion or surprise, constitutes rape."[20] The new law recognized rape within marriage and held that both women and men may be victims of rape. In Norway, the 1902 act on "obscene writings" was replaced in 1985 by a new law in which pornography was defined as "sexual depictions that are offensive or in other ways are likely

---

[19] Kocka, 1996, p. 200.

[20] Author's translation of "Tout acte de pénétration sexuelle, de quelque nature qu'il soit, commis sur la personne d'autrui, par la violence, contrainte ou surprise, constitue un viol." Quoted in Vigarello 1998, p. 255.

to seem degrading or dehumanizing, including sexual depictions utilizing children, animals, violence, coercion and sadism."[21]

Paradoxically, while the mobilizations were successful insofar as the women's liberation movements' framing of rape and pornography as serious social problems was widely recognized, the campaigns were met with criticism and pushback. The criticism also came from actors who claimed to support women's liberation but who interpreted the campaigns as manifestations of puritanism, hatred of men, and authoritarian, oppressive ideology. While "all" proponents of gender equality in the 1970s supported abortion on demand, not all of them wanted to increase the punishment for rape or to ban pornography. In France, there was a widely held opinion on the left that severe penalties for rape would work as a "racist class law" that would affect migrant workers, while allowing men of the bourgeoisie to go free. The obvious argument against the anti-pornography mobilization was that a ban on pornography would be a threat to freedom of expression, which in the long run could affect other subversive—including feminist—publications. Thus, comparing these campaigns exposes ideological contradictions in the feminist movements in a sharper way than would a cross-country comparison of, for example, the mobilization for abortion on demand. The fact that the campaigns against rape and pornography did not lead to immediate success and indeed remain controversial issues for contemporary feminists makes a historical investigation of them particularly intriguing. These cases help to avoid the illusion that historical development progresses in a straight line toward a final, conclusive goal.

The Political Context of 1970s Women's Liberation Movements in France and Norway

There are obvious differences between France and Norway in terms of size and geographical location, political traditions, and state models, which have had an impact on the political opportunities as well as practices

---

[21] Author's translation of "[K]jønnslige skildringer som virker støtende eller på annen måte er egnet til å virke menneskelig nedverdigende eller forrående, herunder kjønnslige skildringer med bruk av barn, dyr, vold, tvang og sadisme." Quoted in Enger, Lill Kristin (2007): "Straffbar pornografi—Har jussen endret seg i takt med samfunnet?" [Criminal Pornography—Has Law Changed According to Societal Changes?], Master's thesis, Faculty of Law, University of Oslo, p. 32.

of women's movements. With around 54 million inhabitants in the 1970s, France had more than ten times the population of Norway. Historically, France was a country with imperialist and colonial ambitions governed by authoritarian and militarist elites that were repeatedly challenged by revolutionary popular uprisings. Norway, on the other hand, is located on the periphery of Europe and has to a larger extent than France been characterized by ideals of equality and a consensus-oriented political culture. Still, in the 1970s, the political cultures of the two countries were different. In France, the political climate was highly polarized, with powerful left-wing movements regularly engaging in violent confrontations with right-wing adversaries. There were regional separatist movements that carried out terrorist actions, as well as racist and fascist groups that threatened and beat up immigrants.[22] French society was still characterized by deep political rifts due to colonial wars against national liberation movements in Indochina (Vietnam) from 1947 to 1954 and in Algeria from 1954 to 1962. In Norway, which had been unaffected by war since the Nazi-German occupation of 1940–1945, the political climate was relatively peaceful. This does not, however, imply that everything was harmonious in Norway. For instance, the battle over Norwegian membership in the European Economic Community (EEC) (the predecessor of the European Union) in 1972 was experienced as politically dramatic by many Norwegians.[23] Nevertheless, compared to France, political life in social democratic Norway was less polarized and confrontational and was characterized to a greater extent by pragmatism and negotiation.

Another difference that shaped the political opportunities of the women's liberation movements relates to social citizenship. In the social democratic Nordic model, social rights have to a greater extent been included in citizenship than in the French Republican model, wherein citizenship has been framed politically as a universal civil right.[24] However,

---

[22] Zancarini-Fournel, Michelle (2008d): "Le début de la fin" [The Beginning of the End], in Artières, Philippe, and Michelle Zancarini-Fournel (eds.): *68. Une histoire collective (1962–81)* [68: A Collective History (1962–81)]. Paris: Éditions La Découverte, pp. 669–670.

[23] Furre, Berge (1991): *Vårt hundreår. Norsk historie 1905–1990* [Our Century: Norwegian History 1905–1990]. Oslo: Samlaget, pp. 344–347.

[24] Siim, Birte (2000): *Gender and Citizenship: Politics and Agency in France, Britain, and Denmark.* Cambridge: Cambridge University Press, p. 46; Bussemaker, Jet (2007): "Vocabularies of Citizenship Since the 1970s," in R. Lister et al. (eds.): *Gendering Citizenship in Western Europe.* Bristol: The Policy Press, p. 61.

it is worth noting that French marriage legislation traditionally made distinctions in the protections offered to men and women. As late as 1965, married women in France did not have the right to take on paid work and to open their own bank accounts without permission from their husbands. "Husband" was defined as "head of the family" until 1970, which implied that the husband exercised sole control over the children and their property, decided on the family residence, and chose where the children should attend school.[25] Further, obtaining a divorce was a daunting process. In Norway, by comparison, gender equality in marriage had been established in 1927.[26] Reproductive rights—or the lack of them—also distinguished the two countries. In the early 1970s, contraception and abortion were still banned in France, as had been the case since 1920. The intention of this restrictive legislation, the so-called *pronatalist* policy, was to increase the population after the excessive human losses during The Great War (World War I, 1914–1918). In 1967, the French National Assembly voted in favor of legalizing contraception for married couples through the so-called *loi Neuwirth*, although the law did not come into effect until 1972. Still, the legislation banned "anti-natalist propaganda"—that is, information about birth control and advertisements for contraceptives.[27] Until abortion on demand was legalized in 1974, the practice was totally prohibited and punishable by imprisonment. In the same period, birth control was fully legal in Norway, and sex education was taught in schools, at least in principle.[28] Although abortion on demand was not adopted until 1978, a 1960 law allowed pregnant women and girls to apply for abortion on medical grounds,

[25] Zancarini-Fournel, Michelle (2008a): "Le champ des possibles" [The Field of Possibilities], in P. Artières and M. Zancarini-Fournel (eds.): *68. Une histoire collective (1962–1981)* [68: A Collective History (1962–1981)]. Paris: Éditions La Découverte, p. 19.

[26] See, e.g., Melby, Kari (2005): "Husmortid" [The Age of Housewives], in I. Blom and S. Sogner (eds.): *Med kjønnsperspektiv på norsk historie* [Gender Perspective on Norwegian History]. Oslo: Cappelen, p. 301; Danielsen, Hilde (2013): "Den kjønnsdelte arbeidsdagen 1913–1960" [The Gendered Work Day 1913–1960], in H. Danielsen, E. Larsen, and I.W. Owesen: *Norsk likestillingshistorie 1814–2013* [Norwegian History on Gender Equality 1814–2013]. Bergen: Fagbokforlaget, pp. 242–246.

[27] Picq 1993, pp. 60–61.

[28] Nordberg Kari Hernæs (2013): *Ansvarlig seksualitet: Seksualundervisning i Norge 1935–1985* [Responsible Sexuality: Sexual Education in Norway 1935–1985]. PhD dissertation in history, Faculty of Humanities, University of Oslo.

including physical or mental illness of the woman, fetal malformation, or genetic disorders.[29] However, it was up to a special medical assessment board—a so-called "abortion board" consisting of two physicians—to decide whether the woman would be permitted to have an abortion or not. The system was dependent on the good will of the physicians in charge and was frequently experienced as degrading by abortion-seeking women. As mentioned earlier in this chapter, the struggle for abortion on demand was doubtless the most important claim of the women's liberation movement in the 1970s, not only in France and Norway, but in many other countries.

State models impact the interaction between governments and social movements. In this study we will see that the French women's liberation movement of the 1970s had very little trust in government reforms that might be of benefit to women, while the Norwegian movement, to a much greater degree, expected the authorities to address its demands. In Norway, there was a tradition of nongovernmental, voluntary organizations partnering in the development of the welfare state, and women's organizations were represented in consultative bodies as well as in government councils and committees.[30] In France, on the other hand, there was no tradition of formalized cooperation between the government and nongovernmental organizations. Welfare schemes were generally implemented "from above" and involved no government consultation with the affected social groups.[31] However, social reforms were often adopted as a response to popular protests and mobilizations. The hostility toward the state and the government was endemic to the French left of the 1970s, as the country had been ruled by right-wing governments since 1955. The Gaullist style of governance was perceived as elitist, authoritarian, and repressive by the left. In Norway, the political scene had been dominated by the Social Democratic Labor Party since World War II, and even

---

[29] "Abortloven" [Law on Abortion], *Store norske leksikon*, http://snl.no, consulted 3 March 2019.

[30] Berven, Nina, and Per Selle (eds.) (2001): *Svekket kvinnemakt? De frivillige organisasjonene og velferdsstaten* [Impaired Woman's Power? The NGOs and the Welfare State]. Oslo: Gyldendal Akademisk; Hernes, Helga (1982): *Staten—kvinner ingen adgang?* [The State—Women No Access?]. Oslo: Universitetsforlaget; Hernes, Helga Maria (1987): *Welfare State and Woman Power: Essays in State Feminism*. Oslo: Norwegian University Press.

[31] Siim 2000.

though the activists of the Norwegian women's liberation movement were skeptical of the government, their view of the state was not overtly hostile. The Norwegian political system, which was based on negotiation between the state and nongovernmental organizations, offered more opportunities for feminist demands to be heard.[32] Of further importance was the representation of women in the supreme legislature. In 1973, women accounted for just 2 percent of the deputies in the French National Assembly, while the percentage of women among Norwegian MPs was 16 percent.[33] Some of the members of the Norwegian National Assembly, the *Storting*, such as Torild Skard and Berit Ås from the Socialist Left Party, were affiliated with the women's liberation movement. Moreover, in the 1970s, several feminists came into leadership positions in the Norwegian governmental bureaucracy.[34]

Cross-national comparisons are valuable in seeking to understand national characteristics. Yet highlighting national differences may be problematic, as there is a risk of overemphasizing particularities and reinforcing stereotypes of "national character." At worst, such an approach may lead to an essentialist understanding of culture as something fixed and innate.[35] It is therefore worth stressing that the differences between the political cultures of France and Norway must not overshadow the fact that

[32] Hernes 1982, p. 62. See also Skjeie, Hege (2013): "Hva var statsfeminisme?" [What Was State Feminism?], in B. Bråten and C. Thun (eds.): *Krysningspunkter. Likestillingspolitikk i det flerkulturelle Norge* [Intersections: Gender Equality Policy in Multicultural Norway]. Oslo: Akademika Forlag, pp. 29–43.

[33] Figures from the period 1973–1978. Assemblée Nationale: Les femmes élues députées depuis 1945 [National Assembly: Women Elected since 1945]: http://www.assemb lee-nationale.fr/elections/femmes-deputees.asp, consulted 3 March 2019; Figures from the period 1973–1977. Representantfordeling Stortinget [Distribution of Members of the Storting (Parliament)]. http://data.stortinget.no/bygger/representantfordeling?dt= Chart&rd=Gender, consulted 3 March 2019. In France, women were not allowed to vote until 1944, more than 30 years after universal suffrage for women was introduced in Norway 1913.

[34] Lønnå 1996, pp. 256–257.

[35] For a critique emphasizing national characteristics, see Bergman 2002, p. 66 and Lamont, Michèle, and Laurent Thévenot (2000): "Introduction: Toward a Renewed Comparative Cultural Sociology," in M. Lamont and L. Thévenot (eds.): *Rethinking Comparative Cultural Sociology: Repertoires of Evaluation in France and the United States*. Cambridge: Cambridge University Press, p. 9.

both countries are modern, Western democracies and welfare states characterized by traditions of dynamic social movements, including women's movements of various kinds.

WHAT ARE WOMEN'S MOVEMENTS?

In this book, women's movements are examined as social movements that, through political mobilization and action, generate historical change. Social movements are driven by ordinary people who aim to change society by challenging and confronting elites, governments, and opponents through collective actions over time, and who develop strategies and solidarity to achieve their goals.[36] These movements are made up of organizations and groups, as well as of people who are not members of any organization but who identify with the movement.

Characteristic of women's movements is the notion that the participants' identity as women constitutes the basis for political organization. Women's movements mirror different tendencies, and in Nordic research it has been customary to categorize and distinguish between women's movements and organizations that work for *equal value* between the sexes, *equal rights*, or *women's liberation*.[37] The first category, which has traditionally attracted the largest number of women to volunteer

[36] Social movements has for several years constituted a comprehensive research field. See, e.g., Eyerman, Ron, and Andrew Jamison (1991): *Social Movements: A Cognitive Approach*. Cambridge: Polity Press; Goodwin, Jeff, James M. Jasper, and Francesca Poletta (eds.) (2001): *Passionate Politics: Emotions and Social Movements*. Chicago: University of Chicago Press; Goodwin, Jeff, & James Jasper (eds.) (2004): *Rethinking Social Movements: Structure, Meaning, and Emotion*. Lanham, MD: Rowman & Littlefield; McAdam, Doug, John D. McCarthy, and Mayer N. Zald (1996): *Comparative Perspectives on Social Movements: Political Opportunities, Mobilizing Structures, and Cultural Framings*. Cambridge: Cambridge University Press; McAdam, Doug, Sidney Tarrow, and Charles Tilly (2001): *Dynamics of Contention*. Cambridge: Camebridge University Press; Tarrow, Sidney (1998): *Power in Movement: Social Movements and Contentious Politics*. Cambridge: Cambridge University Press; Tilly, Charles (2004): *Social Movements 1798–2004*. Boulder: Paradigm Publishers.

[37] Dahlerup, Drude, and Brita Gulli (1985): "Women's Organizations in the Nordic Countries: Lack of Force or Counterforce?," in E. Haavio-Mannila (ed.): *Unfinished Democracy: Women in Nordic Politics*. Oxford: Pergamon Press; Wærness, Kari (1995): "Epilog" [Epilogue], in O. Bjarnar: *Veiviser til velferdssamfunnet. Norske Kvinners Sanitetsforening 1946–1996* [Showing the Way to the Welfare Society: Norwegian Women's Public Health Association 1946–1996]. Oslo: Norske Kvinners Sanitetsforening.

organizations such as housewives' associations, charities, or religious organizations, holds that society should value women and men equally, while accepting the complementary roles of the sexes, typically with men as breadwinners and women as caregivers.[38] The second category is often associated with classic liberal women's rights movements that arose in the second half of the nineteenth century and mobilized for equal rights for women and men in legislation, employment, education, and politics. This tendency advocates legal, social, and political reforms, as well as attitudinal changes, as a means of changing gender roles and ensuring equal opportunities for men and women. The third category, women's liberation, is a more radical project, as it is based on the notion that women constitute an oppressed group that must organize politically *as women* in order to totally transform the established gender order. The goal is not primarily to reform government policies, but to create an entirely different world with a completely new culture and with totally different interpersonal relationships.[39] This book deals chiefly with this type of women's movement, the activists of which were in the forefront in addressing sexuality, abuse, and violence as gender-political issues. The women's liberation movement was, however, anything but homogeneous; rather, it was an amalgam of various groups with different and competing ideologies and political practices.

1970s WOMEN'S LIBERATION MOVEMENTS IN FRANCE AND NORWAY

In 1970, the women's liberation movements in France and Norway made their entrance into the public space with attention-grabbing actions. In August 1970, nine feminists demonstrated at the most sacred national symbol of France, the Arc de Triomphe in Paris, by attempting to deposit a huge wreath of flowers on the Tomb of the Unknown Soldier

---

[38] One example of such an organization is the Norwegian Women's Public Health Association. As the largest women's organization in Norway, it claimed approximately 240,000 members in the mid-1970s. Bjarnar 1995, p. 23.

[39] Jenson 1996, pp. 73–114; Nørve, Siri (1978): "Bevisstgjøring" [Consciousness-Raising], *PaxLeksikon*. Oslo: Pax Forlag, pp. 66–69; Gulli, Brita M. (1979): "Flat organisering" [Flat Organization], *PaxLeksikon*. Oslo: Pax Forlag, pp. 352–356.

in commemoration of "his even more unknown wife."[40] The activists were arrested before they had finished the wreath-laying ceremony, but the action was a media success, and the movement had made its name as the *Mouvement de libération des femmes* (MLF), directly translated from the American *Women's Liberation Movement*. In Norway, the first notable action of the New Feminists (see below) was performed in November 1970, when some 30 women interrupted the radio show "Women, Women" at the Norwegian Broadcasting Corporation's *Store studio* (Big Studio) in Oslo. The feminists argued that the show, hosted by the popular radio personality Mr. Rolf Kirkvaag, was degrading to women because it portrayed them as inferior "instruments of entertainment."[41] Mr. Kirkvaag was told that, beginning now, women were to speak for themselves, and a rose was placed in his mouth. Over the next few years, these kinds of disruptive actions took place regularly. The actions were often performed in places that the feminists regarded as symbols of oppressive male power. In France, they protested outside a women's prison (where, in an act of solidarity with the female prisoners, they allowed themselves to be imprisoned), they demonstrated against prison-like institutions for young, single mothers, protested against the general assembly meeting of the publisher of the ladies' magazine *Elle*, and invaded meetings of the Medical Association (because it was antiabortion) and the antiabortion group *"Laissez-les vivre"* ("Let them live"). In Norway, feminist activists campaigned against beauty pageants, occupied the offices of the publishing house Aschehoug (which had published an anti-feminist book) (Fig. 1.2), and blockaded the hospital of Aker in Oslo as a protest against the form that abortion-seeking women were obliged to fill out and which the feminist activists perceived as degrading. In addition, a number of less spectacular activities were carried out that worked

---

[40] See Picq 1993, pp. 16–17; de Pisan, Annie, and Anne Tristan [pseudonym for Annie Sugier and Anne Zelensky] (1977): *Histoires du M.L.F.* Préface de Simone de Beauvoir [Histories of the M.L.F. Foreword by Simone de Beauvoir]. Paris: Calmann-Lévy, pp. 48–55; Zancarini-Fournel, Michelle (2008c): "Changer le monde et changer sa vie" [Change the World and Change Your Life], in P. Artières and M. Zancarini-Fournel (eds.), p. 436.

[41] Haukaa 1982, p. 25; Lindtner, Synnøve Skarsbø (2013): "Over disk som varmt hvetebrød—Sirene og den norske populærfeminismen" [Over the Counter as Hot Wheat Bread—Sirene and Norwegian Popular Feminism], in H. Danielsen (ed.): *Da det personlige ble politisk. Den nye kvinne- og mannsbevegelsen på 1970-tallet* [When the Personal Became Political: The New Women's and Men's Movement in the 1970s]. Oslo: Scandinavian Academic Press/Spartacus Forlag, pp. 116–119.

Fig. 1.2 In 1973, members of the New Feminists occupied the office of the publishing manager of the Norwegian publishing house Aschehoug, demanding the withdrawal of the Norwegian translation of Esther Vilar's book *The Manipulated Man* (1971). The activists regarded the book as women-discriminatory because it is about how women are oppressing men. To the left, Liv Finstad holding a poster saying "Take the Power Away from the Publishing Manager." To her right, Nina Karin Monsen is seen holding the poster saying "Aschehoug Wants to Make Money on Women Harassment." Subsequently, Aschehoug, as "compensation," published a Norwegian translation of *Freedom, Equality, Sisterhood* (1973) by the Swedish feminists Barbro Werkmäster and Maud Hägg (Photo: Unknown ©The Norwegian Labour Movement Archives and Library (Arbark) [Reprinted with permission])

to consolidate the movement. There were meetings, huge demonstrations for abortion on demand, petition campaigns, and the writing of countless articles.

The women's liberation movement of the 1970s is frequently referred to as "feminist," a term that shares various and contesting definitions of feminism. One definition is that feminism is a *political ideology* that explicitly challenges and confronts gendered power relations. According to sociologist Solveig Bergman, three characteristics tie different forms of feminism together:

> Firstly, that gender is viewed as a primary, but not necessarily the only determining influence upon women's lives and a way of structuring and organising society and cultural life. Secondly, the recognition of the existence of a gender-specific subordination, or of the systematic and institutionalised nature of discrimination against women. Finally, the questioning of the legitimacy of the present gender order and an awareness that collective organising is needed to break down the gendered distribution of power and resources.[42]

Bergman's definition accurately describes the different tendencies of the 1970s women's liberation movement. Nevertheless, it is problematic to label the French and Norwegian movements as "feminist," because key tendencies within these movements on various issues served to forcefully distance themselves from feminism. The most common argument was that feminism was a "bourgeois" ideology that was not sufficiently anti-capitalist. In Norway, some women activists argued that feminism was mistaken because it designated men as "the main enemy." A somewhat different criticism voiced by some activists of the French MLF was that feminism was based on men as the norm and that feminists strove for women to become like men. Despite the criticism of feminism as a political ideology, the women's liberation movement as a whole shared a common goal of liberating women from male oppression. It is also worth noting that, since the 1970s, the meaning of "feminism" has been broadened, so that today it serves more as a collective term for the movement than it did in the 1970s.

Different Ideological Tendencies in the Women's Liberation Movements

The women's liberation movement that blossomed in the United States in the late 1960s was an inspiration to women around the world, including in France and Norway. The feminist groups that emerged in 1970 were

---

[42] Bergman 2002, p. 19.

directly inspired by the American concept of "Women's Lib."[43] Using symbolic and spectacular forms of action, they aimed to conquer traditionally male arenas, whether the Arc de Triomphe in Paris or the Norwegian Broadcast Corporation in Oslo. This feminist current of the movement emphasized that all women have something in common, and that the identity of women and women's specific experiences should form the basis for the struggle against patriarchy, or "the male society," as it was usually called in Norway.[44] The politics was to be developed in consciousness-raising groups without leaders and through participatory democracy in general meetings where everyone was encouraged to partake in decision-making. Formal leadership was rejected in favor of spontaneity and provocation, which were seen as the best means of drawing attention to the groups' political struggles. In Norway, this tendency on the part of the women's liberation movement was represented by the *Nyfeministene* (the New Feminists), a group that was established in 1970 and eventually became a nationwide organization consisting of a number of consciousness-raising groups as well as several thematic groups working with particular issues—for example, sexist advertising. In France, this tendency on the part of the MLF included the *Féministes Révolutionnaires* (Revolutionary Feminists) and an assortment of short-lived local groups. In 1974, however, women from the Revolutionary Feminists established the organization *Ligue du droit des femmes* (the Association for Women's Rights, or LDF) as a response to the general decline of the MLF after the euphoria of the first phase, and a feeling

---

[43] For a comparison of different tendencies in the French and Norwegian women's liberation movements, see Korsvik 2010.

[44] The French sociologist Christine Delphy developed a theory that women comprise a proper social class. In the article "L'Ennemi principal" [The Main Enemy] in *Partisans* in 1970, Delphy explained the material basis for patriarchy as a mode of production, as exploitation of women's unpaid work in the patriarchal family. Christine Dupont [Delphy]: "L'ennemi principal," "Libération des femmes, année zéro" [The Main Enemy, Liberation of Women, Year Zero], *Partisans* (Summer 1970). The article was translated into English in *Gender Issues*, no. 1 (1980). Like the other contributors to this issue of *Partisans*, Delphy did not sign her own name to the article, instead using a pseudonym. In 1977, Delphy, along with Simone de Beauvoir, Monique Wittig, and others, started the theoretical journal *Questions féministes* that further developed the so-called "materialist feminism." Regarding the influence of Simone de Beauvoir on French feminism, see Picq, Françoise (2008): "Simone de Beauvoir et 'la querelle du féminisme'" [Simone de Beauvoir and "The Quarrel of Feminism"], *Les Temps Modernes*, vol. 647–648, no. 1, pp. 169–185.

shared by the LDF's revolutionary feminists concerning the necessity of organizing in a more structured way in order to get things done. Simone de Beauvoir, the author of the feminist "Bible," *The Second Sex* (1949), became the association's first leader. One of the main goals of the LDF was to campaign for an "anti-sexist law" (*loi anti-sexiste*) that they believed could be deployed to eliminate advertising that discriminated against women and pornography, as well as to reform the rape law.[45] The anti-sexist law was, however, never adopted.

In France and Norway, there was also a branch on the part of the women's liberation movement to emphasize class struggle. Activists of this branch believed that class antagonisms are more important than gender, and that women and men of the same class have more interests in common than women of different classes—that is, working-class women and women of the bourgeoisie. At the urging of women from Marxist groups, class-struggle-oriented women's organizations were established in 1971–1972. These groups took a more focused stand against capitalism as part of the women's struggle and had a more structured way of organizing than the New Feminist and Revolutionary Feminist approach. In Norway, the *Kvinnefronten* (The Women's Front), established by socialist students at the University of Oslo in 1972, represented this trend, while in France there were many local groups based in neighborhoods and in workplaces within what was eventually called the "class-struggle tendency." The most important of these groups were *Femmes en Lutte* (Women in Struggle) and *Pétroleuses*, the latter named after the revolutionary women who, during the Paris Commune of 1871, acquired this nickname because they were assumed to have set fire to the property of the bourgeoisie using bottles of paraffin. Women in Struggle and *Pétroleuses* had their roots in Trotskyist parties and endeavored to coordinate local groups on a national level. They failed in this effort, but they did succeed in publishing their own newspapers. In Norway, the Women's Front eventually became the largest organization of the women's liberation movement, with local chapters in all parts of the country.

A common feature of the class-struggle-oriented women's groups in France and Norway was that they regarded themselves as an extension of the nineteenth-century socialist labor women's movement. They were eager to recruit working-class women and to let their interests lead the

---

[45] de Pisan and Tristan 1977, pp. 119-120.

women's struggle. They thus preferred forms of political action that they assumed would appeal to so-called ordinary women—namely, actions that did not appear to be too provocative. The groups of the class-struggle tendency were more firmly structured than the loosely organized feminist groups and became increasingly prevalent throughout the 1970s. It should be noted that the Women's Front remains active to this day (2020).

In France, there was also a third branch of the women's liberation movement, which, in contrast to the other two, had no parallel in Norway. It was called *Psychanalyse et politique* (Psychoanalysis and Politics), a name often shortened to *Psych et Po* or *Psychépo*. Since the ideology and political practice of this group was so singular, it is granted more space here than the other two tendencies, which had equivalents in most countries with active women's movements in the 1970s. The theoretical basis of the Psych et Po was a combination of a Maoist-inspired criticism of imperialism and the theories of Jacques Lacan, a French psychiatrist and psychoanalyst.[46] Like many Parisian intellectuals of the 1960s and 1970s, the unofficial guru of Psych et Po, Antoinette Fouque, underwent psychoanalysis with Lacan. Distinct from classical Freudianism, Lacanian psychoanalysis does not emphasize human drives; instead it sees language as essential for identity formation. According to Lacan, language has phallus (or the masculine) as significant—that is, language is structured according to rules, logic, and grammar. By acquiring the language, the child is placed into "the Law of the Father" or the "Name of the Father" and is thus expelled from the mother's body. Changing the language by breaking the rules of conventional writing, grammar, and syntax was, according to Lacan (and Psych et Po) a revolutionary act. By creating a separate "female language," the group believed that women could overcome the "Law of the Father," the male power, and regain the mother's body.[47] As stated by Psych et Po, the male

---

[46] Roudinesco, Elisabeth (1990): *Jacques Lacan & Co: A History of Psychoanalysis in France, 1925–1985*. Chicago: University of Chicago Press.

[47] The literary theorist and author Hélène Cixous, who was affiliated with Psych et Po in the 1970s, continued to develop the idea of a specific poetic feminine writing, *écriture féminine*, in the essay "Le rire de la Méduse" [The Laugh of the Medusa] (1975). Here she aims to show how feminine writing avoids the discourses that regulate the fallogocentric system. Cixous, Hélène (1975): "Le rire de la Méduse," *L'Arc*, vol. 61, pp. 39–54. English: "The Laugh of the Medusa," *Signs*, vol. 1, no. 4 (Summer 1976), pp. 875–893.

represents "legal, sadistic, patriarchal, pederast, representation, chief, of name, rape, oppression, hatred, greed, owning, knowing, order, individualism, abstract ideas, power," whereas the female represents "giving life, spending, chaos, differences, collective liberties, opening, bodies, recognitions, away with prohibitions, desires, outside law, able-to-act-think-do-for-all."[48] This nongrammatical way of articulating the male and the female also works as an illustration of the so-called female language.

Psych et Po strongly criticized feminism, especially the type represented by Simone de Beauvoir, for being reformist and universalist and aiming to assimilate women into male power to the point that they ceased to be women. Psych et Po believed that women were completely different from men by virtue of their uteruses.[49] As an alternative to feminism, Fouque developed a so-called "féminitude" philosophy.[50] That women "have always been slaves, beaten, raped and sold," was declared to be the result of an interaction between corporal and capitalist exploitation of women which, together, had created a phallocentric society dominated by a masculine bourgeois ideology. According to this theory, the phallus worked both as a tool for raping women and as a symbol of a conformist and hierarchical mentality that Fouque delineated as male. Women ought to be liberated from such a male mindset, which she considered to be widespread among women and especially among feminists, by "chasing phallus out of the head" through therapy with Fouque. According to Fouque, men's unconscious "envy of the uterus" is the basis for men's misogyny and their desire to control women. Women, as well, have internalized the misogyny, Fouque maintained, as they carry with them an

---

[48] "d'une tendence..." [about a tendency...], *Le Torchon Brûle*, no. 3 [1972], [no page numbers]. On the history of Psych et Po seen from their own perspective, see Fouque, Antoinette, et al. (eds.) (2008): *Génération MLF 1968–2008* [The MLF Generation 1968–2008]. Paris: Des femmes—Antoinette Fouque.

[49] After Simone de Beauvoir died in 1986, Antoinette Fouque published the article "Moi et elle" [Me and Her] in *Libération*. Here she claimed that the death of de Beauvoir was a liberating turning point in women's history. For Fouque, de Beauvoir represented a feminism of equality derived from an "intolerant, assimilating, hateful, sterilizing and reducing universalism." She maintained that the death of de Beauvoir envisaged a new era for women that was more open to diversity and to fruitful sex differences. Rodgers, Catherine (2000): "Elle et Elle: Antoinette Fouque et Simone de Beauvoir" [She and Her: Antoinette Fouque and Simone de Beauvoir], *MLN*, no. 4 (French Issue), p. 741.

[50] "Femmes, sexualité, politique" [Women, Sexuality, Politics], flyer by Antoinette Fouque, 1970, referenced in Fouque et al. (eds.) 2008, p. 418.

unconscious desire to kill their mothers. However, there was still reason for hope, since the "geography" of the female body makes women more open, antiauthoritarian, life-giving, and so on. A woman could be liberated by cultivating her female *"geni(t)alité"*—a genius based on the female body—and by learning to love her mother, the first person with whom, as a little girl, she had a sexual relationship.[51]

Psych et Po adherents believed that their psychoanalytical work and creativity through poetry and the creation of a "female language" had made them "transcend the history."[52] In terms of organizational model, Psych et Po differed from other groups of the MLF by practicing a form of master-discipleship in which the charismatic psychoanalyst Antoinette Fouque acted as a guru. Thus, the group was often described as a sect by its feminist opponents.[53] Thanks to funding by the wealthy heiress Sylvina Boissonnas, Psych et Po had access to exceptional financial resources compared to other groups of the MLF. For example, it was the only MLF group that had a permanent address and a telephone. From the mid-1970s on, Psych et Po owned the professional publishing house Des femmes (Women) as well as several bookstores with the same name. It also published the women's journal *Le quotidien des femmes* (Women's Daily) and later *Des femmes en mouvements* (Women in Movements). With a circulation of over 100,000, *Des femmes en mouvements* was the most widely read journal of the MLF in the late 1970s.[54] The journal presented a world of women who were revolutionary, struggling, working, and

---

[51] Op. cit., pp. 15–28.

[52] *Le quotidien des femmes*, no. 4 (1975), p. 1.

[53] "Librairie des Femmes" [Women's Bookstore], *Les Pétroleuses*, no. 7 (1976), p. 34; Nadja Ringart: "La naissance d'une secte" [The Birth of a Sect], *Le Monde*, 1 June 1977; and Marie-Jo Dhavernas: "Des divans profond comme des tombeaux" [Couches Deep as Tombs], *La Revue d'en face*, no. 8 (1979), both published in *Association du Mouvement pour les luttes feminists* [Association of the Movement for Feminist Struggles] (1981): *Chroniques d'une imposture. Du mouvement de libération des femmes à une marque commercial* [Chronicles of a Deception: From the Women's Liberation Movement to a Commercial Brand]. Paris [author]; Guadilla, Naty García (1981): *Libération des femmes: le M.L.F.* [Women's Liberation: The M.L.F.]. Paris: Presses Universitaires de France, pp. 64–100; Jenson 1996, p. 79. Storti 2010, pp. 66 and 126.

[54] Psych et Po's publishing house, Des femmes (est. 1973), was, according to Psych et Po, Europe's first women's publishing house. The journal *Le Quotidien des femmes* was published from 1974 to 1976, and *Des femmes en mouvements* from 1977 to 1982. It can be noted that Fouque received the Legion d'Honneur medal in 2006. Fouque et al. (eds.) 2008.

creative, yet beautiful and in harmonious community with other women. In 1979, *Des femmes en mouvements* was converted to a weekly magazine but ceased publication when Fouque moved to the United States in 1982. In the late 1970s, Psych et Po—and Fouque in particular—enjoyed great public visibility, and the media often let them speak on behalf of the women's liberation movement. In addition, internationally known gender theorists such as Hélène Cixous and Luce Irigaray frequented the group in the 1970s. Ironically, in the 1980s their Fouque-inspired, post-structuralist gender theories became known under the name "French Feminism" in the United States, despite the fact that this tendency stood in explicit opposition to feminism.

Political Conflicts

The French and Norwegian women's liberation movements were both characterized by strong internal political disagreements. Anglo-American scholars who have written about the French MLF have emphasized how it was unusually divided and sectarian compared to women's liberation movements in other countries.[55] Years of bitter conflict between Psych et Po and feminists of various kinds peaked in 1979, when Psych et Po copyrighted the name *Mouvement de libération des femmes* and the acronym MLF both as an association and as a commercial trademark. In doing so, Psych et Po gained the legal right to call itself *Mouvement de libération des femmes*/MLF and denied other rival feminist groups' claims that they were part of the women's liberation movement. The copyrighting of the MLF as a commercial trademark and legal association caused much anger among feminists, but the antagonism between them and Psych et Po had already existed for several years.

Radical (or revolutionary) feminists and Marxist feminists disagreed on many political matters but shared their condemnation of Psych et Po. The latter was criticized for idealizing and mystifying "the Woman," for doing nothing politically, and for being a totalitarian sect wherein there was no room for doubt or debates, and all were supposed to be kind and beautiful.[56] As a disenchanted former follower of Psych et Po declared

---

[55] Jenson 1996, p. 77; Mazur, Amy G. (1996): *Gender Bias and the State: Symbolic Reform at Work in Fifth Republic France*. Pittsburgh, PA: University of Pittsburgh Press, p. 8.

[56] Marie-Jo Dhavernas, in *La Revue d'en face*, no. 8 (1979).

in 1977, the participants followed the leader Fouque in every way, tried to speak in her obscure psychoanalytic way, broke with the social life outside of the group, and sacrificed their lives for Psych et Po. Persons who voiced a dissenting viewpoint were accused of not having achieved the proper insight—that is, they had failed to "chase the phallus out of their heads."[57] Other feminist opponents pointed out that Fouque acted simultaneously as a political leader, a psychoanalyst, and an employer of employees in the publishing house and the Des femmes bookstores, as well as a mistress for certain chosen ones. The critics argued that this confusion of roles facilitated the manipulation of the followers, who were pitifully characterized as "analyzed, fucked, exploited and domi-nated."[58] Some labeled the psychoanalytic practice of Psych et Po as a "Stalino-Lacanian" terror against those exposed to it.[59]

The disapproval was mutual. In the late 1970s, Psych et Po's condem-nation of feminists was almost frenetic, as it accused feminists of spreading American imperialism to Third World countries and for facilitating capi-talist exploitation. The criticism also took on a Lacanian psychoanalytic touch when feminists were called "sons" of "the father"—specifically of the feminists' "father," Simone de Beauvoir.[60] When feminists passed judgment on Psych et Po, their action was characterized as a subcon-scious desire to rape "the mother." To prevent feminists from "abusing" the women's liberation movement, Psych et Po had considered it neces-sary to secure legal and commercial copyright protection for its name and the abbreviation MLF.[61]

---

[57] Nadia Ringart, in *Le Monde*, 1 June 1977.

[58] "Librairie des Femmes" [Women's Library], *Les Pétroleuses*, no. 7 (1976), p. 34.

[59] Storti, Martine (2010): *Je suis une femme, pourquoi pas vous? 1974–1979. Quand je racontais le mouvement des femmes dans Libération* [I Am a Woman, Why Not You? 1974–1979: When I Told About the Women's Liberation Movement]. Paris: Éditions Michel de Maule, pp. 66 and 126.

[60] Psych et Po's criticism of feminism was particularly prominent in the 1978 annual volume of *Des femmes en mouvements—mensuel*, particularly in nos. 2, 3, 10, and 12–13. The justification for the accusation of feminists spreading American imperialism was that the First Lady of the United States, Rosalynn Carter, claimed to be a feminist.

[61] The divisions between former activists of the MLF continued into the 2000s. In *Génération MLF 1968–2008*, Fouque claims that she personally created MLF in 1968, whereas feminists of different political affiliations argue that the MLF did not exist until 1970. See, e.g., Storti 2010 and the thematic issue of *ProChoix* no. 46 2008 on "MLF le mythe des origines" [MLF the Myth of Origins].

In addition to the fact that the copyright action of Psych et Po seems to have had no counterpart in other countries' women's movements, the Norwegian women's liberation movement was also distinguished by a high level of conflict.[62] In Norway, however, the lines of conflict revolved around contending views of Marxist-Leninism. In 1972, the Women's Front was established by socialist women who were not satisfied with the politics of the New Feminists and who believed that the women's struggle must be connected to the class struggle. However, in 1974, women from the small but hyperactive Maoist Worker's Communist Party (Marxist-Leninists)—abbreviated AKP (m-l)—took over the leadership of the Women's Front, a "coup" that caused many women to leave the organization. Eventually, in 1975–1976, some hundreds of former members of the Women's Front who sympathized with the Socialist Left Party—abbreviated SV—established the nationwide organization Bread and Roses.[63] Despite the Women's Front being controlled to a large extent by the Marxist-Leninists of the AKP (m-l), as well as its own loud declarations that it was not feminist, it remained the largest organization of the women's liberation movement in Norway. It was able to do so because the Women's Front was more structured and expected its members to be strongly committed to political activity, unlike the more loosely organized feminist groups. The New Feminists, for their part, seriously feared that the Marxist-Leninists of the Women's Front would take over their organizations and use the women's mobilization to build the AKP (m-l) party. The political conflicts were tough but not entirely destructive, as they led to dynamic debates and development of theory. As pointed out by sociologist Runa Haukaa, herself a "defector" from the Women's Front, in her book on "the new women's movement" from 1982, the political conflicts served to prevent the movement from stagnating. Indeed, the strength of the movement increased the most during periods when political conflicts reached their peak. The disagreements were signs of the women's movement being considered important, according to Haukaa.[64]

---

[62] Regarding the political divisions in the French and Norwegian Women's movements, see Korsvik 2010.

[63] Haukaa 1982, pp. 119–121. The Socialist Left Party (SV) was a non-Leninist socialist party whose forerunner, the Socialist People's Party (SF), was established in 1961 and was represented in Parliament.

[64] Haukaa 1982, p. 79.

Despite these differences, both the French and Norwegian move-ments shared the fact that the toughest conflicts revolved around political ideology and organization. Though dissimilar, the French Psych et Po and the Norwegian Women's Front were both resourceful and well-organized movements; they had authoritarian leadership and denounced feminism as an ideology; and they constituted a dominant part of the women's liberation movement and were thus feared by the more loosely orga-nized feminist groups. This was a source of conflict that differed from, for example, the U.S. women's liberation movement, where conflicts instead revolved around identity—that is, sexuality and race. In the United States, lesbian and heterosexual feminists, as well as black and white feminists, established separate groups.[65] Although some lesbian and migrant women began their own groups in Norway and France, they continued to coop-erate with other women's groups. The political and ideological conflicts overshadowed those based on ethnicity and sexuality.

The Activists

It is impossible to know the number of people who identified themselves as part of the women's liberation movement. The activists wanted the movement to be for "all" women, but it was too avant-garde to become a mass movement.[66] Nonetheless, there are reasons to believe that the Norwegian women's liberation movement was more of a "popular" movement than its more elitist French counterpart. In Norway, local chapters of the Women's Front were established in rural areas of the country, whereas the French MLF was more of an urban phenomenon. The Norwegian activists were generally younger than their French coun-terparts: most of them were in their twenties, and many of them were students.[67] Moreover, the presence of intellectual, avant-garde activists

---

[65] Rosen 2000, p. 239.

[66] In France, the groups of the MLF did not register membership lists. Haukaa (1982) found that there were approximately 5000 members in the Women's Front and the New Feminists nationwide in 1974. In addition, there were approximately 800 members of Norsk Kvinnesaksforening (The Norwegian Association for Women's Rights) and approximately 1200 in Norsk Kvinneforbund (The Norwegian Women's Federation).

[67] Lønnå 1996, p. 233. On the French participants, see Picq, Françoise (1987): *Le Mouvement de libération des femmes et ses effets sociaux. Rapport de recherché* [The Women's Liberation Movement and Its Social Effects: Research Report], CNRS, ATP "Recherches féministes et recherches sur les femmes" [Feminist Research and Research on Women]. The study is based on a survey of 122 former activists and in-depth interviews with approximately 20 women.

was less prevalent in the Norwegian than in the French movement. For instance, while the New Feminists who protested the above-mentioned radio show in 1970 were all young newcomers to the public scene, the nine feminist protesters involved in the famous Arc de Triomphe action in Paris in 1970 all came from literary and artistic avant-garde milieus, and included two award-winning authors, Monique Wittig and Christiane Rochefort, the future acknowledged sociologist Christine Delphy, and the French-American actress and folk singer Julie Dassin.[68] Soon after, the author and philosopher Simone de Beauvoir, then in her sixties, joined the movement. Along with Rochefort, she was a central figure behind a famous manifesto for abortion on demand, signed by 343 distinguished women, including the film star Catherine Deneuve, who revealed that they had had illegal abortions and demanded a change in the law. The so-called *Manifeste de 343*, published in the mainstream, left-wing weekly magazine *Le Nouvel Observateur* on 5 April 1971, was crucial to the abortion issue being placed on the political agenda in France.[69] In case the 343 signatories were to be prosecuted—which they were not, despite abortion being forbidden—the lawyer Gisele Halimi, herself a co-signer of the manifesto, established the organization *Choisir* (Choose) in July 1971. Simone de Beauvoir was also affiliated with Choisir, which mobilized politically within the domain of the law both by working to change the abortion law and by defending those who had been accused of performing abortions. Halimi acted as defense attorney

---

[68] In 1964, Wittig won the literary Médici Prize for her first novel, *L'Opoponax*. Her book *Les Guérillères*, from 1969, about a war between the sexes in which women engage in bloody, victorious battles against men, became world famous. Rochefort was known for the books *Le repos du guerrier* [Warrior's Rest] from 1958 (adapted to the screen in 1962, directed by Roger Vadim and starring Brigitte Bardot in the lead role) and *Les petits enfants du siècle* [Children of Heaven] from 1961. The other activists included translators, writers, and musicians. Lasserre, Audrey (2010): "Les héritières. Les écrivaines d'aujourd'hui et les féminismes" [The Heiresses: Today's [female] Writers and the Feminisms], www.revue-analyses.org, vol. 5, no. 3.

[69] Pavard, Bibia (2012): *Si je veux, quand je veux. Contraception et avortement dans la société française (1956–1979)* [If I Want, When I Want. Contraception and Abortion in French Society (1956–1979)]. Rennes: Presses Universitaires de Rennes, pp. 135–153; de Pisan and Tristan 1977, pp. 63–69. The idea of the manifesto was clearly inspired by the "Manifeste de 121" from 1960, in which 121 well-known personalities, including de Beauvoir and Jean-Paul Sartre, demanded that France withdraw from its colonial war in Algeria and supported active assistance to the Algerian National Liberation Front, FLN. Ever since the Dreyfus affair at the turn of the twentieth century, signing manifestos has been a classic means of protest for the French intellectual left.

in the much-publicized "Bobigny case" in 1972, where she successfully secured an acquittal for a 16-year-old girl who had been charged with having an illegal abortion after being raped by a classmate. After this extensively publicized trial, there were no further convictions of girls or women who underwent illegal abortions in France.[70]

Far from all activists of the French MLF were famous, but most of them shared the student and worker revolt of May–June 1968 as a politically formative experience. In Norway, 1968 passed relatively quietly, and although some of the Norwegian activists had gained political experience from, for example, radical student groups and Vietnam committees, there were also quite a few activists with no political experience at all, especially among the New Feminists.[71] The experience gained by the French MLF activists during the revolutionary upheavals of May–June 1968 was reflected in their rhetoric, aesthetics, and political practices. They were considerably more avant-garde than the generally more serene Norwegian activists, and many of them were willing to break with all kinds of convention. This meant, for example, that they conducted their noisy meetings without any chairperson, and that there was strong opposition to planning and "organization." In their experimental publications, of which the magazine *Le Torchon Brûle* (published 1971–1973) remains the most iconic visual expression of the MLF, the ideal was to break down the boundaries between reader and writer, between amateurs and professionals, between the individual woman and the collective movement (Fig. 1.3). Therefore, none of the articles were signed, and many of them were written collectively. Moreover, MLF introduced new and cheerful forms of demonstration with singing and dancing, balloons, flowers, and children on floats. The invention of new forms of protest was politically conscious, because they were intended to be alternatives to "male and fallocratic" demonstrations involving confrontations between male protestors and policemen.[72]

---

[70] Pavard 2012, pp. 153–154.

[71] Haukaa 1982, p. 19; Live Brekke: "Nyfeministene og politikk" [New Feminists and Politics], *Oslofeministen*, no. 3 (1975). In this article the author, herself a member of the New Feminists, writes that the general trend was that women with political experience participated in the Women's Front, whereas the members of the New Feminists generally lacked political experience.

[72] "viet-nam samedi 20 janvier" [Viet-nam Saturday 20th January], *Le Torchon Brûle*, no. 5 [1973].

Fig. 1.3 *Le Torchon Brûle*, the joint journal of the Movement de libération des femmes (MLF), no. 1, 1971. The journal had no chief editor, none of the articles were signed, and many of them were written collectively. None of the illustrations were signed either, but, in fact, this iconic front-page was made by the artist Raymonde Arcier

Relations with the Established Women's Organizations

When the women's liberation movement entered the political scene in the early 1970s, there was already an established women's movement in place. Nineteenth-century social-liberal women's associations—such as the *Ligue Française pour le Droit des Femmes* (French League for Women's Rights, LFDF), established in 1882, and the *Norsk kvinnesaksforening* (The Norwegian Association for Women's Rights, NKF), established in 1884—were still active in the 1970s. In addition, there were socialist, communist, and conservative women's organizations, as well as apolitical humanitarian, religious, and professional women's associations. In France, the communist *Union des femmes françaises* (Union for French Women, abbreviated UFF) was the largest women's association, claiming approximately half a million members.[73] UFF had been founded in 1944 by women from *la Résistance* (i.e., the French resistance movement that fought against the Nazi-German occupation and its collaborators), and was affiliated with the Soviet-oriented French Communist Party (PCF), which was the largest political party of the French left in the 1970s. Through its adherence to the communist Women's International Democratic Federation (WIDF), UFF was a sister organization of the *Norsk kvinneforbund* (The Norwegian Women's Federation), which was considerably smaller, claiming only 1200 members.[74] The major women's organization in Norway was the *Norske Kvinners Sanitetsforening* (The Norwegian Women's Public Health Association), which had around 240,000 members in the 1970s—an impressive number considering that the population of the country at large was only 4 million.[75] The second principal women's organization was the *Norsk Husmorforbund* (The Norwegian Housewives' Association), with about 60,000 members. The primary objective of this rather conservative group was to strengthen the

[73] Chaperon, Sylvie (2000): *Les années Beauvoir (1945–1970)* [The Beauvoir Years 1945–1970]. Paris: Fayard, p. 363.

[74] The Norwegian Women's Federation was established in 1954 as a merger of the Communist Party-affiliated *Norges Husmorlagsforbund* [the Norwegian Housewife League] (established 1937) and the *Norges Demokratiske Kvinneforbund* [the Norwegian Democratic Women's Federation] (established 1948). Clayhills, Harriet (1980): "Kvinneforbund, Norsk" [Women's Federation, Norwegian], *PaxLeksikon*. Oslo: Pax Forlag, p. 66.

[75] Bjarnar 1995, p. 23. The Norwegian Women's Public Health Association was established in 1896.

position of women as housewives and to protect the family.[76] In France, the Gaullist women's organization *Femmes Avenir* (Women Future), with its approximately 20,000 members, had a similar objective. In its journal, it was claimed that when women have children, they must stay home and look after them.[77] In both countries there were also a number of women's organizations connected to political parties, religious congregations, and various professional women's associations.

The relationship between the organizations of the "old" and the "new" women's movements was somewhat different in France than in Norway, and considerably more strained in the former. In France, the new generation of the MLF perceived the established women's organizations as uninteresting, even boring. They did not recognize their rational analyses and steady work for gradual reform; instead, they wanted to direct all of their passion toward their revolutionary and utopian struggle to crush the system.[78] The relationship between MLF and the large communist women's organization UFF was particularly hostile. UFF perceived the feminists of MLF to be a handful of rebellious and spoiled petty bourgeois who did not serve the interests of working women.[79] They appealed to women as mothers, and their ideas regarding gender, sexuality, and family differed fundamentally from those of the MLF. The UFF opposed abortion on demand and rejected the sexual revolution because they perceived it as granting the "freedom to be unfaithful" and as providing a means to

[76] The Norwegian Housewives' Association was established in 1917. Berven, Nina, and Per Selle (2001): "Kvinner, organisering og makt" [Women, Organization, and Power], in N. Berven and P. Selle (eds.): *Svekket kvinnemakt? De frivillige organisasjonene og velferdsstaten* [Impaired Woman's Power? The NGOs and the Welfare State]. Oslo: Gyldendal Akademisk.

[77] Chaperon 1995, p. 71; Storti 2010, pp. 202–203. The Gaullist women's organization *Femmes Avenir* (Women Future) was established in 1966.

[78] Picq 1993, p. 27. The lack of recognition of the established women's movements by MLF can be seen in the fact that when revolutionary feminists established the *Ligue du droit des femmes* [the Association for Women's Rights], LDF, in 1974, they more or less stole the name of the *Ligue Française pour le Droit des Femmes* [French League for Women's Rights], or LFDF. According to Chaperon (1995, p. 72, note), LFDFs letter of protest against the theft of its name was not even answered.

[79] Issorel, Irène (2000): "Le mouvement de libération des femmes vu par la presse nationale française 1970–1972" [The Women's Liberation Movement Seen by the French National Press 1970–1972]. Master's thesis in history, University of Toulouse-Le Mirail, p. 105.

destroy the family.[80] By contrast, the MLF's goal was to crush the nuclear family and promote homosexuality and free abortion. For members of the UFF, the feminists' forms of protest appeared crazy and disrespectful, and their lifestyle was perceived as bohemian. In short, the avant-garde political style of the MLF could seem alien to many so-called ordinary women. The hostility was mutual, and in the MLF there was a general opinion that the communist movement was made up of male chauvinist Stalinists who promoted "*travail, famille, parti*" (work, family, party), referring to the fascists' slogan "*travail, famille, patrie*" (work, family, fatherland).[81] Thus, opposing ideas about sexuality and family were at the core of the antagonism between the UFF and the MLF.

In Norway, the relations between the established women's organizations and the newcomers were less hostile. In fact, the groups cooperated pragmatically on particular issues. For instance, the New Feminists and the Women's Front worked with the Housewife Association to increase the proportion of women in political representation. Further, they worked with the Farmers' Women's Association against Norwegian membership in the EEC, and with social democratic and communist women's organizations for abortion on demand.[82] When the famous American feminist Jo Freeman came to the University of Oslo in the fall of 1970

---

[80] Chaperon 2000, p. 363.

[81] *Libération* 10.5 (1976), p. 2.

[82] In the 1971 election, women's organizations across the political spectrum cooperated in a campaign to increase the number of women in municipal councils. The method was a so-called "cumulating campaign," which was designed to give extra votes to female candidates while erasing the names of male candidates on the election lists. The campaign was a success, and in three municipal councils—Asker, Oslo, and Trondheim—a majority of the elected representatives were female. In six other municipal councils, the proportion of female representatives was 40 percent and above. After the 1971 election, the number of municipal councils with no representation of women dropped from 78 to 22. Several male politicians complained about the so-called "women's coup" and presented it as a mockery of democracy. Before the next elections, the law was changed so that it was no longer possible to erase names of candidates on the election lists (Haukaa 1982, p. 30). About the "women's coup" in Asker, see Ryste, Marte (2003): "Kvinnekupp i Asker" [Women's Coup in Asker], Kvinnehistorie.no. In 1971, the socialist politician Berit Ås and other women initiated The Women's Action against Norwegian Membership in the EC, which included a number of women's organizations of different political affiliations (Haukaa 1982, pp. 37–41; "Den nye kvinnebevegelsen" [Women's Liberation Movement], *Kontrast*, no. 8 (1972), pp. 8–9. About the cross-political cooperation in the abortion campaign, see, e.g., Haukaa 1982, pp. 95–100; Aanesen, Ellen (1981): *Ikke send meg til en "kone," doktor! Fra tre års fengsel til selvbestemt abort* [Do Not Send Me to a "Wife"

to be the main speaker at what was eventually referred to as a feminist "revival meeting" that led to the establishment of the New Feminists, her appearance was actually at the invitation of the Oslo chapter of the old Norwegian Association for Women's Rights.[83] Several feminist activists were members of both the Norwegian Association for Women's Rights and the New Feminists. However, there were generational differences. Looking back, a former member of the New Feminists recalled, "We were wild and free.... We saw ourselves as a kind of guerrilla movement."[84] The younger generation of feminist activists saw the established women's movement as overly polite, academic, bureaucratic, and boring. They represented a different political style that was influenced by the youth revolt and the antiauthoritarian movements of the 1960s in regard to participants and collective identity, as well as to political ideas, claims, and forms of protest.

CONSTRUCTING A POLITICAL FIELD

In the early 1970s, the sexual exploitation and abuse of women, pornography, and rape were generally regarded as issues concerning sexual morality that had nothing to do with politics. Ten years later, it had become mainstream to regard such phenomena as manifestations of male dominance and the sexualized oppression of women. How did this transformation come about? In research on how social movements mobilize and construct political fields, the analytical concept of *framing* is widely used. The term is attributed to the sociologist Erving Goffman, who used it to describe the "schemata of interpretation" that people and groups use to organize and construct meaning from their experiences.[85] Researchers on social movements emphasize that grievances and conflicts

Doctor: From Three Years of Prison to Abortion on Demand]. Oslo: Oktober; Schrumpf, Ellen (1984): *Abortsakens historie* [The History of the Abortion Campaigns]. Oslo: Tiden.

[83] The Freeman meeting at the University of Oslo on 7 September 1970 is, for example, referred to in Haukaa 1982, pp. 22–23; Lønnå 1996, pp. 230–231; Hagemann 2004, pp. 275–276; Korsvik, Trine Rogg (2008): "Sekstiåtter med rosa løpesedler. Intervju med Gerd Brantenberg" [Sixty-Eight-Year-Old with Pink Leaflets. Interview with Gerd Brantenberg], in T.E. Førland and T.R. Korsvik: *Ekte sekstiåttere* [Real Sixty-Eight-Year-Olds]. Oslo: Gyldendal Akademisk, p. 65.

[84] Lønnå 1996, p. 234.

[85] Goffman, Erving (1974): *Frame Analysis: An Essay on the Organization of Experience*. Cambridge: Harvard University Press, p. 21.

alone do not necessarily move people to take political action. Social phenomena first become political problems when actors make them political through meaningful activities that inspire, justify, and legitimize collective political protest.[86] The process of politicizing begins with the identification of a social phenomenon as a *problem* that it is connected to other phenomena with which one is dissatisfied, and that someone or something is identified as responsible for the problem—in other words, that the "enemy" is defined. For a social movement to succeed, it is also crucial to propose solutions to the identified problems. Goals must be defined, along with strategies for reaching those goals. At this stage, it is important to form alliances. Further, for social movements to be successful, it is also essential to motivate people to political action over time. To achieve this, participants must have a common goal and develop collective identities and solidarity with one another.[87]

Frame analysis is beneficial in studying processes of politicization of social phenomena and for analyzing how one and the same phenomenon may be interpreted in different ways. The different interpretations, or framings, of a phenomenon will typically have consequences for the formulation of specific political allegations. An example is how different framings of abortion may lead to different assertions. Abortion can be framed as an issue concerning the *protection of unborn life*, which typically leads to the conclusion that abortion is murder and should not be tolerated. Alternatively, abortion can be framed as a *social question regarding the life and health of the pregnant woman*. In the latter case, however, the question remains as to whether doctors are to decide whether a pregnant woman who wants an abortion should or should not be granted

---

[86] See Eyerman and Jamison 1991; Dahlerup 1998; Tarrow 1998.

[87] In 1968, French sociologist Alain Touraine defined a social movement as follows: (1) it has a clearly defined enemy; (2) it has a clearly defined aim; and (3) it creates identification and solidarity within the group. See Touraine, Alain (1968): *Le mouvement de mai: ou le communisme utopique* [The May Movement: Or the Utopian Communism]. Paris: Editions du Seuil. The concept of framing was developed during the 1980s by David A. Snow and Robert Benford, who created a model for how framing processes within social movements take place: (1) diagnosis, that is, defining the problem; (2) prognosis, that is, figuring out what has to be done to solve the problem; and (3) motivation to political action. Snow, David A., and Robert Benford (1988): "Ideology, Frame Resonance, and Participant Mobilization," in B. Klandermans, H. Kriesi, and S. Tarrow (eds.): *From Structure to Action: Comparing Social Movement Research across Cultures*, in *International Social Movement Research*, vol. 1 (1988). Greenwich: JAI Press, pp. 197–217.

one, or whether she herself is entitled to make the decision. When the women's liberation movement of the 1970s framed abortion as a matter of *a woman's right to control her own body*, the call for abortion on demand was given voice. Different ways of framing may thus point toward a specific demand, but not always. As frame analysis primarily describes *how* a phenomenon is interpreted, it does not explain *why* it is framed in a certain way. In their research on social movements, Myra Marx Ferree and David A. Merrill argue that political *ideology* must be taken into account when analyzing framing processes. The concept of gender, for instance, can be framed as biological sex differences and as social constructs, but it remains to be seen whether the attendant political demands will turn out to be either feminist or anti-feminist.[88] Later in this book, we will see that the various ideological tendencies of the women's liberation movement framed the phenomena of rape and pornography differently. Marxism was the major political reference for French and Norwegian 1970s left-wingers, but it was challenged by feminist ideas.

Frame analysis has been criticized for ignoring the emotional aspects of political struggle. Scholars have argued that emotions such as anger, fear, hate, outrage, joy, and love must be taken into account in research on social movements and protests.[89] For instance, do Michèle Lamont and Laurent Thévenot criticize frame analysis for presuming that social movement actors are manipulative and have "hidden self-interests".[90] They claim that that it is essential to recognize that social movement actors are motivated by genuine moral criticism of injustice. There is no doubt that emotions are important motivations for people to act politically, but this fact does not necessarily lead to the conclusion that frame analysis is an irrelevant tool. Frame analysis helps one to understand the production of

---

[88] Ferree, Myra Marx, and David A. Merrill (2004): "Hot Movements, Cold Cognition," in J. Goodwin and J. Jasper (eds.): *Rethinking Social Movements: Structure, Meaning, and Emotion.* Lanham, MD: Rowman & Littlefield, p. 249.

[89] Goodwin et al. 2001; Goodwin et al. 2004; Goodwin, Jeff, James M. Jasper, & Francesca Poletta (2006): "Emotional Dimensions of Social Movements," in D.A. Snow et al. (eds.): *The Blackwell Companion to Social Movements.* Malden, MA: Blackwell. This perspective is also discussed by the Swedish sociologists Lars Dahlgren and Bengt Starrin (2004) in the book *Emotioner i vardagsliv & samhälle. En introduktion til emotionssosiologi* [Emotions in Everyday Life and Society: An Introduction to the Sociology of Emotions]. Malmö: Liber, especially in Chap. 11, "Emotioner i sosiala rörelser" [Emotions in Social Movements].

[90] Lamont and Thévenot 2000.

meaning that justifies and inspires people to collective action. The intention of social movements is to mobilize people to collective action with the purpose of changing society, and there need not be any contradiction between the emotional and the rational in political practice.[91] Political grassroots activism is often triggered by a "righteous anger that puts fire in the belly and iron in the soul,"[92] but that does not mean that the activists are unable to think strategically. When women threw themselves into the women's liberation struggle, it was because they were both angry at injustices perpetrated on women and delighted to participate in a community of women; what's more, they were determined to change the world.[93]

STRUCTURE OF THE BOOK

The following chapters explore how the women's liberation movements in France and Norway constructed rape and pornography as gender-political issues. Chapter 2 deals with the early phase of the mobilization against rape and pornography. It outlines the historical context of those issues as social phenomena, including in the judicial system, in France and Norway, respectively, showing how the different contexts impacted the way in which the women's liberation movements framed these issues. Identifying rape and pornography as gender-political problems began inside the women's liberation movements, but movement activists soon began to communicate explicitly to the outside world that sexual exploitation of women is a political problem that must be solved. In doing so, they took advantage of various strategies of legitimization that could appeal to the left, such as framing rape as a form of imperialism or fascism, or pornography as capitalist exploitation nourished by Christian morality that equates sex with sin.

---

[91] Goodwin et al. 2001, 2004, and 2006.

[92] Gamson, William A. (1992): "The Social Psychology of Political Action," in A. Morris and C. McClurg Mueller (eds.): *Frontiers in Social Movement Theory*. New Haven: Yale University Press, p. 32.

[93] Taylor, Verta (1995): "Watching for Vibes: Bringing Emotions into the Study of Feminist Organizations," in M. Marx Ferree and P.Y. Martin (eds.): *Feminist Organizations: Harvest of the New Women's Movement*. Philadelphia, PA: Temple University Press.

Chapter 3 delves into the next phase of the mobilization against rape and pornography—that is, when activists of the women's liberation movement took to the streets and through direct action brought these issues into the public political space. Movement activists made use of established forms of protest such as marches, rallies, distribution of flyers, petitions, and publication of opinion pieces in the newspapers. But they also invented new forms of action. These actions were typically disruptive and highly symbolic, and broke with cultural expectations of what women should say and do, creating new protest rituals. Although the forms of protest were generally nonviolent, it happened that activists sometimes attacked private property. The intention of direct actions is evidently to draw attention to political claims, to provoke public debate, and to make the movement visible. Also, they work as means to strengthen unity among the activists and to create heroic myths about themselves. In addition, direct actions are important learning processes. The planning and carrying out of actions contribute to the development of political theory, not least because they are crucial to identifying both allies and adversaries of the cause. Large protest marches show strength, but direct militant actions performed by a small group may be more effective in gaining attention, as illustrated by the impact of the Norwegian women activists' public burning of pornography magazines. At the same time, activists have no control over how the outside world interprets their actions. Some actors interpreted the mobilizations against rape and pornography as manifestations of puritanism and a totalitarian ideology.

The breakthrough for the campaigns against rape and pornography is the subject of Chapter 4. The women's liberation movements' framing of rape and pornography as serious gender-political matters was acknowledged by large segments of the media, by other social movements, by the political elite, and by the judicial system. However, the success was ambiguous. In France, many feminists interpreted the breakthrough not as a victory, but as a sign that they had walked into a trap set by the bourgeois state, which now imposed increasingly strict penalties on rapists. In Norway, the success of the anti-pornography campaign led to a bitter media debate about whether the women's movement was driven by hatred of men. Despite these paradoxes, legislative changes were made in response to the mobilizations of the women's movements, but it was not clear that the women's liberation activists would interpret this as a victory. In any case, the political mobilizations surrounding these issues declined after the legislative changes. But that was in the 1980s, a decade with a markedly different political climate than the rebellious 1970s.

The mobilizations against rape and pornography were by no means unique to the French and Norwegian women's liberation movements. In all Western countries with vibrant radical women's movements, these issues were politicized in various ways and to varying degrees in the 1970s, along with other phenomena that feminist activists defined as sexualized violence against women. Despite the fact that this was a transnational trend, however, there were national and local variations as to which aspects of the sexualized violence were emphasized by the women's movements. By looking toward other countries to which reasonable comparisons could be drawn, Chapter 5 explains why the mobilization against sexual exploitation and abuse of women was predominantly articulated as a struggle against rape in France and as a struggle against pornography in Norway. The chapter discusses whether rape and pornography were, in fact, experienced as more severe problems in one country than in the other, and the extent to which there were distinctive features of the movements—including how they interacted with other societal actors—that led to these issues being prioritized. Emphasis is placed on the importance of forms of protest, individuals, alliances, and opponents, as well as on media coverage. In addition, the chapter traces historical connections from the 1970s women's liberation movements to the contemporary feminist movements in France and Norway. Using interviews with feminist activists, the chapter explores the position and the framing of rape and pornography as gender-political issues in French and Norwegian feminist movements of the 2000s, as compared to the 1970s and 1980s. The chapter concludes with a discussion of enduring dilemmas connected to feminist political mobilization against sexual exploitation and the abuse of women.

CHAPTER 2

Addressing the Problem: Rape and Pornography Become Feminist Political Issues

In the early 1970s, rape and pornography were not widely perceived as relevant political issues but rather as phenomena having to do with sexual morality, especially about men's unruly sexual urges. However, there were considerable differences in terms of the position that rape and pornography held in the public discourse in France and Norway, respectively. While there was general silence about rape in France, pornography was extensively discussed in Norway. In left-wing liberal circles, many people looked positively on pornography, regarding it as a healthy expression of sexual liberation and a much-needed corrective to old-fashioned prudishness. The most vocal opponents of pornography were found among Christians and conservatives, who believed that sex outside of marriage was sinful and worthy of shame.

Despite these different beginnings, the politicization of rape and pornography developed in similar ways in France and Norway. The shared process, which had its roots in the countries' women's movements, began by addressing these phenomena as gender-political problems that required resolution. As was typical of the 1970s women's liberation movements, the personal experiences of women were key to the development of politics. When activists set about to explain the problems, they made use of concepts and theories that were commonly employed by the contemporary left, particularly explanations inspired by Marxism, the major frame of reference for 1970s radicals.

© The Author(s) 2021
T. R. Korsvik, *Politicizing Rape and Pornography*,
Citizenship, Gender and Diversity,
https://doi.org/10.1007/978-3-030-55639-6_2

47

For rape and pornography to become political issues, however, it was insufficient to simply discuss the problems solely within the women's movement; the questions had to invoke a wider public debate. In both countries, this debate initially took the form of newspaper exchanges that feminists initiated in the wake of specific events. In France, the triggering event was the rape of a woman who was active in the anti-racist movement. When one of the raped woman's revolutionary feminist friends wrote an opinion piece about the rape in the left-wing newspaper *Libération*, it became a topic of public discussion. In Norway, the debate on pornography as a gender-political issue was ushered in by three members of the New Feminists who visited a strip club and later wrote an opinion piece about their experiences for the liberal newspaper *Dagbladet*. The fact that young feminists wrote in leading newspapers about rape, pornography, and sexual exploitation of women was sensational and led to intense debate about sexuality, sex roles, men's sexism, and the "right to use" women. Women and men—ordinary people and intellectuals alike—posted letters to the newspapers in which they aired their opinions on the subject. In France, philosopher Jean-Paul Sartre, one of society's most influential left-wing intellectuals of the period, engaged in the debate on rape, taking the side of feminists. In Norway, law professor Anders Bratholm publicly adjudicated the myths regarding men's unruly urges. Once the discussion expanded to include the voices of elderly men of authority, it lent an aura of seriousness to the subjects of rape and pornography as topics of public discourse.

Despite the differences in France and Norway in the public attitudes concerning rape and pornography, targeting them as feminist political issues was not easy. To understand why, it is useful to take a closer look at the historical context of rape and pornography in France and Norway, respectively, regarding legislation, judicial practices, and public debate.

Rape in France

In France, the prevailing rape legislation in the 1970s dated back to 1832. The law provided no clear definition of rape, but following an 1857 verdict, it became customary for the courts to define rape as "illegal intercourse with a woman whom one knows does not consent"[1]—"illegal

---

[1] "Coït illicite avec une femme qu'on sait n'y point consentir." The following information on court proceedings in rape cases is taken from Mossuz-Lavau, Janine (1991): *Les*

intercourse" in this context meaning sex outside of marriage. The concept of rape within marriage did not exist, for it would involve questioning the "obligation of marriage," that is, the spouses' mutual duty to engage in intercourse with one other, the failure with which to comply was grounds for divorce. According to this interpretation of the law, rape would only have taken place if there had been forced vaginal penetration of a woman who was not the man's wife. Other types of sexual assault were considered "indecent assault" (*attentat à la pudeur*), with lighter sentencing ramifications. The verdict of 1857 had established that the magistrate in each case should determine whether rape had taken place, based on the severity of the incident and the consequences to the victim and to the "honor of the family." The old-fashioned notion of the "honor of the family" referred to the possible adulterous pregnancy in which the rape could result—a shame for the family.

According to the law, rape should be punished severely, by a prison sentence of 10–20 years. In practice, however, there were almost no convictions for rape, and there were few victims who reported being raped to the police. In 1970, 1030 rapes were reported in France, of which 290 led to convictions. Four years later, in 1974, the number of reported rapes had increased to 1538, while the number of convictions had dropped to 249. How many rapes were actually committed is unknown. In the 1970s, experts estimated that there were about 10 or even 20 times more rapes than were reported.[2] The reason for the serious underreporting of rapes was the shame attached to describing the event, as well as the ordeal involved in the detailed interrogations of a trial, the psychiatric observations, and the investigations of one's morals, all of which were required by the judicial process. The parameters of what was considered rape were rigorous: it had to be proved that gross violence had taken place, that the penis had penetrated the vagina, and that the defendant *knew* that the alleged rape victim did not consent. Among those on the political left, there was an additional factor that limited the rate of reporting—namely, that they were opposed to involving the "bourgeois" judicial system in rape cases.

lois de l'amour. Les politiques de la sexualité en France (1950–1990) [The Laws of Love. The Politics of Sexuality in France (1950–1990)]. Paris: Payot, pp. 189–193.

[2] Senate Report no. 442, cited in Mossuz-Lavau 1991, p. 192.

Court practices intricately drive societal attitudes. Scholars who have investigated how rape has historically been perceived in France emphasize the tacit acceptance of rape, a state of affairs that persisted into the 1970s.[3] Victims of rape were generally perceived as accomplices in the act they had been subjected to—that is, that they had been "careless" or had a "free" lifestyle and thereby provoked the assault. According to gender historian Anne-Marie Sohn, rape was excused and interpreted as a "classical manifestation of manliness," and the victims were perceived as consenting, or responsible for "the urges they had stirred."[4]

Historian Georges Vigarello claims that the women's liberation movement of the 1970s was the first to challenge "the relative tolerance" of rape in France.[5] In his work on the history of rape in France from the sixteenth century to modern times, Vigarello analyzes the historical background of this tolerance. During the *Ancien Régime*—that is, prior to the French Revolution of 1789—rape was not designated a violent crime, but instead a crime of blasphemy against God in the same manner as sorcery, witchcraft, adultery, infidelity, sodomy, and bestiality, i.e., sexual intercourse with animals. Unique to blasphemy crimes was that one did not distinguish between victims and abusers: the victim was perceived as an accomplice to the act. There were exceptions to the rule, of course, and in the *Ancien Régime* the "quality" of the victim, as well as of the offender, was decisive. If a servant raped his master's wife, the crime called for the death penalty, but a gentleman's rape of a maidservant would pass. Thus, the application of law was driven not by the cruelty of the act, but by the social status of the offender and the victim.[6] Moreover, the punishment was determined by the degree of the rape victim's "innocence": the rape of an "honorable" virgin was punished more severely than that of an adult woman. In principle, the punishment for raping a marriageable virgin was

<hr />

[3] Mossuz-Lavau 1991; Sohn, Anne-Marie (2006): "Le corps sexué" [The Sexed Body], in A. Corbin, J. Courtine, and G. Vigarello (eds.): *Histoire du corps. Les mutations du regard. Le XXe siècle* [History of the Body. The Mutations of the Gaze. The Twentieth Century]. Volume 3. Paris: Éditions du Seuil, p. 125; Vigarello, Georges (1998): *Histoire du viol. XVIe–XXe siècle* [A History of Rape: Sexual Violence in France from the 16th to the 20th Century]. Paris: Éditions du Seuil; Welzer-Lang, Daniel (1988): *Le viol au masculin* [Masculine Rape]. Paris: Editions L'Harmattan.

[4] Sohn 2006, pp. 125–126.

[5] Vigarello 1998, p. 7.

[6] Op. cit., pp. 24–26.

the death penalty—specifically, mangling with steep and wheel.[7] The logic of such strict sentencing was that the girl's virginity was a prerequisite of her family's ability to marry her off. A "deflowered" girl was considered "damaged fruit" that was no longer acceptable in the marriage market. Therefore, it was important to keep any rapes hidden.[8]

The point of outlining this historical background on rape is to illustrate the persistence of mentalities. Thus, despite the French Revolution's abolition of all the old blasphemy laws and the privileges of the nobility and the clergy, and its ushering in of legislation that declared every citizen to be an independent legal entity, the old mentalities persisted into the twentieth century. For example, many doctors and lawyers continued to believe that it was physically impossible for a single man to rape an adult woman, and that there must be a "hidden consent" behind the act.[9] Until the 1970s, the courts generally doubted the victim, and for the offender to be convicted, the rape must have taken place in a public space and needed to have been observed by witnesses. At the same time, the rape should not have happened in *too* public a space—for example, along a country road—at least not if the victim had a questionable reputation.[10]

On the other hand, historical changes indeed occurred in terms of the perception of perpetrators and victims of rape. With the development of medicine as a modern science during the 1800s, rapists became objects of research. Mental defects of the rapists were identified and often considered to be indicators of insanity. In line with new theories of evolution, rapists and other criminals were viewed as primitive and degenerate holdovers from an earlier stage of evolution. Another view of rape, a sociologically oriented one, gained prominence beginning in the 1890s. Rape was explained as the result of social conditions, including miserable living conditions in working-class environments, alcoholism, and "urban promiscuity."[11] During the 1900s, the science of psychiatry became increasingly aware of the psychological profile of the rapist. It became

---

[7] In mangling with steep and wheel, the criminal's arms and legs were first crushed with a mallet, and then the criminal was tied onto a wheel placed at the top of a pole.

[8] In the period 1540–1692, there were only 49 reports of rape in the Paris Parliament, which represents an average of less than three rapes per decade. Most of these reports involved extremely violent rapes of young children. Vigarello 1998, p. 69.

[9] Op. cit., p. 243.

[10] Op. cit., p. 180.

[11] Op. cit., pp. 215–216.

customary to perceive him as a victim of "uncontrolled sexual drives" and sexual frustration.[12] Or, to state it another way, instead of seeing the rapist as a savage, he was rather seen as a deficient man. Attention was turned to marginalized men, vagabonds, foreigners, and frustrated men living in isolated villages. In the 1970s, it was commonplace to explain rape as a result of *la misère sexuelle*, or "sexual misery."

Society's perception of the victims changed as well. While rape victims, including children, were regarded during the *Ancien Régime* as "tempters," they came to be perceived more as innocent victims in the nineteenth century. However, in court, this did not apply to the rape of "free" women—that is, women who were not virgins or married. Men who raped such women were most often acquitted.[13] The traumatic effects of rape were not considered until the late 1970s, the change being a result, according to Vigarello, of the women's liberation movement's campaign against rape.

In her book on French laws regarding sexuality from 1950 to 1990, Janine Mossuz-Lavau offers many examples of how rape continued to be accepted into the 1970s. For example, a popular radio host of a program on the state channel declared that rape could be a woman's "best memory in life."[14] And one of the country's most renowned sexologists, Michel Meignant, claimed that women who walk alone or hitchhike have an unconscious desire to be raped:

> One doesn't just rape anybody, and the men aren't as guilty as is claimed. The woman who hitchhikes, and the one who walks in shorts in the evening in a deserted suburb, puts herself unconsciously in a position where she can be raped, with a subconscious desire to be raped.[15]

It was customary to argue that sexual liberation provoked rape. As stated by a defense attorney for a rapist: "Women know what they are doing

---

[12] Op. cit., pp. 225–227.

[13] Op. cit., p. 182.

[14] Mossuz-Lavau 1991, pp. 198–203.

[15] Quotation in Storti 2010, p. 115. From the article "*Le Viol*, un titre, deux livres, l'un par Susan Brownmiller, l'autre par Marie-Odile Fargier" [The Rape, One Title, Two Books, One by Susan Brownmiller, the Other by Marie-Odile Fargier], *Libération*, 25 November 1976.

when they abandon their traditional submissiveness."[16] Another defense lawyer of a rapist who, in concert with a friend, had abused and raped a 23-year-old woman they had met at a nightclub in Paris, said in defense of his client that "If a woman finds herself in a nightclub with a girlfriend at three o'clock in the morning and agrees to talk with two men, then she knows how it will end. Such women are not respectable." Moreover, in the defense speech the lawyer continued:

> Rape is the carnal sin that is the least serious, dating back to Adam and Eve. Those who have never sinned can throw the first stone (...) Rape is the result of a looser morality, the women being too loose. Besides, the man is made to enjoy the woman. A woman at three o'clock in the morning is a surprise gift.[17]

In view of these prevailing attitudes, the authorities did not take rape particularly seriously, nor did the men who were convicted of rape. The general attitude was that they did not understand that they had done anything wrong. A study of convicted rapists from the 1970s revealed that few of them understood why they were in prison; they had just wanted to have some fun.[18] Mossuz-Lavau claims it was quite common to show compassion for rapists and their possible "sexual misery" and frustrations. There was little consideration of the traumatic effects of the rape on the victims. Men who had been convicted of rape seldom understood that they had done anything wrong. Many of them said that on their part it had only been intended as a "joke."

Court Proceedings in Rape Cases

According to France's 1832 Criminal Code, which was in in effect until 1980, rape cases should be dealt with in the Assize Court (*Cour d'Assises*), along with other serious felonies such as murder and armed robbery. The penalty for felonies was prison or detention of a duration ranging from ten years to life and also included, until 1981, the death penalty by means of the guillotine. Nevertheless, rape cases were most often dealt

---

[16] Mossuz-Lavau 1991, p. 202. Quotation from *Rouge*, 26 June 1976.

[17] Quotation from Ginou Richard: "Viol: trois ans de lutte, pourquoi?" [Rape: Three Years of Struggle, Why?], *F magazine*, no. 6, juin 1978, p. 31.

[18] Mossuz-Lavau 1991, p. 198. Quotation from *La Croix*, 11 April 1980.

with in the Correctional Tribunal (*Tribunal Correctionnel*), along with less serious offenses (misdemeanors) such as theft, fraud, embezzlement, traffic offenses, and assault. Here, rape cases were treated under the category of "gross indecency" (*outrage à la pudeur*). The "declassification" of rape from felony to misdemeanor was, according to Vigarello, a legal compromise that served to increase the chances of the defendant being convicted.[19] The evidentiary requirements of the Assize Court had been so strict that the cases rarely led to conviction. The judge had to find evidence that the victim had not consented, and that the defendant *knew* she did not consent. In addition, the penalties were so severe that this, in itself, often led to acquittal. The transfer of rape cases to the Correctional Tribunal ensured that they were handled more quickly and were more likely to result in conviction, but with a limited penalty.[20]

As we will see later on, the activists of the MLF were dissatisfied with rape being treated as a misdemeanor, viewing it not as a felony but more akin to thefts of mopeds or drunken brawls. Thus, one of their main demands was that rape be handled in the Assize Court, which they believed would lend it appropriate recognition as a felony and a grave social problem. This demand, however, was not pressed until the mobilization against rape was well underway in the mid-1970s.

Pornography in Norway

Pornography was subject to considerably more debate in Norway than rape was in France. At the same time, however, Norwegian legislation on pornography in the 1970s was quite archaic. Section 211 of the Penal Code, the so-called pornography clause from 1902, reads as follows:

> With fines or with imprisonment for up to one year, anyone who holds public lectures or arranges public performances or exhibits of obscene content or who contributes to such lectures, performances, exhibitions, will be punished.

---

[19] Vigarello 1998, p. 193.

[20] For arguments supporting the use of the Correctional Tribunal, see the accusation by the public prosecutor Perfetti in "Le réquisitoire" [The Indictment], in Choisir la cause des femmes (1976): *Viol. Le procès d'Aix* [Rape. The Process in Aix]. Paris: Gallimard, pp. 253–255.

Likewise, the person who causes or contributes to the fact that obscene writings, images, or the like are publicly peddled, exhibited, or otherwise disseminated among the public, will be punished.

If someone in his business activities within two years performs such crimes as mentioned above, he may be deprived of the right to continue the business.[21]

In this statutory provision (which, with certain amendments, was in force until 1985), "obscene" referred to all sorts of sexual representations, except in medical and legal publications, that were, in principle, forbidden. In practice, however, such was not the case, because it was up to prosecutors and the courts to decide what was "obscene." In fact, there was no clear definition of pornography. For example, there was no distinction between erotica and "hard" or "soft" pornography.

The definition of pornography has changed throughout the ages. Etymologically, the term is derived from the Greek words *porne*, meaning prostitute, and *graphein*, meaning writing, as in descriptions of prostitutes. The term was originally applied in England and France in the eighteenth century to writings dealing with prostitution as a social hygiene problem, but was also used as a term for describing the sexual depictions that had been found during the archeological excavations in Pompeii.[22] By its modern definition, pornography refers to depictions whose main purpose is to provoke sexual arousal, a characteristic that distinguishes it from art and literature with erotic content. In the 1970s, the debate surrounding pornography as we know it today had been settled. In general, distinctions were made among "soft pornography," "real pornography," and "hard-core pornography." Hard core included pornography that showed sexual violence, children engaging in sexual intercourse with adults, and women engaging in sexual intercourse with

[21] "Med bøder eller med fængsel indtil 1 aar straffes den, som holder offentlig foredrag eller istandbringer offentlig forestilling eller udstilling af utugtigt indhold, eller som medvirker til, at saadanne foredrag, forestillinger eller udstillinger finder sted.

Paa samme maade straffes den, som bevirker eller medvirker til, at utugtige skrifter, billeder eller deslige offentlig falholdes, udstilles eller paa anden maade søges utbredte blant almenheden.

Forøver nogen som sin næring i løbet af 2 aar tvende gange saadan forbrydelse som oven nævnt, kan retten til at fortsætte næringen frakjendes ham." Quoted in Århelle 1981, p. 8.

[22] Rollnes, Kjetil: "Pornografi" [Pornography], *Store norske leksikon*, http://snl.no; "Pornography," *Oxford Dictionaries*.

animals. In the mid-1970s, after most limits had been tested, the final genre was "snuff" pornography, which allegedly showed actual sexual murders.[23]

Still, pornography existed before the 1970s. In Norway, commercial, mass-produced pornography came on the market after World War II, in particular after the rationing of paper ended in 1952. As part of the Marshall Plan, a new type of "entertainment magazine" was imported from the United States, including comics, celebrity gossip sheets, pin-up magazines, and crime magazines offering "real-life stories" about gangsters, drugs, prostitution, executions, rapes, and sexual murders. Soon thereafter, Norwegian magazines began to mimic the American models, such as the pin-up magazines *Cocktail*, *Bikini*, and *Krydder* (Spices), as well as the *Kriminaljournalen* (the Criminal Journal), a magazine that was described as a "poison cesspool" by the Social-Democrat newspaper *Arbeiderbladet*.[24] The concern over these developments was great, not only in Christian environments, but also among parents, women's organizations, politicians, and intellectuals who opposed the new commercial popular culture imported from America. A broad-based movement against pornography, or "dirt magazines," which they were often called in the 1950s, was born. This movement focused primarily on the harmful influence the magazines might have on children and adolescents. Notifications to the police about the "dirt magazines" rarely brought any response, but several magazine dealers refused to sell them, and sales appeared to decline.

In 1955, the Norwegian Parliament (the *Storting*) discussed what could be done to limit the spread of magazines that, because of content of a "sexual, criminal and sadistic nature, have an unfortunate influence, especially on children and adolescents."[25] The discussions resulted in the appointment by the Labor Government of a committee led by the radical pedagogue and Chairman of the Norwegian Broadcasting Council, Eva Nordland, to weigh in on a dozen publications of "inferior" literature

---

[23] The account of the content of the pornography in this period is based on Tessem, Liv Berit, and Kjetil Wiedswang (1984): *Pornorge. Krigere og kremmere på pornomarkedet i 30 år* [PorNorway. Warriors and Peddlers on the Porn Market for 30 Years]. Oslo: Universitetsforlaget, pp. 85–88.

[24] On the pornography debates of the 1950s, see Tessem and Wiedswang 1984, pp. 22–27.

[25] From the debates at the *Storting*, quoted in Tessem and Wiedswang 1984, p. 25.

in the genres of crime, cowboys, and pin-ups. The so-called Nordland Committee did not support prohibition, but in 1957 the Criminal Law Council recommended expanding paragraph 211 thusly: "Obscene writings" should also apply to publications "that are obviously offensive or likely to be seen as corrupting or vulgarizing children or adolescents; or, when their purpose is considered to be a predominantly economic exploitation of interest in sexuality, violence or crime."[26] The recommendation of the council was rejected by advisory bodies, including the Publisher Association, the Author Association, and the Bookstore Association, as well as the liberal newspaper *Dagbladet*, all of which held that it amounted to censorship and an attack on intellectual freedom. Thus, it was abandoned. Of significance in this decision was the fact that, at the same time, the prosecuting authorities were about to prepare a lawsuit against the author Agnar Mykle, whose 1957 novel *The Song of the Red Ruby* was confiscated and banned because of its daring sex scenes. The new proposal on "obscene writings" could be perceived as a plea in court.

The Mykle case was controversial, since it was the first time in 70 years that the Norwegian prosecuting authorities had brought proceedings against a literary work for obscenity. The last time this had occurred was in 1886, when the artist Chr. Krohg's socially critical novel *Albertine*, about a young seamstress who was raped by a police officer and subsequently forced into prostitution, was seized and banned.[27] In 1957, Mykle and Harald Grieg of the publishing house Gyldendal were convicted on the obscenity charges, but were acquitted in 1958 by the Supreme Court. Meanwhile, the Norwegian translation of American writer Henry Miller's autobiography *Sexus* was banned. In the context of these court cases, the attention shifted from protecting children and adolescents from "inferior dirt magazines" to fiction. This led to a weakening of the popular movement against pornography.[28] The cases against the literary works also added to the impression that Norway led an active censorship policy. Upon closer inspection, however, the censorship was not so strict in

---

[26] "Forandringer i straffebestemmelsene om pornografi m.v." [Changes in the Penalties Regarding Pornography etc.]. Tessem and Wiedswang 1984, p. 27.

[27] Korsvik 2014, p. 18. For the protests by the Norwegian Association for Women's Rights against the seizure, see Moksnes, Aslaug (1984): *Likestilling eller særstilling? Norsk Kvinnesaksforening 1884–1913* [Gender Equality or Unique Position? Norwegian Association for Women's Rights 1884–1913]. Oslo: Gyldendal, p. 128.

[28] Tessem og Wiedswang 1984, pp. 22–27.

practice: the lawyer Tone Århelle's research on Norwegian court practice in pornography cases from 1953 to 1978 revealed that the Mykle and Miller cases were actually the only pornography trials in the period 1954–1966.[29] In 1967, however, a new author, Jens Bjørneboe, was convicted on charges stemming from his erotic novel *Without a Thread*. The book was originally published anonymously by the obscure publisher Scala in 1966, but it soon became known that the "famous author" who had written the book was Bjørneboe. Both the author and the publisher were convicted, first in the Oslo District Court, and then in the Supreme Court. The book was confiscated and placed on the index of forbidden books. The Supreme Court's argument was that *Without a Thread* "grossly violated the decency of the ordinary woman and man in our country."[30] The Supreme Court referred to the Mykle and Miller cases as precedents.

The Bjørneboe case was the final time in which the Norwegian pornography debate centered on what should and should not be allowed in erotic descriptions in fiction. One of Bjørneboe's main points in the highly publicized trial was that it was striking that his book, which was "a sole attack on the male society's view of women—the woman as a private property," was banned at a time when one could freely purchase magazines that depicted "young girls raped by baboons," in which women are portrayed as "sheer commodities, as passive females ... humiliated as beings without an existence of their own ... and proper human life."[31] This point was emphasized by the defense, which presented evidence

[29] In 1953, however, there were two convictions for image pornography. Århelle, Tone (1981): *Pornografiens vilkår i Norge. En undersøkelse av domstolspraksis i Oslo 1953–78.* Institutt for offentlig retts skriftserie [Conditions of Pornography in Norway. An Investigation of Court Jurisdictions in Oslo 1953–78. Department of Public Law, University of Oslo]. Oslo: Universitetsforlaget, pp. 16–42.

[30] Rem, Tore (2010): *Født til frihet. En biografi om Jens Bjørneboe* [Born to Freedom. A Biography on Jens Bjørneboe]. Volume 2. Oslo: Cappelen Damm, p. 276. The penalty in the city Court of 16 June 1967 was a symbolic 100 NOK fine for Bjørneboe and 10,000 NOK for the publisher, in addition to the legal expenses and cost of confiscation of the books. Both the defendants and the prosecution appealed the verdict, and when the case was settled in the Supreme Court on 15 December 1967, the penalty was raised to 1000 NOK for Bjørneboe and 50,000 for the publisher, in addition to the legal fees and costs of confiscation.

[31] Bjørneboe, Jens (1966): "Istedenfor en forsvarstale" [Instead of a Defense Speech], in A. Nordhus et al. (eds.): *En tråd. Seks innlegg om pornografi* [A Thread. Six Posts about Pornography]. Oslo: Pax Forlag, pp. 43, 52–53.

in the form of pornographic magazines, books, and films that were far more "obscene" than Bjørneboe's book but were still freely available for purchase. Although fiction was no longer subject to prosecution following this trial, films containing sexual content were censored. In the rebellious year 1968, the Public Movie Control (*Statens Filmkontroll*) decided to censor parts of Swedish film director Ingmar Bergmann's films *Silence* and *The Virgin Spring* and to ban the Swedish experimental, socially critical film *I Am Curious (Yellow)* (*Jag är nyfiken—gul*).[32]

The censorship policy triggered the pornography debates of the late 1960s. The pornography dealer Magne Severinsen, who had become famous after testifying in the Bjørneboe trial and, moreover, was something of a rare figure as an openly gay man, travelled the country and debated pornography with priests and teachers in high school societies and local youth party chapters.[33] Bjørneboe himself visited the Norwegian Student's Society, where he attacked authoritarian views on sexuality. In the cultural debates, the *Without a Thread* case was perceived as a struggle for the new era.[34] Psychoanalysis was fashionable among cultural radicals of the time, who saw in pornography opportunities to help people bring their dark sides to light. Pornography was seen as a means of mental purification, a way to rid one's mind of Christian morality, and it became a symbol of the struggle against what cultural radicals perceived as a distinctly Norwegian tradition of censorship and the forces of obscurantism.[35] In the Danish debates on whether to allow pornography, which undoubtedly influenced Norwegians who held liberal views on sexuality,

---

[32] "Jag är nyfiken—en film i gult" [*I Am Curious (Yellow)*], from 1967, was directed by Vilgot Sjöman. The 1968 sequel, "Jag är nyfiken—en film i blått" [*I Am Curious (Blue)*], was recorded simultaneously. Lena Nyman played the lead role of a political agitator who exposed the Swedish "class society"—that is, a society in which the bourgeoisie exploits the working class.

[33] Tessem and Wiedswang 1984, p. 41. In the Pax-book *En tråd* (A Thread) there is an extended overview of Severinsen's assortment of "magazines, books and phonograph records from Six magazine store, Oslo."

[34] Rem 2010, p. 276.

[35] Århelle 1981, p. 31. See also Kvam, Ragnar (ed.) (1966): *Norske sengehester. Uskyske noveller* [Norwegian Bedhorses. Unchaste Short Stories]. Oslo: Pax Forlag. The contributors were Lars Berg, Jan Bull, Lisbeth Bull, Ketil Gjessing, Helge Hagerup, Carl Hambro, Axel Jensen, Georg Johannesen, and Ragnar Kvam. In Norwegian, the word "mørkemann" (shadowman) refers to Christians who oppose enlightenment and spiritual freedom.

it was argued that pornography could work as a "safety valve" for sexually frustrated men.[36] The idea was that instead of raping women and children, they could have an outlet through pornography.

In the 1960s, the act of supporting pornography was perceived as being modern and radical, and opposing it as being old-fashioned and puritan.[37] The prototype of the pornography opponent of the time was the evangelist Aril Edvardsen. In the summer of 1969, he organized an anti-pornography march in Saron's Dal (Saron's Valley) in Southern Norway that drew some 12,000 Pentecostals carrying banners with slogans that read, for example, "Norway—remember Sodom and Gomorrah" and "Away with the pornography plague, love is pure."[38] Looking closer at the pornography debates of the 1960s, however, the picture becomes more complex. Although cultural radicals were opposed to banning pornography, several of them were critical of the visual pornography that was increasingly available on the market. Above we saw how Bjørneboe criticized representations of women as "sheer commodities" and "passive females" without an existence of their own. The author Axel Jensen revealed a somewhat different perspective in his criticism of pornography when, in an anthology on pornography edited by Bjørneboes's lawyer Alf Nordhus in 1966, he argued that it represented a "one-sided and distorted perspective on human reality":

> Its worship of the body, and particularly the reproductive organs, ultimately becomes derisive of the body, for it is a prerequisite of pornography to cultivate the body as a piece of flesh laden with adrenaline, not as something unknown, something miraculous, something which we are yet to discover.[39]

[36] Gulli, Brita M. (2007): "Gjenerobring av kvinnekroppen" [Reclaiming the Female Body], Kvinnehistorie.no.

[37] Rustad, Unni (2007): "Kampen mot pornografi på 1970-tallet: Unni Rustad forteller" [The Struggle Against Pornography in the 1970s: Unni Rustad Relates]. Kvinnehistorie.no. See also Århelle 1981; Hompland 2003; Tessem and Wiedswang 1984.

[38] Hompland 2003, p. 282; Rustad 2007; Tessem and Wiedswang 1984, p. 60.

[39] Jensen, Axel (1966): "Bølgen" [The Wave], in A. Nordhus et al. (eds.): *En tråd. Seks innlegg om pornografi* [A Thread. Six Posts About Pornography]. Oslo: Pax Forlag, p. 64.

Heavily influenced by 1960s anti-authoritarian, liberatory ideals, Jensen criticized pornography for "producing man and woman as synthetic arti-facts, as commodities, as commercial products. What is worrying about pornography is that it is a child of its time."[40] Jensen's objections were thus formulated as a criticism of contemporary society, of a time of alien-ation, of plastics and cellophane, as many other hippie-inspired critics interpreted it.[41] He was not concerned with gendered power relations reflected in pornography, but rather with the depiction of an alienated and synthetic sexuality devoid of the "miraculous" and "undiscovered." Despite his qualms, Jensen was opposed to censorship. Like other "sexual liberals," he argued that pornography would be redundant once society adopted a more open attitude toward sexuality. As the radical sociolo-gist and Reichian Erik Grønseth put it, the "porn troll" would burst if it came to light.[42] The idea was that people would quickly lose interest once pornography was made available: "'The pornography wave' will reach a peak and then drop. It will lose its power," as Alf Nordhus, the defense lawyer for Bjørneboe, wrote in the anthology he edited on pornography in 1966.[43] Nordhus believed that the "pornography wave" was a result of Christianity, Puritanism, and Pietism, and that police and court inter-ference led only to artificially keeping up public curiosity and interest in it.

"The pornography wave" that Nordhus referred to in 1966 developed into a "pornography flood" after 1969, when Denmark sanctioned all forms of pornography, including depictions of children, animals, and violence. The following year, Sweden followed suit. On the one hand, the justification for the liberalization was that free access to pornography

---

[40] Op. cit., p. 65.

[41] A collection of essays that offers a good example of this kind of social criticism is Gudevold, Rolf J. (1978): *Strømninger: mellom tradisjon og apokalypse: tidskritikk 1966–1978* [Currents: Between Tradition and Apocalypse: Time Criticism 1966–1978]. Oslo: Lanser Forlag.

[42] The designation of Grønseth as a Reichian refers to the fact that he was inspired by the theories of Wilhelm Reich (1897–1957), an Austrian doctor, psychotherapist, and student of Sigmund Freud. After the Nazi takeover in 1933, Reich fled from Germany. He spent some time in Norway, where his very radical ideas regarding sexual liberation influenced Norwegian intellectuals such as the author Sigurd Hoel and the psychiatrist Nic Waal. See Wilhelm Reich, https://snl.no/Wilhelm_Reich.

[43] Nordhus, Alf (1966): "Pornografiparagrafen" [The Pornography Clause], in A. Nordhus et al. (eds.) 1966, p. 22.

was a "safety valve" for sexually frustrated men, and on the other, that the curiosity regarding pornography would diminish if it were made freely available. The assumption was that the sales would rise in the beginning, then flatten out or sink.[44] But this was not the reality. Both its production and sales increased year by year, and—especially in Denmark—pornography became an important export item. The first years of the 1970s have been referred to as the "golden age" of the Scandinavian porn industry.[45] In Copenhagen and Stockholm, sex shops, porn cinemas, brothels, and porn clubs displaying actual intercourse on stage became important parts of the tourist industry. Although Norwegian policy was much less liberal than that of neighboring countries, the significantly smaller Norwegian porn industry changed in order to meet the competition. Established pin-up magazines from the 1950s, such as *Cocktail*, became more explicit, and at the beginning of the 1970s new magazines were launched, with titles such as *Proff*, *Puls*, and *Lek* (Play).

Despite the growth in the market, the Norwegian pornography debate had lost its urgency by the early 1970s, at least on the part of left-wingers. For them, other political issues had come to the forefront, such as the struggle against Norwegian membership in the European Economic Community (EEC) and against the U.S. war in Vietnam.[46] Among Christians, however, the campaign against pornography was still alive. In 1973, a "Common Christian action against fornication and wickedness" was launched, involving several congregations within and independent of the Norwegian State Church.[47] Among the supporters of the action was Prime Minister Lars Korvald of the Christian Democratic Party. The campaign was not only aimed at stopping the "porn flood," but also at abortion, as well as "profane and immoral" radio and television programs. Christian youths campaigned by visiting pornography dealers and telling them to stop selling pornography or face prosecution. In connection with the election campaign of 1973, thousands of Christians participated in a demonstration in Oslo against pornography and abortion on demand.

---

[44] Århelle 1981, p. 57.

[45] Tessem and Wiedswang 1984, p. 49.

[46] Gulbrandsen, Barbara, Lise Kari Holøs, and Anne Britt Bertelsen (1984): "Pornografi. Menns makt – kvinners avmakt?" [Pornography. Men's Power—Women's Powerlessness?]. Term paper in journalism. Oslo: Norwegian School of Journalism, p. 11.

[47] Regarding this action see Tessem and Wiedswang 1984, pp. 61–65.

According to Hans Bratterud, pastor of the Pentecostal Church, a shared "unchristian spiritual current" was behind both efforts.[48]

In 1974, pornography was discussed in Parliament. An MP from the Christian Democratic Party, Kjell Magne Bondevik, asked what the government was going to do to stop the "porn profiteers," and Lars Roar Langslet from the Conservative Party expressed concern about the fact that the reach of "the so-called free-spirit" in Sweden and Denmark had extended so far that almost all barriers had collapsed and "a sultry stream of speculation in violence and sex has extended outward and settled into a swamp of drugs and crime."[49] The Minister of Justice, Inger Louise Valle of the Labor Party, responded that there was nothing more to do than had already been done. This time, the Socialist Left Party took an active part in the debate. Otto Hauglin, MP of the Social Left Party and a Christian Socialist, who five days after this parliamentary debate ensured, by his vote, that the law on abortion on demand was *not* adopted, brought up the discriminatory attitude toward women reflected in pornography. His party comrade, Arne Kielland, took to self-criticism, stating that socialists and social-democrats in cultural politics had for too long been "cultural-radical or cultural liberal instead of socialists."[50]

Court Proceedings in Pornography Cases

The verdicts against the books of Mykle, Miller, and Bjørneboe, as well as the prohibition of the Swedish *I Am Curious* films, gave the impression that Norway was a very strict country when it came to the enforcement of the "obscenity clause," which had remained more or less unchanged since 1902.[51] However, because the latter cases had received so much attention, the fact that there were very few pornography trials in Norwegian courts was much overshadowed. Århelle's overview shows that in the 25 years from 1953 through 1978, there were 22 violations of the "obscenity clause" handled in the Oslo City Court and the Supreme Court—thus, on average, less than one case per year, including the cases

---

[48] *Aftenposten*, evening issue, 30 August 1973, p. 16.

[49] Minutes from Parliament negotiations, 25 October 1974, quoted in Tessem and Wiedswang 1984, p. 64. See also Hompland 2003, pp. 280–281.

[50] Tessem and Wiedswang 1984, p. 64.

[51] Århelle 1981, p. 9.

against Mykle, Miller, and Bjørneboe. Most of the defendants in these cases were not writers, but magazine dealers who sold image pornography, often of the rougher sort. In the few cases that ended up in court, sentencing was generally lenient, with modest fines and suspended prison terms of 21–45 days. In reality, the porn dealers could operate largely undisturbed, and the stores usually reopened a few days after a raid. The porn dealers paid customs duties and VAT on their products, and any fines were figured into the business.[52] The disparity between the strict legislative regulation and the liberal legal practice, and law enforcement's choice not to prioritize such cases, can be explained as a result of a development within the judicial system with respect to what matters the state should and should not interfere in. However, it can also be seen as a manifestation of the fact that the concept of obscenity was vaguely defined. It was up to the courts to make a discretionary assessment of what the term encompassed—that is, to assess what at any time "violates people's sense of decency."[53] As a consequence, the application of anti-pornography judgments was generally characterized as arbitrary.

RAPE AND PORNOGRAPHY BECOME FEMINIST POLITICAL ISSUES

As the previous overview illustrates, there were different starting points in the early 1970s in terms of how much rape and pornography were discussed by the French and Norwegian public, respectively. However, there were also similarities. In both countries court proceedings were characterized by inconsistency because the legislation was outmoded and unclear. In principle, the laws were very strict, but they were observed only to a certain degree, and it was left to individual judges to decide their application on a case-by-case basis. Another common feature was that women were virtually absent from the public debates on rape and pornography. This was about to change, however, as a new generation of feminists brought the sexual exploitation of women as a gender-political issue into the public domain. There were, as mentioned, concrete events that motivated feminist activists to write opinion pieces in agenda-setting newspapers in which they confronted men and their sexist attitudes

---

[52] Op. cit., p. 42; Tessem and Wiedswang 1984, p. 8.
[53] Århelle 1981, p. 16.

toward women. In France, the first public debate on rape, in *Libération*, was triggered by a rape that had taken place in an anti-racist activist environment. In Norway, meanwhile, three feminists who had visited a strip club at the invitation of the owner as "company" for the male guests, wrote a critical opinion piece about men's sexuality in *Dagbladet*. Although pornography had been more extensively debated in Norway than rape had been in France, the French MLF activists were earlier than their Norwegian counterparts in addressing sexual exploitation of women as a gender-political issue.

Personal Rape Stories in MLF

Rape was addressed in one of the first important texts written by MLF activists, "*Libération des femmes année zero*" [Women's Liberation Year Zero], a 250-page special issue of the anti-colonial journal *Partisans*, published in October 1970 by François Maspero, a publisher who was highly respected by leftists.[54] This issue, which aroused interest because all of its articles were written by women, set the political tone of the new women's movement. The articles were based on the writers' personal experiences, and here it was documented how rape, like the ban on abortion, was a problem that specifically affected women. In one article, one of the women, who had participated in the feminist demonstration at the *Arc de Triomphe* (cf. Chapter 1), wrote about a rape she had been subjected to in the home of a man she had met. She related how she had not offered much resistance because she was afraid for her life, and about not reporting the rape for fear of being accused of behavior that proved she had "encouraged" the attack. She interpreted this as a typical expression of the myth of passive female sexuality and the notion that women really want to be raped: "A woman who says nothing, agrees. A woman who says no, says maybe. A woman who says maybe, says yes."[55]

---

[54] The publication was strongly inspired by the American collection of writings *Notes from the Second Year: Women's Liberation*, which was published by the New York Radical Feminists the same year. The title "Women's Liberation Year Zero" illustrates how, in 1970, the activists themselves believed they represented something completely new and had no relationship with the "shy and conformist" women in the established women's movement up to that time. Picq 1993, p. 12.

[55] "Le viol" [Rape], *Partisans*, nr. 54–55, 1970, published in Bernheim, Cathy, Liliane Kandel, Françoise Picq, and Nadia Ringart (eds.) (2009): *Mouvement de Libération des*

Experience-based rape stories were frequent in *Le Torchon Brûle*, the MLF's joint publication of the period 1971–1973. These texts were based on painful and detailed stories of sexual abuse experienced by the authors themselves or by other women. Articles related how girls and women were raped and beaten by fathers, brothers, doctors, priests, bosses, pimps, and policemen; that women could not walk in peace on the street without being evaluated, commented on, pinched, and, most frighteningly, raped; and how even comrades in the communist trade union CGT warned striking female workers that they would be raped if they participated in the occupation of the Renault factory at night.[56] This genre of personal rape stories, which may be characterized (somewhat insensitively) as stories of misery, also echoed in the movement's own "Hymn of the MLF," a combat song that encouraged women to rise up and break their chains. The second verse of the song is:

Women, slave-bound, humiliated
Bought, sold, raped
In all homes are women
Controlled, outside the world.[57]

The early experience-based texts presented rape in all its horror. The accounts can be seen as an expression of a need to confess the painful and shameful experiences women had previously kept to themselves. In this period, the movement was in an early stage of exploration and discovery, and the stories of misery served to highlight the problems many women experienced. When the MLF organized its first major rally in 1972, rape as a women's problem took center stage.

Rally in Paris Against Crimes Against Women

In 1972, the MLF was at a euphoric stage in its growth. A number of new women's groups were formed around the country, and the level of

Femmes. Textes premiers [Women's Liberation Movement. First Texts]. Paris: Stock, p. 239. The article was unsigned in 1970, but was written by Emmanuelle de Lesseps.

[56] The occupation at Renault is presented in *Le Torchon Brûle* 1 [1971]. The other examples are from *Le Torchon Brûle* 2 [1971] and 4 [1972].

[57] "Asservies, humiliées, les femmes/Achetées, vendues, violées/Dans toutes les maisons, les femmes/Hors du monde régulées," "Hymne du MLF," *Le Torchon Brûle* 3 [1972].

activity was at its peak. That spring it was decided to mobilize the activists for a major event in Paris. At the chaotic preparatory meetings, the same group of people seldom showed up, but after several months of discussion and planning, they finally agreed on a format in which women were to give personal testimonies dealing with women's oppression, abortion, motherhood, rape, and oppression of homosexuality. The event *Journées de dénonciation des crimes contre les femmes* [Days to Condemn Crimes Against Women] was held in Paris's political "Grand room," Mutualité, in the Latin Quarter on May 13–14, 1972. Almost 4000 women were present, and some men—who, on this occasion, instead of speaking, were assigned the task of looking after children.[58] The rally was anarchist in style. There were no lists of speakers and no moderators. The chairs were removed from the hall, and everybody sat on the floor, including the 64-year-old Simone de Beauvoir (Fig. 2.1). There were balloons and Indian rugs and the non-stop projection of activist films on the walls. The left-wing press was enthusiastic. *Le Nouvel Observateur* wrote, "MLF is going to win!" For while the revolutionary movements of the 1968 uprising had been contaminated by dirty games of power, the joy, festivity, and enthusiasm of May 1968 were revisited in Mutualité, the magazine stated.[59]

Despite the enthusiasm, the themes of the event were grim and focused on the condemnation of crimes against women. In the flyer announcing the meeting, such crimes were portrayed as "legal crimes, daily crimes, invisible crimes, and perfect crimes, so perfect that their victims are not aware of them or believe that they themselves are guilty of them."[60] The flyer concluded that the fundamental crime is that one half of the world is subordinate to the other because of their sex. The subordination is manifested in employment discrimination, burdensome housework, rape in marriage, forced motherhood, denial of women's sexuality, and an upbringing that demands obedience and the suppression of personal creativity.[61]

[58] de Pisan and Tristan 1977, pp. 85–91; Picq 1993, p. 145.

[59] "M.L.F. vaincra!" [M.L.F. Is Going to Win!], *Le Nouvel Observateur* 22.5, 1972. Published in Fouque et al. (eds.) 2008, pp. 472–473.

[60] "Les 13 et 14 mai 1972: Dénonciation des crimes contre les femmes" [13 and 14 May 1972: Denunciation of Crimes Against Women], leaflet published in Fouque et al. (eds.) 2008, p. 461.

[61] "La Mutualité" [Mutuality], in Fouque et al. (eds.) 2008, pp. 107–108.

Fig. 2.1 When in her sixties, Simone de Beauvoir, author of the feminist "Bible," *The Second Sex* (1949), joined the new women's liberation movement. She adhered to the revolutionary feminist branch of the movement, and was constantly criticized by the *féminitude* group Psychanalyse et politique (Photo: Unknown © Alamy)

Rape was a prominent topic at the meeting. Several women spoke about rapes they had been subjected to. But not all the participants had a taste for this form of personal testimony. In particular, the group *Psychanalyse et politique* (Psych et Po), which had not been part of the planning, strongly opposed these individual testimonies about rape. Instead, they chose to sit in a circle on the floor and read—one after another—a collectively written text about rape.

2 ADDRESSING THE PROBLEM: RAPE AND PORNOGRAPHY ... 69

Psych et Po: "They Rape Because They Are the Law"

The collectively written text "Le viol" [The Rape] presented an understanding of rape that was inspired by the psychoanalytic theories of
Jacques Lacan. As mentioned in Chapter 1, Lacan claimed that language,
with its rules, logic, and grammar, has phallus (symbol of the masculine)
as significant, and that the child, by acquiring the language, is inserted
into the "Law of the Father." Psych et Po, however, further developed
Lacan's theory of the "Law of the Father" and stressed that rape functions
as the means to draw girls into this law:

> They rape because they have the law—They rape because they are the
> law—They rape because they make the law—They rape because they are
> guardians of calm, order and of the law—They rape because they have the
> power, the word, the money, the knowledge, the power, a penis, phallus.[62]

In this passage, the link between the "Law of the Father" and the phallus
is almost overstated, for while phallus for Lacan was an abstraction and
a metaphor for (masculine) power, for Psych et Po it was perceived as a
tangible and significant organ that bequeaths undeserved power on those
who hold it. As stated in another passage:

> Fathers are raping their daughters at home—Husbands are raping their
> wives in the peace and quiet of their marriage bed—Bosses are raping their
> secretaries at the office desk (...)—Stablemen are raping the bourgeois
> women in the straw of the stables—Doctors are raping the nymphomaniacs
> in the psychiatric hospitals because they say that they need it. (...)—Black
> American men are raping white women—American soldiers are raping Viet-
> namese female warriors—Rape is always a risk for a woman, no matter what
> class she belongs to.

The text gives the impression that all men, empowered by their penises,
are raping women. However, one exception to this rule is mentioned:
the schizophrenics. Because they are affiliated with a "different world,"
they are "outside the law." According to Psych et Po, schizophrenics are
characterized by their refusal to enter the patriarchal and phallocentric
world; they reject entry into the "Law of the Father" and remain in their

---

[62] "Le viol" [Rape], *Le Torchon Brûle* 4 [1972] [unpaged]. Unless otherwise noted,
the following quotes are from this text.

first relationship, which was with their mother. The women of Psych et Po frequently repeated that they were "outside the law," and an important project in the group was to learn to love their mothers through loving other women.[63]

Psych et Po held that rape had the specific purpose of bringing girls and women under the "law," where women were to be locked in, and rape was understood as the symbolic murder of the woman. At the same time, rape was framed as more far-reaching than in the customary understanding. The collective text asks, "How many little girls have not been raped by the simple fact that men show off their genitals in the parks?" The understanding of rape went even further when it was rhetorically asked: "Why isn't a woman a 'real woman' without being raped?" The cultural notion that a woman is not a "real woman" before she has slept with a man is widespread, and this rephrasing may indicate that Psych et Po perceived every instance of vaginal intercourse as rape. It seems that the group believed that violent sexuality was an embedded trait of men, unless they were schizophrenic and "outside the law." The possibility that men could change was not discussed. On the contrary, men were not perceived as particularly interesting. Psych et Po would rather cultivate its own internal women's community.

When this text was written in 1972, Psych et Po was opposed to engaging in public debates and actions. Although rape is largely related to men, the group had no intention of discussing it with them. The revolutionary feminists were different, though: they wanted to initiate a debate through provocation. When the discussion of rape was taken up by the wider public in 1973, the trigger was a fierce feminist newspaper article.

---

[63] The idea of schizophrenia as a kind of authentic rebellion against a sick, authoritarian society echoes the view of the anti-psychiatry movement of the 1960s and 1970s. See Gros, Frédéric (2008): "L'antipsychiatrie: la folie change de visage" [Anti-psychiatry: Madness Changes Face], in P. Artières and M. Zancarini-Fournel (eds.), *68. Une histoire collective (1962–1981)* [68. A Collective History]. Paris: Éditions La Découverte, pp. 592–599. See also Davidsen, Silje, and Trine Rogg Korsvik (2006): "Hippielegen. Jan Greves psykedeliske kamp mot autoriteter" [The Hippie Doctor. Jan Greve's Psychedelic Struggle Against Authorities], in T.E. Førland and T.R. Korsvik (eds.): *1968. Opprør og motkultur på norsk* [1968. Rebellion and Counterculture in Norway]. Oslo: Pax Forlag, pp. 76–77.

Annie Cohen: "For Many, the Revolutionary Consciousness Stops at the Bedroom Door"

In the name of the revolution, women are told to be silent about the constant humiliation they are subjected to. It is true that immigrant workers live in great sexual distress. Should we pay for that? Should we feel guilty if we reject the approaches of an Algerian or a Black and hear that we are racists? We are blamed for talking about this rape because it was a black man.[64]

This provocative statement appeared in an opinion piece in the left-wing newspaper *Libération* in November 1973. The author of the piece was Annie Cohen, an activist in *Féministes révolutionnaires*, the revolutionary feminist branch of the MLF. Cohen wrote about the reaction of an anti-racist community in Paris after a female activist reported at a meeting that she had been raped in her home by a male co-activist. Both had been active on a committee working in support of so-called immigrant workers who were being threatened with deportation. The problem was that the rapist was black. Fearing that her story would lead to heightened racism, the raped woman, who also had an immigrant background, had waited for several days before reporting the event. When, with the support of friends from the MLF, she told about the rape at a meeting of the support committee, she was told that her story was harmful to the cause and would serve only to aggravate racism.

Cohen's attack on the hypocrisy of the revolutionaries in the anti-racist movement regarding the sexual abuse of women now became a public issue. Her opinion piece triggered a passionate debate about rape in *Libération* in the fall of 1973. The newspaper had recently been established by a group of male Maoists, with the elderly philosopher Jean-Paul Sartre as editor-in-chief. It was supposed to be "the mouthpiece of the oppressed" and actively encouraged its readers to engage in debate.[65] Eventually, the rape victim herself, Maï, wrote a 22-page article detailing the rape in a special issue of the prestigious left-wing literary journal *Les*

[64] Cohen, Annie: "Au nom de la révolution" [In the Name of the Revolution], *Libération*, 8 November 1973, p. 8.

[65] On the founding of the original Maoist newspaper *Libération*, see Guisnel, Jean (2008): "Trois fois rien sur *Libération*" [Three Times Nothing on Liberation], in P. Artières and M. Zancarini-Fournel (eds.), pp. 688–692.

Temps modernes, edited by, among others, Jean-Paul Sartre and Simone de Beauvoir. Since 1973, Beauvoir had edited the column "*Le sexisme ordinaire*" (Ordinary Sexism), to which readers were invited to submit stories of sexism they had experienced.[66] In the article "*Un viol si ordinaire, un impérialisme si quotidien*" (A Rape so Ordinary, an Imperialism so Everyday), Maï analyzed the rape using an anti-imperialist perspective.

The opinion piece by Cohen in *Libération* was thought-provoking, went straight to the point, and had a simple message: "What we condemn is rape. No matter if it comes from a white man or a black man, or even more so, if it comes from a 'revolutionary.'"[67] Cohen interpreted the fact that Maï was told that it was politically incorrect for her to report the rape as a manifestation of the notion that women "in the so-called name of the revolution" must remain silent about problems that could harm oppressed men. Her criticism was not only aimed at revolutionary French men who fought in solidarity on behalf of others, but also against oppressed immigrant men, whom she claimed profited from the oppression of women:

> Women recognize different types of oppression and participate in the struggle of the oppressed: that was the case with our friend. However, the very same oppressed ignore or will ignore the oppression of women (because they are served by it). Not only that, they will forbid us to fight for ourselves under the pretext that our struggle may damage the "main combat." That was what they told us at the immigrant workers' house. For many, the revolutionary consciousness actually stops at the bedroom door.[68]

According to Cohen, the revolutionaries were hypocrites because they pretended to fight for all the oppressed, for the "liberation of mankind," while themselves oppressing—with no pangs of conscience—women. She

---

[66] de Beauvoir, Simone: "Le sexisme ordinaire" [Ordinary Sexism], *Les Temps modernes*, no. 329, December 1973, quoted in Laubier, Claire (ed.) (1990): *The Condition of Women in France 1945 to the Present. A Documentary Anthology*. London: Routledge, p. 77. The issue of Maï's article that I refer to here, however, is from the feminist anthology *Les femmes s'entêtent* [Stubborn Women] from 1975. Maï (1975): "Un viol si ordinaire, un impérialisme si quotidien" [A Rape so Ordinary, an Imperialism so Everyday], *Les femmes s'entêtent* [Stubborn Women]. Paris: Éditions Gallimard, pp. 188–210.

[67] Cohen, *Libération*, 8 November 1973, p. 8.

[68] Ibid.

claimed that the expectation that women should be sexually available to oppressed men was a manifestation of the revolutionary men's oppression of women. Because their sexist prejudices directed at women were not fundamentally different from the prejudices that racists hold about how Blacks "are," she argued that the revolutionaries were no better than fascists.

Cohen's article received a mixed reception. According to *Libération*, it led to a racist campaign in the "bourgeois press."[69] At the same time, several women wrote letters to the editor saying that Cohen had identified an important problem. However, as *Libération* wrote in its summary of the readers' letters, rape is also about men: "Many of them have begun to question the sexuality they have always imposed on women," the newspaper stated. On the other hand, the initial reactions from male readers to Cohen were hostile. Some of them argued that her accusations against revolutionary men, specifically her equating them with fascists, showed that she despised men. Other men felt less personally attacked and chose to handle the issue on a more philosophical level. One of them was Jean-Paul Sartre, who in a lengthy interview discussed the following questions: Where does a rape begin? Is every sexual intercourse a rape? Does the woman have to deal with male power, or is there a revolutionary path to sexuality?[70]

Sartre: "Is There Is a Revolutionary Path to Sexuality?"

In the early 1970s, the aging existentialist philosopher Jean-Paul Sartre was among the honored intellectuals who "systematically defended the children of May 68."[71] He was in attendance at most of the major

---

[69] "...et le courrier de lecteurs à propos de l'article 'Au nom de la révolution'" [...and the Readers' Opinion Pieces About the Article "In the Name of the Revolution"], *Libération*, 15 November 1973, p. 4. The opinion pieces in *Libération* (as in this case) were often summarized by the editors instead of the entire texts being published.

[70] "La chronique de Jean-Paul Sartre: 'Où commence le viol? Est-ce que tout acte sexuel est déjà un viol? La femme doit-elle composer avec le pouvoir mâle?... Ou y-a-t-il un chemin révolutionnaire à la sexualité'?" [The Opinion Piece of Jean-Paul Sartre: "Where Does Rape Begin? Is Every Sexual Act Already a Rape? Does the Woman Have to Deal with Male Power?... Or Is There a Revolutionary Path to Sexuality?"], *Libération*, 15 November 1973, p. 4.

[71] Bourseiller, Christophe (1996): *Les Maoïstes: la folle histoire des gardes rouges français* [The Maoists: The Crazy Story of the French Red Guards]. Paris: Plon, p. 157.

demonstrations organized by the Maoists; he signed their petitions and acted as editor-in-chief of their publications, including *Libération*. Sartre generally supported liberation movements on the basis of existentialism's idea that because humans are free and responsible, they should act in a way that encourages and protects "the other's" freedom.[72] The women's liberation movement was no exception. He believed that it could change both men and women and the relationships between them. Sartre was, after all, the life companion of Simone de Beauvoir and was undoubtedly influenced by her feminist political analyzes. Like revolutionary feminists such as Annie Cohen, Sartre argued that only women could free themselves, but he also believed that it was absolutely essential that "the woman liberate the man" by forcing him to take responsibility.[73]

In the *Libération* interview, Sartre discussed rape by means of philosophical questions. He claimed that the question of whether every sexual intercourse is a form of rape was "immensely important," as was the question of whether it is possible to offset men's male chauvinism—and whether women truly want that. According to Sartre, there is an element of aggressiveness in every penetration; therefore, women have the right to believe that intercourse with a man is, in effect, "dealing with the male chauvinist power." Sartre did not believe that the aggressiveness could be completely eliminated from sexuality, as aggression is human, and sexual intercourse that is totally lacking in aggression would imply "a completely different man than today's man." In order to find the "revolutionary path to sexuality," Sartre relied on the women's liberation movement as a segment along the revolutionary path. He believed that "the new woman," who no longer accepts rape, was about to be born through the women's revolt. Through their own liberation, he stated in the interview, women could free men from their "inclination to rape."

Sartre also commented on the specific rape case. Among feminists, including Maï, this was perceived as a turning point, after which rape was taken seriously as a problem.[74] Sartre declared that the rapist was not a

---

[72] See Flynn, Thomas (2012): "Jean-Paul Sartre," in E.N. Zalta (ed.): *The Stanford Encyclopedia of Philosophy*.

[73] "La chronique de Jean-Paul Sartre...," *Libération*, 15 November 1973, p. 4. The following quotations from Sartre are from the same article.

[74] Maï (1975): "Un viol si ordinaire, un impérialisme si quotidien" [A Rape so Ordinary, an Imperialism so Everyday], *Les femmes s'entêtent* [Stubborn Women]. Paris: Éditions Gallimard, p. 204.

true revolutionary, but a male chauvinist. However, he did not think that the rapist should be reported to the police, an opinion shared by most French leftists of the time. Instead, Sartre argued, one could make the rapist change by engaging in a rational discussion with him. In forcing him to realize his mistakes, he would change his behavior, according to Sartre. The goal of any revolutionary organization is not only to work toward revolution, but to improve each activist: "In fact, it's the only way to make a revolution," Sartre claimed.[75]

As an elderly male intellectual with a prestigious reputation and with a philosophical approach to rape, Sartre inspired several male readers of *Libération* to reflect on the issue. One of them wrote a letter to the newspaper in which he urged men to take action and change their behavior toward women straightaway, without waiting for the revolution. This was a fairly radical position at a time when a widespread belief on the French left was that men could not be held responsible for sexual assault because they suffered from "sexual misery" brought on by the capitalist society and the bourgeoisie.[76] Another male reader disagreed that every instance of intercourse is rape: exceptions include, for example, "if the penetration was desired by the woman as a path to orgasm." Female readers also engaged in the debate. A woman wrote that she "totally agrees with Sartre, every sexual intercourse is rape. When the man penetrates for the first time, it is even an act of perforation. For him it is good, while she does it only to feel she is desired." However, she added that this form of "minimal rape" was acceptable because it was based on love. That particular reader's response illustrates how Sartre's approach could lead to an inflation of the concept of rape. As a "woman over forty" wrote, there was no real difference between marriage and rape, because both have as a prerequisite that the value of women is as an object to be used by men. The only difference is that the one is legal and the other is not, she claimed. Thus, it was understandable that women "do not fancy their oppressors" and instead choose homosexuality in their quest for freedom.

The conceptual discussions concerning rape can be interpreted in the context of the vague definition of rape of the period. For example, as

[75] "La chronique de Jean-Paul Sartre...," *Libération*, 15 November 1973, p. 4.

[76] "Courrier sur la sexualité (suite) 'Où commence le viol?'" [Letters on Sexuality (Continued). "Where Does Rape Begin?"], *Libération*, 20 December 1973, p. 8. The following quotes are from this review article of the various opinion pieces.

previously mentioned, rape in marriage was not illegal, as the "obligation of marriage" (i.e., sexual intercourse) was embodied in the law. The
issue of whether any heterosexual intercourse was actually rape was also
forwarded by Psych et Po. Such a definition created a dilemma. On the
one hand, the goal was to bring an end to sexual abuse; on the other,
however, if every instance of heterosexual intercourse was considered
abuse, one was in danger of trivializing what was usually perceived as
rape, namely that someone forces or threatens another in the pursuit of
sex. However, this was not a dilemma that was addressed in these debates.
In the early 1970s, rape was new as a political topic, and few political
theories had thus far developed to explain rape. One of the ways to cultivate theory in this field was to make use of familiar ideological concepts
and expand their meaning. An example was the way in which Maï, in her
article in *Les Temps modernes*, portrayed the rape she had been subjected
to as a form of imperialism and colonialism.

Maï: "A Rape so Ordinary, an Imperialism so Everyday"

Maï had been subjected to a typical rape in which the man, using physical violence and threatening to kill her, forced himself on her. In the
22-page article "A Rape so Ordinary, an Imperialism so Everyday," Maï
wrote in detail about what happened and what was said, beginning from
the time the man invited her to a café, then followed her to her home
and raped her, to the eventual confrontation in the support committee
for illegal immigrants. The way she drew a connection between rape and
imperialism is intriguing, as the whole affair actually began with the man
inviting her to a café to discuss imperialism and the Vietnamese people's
struggle against the United States, which eventually proved to be a pretext
for sex. Moreover, the rapist and Maï both had experienced French colonialism: she had a Vietnamese background, while he was a revolutionary
student from one of the French Caribbean colonies. Thus, imperialism
was a frame of reference they shared. In the article, Maï recounts that
before, during, and after the rape she tried to explain to him that his abuse
of power was the equivalent of American imperialist warfare in Vietnam:
"He took possession of my body as one conquers a country with violence,
and would punish me for having resisted his male politics of dominance."
Just as President Richard Nixon punished the Vietnamese with bombs,
rapists use the phallus as a weapon to make women obey. According to

Maï, "the power grows out of the phallus; he confirmed this when he raped me and thereby claimed his 'fascist manliness.'"[77]

By framing rape as "everyday imperialism," Maï drew parallels between the imperialists' exploitation of the colonies' resources and men's exploitation of women's bodies and their ability to make children, which society relies on to exist. Her argument was that "The Vietnamese people and every dominated people must fight against foreign imperialism to regain their identity and their independence. For women to regain their identity and independence, they must fight against masculine imperialism."[78] As stated by Maï, her equating rape to imperialism was a deliberate legitimation strategy toward the leftists, because, at the meeting of the support committee where Maï and her feminist friends had told about the rape, the prevailing attitude had been that one should not talk about it because it would harm the anti-racist struggle, and, further, that rape was not a political problem.[79] This attitude was also shared by several of the meeting's female participants. According to Maï, one of them said that rape was so common that it was pointless to talk about it. Her boss raped her every day, and besides, there were so many other important issues to address. Another woman said that all women who are raped encourage it themselves, while a third woman argued that only this particular rape was wrong because it had happened within the support committee. (The man should have raped someone who was not a member!) The fact that even politically conscious women declared that rape was not a real problem illustrates how taboo the subject was at the time. Even in political milieus that struggled against racism and the oppression of the working class, rape was something not to be talked about or problematized.

League for Women's Rights (LDF): Rape as a Class Crime

From its foundation by revolutionary feminists in 1974, the fight against rape was a major issue for the League for Women's Rights (*Ligue du droit des femmes*, LDF) (cf. Chapter 1). The inaugural issue of the LDF journal

---

[77] Maï 1975, p. 198. The quote that the power grows out of the phallus—"Le pouvoir est au bout du phallus"—was an MLF slogan and a rephrasing of Chairman Mao's quote "Le pouvoir est au bout du fusil" [Political *Power* Grows Out of the Barrel of a *Gun*].

[78] Maï 1975, p. 210.

[79] de Pisan and Tristan 1977, p. 161. In this book, Maï is called Louison.

Les Nouvelles féministes dealt with two rape trials that the association had engaged in politically.[80] One was the internationally known case of Inès Garcia from California, who had killed one of two rapists in self-defense. While she was sentenced to five years in prison for murder, the surviving rapist went free. An international support campaign for Garcia was initiated. French feminists went to the office of the American newspaper *The International Herald Tribune* in Paris, where they handed over a statement in support of Garcia and against rape in general. The leader of the LDF, Simone de Beauvoir, wrote an open letter to Garcia, to whom she lent her full support for having "taken justice into her own hands."[81] The other rape case involved a well-known judge from Lille, Monsieur Dujardin, who was held in high esteem by leftists. He had declared that he was very pleased by the acquittal of a youngster who had been charged with rape. While the girl had reported that she was raped, the boy claimed that she had "consented" and just said "no" because she was afraid of her father. Besides, he would not have raped her had he known she was a virgin. *Les Nouvelles féministes* interpreted this as evidence that rape is only recognized when the victim is a virgin, that is, "when her most important capital, the capital of virtue, is available to the one who takes it and becomes the owner of it."[82]

The theoretical foundation of the LDF was the form of feminism that Simone de Beauvoir had outlined in her classic work *The Second Sex* from 1949. According to this perspective, rape is a result of the woman being "the other," as defined in relation to men and their desires. The following statement appeared in the first issue of the LDF's journal: "As a virgin she watches out for him—as a married [woman] she belongs to him—as a "free" [woman] she belongs to all."[83] "Men always think in terms of property," it continued, and women are not considered as separate individuals. A woman who does not already belong to a man through marriage, or is a virgin and must take care of her virtue, is thus subject to the free enjoyment of all men. According to the article, the free access to and abuse of women had been made even easier with the availability

---

[80] "Le viol" [Rape], *Les Nouvelles féministes*, no. 1, December 1974, p. 11–13.

[81] Simone de Beauvoir in "Le viol," *Les Nouvelles féministes*, no. 1, December 1974, p. 11.

[82] "Le viol," *Les Nouvelles féministes*, no. 1, December 1974, p. 12.

[83] Ibid.

of the birth control pill. Now that the fear of unwanted pregnancy was eliminated, men didn't see any reason for women to say "no."

LDF was also inspired by the feminist theory of sociologist Christine Delphy, which held that women and men belong to different classes. Accordingly, rape was described as a "class crime":

> Rape is a class crime: men as a group against women as a group. Any woman can be a victim of rape: a child, a youth, a single woman, a married woman, an old woman...even a dead woman. Society accepts rape and is complicit because it allows a persistent situation of insecurity for women.[84]

According to the LDF, rape was a form of terror that men, as a group, imposed upon women, as a group, to prevent them from rebelling. Although not all men rape women, all who rape women are men. The LDF's view on this matter was also reflected in the claim that the judicial system in rape cases served as a "class court" or as a "sex court" whose function is "to uphold men's unreasonable privileges and the sadomasochistic relations they maintain towards women."[85] Although the revolutionary feminists of the LDF believed that the purpose of the judicial system was to assure continued male dominance, they nonetheless argued for taking advantage of it. Their view of involving the judicial system in rape cases was controversial on the left, as will be discussed in greater detail in the next chapter.

The simple act of problematizing rape was considered radical in early 1970s France. Rape was a problem that went unmentioned and was even accepted as part of the "erotic play" in which the conquering man insists and the woman rejects until she "gives in." While rape comprised a new topic of public debate in France, the context of the discussion of pornography in Norway was different. Though pornography was clearly established as a topic of Norwegian cultural debate, it was nevertheless radical to problematize pornography from a feminist perspective.

---

[84] "Tribunal international" [International Tribunal], *Les Nouvelles féministes*, no. 12, Mai 1976 [unpaged].

[85] "Le viol," *Nouvelles féministes*, no. 1, December 1974, p. 13.

PORNOGRAPHY AS PART OF THE SEXUAL
OPPRESSION OF WOMEN

As early as the 1950s, women's organizations such as The Norwegian Housewives' Association had engaged in attempts to limit the spread of "inferior dirt magazines" and pornography. Their rationale was not that pornography was oppressive to women, but that it transmitted attitudes that were incompatible with the norms that families and schools were charged with cultivating among the younger generation.[86] In the early 1970s, resistance to pornography was a cause primarily fronted by Christians and conservatives. They combined the struggle against pornography and against abortion on demand in a crusade against "unchristian spiritual currents." For young, radical women activists who advocated sexual liberation, sex outside of marriage, and abortion on demand, the conditions were not particularly favorable for initiating a fight against pornography as a progressive project. However, when the new women's liberation movement assembled for the International Women's Day rally in Oslo 8th of March 1973, "Pornography Is Contempt for Comen" and "No to Woman as Merchandise and as Sexual Object," were among the main slogans.[87] These demands, however, were overshadowed by calls for abortion on demand, equal right to work, day care centers, and similar matters.

Although pornography was not a prominent issue, the Women's Front (*Kvinnefronten*) tagged it as a problem it in its first publication, the hand-printed *Om Kvinnefronten* (About the Women's Front) from 1972. This document consists of ten pages of minutes, including a proposal for a work program, from the Women's Front Conference of March 19, 1972, when 150 women gathered and agreed to form "a broad

---

[86] Tessem and Wiedswang 1984, p. 33.

[87] *Universitas*, no. 4–5, 1973, last page. Other slogans were "Alle kvinner med i kvinnekampen" [All Women Join the Women's Struggle], "Vi vil ha menneskelønn, ikke kvinnelønn" [We Want Human Wages, Not Women's Wages], "Fri abort er en kvinnerettighet" [Free Abortion on Demand Is a Women's Right], "Daghjem og fritidshjem til alle barn—følg også industriens arbeidstider" [Day-Care Centers and Leisure Centers for All Children—Follow Also the Working Hours of Industry], "Alle kvinners rett til smertefri fødsel" [Every Woman's Right to Painless Delivery], "Nei til dobbeltarbeid for kvinner: Halve arbeidsbyrden i hjemmet er mannens" [No to the Double Workload of Women: Half the Workload at Home Belongs to the Man]. There were also slogans about equal rights to education and work, social security and pensions, and the right to contraception guidance and free contraceptives.

women's organization" under the slogan "Fight all Women's Oppression—for the Liberation of Women."[88] In the proposal for a work program, pornography was linked to other "material manifestations of women's oppression" such as the representation of women in advertising, the position of women in the labor market, the shortage of maternity wards, and the general price increase. Here the use of women as "merchandise" in pornography and advertising was identified as a problem. The framing of pornography primarily as a financial issue was typical of the Women's Front, as the slogan "No to Woman as Merchandise" illustrates. However, this was not the only context in which pornography figured in the proposed work program. Pornography was also presented as a manifestation of "the sexual oppression of women":

> Women are commodified as sex objects; they are valued only by entirely external criteria and for the enjoyment of others. She ought to be the passive one, she ought to be one who is chosen, not the one who herself takes the initiative and chooses. Whether the women enjoy their own sex lives is given less significance, and many women do not have the courage to call for it. (...)
>
> We must fight the ideal of woman in advertising and pornography, because it is an ideal that is impossible for any normal woman to live up to, and an ideal that no doubt creates the feeling of inadequacy in us.[89]

As the quotation illustrates, neither the contempt for women reflected in pornography nor the violent humiliation of them was pointed out as problematic; rather, it was the "inadequacy" felt by women faced with unattainable (beauty) ideals that were emphasized. The strategy for fighting these ideals was, according to the work program, "to require honest and non-discriminatory sexual education and contraceptive guidance in all schools, in television and radio, at health centers and maternal centers, etc."

---

[88] Arbeidsutvalget in KVINNEFRONTEN: *Om Kvinnefronten* [The Working Committee of the WOMEN'S FRONT: About the Women's Front] (1972). ABA. This hand-print contains, in addition to minutes, proposals for a work program for groups of the Women's Front, and a list of recommended literature. The source material from the New Feminists, established in 1970, is sketchy, so it's difficult to establish whether or not they had a policy on pornography during the early years.

[89] *Om Kvinnefronten* (1972), pp. 7–8. The following quotations are from the same source.

One finds in the 1972 proposal for a work program much space devoted to concrete and detailed descriptions of how to "fight against women's roles and men's roles that entail the man oppressing the women, while the women allow themselves to be oppressed." At the same time, it was stated that men "gain little from the oppression (...). Therefore, we must not make our men the enemy, but try to solve the problems with them." The confrontation with "our men" had to be done delicately, without "scaring the hell out of them." The Women's Front did not reject the nuclear family or marriage, as some of the New Feminists did.

"No to Women as Merchandise"

The proposed work program of the Women's Front did not call for action against pornography, but instead against commercials. The long-term goal was to make it "politically impossible to use women as sex objects in advertising, film, literature and the like, in the same way as it has become politically impossible to ridicule and degrade people because of skin color." To achieve this goal, several actions were proposed. In addition to writing opinion pieces to newspapers, women were encouraged to point out "reactionary views on women in all contexts" and to campaign against commercials in movie theaters: "Get up in front of the screen with banners." In May 1972, several members of the Women's Front and the New Feminists campaigned against sexist commercials in movie theaters in Oslo.[90] Before and after each movie, the activists handed out leaflets encouraging people to notice how women were portrayed in the commercials. During commercials that the activists regarded as particularly oppressive to women, they began booing and stood up in front of the screen with banners inscribed with the message "No to Women as Merchandise!" in fluorescent paint. According to members of both the New Feminists and the Women's Front, the protests were well received by the audience. Similar movie protests are said to have been carried out, also outside Oslo.[91]

---

[90] *Kvinnefronten*, no. 2, 1972; Rytter, Kirsten, and Inge Ås (1973): "Om å være heks på Karl Johan. Feminisme og motkultur" [About Being a Witch on Karl Johan (main street of Oslo). Feminism and Counterculture], *Kvinnens årbok 1974* [The Women's Yearbook 1974]. Oslo: Pax Forlag, pp. 16–17; Haukaa 1982, p. 103.

[91] Haukaa 1982, p. 103.

Although the movie protests were not about pornography, they addressed a similar issue—namely, the depiction of women as merchandise. The above slogan was taken up again a few years later once the fight against pornography became a priority of the Women's Front. The economic perspective was also apparent when the Women's Front explained the causes of women's oppression. In the 1972 article "Speaking of the slogan 'No to Woman as Merchandise'" in the organization's internal journal *Kvinnefronten*, an anonymous but obviously young member wrote about the use of "the woman as a sex object" in the media and commercials, and how this is reflected in the relationships between girls and boys in different youth environments, whether in the hippie culture or the "pop milieus." Even the "politically conscious boys," "well into the ranks of the Marxist-Leninists," were "hung up" on girls' appearances, the young member of the Women's Front claimed. The cause was, according to her, "monopoly capital that is looking for profit. It speculates in the girls' trained vanity and does everything possible to squeeze the most money out of her. (...) Monopoly capital has an economic interest in maintaining and intensifying the women's oppression."[92] Pointing to monopoly capital as the cause of most things wrong in society was a customary analysis among Marxist-Leninists of the 1970s. And, as the young member of the Women's Front put it, women and men together had a common interest in combating it. For the Women's Front it was important to avoid designating men as enemies, and the organization did not prioritize mobilizing against pornography until it became a major issue in 1977 (Fig. 2.2). When pornography became a topic of public debate in the realm of women's issues in 1974, the initiative was taken by members of the New Feminists.

The 1974 Debate "Is Man a Pig?"

The opinion piece "Sexual Liberalism and Women's Oppression in Male Society" in the liberal newspaper *Dagbladet* in 1974 is regarded as the first New Feminist analysis of pornography in Norway.[93] In this period,

---

[92] "Apropos parolen 'nei til kvinnen som salgsvare'" [Speaking of the Slogan "No to Woman as Merchandise"], *Kvinnefronten*, no. 2, 1972.

[93] Haukaa 1982; Hompland 2003; and Karlsen, Torill Enger (1991): "Antipornokampen i Norge gjennom 15 år (1974–1990)" [Anti-Pornography Campaign in Norway Throughout 15 Years]. Published by the Women's Front of Norway.

Fig. 2.2 Poster to recruit members to the Women's Front from 1976, saying "Fight – but not alone! Sign up for the Women's Front." The uphill testifies what the Women's Front regarded as the most important problems facing women in their daily life: low wages, few and unsafe working places, too short maternity leave, too few and too expensive day care centers, too expensive food, housing, and public transportation, as well as traffic danger. Sexual oppression of women was not yet in the forefront in 1976

the opinion pieces in *Dagbladet* were important trendsetters in the public conversation, and the so-called "Is Man a Pig?" debate, named after the title of one of the pieces, raged for a full month during the winter of 1974. The initial opinion piece that triggered the debate was written by three members of the New Feminists; Birgit Bjerck, Kari Melby, and Brita Gulli, who wrote about their experience when they attended a striptease show in Oslo. The piece begins with the following story:

> We are at a restaurant after a [New Feminist] consciousness-raising group meeting. A yellow note drops on our table—"two ladies free entrance, greetings Thor" is written at the top right corner. It turns out to be an invitation to a show in Oslo New Club where there will be "fresher things than ever." The entrance fee is in fact 100 Crowns. Signed: *T. Thorsen.*
>
> Thorsen tells us that there is always a lack of ladies—so we will be admitted free. We learn that similar notes have been distributed to women working in the Post Office and in the banks. He asserts that there is no obligation in coming—we can just come and enjoy ourselves, eat the food included in the admission ticket, dance a bit and leave if we do not like it. The entertainment is striptease.[94]

The three women wrote that the manner in which Thorsen tried to "pick us up" reflected his contempt for women. He was deliberately trying to lure women in low-wage jobs who "say yes to all free offers", lonely women who might be new in town and who probably would "swallow the striptease" in exchange for male company. In looking back, Birgit Bjerck shares that they already knew that Thorsen was running strip clubs and was a porn dealer, and that they wanted to check out what it was all about.[95] Their report in *Dagbladet* was rather unglamorous:

> The show takes place at "Kongen" (The King), and the room is freezing cold and unpleasant. "The gentleman follows you to a table," we are instructed, and the gentleman tries to guide us to a long table filled with

[94] Birgit Bjerck, Kari Melby, and Brita Gulli: "Kjønnsliberalisme og kvinneundertrykkelse i manns-samfunnet" [Sexual Liberalism and Women's Oppression in Male Society], *Dagbladet*, 21 February 1974 [emphasis in original].

[95] Conversation with Birgit Bjerck, 28 June 2010. The following year, Thorsen was convicted of pimping after the sex club he ran in Brugata 17, Oslo—Club Blue Heaven—was closed by the police. Århelle 1981, pp. 30–32; Fjeld-Pedersen, J.J. (1976): *Hele verden på et sølvfat* [The Whole World on a Silver Platter]. Oslo: Zenith Forlag, pp. 132–133. See also Chapter 3 herein.

rather drunken men. We resist this and manage to get a table for ourselves. The serving consists of two small sandwiches (on a paper plate) and half a bottle of beer. (...) We look around us: 60–70 men and 10 women at the most, including us. We can confirm what we hoped for: women do not come to sex clubs even though it is for free and despite Thorsen's personal efforts at restaurants and at typical women's workplaces.

We didn't want to dance—something that aroused great astonishment and demand for explanation. Rejected. The dance invitations were on top after every striptease appearance, which came every half hour. (...) The striptease played on two types of women (or myths about women). One approached the men directly, signaling that she could be gotten. The other represented a kind of upper-class "coolness," remoteness, and inaccessibility.[96]

Next, the three New Feminists went on to analyze the striptease: what kind of sexuality it expressed, and what sort of role women were supposed to play at the strip club. They stated that striptease played on "conservative prejudices against sexuality" and represented a "depersonalized sexuality." "It is not liberated, but deeply reactionary because it reinforces traditional attitudes and actions." They perceived striptease as an "extreme commodification of women as sexual objects and as a means of satisfaction." They interpreted the intention of the dancing as that the women should "take care of" the excitement aroused by the striptease.

In the opinion piece, the New Feminists viewed striptease in the context of "pornographic literature." "This literature is the exact expression of the same: to excite, playing on sexual taboos, giving women status only by virtue of their genitals. Only with this view of women and of sexuality is pornography in its various forms possible." This view of women and of sexuality, which permeated the entire society, drove the "women industry" of pornography, striptease, and brothels. "In short: commercialized sex. The woman is the commodity," they argued. As previously mentioned, the women's liberation movement had already framed pornography as an expression of the "woman as merchandise."

What was new in this opinion piece was that the three feminists explained the "conservative and reactionary" view of sexuality, which

---

[96] Birgit Bjerck, Kari Melby, and Brita Gulli: "Kjønnsliberalisme og kvinneundertrykkelse I manns-samfunnet" [Sexual Liberalism and Women's Oppression in Male Society], *Dagbladet*, 21 February 1974. Unless otherwise notes, the following quotes are from this opinion piece.

made women into sexual objects, as an interaction among capitalist society, patriarchy, and Christian sexual morality. Pornography and striptease were expressions of "the tendency of capital to penetrate all interpersonal relationships and to make them into commodity relations." When sexuality was thus disconnected from the human, it could be more easily exploited as a commodity in the capitalist market. The result was a commodification of women as merchandise and as objects of pleasure for men. The specific feminist thrust of the article was, however, the claim that capitalism needs the help it receives from patriarchy's attitude toward and use of women as sex objects:

> Capital can apply patriarchy's view of women and *praxis*. This praxis consists of the fact that patriarchy uses, and not only views, women as sex objects. Capitalism needs patriarchy to survive, just as patriarchy needs capitalism to survive.

Christianity also received its share of the blame:

> Pornography splits humans in two: one physical part and one mental/spiritual part, where the latter is of no significance. Christian sexuality operates with a similar distinction, but for Christianity it is the *physical* part that is the problem, and should preferably be subordinated to reproduction, and at least kept within marriage. *Outside* this framework, sexuality is a *sin*. We believe these frameworks are as destructive as the frameworks of pornography.

The solution promoted by the New Feminists was this: "In our feminist struggle, we must work to ensure that people, including men, become integrated people. Sexuality is a meeting between two whole people. Whole people are people in whom the physical and the spiritual are integrated and who are *alive*." At the same time, the New Feminists addressed men directly: "The visit to the club triggered new concerns about men's sexuality toward us. We've asked a number of questions, but we do not get the answers until the men themselves begin a real consciousness-raising." They also rejected the claim that pornography and strip clubs could work as a "safety valve that benefit women," which is one of the arguments for making pornography available, and asked, "Do men see their own sexuality as a steam engine?"

There were two main aspects of the opinion piece "Sexual Liberalism and Women's Oppression in Male Society" that provoked the readers of

Dagbladet to seize their pens: the attack on Christianity and the feminist criticism of men's sexuality. The anti-capitalism issue apparently provoked no one.

In one response, three feminist Christian socialists protested the idea that Christianity is to blame for being a cause of pornography. In their view, it was sufficient to explain pornography as a form of women's oppression based on capitalist principles. According to them, Christian sexual morality played no part in dividing the physical and the spiritual aspects of humans. That division was attributed to Hellenistic dualistic thought that "unfortunately penetrated Christianity in an early era". Christian ethics takes a positive view of sexuality, they wrote, as it "connects man and woman in the closest and most intimate form of *personal, whole-human community.*"[97] In their opinion piece, the Christian socialists chose not to weigh in on whether this "whole-human community" could also take place outside marriage, something the three New Feminists eventually pointed out.

However, it was the New Feminists' criticism of men's sexuality that really lent momentum to the debate. A male reader argued that feminists should be friendlier to lonely men at sex clubs. Instead of verbally harassing the men, they should meet them, talk to them, and invite them home, he claimed, calling for "some respect for the man's loneliness and some human compassion."[98] Another male reader, the renowned professor of classical philology Knut Kleve, accounted for "the heterosexual man's sex life" by taking advantage of a Greek myth, namely, Aristophanes' speech regarding the origin of Eros in Plato's *Symposium*.

The myth relates how man was originally one person—man and woman fused into one individual—but because the gods divided them into two, humans were left to spend their lives finding their "better half." That is why the man walks around with a constant itching or burning that he is desperately seeking to quench in one way or another—for example, by watching striptease and pornography, the professor claimed. He argued:

> It is necessary to emphasize the strength and the persistence of the male's sexuality. If one is not aware of this, one will not be able to understand

[97] Edel Hildre, Sidsel Thoresen Øistad, and Inger Lise Breivik: "Kristen seksualetikk" [Christian Sexual Ethics], *Dagbladet*, 28 February 1974 [emphasis in original].

[98] Kay Jacobsen in *Dagbladet*, 5 March 1974.

him. It is important to know that a man really *cannot* be without a woman (...) When, for example, our feminists believe that man can "cut out" his sexuality at will, it is ignorance. When, for example, a monk claims that he masters his sexuality, it is dishonesty.[99]

According to the professor of philology, women have to understand that men's sexuality cannot be controlled, and he was concerned about what gender equality might lead to: "she must *not* become a new kind of man. Then we can stop all searching and just all become homosexuals."

The two male readers' opinion pieces provoked a number of responses from both female and male readers. Common to these was their criticism of the call for women to try to understand men and to reach out to them, as well as the idea of sexuality as a biological function detached from social conditions. Instead, it was argued that sexuality is socially constructed, and that the dominant male culture teaches men to see women strictly as bodies and as objects of desire. Another principal argument was that it is a myth that men have stronger sexual drives than women. On the contrary, men have had greater power to live out their desires, and this power has been abused by using women as objects of sexual satisfaction.[100]

A male reader wrote: "As a man, I feel ashamed of the antifeminist attitude of the opinion pieces."[101] He was upset by the argument that feminists should be friendlier to men at sex clubs and asked, rhetorically, "Who would ask the same question to other oppressed groups? Who would, for example, claim that people of color now have to be friendlier to white oppressors?" He speculated that although some of the men who visit sex clubs might be lonely, unhappy, and exploited by the club owners, the women who work there are much worse off. This particular reader called on other men to realize that "pornography is the expression of contempt for women" and that it was "justified that women finally renounce our (ab-)use of their bodies to satisfy our, according to Kleve (...), such unruly drives." Like other readers, he thought it was a myth

[99] Knut Kleve: "Er mannen en gris?" [Is Man a Pig?], *Dagbladet*, 9 March 1974.

[100] Alice Braadland: "Hvem skapte grisen?" [Who Created the Pig?"]; Runa Haukaa: Myter og menn" [Myths and Men]; Merle Endresen: "Gris eller helt" [Pig or Hero]; Lars Maanum: "Menn vil gjøre kvinnen til mann" [Men Want to Make the Woman a Man]; Anders Bratholm: "Er kvinnen også en gris?" [Is the Woman also a Pig?], all in *Dagbladet*, 12 March 1974, p. 12.

[101] Lars Maanum: "Menn vil gjøre kvinnen til mann" [Men Want to Make the Woman a Man], *Dagbladet*, 12 March 1974.

that men have stronger sexual urges than women but conceded that "We have abused our power to make women temporary objects of satisfaction for our (still, according to Kleve) itchy and erect penis. It is time—as feminists have realized—to stop living up to the horny sex creature à la Tarzan." He encouraged men to find solidarity with the women's struggle instead of "mobilizing all powers for self-defense and verbal harassment."

Also joining the debate was the distinguished law professor Anders Bratholm. He wrote that it was "ungallant" to ignore women's sexuality, and claimed, as had the other participants in the debate, that sexual needs are independent of gender.[102] He also argued for the blessings of masturbation. If one only "removed the silly feeling of guilt and secrecy that still surrounds masturbation," it would reduce the incidence of sex crimes and prostitution, which he believed was "of little joy to the man and much harm to the woman."

The three New Feminists had the last word in the debate they had initiated. In their final opinion piece, they outlined a feminist liberation strategy that was quite different from that of the Woman's Front.

> We cannot fail to oppose the oppression of women, even if it entails opposing men. We cannot effectively fight the oppression by acting within our traditional roles: helping men, supporting men, and suppressing our own needs and political demands. We have the right to fight. We will no longer suppress or smooth over the symptoms, but strive to remove the cause of the evil. In this case, the cause is the entire male society and its view of women.[103]

Although they believed that in the long run women's liberation might lead to the liberation of men, they claimed that it was not the task of the women's liberation movement to help men. Instead, they argued for concentrating on "our need to free ourselves, together with other women." In practice, this implied that "today, we will not cooperate with men on the terms of the male society."

The debate faded for the time being, but within the New Feminists, Birgit Bjerck seized the initiative to establish a "theme group on

[102] Anders Bratholm: "Er kvinnen også en gris?" [Is the Woman also a Pig?], *Dagbladet*, 12 March 1974.

[103] Birgit Bjerck, Brita M. Gulli, and Kari Melby: "Vi kan ikke lenger være barmhjertige samaritanere" [We Can No Longer Be Merciful Samaritans], *Dagbladet*, 23 March 1974.

pornography" to map out what was being peddled in Norway by "hard" pornography, in which "violence and extreme contempt of women are the main ingredients," as she wrote in the internal journal of the Oslo chapter of the New Feminists. "I think most people have too rosy an image of what pornography is about, and I want to smash that image."[104] Unfortunately, no evidence is available as to what this group was doing at the time, since there were no major actions taken against pornography during this period. However, in the internal journal *Oslofeministen*, it appears that some smaller actions were taken against the new "men's magazine" *Nye Alle Menn*, launched by the Swedish publishing company Bonnier in 1975. For example, some New Feminists protested against the magazine's promotional posters showing Julie Ege and Brigitte Bardot by posting pictures of naked men on them.[105]

Breaking the Silence

Breaking the silence and eliminating the shame was the first step in politicizing the sexual exploitation of women. It was necessary to highlight sexual exploitation of women as a true problem before it could become a real political issue with strategies for change. Consciousness-raising and problematizing of matters that had previously been viewed as normal as, in fact, manifestations of "women's oppression," was fundamental for the women's liberation movement of the 1970s.

The public responses to the Norwegian New Feminists' condemnation of pornography as a gender-political problem differed from the reactions to the French revolutionary feminists' public denunciation of rape. Although not all agreed with the New Feminists' analysis of the "women industry" as manifested in pornography, striptease, and prostitution, no one outlawed debate on it by claiming that it was politically irrelevant

---

[104] Birgit: "Temagruppe om pornografi" [Theme Group on Pornography], *Oslofeministen*, no. 2, 1974, p. 16.

[105] Konny Krogh: "Aksjoner" [Actions], *Oslofeministen*, no. 10, 1975, pp. 10–11. According to the article, other actions had also been carried out. For example, it is mentioned that some unknown people had put stickers on the same commercial posters of *Nye Alle Menn* that read "Sister Solidarity. Crush *Nye Alle Menn*. Crush the Pornography Industry. Long Live the Women's Front. Julie Ege Is the Trueborn Child of Capital" [Søstersolidaritet. Knus Nye Alle Menn. Knus pornoindustrien. Leve Kvinnefronten. Julie Ege kapitalens ektefødde barn]. The author wanted to cooperate with the activists on future actions against advertising for *Nye Alle Menn*.

or was destroying the "main struggle." After all, pornography had been publicly discussed for years in Norway. Previously, however, the public conversation pertaining to it had been dominated by men, just as the users of pornography were predominantly male. In fact, according to Danish research, men comprised 98 per cent of pornography users in that country.[106]

There were, however, common features of these early debates on the sexual exploitation of women. For the first time women publicly problematized men's sexuality and directly confronted their sexual relations with women. This provoked anger on the part of some men, while others met the challenge and distanced themselves publicly from men's sexual exploitation of women. Another common feature was that activists in both countries drew parallels to racism as a way of encouraging the public to take the issue seriously. The crux of the argument was that, in the same way as prejudice against people of color legitimizes racism, prejudice against women legitimizes sexual exploitation. Discrimination and abuse based on sex had to be taken as seriously as discrimination and abuse based on skin color.

When women's liberation activists began to theorize about rape and pornography, they often used concepts that were common to contemporary left-wing radicals. Among French intellectuals, Lacan's theories held sway, and Psych et Po extended his abstract notion of "the Law of the Father" to include rape—not just language—as a way in which women are subjected to this law. In order to get Marxists to understand that rape was a problem, Maï used a deliberate strategy of presenting it as a form of imperialism. In Norway, the activists used the Marxist concept of commodification to protest the use of women as merchandise in the pornography industry. In both countries, radical feminists were less reliant on left-wing discourse and confronted men more directly than Marxist women did. Admittedly, the French revolutionary feminists used the Marxist notion of class, but in a different way than the "pure" Marxists did. Instead of seeing class conflict as a struggle between the bourgeoisie and the proletariat, the revolutionary feminists argued that the main conflict was between the sexes. According to them, rape served as a weapon that men as a class used to oppress women as a class. The Norwegian New Feminists also viewed sex as a fundamental conflict, but

---

[106] Tessem and Wiedswang 1984, p. 98.

they emphasized that women's oppression was due to a combination of patriarchy and capitalism, and that Christianity was a driving force of sexual repression. Although France is a predominantly Catholic country and French activists of the MLF constantly criticized religion, Christianity was a less prominent element in political discussions. This was likely due to the fact that French society was more secular, with an absolute distinction drawn between religion and the state (the *laïcité*), while Christians remained a significant political force in 1970s Norway.[107] Strong Christian movements prevented the adoption of the law securing abortion on demand in 1974. In 1978, however, the new abortion law passed by the slimmest of margins—one vote—four years after abortion on demand was introduced in France (cf. Chapter 1). Opposing pornography had mainly been a Christian cause in Norway, and for radical feminists it was important to distance themselves from that group.

The early feminist debates on the sexual exploitation of women did not immediately lead to public protest or political action. It was only after the women's liberation movements mobilized people to take to the streets to demonstrate against rape and pornography that these issues gained momentum.

---

[107] Haase-Dubosc, Danielle et al. (2003): "An Introduction by the French Editors," in D. Haase-Dubosc et al. (eds.): *French Feminism: An Indian Anthology*. New Delhi: Sage, p. 23.

CHAPTER 3

The Women's Liberation Movement Takes to the Streets Against Rape and Pornography

When women activists began to take to the streets in the second half of the 1970s to protest the sexual exploitation of women, the result was far more dramatic than when the fight was limited to the newspaper columns. Activists ended up in physical, sometimes violent confrontations with opponents, whether they be police, trade unionists, or porn dealers. The drama and the spectacle of the confrontations caught the media's attention. Media coverage in Norway, where militant political actions were far less common than in France, could be particularly intense. Although the women activists and their street forays were not necessarily presented in a favorable light, the media coverage made the public aware of their cause.

Though street demonstrations against rape in France began a couple of years earlier than the anti-pornography actions in Norway, the two activities shared a common feature—namely, that the actions were triggered by the fact that women associated with the women's movements had been victims of abuse, albeit of different kinds. In France, the rape of two Belgian tourists named Anne and Araceli who were hiking on the outskirts of Marseille led to demonstrations outside courts during rape trials as a widespread form of protest. In Norway, the suspension of Liv and Rannveig, two female conductors on the Holmenkollen metro line in Oslo who had torn down promotional posters for the "men's magazine" *Nye Alle Menn* (New All Men) and subsequently lost their jobs, triggered support campaigns and anti-pornography demonstrations. When the first

© The Author(s) 2021
T. R. Korsvik, *Politicizing Rape and Pornography*,
Citizenship, Gender and Diversity,
https://doi.org/10.1007/978-3-030-55639-6_3

porn burning took place in Oslo in August 1977, it was in support of Liv and Rannveig. Thereafter, porn burnings as a form of protest took on a life of their own.

Anne and Araceli in France and Liv and Rannveig in Norway came to personify the fight against rape and pornography in their respective countries. In both cases, the women were victims of abuse, but they were not victims of the passive type. They had friends in the women's liberation movement and initiated support campaigns for themselves. From the very beginning, they made clear that their campaign was about more than their individual cases; indeed, it was about building a movement that denounced sexual abuse against women as a social problem.

THE FRENCH CAMPAIGN BEGINS

Beginning in the autumn of 1975, the fight against rape metamorphosed from a cause undertaken primarily by engaged dedicated women activists to one that became an issue for the wider public. The Mouvement de libération des femmes (MLF) activists carried out direct actions, particularly demonstrations in front of courts during rape trials. The demonstrations outside these heavily symbolic "male bastions" made the MLF visible in a different way than articles and debates in women's liberation movement and left-wing publications had previously done. In street demonstrations, ordinary, less intellectually sophisticated women could actively participate and show their support for the claim that rape was a crime that women would no longer accept. On May 1, 1976, the MLF participated for the first time in the labor movement's Workers' Day rally in Paris, using slogans against rape. This led to fiery confrontations with male trade unionists, who believed that such slogans had nothing to do with the labor movement. The same year, MLF activists organized a feminist mass rally against rape in Paris that they called Ten Hours Against Rape (*Dix heures contre le viol*), which attracted 3000–4000 women. Feminists from the League for Women's Rights (*Ligue du droit des femmes*, LDF) were also active in putting together the International Tribunal on Crimes against Women in Brussels in 1976.

Both the mobilization and cooperation against rape were characterized by anything but harmony. As was typical for the MLF, the conflict level was intense. There were strong disagreements about the causes of rape and how it was to be fought. Nevertheless, activists from different branches of the MLF agreed that there was a connection between rape and pornography, and that it was necessary to confront men's sexist attitudes. Their meetings and protest activities became important learning opportunities in terms of developing both political practice and theories of rape.

"Fascism Is Permanent Rape; Rape Is Unrecognized Fascism"

The first major street demonstration against rape took place not in Paris, but in the small Basque town of Hendaye, close to the Spanish border. At the time, Spain was still a fascist dictatorship under the rule of General Francisco Franco. On October 5, 1975, about a thousand women demonstrated in Hendaye under the slogan "Fascism is Permanent Rape; Rape is Unrecognized Fascism." All of the different political branches of the MLF joined the event, which was organized in collaboration with Basque women.

The inspiration for this particular women's demonstration was a major international protest campaign against the execution of five Spanish opponents of the Franco regime.[1] Several activists from the Basque separatist group ETA and the Marxist-Leninist organization FRAP[2] were awaiting convictions, and in Spanish prisons more than 400 political prisoners were on hunger strike in solidarity with them. One of these was Eva Forest, a well-known opposition writer, activist, and ETA sympathizer, who had become a symbol of the struggle against fascism. She was incarcerated without trial in the infamous Yeserias prison in Madrid for allegedly having taken part in a bomb attack in 1974. A support committee on her behalf, *Collectif Eva Forest*, had been formed. In addition to revolutionary French and Spanish organizations, it included women's groups

---

[1] The European Commission recommended that the Council of Ministers break off negotiations with Spain on a free trade agreement, and the EC diplomats decided to boycott a ceremony that would mark General Franco's 39 years in power. In Sweden, Prime Minister Olof Palme condemned the executions, and typographers in *Dagens Nyheter* refused to print ads promoting holidays in Spain. Throughout Europe, there were demonstrations against the Franco regime. See the articles "Quinze militants de l'ETA seront jugés par tribunal civil" [Fifteen ETA Activists Will Be Tried in Civil Court], *Libération*, 6 October 1975, p. 7; "Marche sur Hendaye le 1er novembre" [March on Hendaye on November 1st], *Libération*, 30 October 1975, p. 2; "En espagne" [In Spain], *Le quotidien des femmes*, no. 7, 10 October 1975, p. 4.

[2] ETA (Euskadi Ta Askatasuna) was established in 1959. The Marxist-Leninist FRAP (Frente Revolucionario Antifascista y Patriota) was formed in 1971.

such as *Psychanalyse et politique* (Psych et Po) and the Trotskyist feminist groups *Les Pétroleuses* and *Cercle Elisabeth Dimitrev*.[3] While imprisoned, Forest wrote about the anti-fascist struggle and about the torture that was taking place in the prisons. Her texts were published in Psych et Po's newspaper, *Le Quotidien des femmes*, and its publishing company, Des femmes, issued her prison diary and letters.[4] Forest's description of how rape was used as a means of torture against the female prisoners underscored the connection between rape and fascism.

The idea behind a separate women's march in Hendaye was to show that the women's struggle was part of the anti-fascist struggle, and that fascism particularly affects women. By marching to the Spanish border, the organizers wanted to show that women cross borders, both literally and figuratively, and that there were no limitations to their solidarity with the struggling Spanish people. Participating in the fight against fascism was also liberating for the individual: "The more you become politicized, the stronger the woman you are, the more you become a woman. The more woman you become, the more you fight," as had been vigorously stated in Psych et Po's newspaper.[5]

The planning of the women's march was characterized by spontaneity, and thus, in Hendaye, disagreements immediately arose on how to demonstrate.[6] The serious character of the demonstration ran counter to the festive atmosphere of balloons and funny songs and performances that was typical of MLF demonstrations. Some wanted to introduce a new and silent form of protest that did not reinvent the traditional left-wing rallies in Paris, with clenched fists and megaphone slogans. According to one of the many critical letters to the publisher in *Liberation* after the women's rally, the demonstrators wanted to show that "another anger was possible," one that avoided a "male" form of demonstration in which

---

[3] *Libération*, 30 October 1975, p. 2.

[4] Forest, Eva (1975): *Journal et lettres de prison* [Journal and Letters from Prison]. Paris: Des femmes.

[5] "Voix plurielle..." [Plural Voices], *Le quotidien des femmes*, no. 7, 10 October 1975, p. 7.

[6] "1000 femmes manifestent à la frontière" [1000 Women Demonstrate at the Border], *Libération*, 6 October 1975, p. 7.

the aim was to confront the riot police.[7] Instead, they preferred imaginative slogans such as "Machismo Makes the Bed for Fascism" and "Franco, Half the Sky Is Falling on Your Head," as well as a slogan declaring that fascism is tantamount to permanent rape, and rape is an unrecognized form of fascism.[8] Psych et Po was among those who wanted to introduce this new "female" way of demonstrating: "To oppose the violence with violence, is to remain in the order of death. But to get into the order of life it is not enough to use silence and non-violence. You have to arm yourself with a wild imagination."[9]

Women associated with far-left groups did not like the idea of a "female"-style demonstration. The Trotskyist feminists in *Les Pétroleuses* were disappointed that there was not more of a confrontation with law enforcement upon their arrival at the border crossing, which was heavily guarded by the French riot police CRS. The fact that half of the demonstrators sat down on the ground and were peaceful instead of belligerent meant that "the coppers didn't see us as protesters, but as women's holes, weak and defenseless."[10] In their view, the struggle was about breaking down the traditional roles in which men represent death and war and women represent fertility and peace. Women must "take their share of the violence" in order to create a society without violence. Their solidarity with the Spanish women, who risked so much in their struggle, represented solidarity between struggling women, not "between uteruses," according to the Trotskyist feminists.

Although there were disputes over how to demonstrate, the different political branches of the MLF all agreed on the slogan "Fascism is Permanent Rape; Rape is Unrecognized Fascism." An obvious reason why rape and fascism were seen to be related was that Eva Forest and other political prisoners had documented how rape was a common means of torture in

[7] Les effrontées du car no 7 [The Impudent from Bus Number 7]: "Le fascisme est un viol permanent, le viol est un fascisme non reconnu" [Fascism Is a Permanent Rape, Rape Is an Unrecognized Fascism], *Libération*, 28 October 1975, p. 2.

[8] In original: "Le machisme fait le lit du fascisme" [Machismo Makes the Bed for Fascism], "Franco, la moitié du ciel te tombe sur la tête" [Franco, Half the Sky Is Falling on Your Head]. In French, slogans are called "mots d'ordre," while some parts of the women's movement instead called them "mots de désordre," meaning disturbing or messy words.

[9] "à hendaye" [in Hendaye], *Le quotidien des femmes*, no. 7, 10 October 1975, p. 6.

[10] Mina, Dominique, Sophie: "Hendaye. Femmes contre le fascisme" [Hendaye. Women Against Fascism], *Les Pétroleuses*, no. 4, 1975, p. 23.

the Spanish prisons. Also, the fascist ideal of women centered on the three Ks: *Kinder, Küche, Kirche* [children, kitchen, and church], and the trinity of the Family, the Church, and the Fatherland was the exact opposite of what the MLF stood for. At the same time, the international campaign against torture and executions in Franco's Spain mobilized the anti-fascist struggle, and that campaign in turn influenced MLF activists, who began to interpret many phenomena as expressions of fascism. Fascism was not perceived merely as a specific political ideology or mode of governance in dictatorships such as Spain, but as a coercive, violent, and patriarchal system that concerned all women and was most clearly manifested in the abuse and rape of women.[11] Sexual violence against women was often referred to as "sexual fascism" and included violent pornography, which the MLF, from this point on, campaigned against.

Violent pornography was becoming widespread just as the anti-fascist struggle reached its peak. In the fall of 1975, the erotic movie *Story of O* (*Histoire d'O*) premiered in France. The film tells the story of a young woman who is held captive in a castle by an elderly rich man, bound and chained in various ways, and tortured and raped. Gradually, the woman, called "O," begins to enjoy her slave existence. The movie was considered a high-quality erotic film, not least by the left, as illustrated in its praise by the left-wing weeklies *L'Express* and *Le Nouvel Observateur*.[12] Just prior to the women's rally in Hendaye, the different branches of the MLF, despite their generally strong disagreements, issued a joint statement criticizing these weeklies. In the petition "Story of O or Sexual Fascism," *L'Express* and *Le Nouvel Observateur* were condemned

---

[11] See "à hendaye" and "voix plurielle...," *Le quotidien des femmes*, no. 7, 10 October 1975.

[12] *Histoire d'O* is based on Pauline Réage's book of the same name from 1954. When the film premiered in 1975, it was the cover story of *L'Express*. A feature of the case that made it especially intriguing was that the State Secretary responsible for "the feminine condition" (i.e., the position of women), Françoise Giroud, was also chairman of *L'Express*. Instead of criticizing the article about the *Story of O*, she resigned as chairman of the weekly, stating that it was damaging to mix the role of representative of the government with public debate, according to de Pisan and Tristan 1977, p. 185. See also "le lendemain du ressemblement à hendaye, une réunion..." [The Day After the Rally in Hendaye, a Meeting...], *Le quotidien des femmes*, no. 7, 10 October 1975, p. 9.

for promoting rape under the guise of sexual freedom.[13] The petition linked sadomasochistic pornography to the rape of female prisoners in fascist dictatorships. The MLF argued that it was hypocritical for the weeklies to dissociate themselves from fascism while promoting a film that glorified the torture of a woman. A movie wherein blacks were chained and mistreated would never have been accepted as high-quality erotic art, the petition stated. Torture pornography was portrayed as a fascist counter-offensive to the progress of the women's liberation movement; the opponents of women's liberation did not accept that women had become active and began to protest, and now they wanted to punish them. To attract attention to the petition, about one hundred women invaded the editorial office of *L'Express*, writing slogans with lipstick on the wall and offering the editor a whip. Afterward, the protesters continued on to a cinema on the Champs-Elysées, where a massive police presence prevented them from entering.[14]

The Rape Victims Anne and Araceli

In the petition against *Story of O*, the rape of the two Belgian tourists on the outskirts of Marseille was also referred to as an example of "sexual fascism." At first, the case was hardly sensational; after all, no one had been killed or grossly mutilated. Rather, it was a fairly routine case of sexual abuse in a holiday resort. What was exceptional about the case was that the two victims, Anne Tonglet and Araceli Castellano, had actually reported the rape to the police and, further, that they went public and organized a campaign in support of themselves and against rape in general. Their claim was that rape should be dealt with as a felony in the Assize Court and not as a misdemeanor in the Correctional Tribunal. The maneuvering for support for Anne and Araceli became a driving force in the campaign against rape, which was attracting an increasing number of people. At first, activists of the MLF began to demonstrate in front of courts where rape trials were taking place. Next, others joined the

---

[13] "Histoire d'O ou le fascisme sexuel," petition signed by Les Pétroleuses, Ligue du droit des femmes, Politique et Psychanalyse, Librairie des femmes and Tribunal international contre le violence contre les femmes. Printed in *Les Pétroleuses*, no. 4, 1975, p. 4.

[14] Valérie: "Sado-Machisme" [Sado-Machismo], *Les Pétroleuses*, no. 4, 1975, p. 4; de Pisan and Tristan 1977, pp. 188–191.

campaign, including feminist lawyers, activists from the labor union movement and human rights organizations, intellectuals, left-wing parties, and
top-level politicians. Anne and Araceli became symbols of women who no
longer kept silent about the assaults they had been subjected to, choosing
instead to resist. Historian Georges Vigarello claims that this particular
case led to a change in attitudes in France, where more and more people
began to see rape as a societal problem.[15] It was the first time that rape
victims themselves, acting in public and identified by their real names,
took control of a judicial process and set the stage for the debate. At the
same time, the campaign acquired a controversial character because of
the opinion that rape should be handled as a felony in the Assize Court.
This claim was not supported by large segments of the left, where the
general attitude was that the judicial system was the oppressive tool of
the bourgeoisie.

The case of Anne Tonglet and Araceli Castellano became known to the
public in the fall of 1975, but the rape had occurred one year earlier. The
two Belgian women, then 24 and 19 years old, respectively, had camped
out in a tent on the Morgiou, a bay near Marseille. A 400-page book on
the trial, published after the final conviction in 1978 (Fig. 3.1), describes
what happened from the young women's point of view:

> Immediately upon their arrival at the parking lot in Morgiou, where they
> are unloading from the 2CV, they are accosted by a local "bully," Serge
> Petrilli, whom they ask to get lost. The next day Petrilli sneaks around
> their tent and approaches them again. For the second time, he is brutally
> rejected. He is deeply offended and thinks only of revenge. In the evening
> (21 August), he informs two of his friends, Guy Roger and Mouglalis, that
> there are two girls alone in a waterfront tent, some distance away from
> the village. Petrilli proposes a punishing expedition. Roger and Mouglalis
> hesitate for a moment. But Petrilli insists. And soon the three boys are
> heading over the cliffs to the remote tent, where Anne and Araceli lie
> asleep.[16]

[15] Vigarello 1998, pp. 248–255.

[16] Choisir la cause des femmes (1978): *Viol. Le procès d'Aix*. Paris: Gallimard, p. 29.
The bulk of the book consists of the transcribed court proceedings. However, two of the
three defense attorneys refused to publish their defense speeches. In addition to the story
of the rape and what happened afterward, the book contains a longer article by Anne
and Araceli's assistant attorney, Gisèle Halimi, in which she argues why rape should be
punished as a felony, as well as a response that Anne and Araceli wrote to *Libération*

Fig. 3.1 The feminist lawyer Gisèle Halimi flanked by the two Belgian rape victims Anne Tonglet (left) and Araceli Castillano (right). Facsimile of the book about the rape trial in Aix-en-Provence 1978, when the case of Anne and Araceli was settled. In 2014, a new book about their case was published by Jean-Yves Le Naour and Catherine Valenti, *Et le viol devint un crime* (Editions Vendémiaire). Based on the book, the documentary *Le procès du viol* by Cédric Condon and the Belgian TV drama *Le viol* by Alain Tasma were both launched in 2017 (© Editions Gallimard [Reprinted with permission])

The three men crawled into the tent, and after Anne hit one of them over the head with a hammer, she was hit by a fist in her face, and the "nightmare" began. As the book describes the events: "For four hours,

in which they refute the newspaper's representation of the case, as well as the feminist association Choisir's proposal for new rape legislation.

they keep on, on top of the two young women, who, exhausted, terrified and strangled by horror, as if dead, undergo the most serious acts of violence...".

As soon as the three men left early the next morning, the two girls drove to the gendarmerie and reported the rape. In the preliminary judicial investigation, the two were subjected to a "biased and suspicious" female interrogation judge. She commented that Anne and Araceli were lesbians and, as naturists, had a "free" way of life. The judge accepted the three men's explanation that the women had "consented" after the first melee with the hammer. Her reasoning was that the two lesbian girls had given themselves to the men and later regretted it. Thus, the interrogation judge did not consider it to be rape, but abuse, and transferred the case to the Correctional Tribunal as a misdemeanor. Anne and Araceli protested this decision. They argued it was indeed rape, and thus should be handled as a felony in the Assize Court. The Correctional Tribunal in Marseille accepted their claim in the fall of 1975. Still, it took an unusually long time—almost four years—before their case was handled by the Assize Court in Aix-en-Provence in 1978.

The controversial aspect of the case was that the defendants claimed that the girls had "consented" and "joined the game," while Anne and Araceli said they had given up resisting because they were stunned by the horror of the attack and were "like dead." What the three men said had been a little rough, but otherwise normal sexual intercourse was described by the two women as a "depraved act of violence" from which they were so traumatized that they became like "automatons." After the rape, both of them struggled with trauma, anxiety, and depression, took tranquilizers, and quit their jobs. Araceli had also become pregnant and had an abortion.

The case of Anne and Araceli became known to the MLF in connection with the first trial in Marseille in September 1975. The two had not appeared in person because they felt that they were not taken seriously and that the interrogation judge had misinterpreted and manipulated what they had said. Further, they had declined to participate in a trial in which only the abuse, and not the rape, was recognized.[17] Outside the court-house, several women's groups demonstrated. Psych et Po's newspaper encouraged readers to engage in the solidarity campaign for Anne and Araceli, a campaign that the two women themselves coordinated. They had crafted a petition, to be sent to Anne's address in Brussels, that made the following demands: (1) that the judiciary system recognize rape as a felony; (2) that the promise of a trial be used to encourage women to report rape; and (3) that the "false masculinity" of men who daily rape women, girlfriends, wives or others had to end.[18] The question of using the judicial system in rape cases was now added to the gender-political agenda. Previously, activists in the MLF had not supported reporting rape to the police, as doing so was considered useless, and besides, the move-ment had no confidence in institutions and punishments. From now on, however, the different branches of the MLF would support using the judi-cial system, whether or not they thought it worked as a tool to protect the privileges of men or of the bourgeoisie. The argument for using the judicial system was not to send rapists to jail, but to break the silence and shame of the victims and make rape recognized as a crime against women. For feminists associated with left-wing, Marxist groups, this was politically challenging and posed a difficult dilemma. On the one hand, they encouraged women to report rape to the police; on the other, they strongly opposed the "bourgeois" judicial system. Radical feminists had a more pragmatic approach to making use of it.

Political Challenges for the Class-Struggle Feminists

Femmes en lutte (Women in Struggle) was one of the groups adhering to the so-called class-struggle tendency of the MLF, and they grappled with the dilemma about using the judicial system in rape cases. The group aimed to organize working-class women and was mainly concerned with that group's conditions and struggles in the workplace. Now, however, rape became a prominent issue for the group. Their newspaper was clearly siding with Anne and Araceli by pointing out how, during the trial, it

---

[17] Anne Tonglet and Araceli Castellano: "Lettre adressée à M. le Président et Messieurs les Juges" [Letter Addressed to the President and the Judges], *Le Quotidien des femmes*, no. 5, 22 September 1975, p. 16; Martine Storti: "Dans la mouvance d'une mobilisation" [In the Movement of a Mobilization], *Libération*, 26–27 June 1976, p. 8.

[18] "Pétition" [Petition], *Le Quotidien des femmes*, no. 5, 22 September 1975, p. 16.

had been stated that they were lesbians who were active in the fight for
women's liberation, and that their "unusual way of life" involved risk. The
newspaper stated that this indicated that "women don't have the right
to move about freely."[19] Though Women in Struggle wanted to engage
working-class women in the fight against rape, this challenge turned out
not to be that simple. In an article about discussions they had had with
working-class women, it appeared that the latter, who were characterized
by resignation and fatalism, had difficulty condemning rape. They said
things like: "Men are just like that" and "He who rapes you is even more
miserable than you, so what is it you really want to denounce?"[20] After
the Women in Struggle activists succeeded in convincing the working-
class women that "daddy's girls with cars and connections" (such as
Anne and Araceli, presumably) were not the ones most exposed to rape—
instead, the real targets were working-class women who worked shifts
and were obliged to walk alone to and from work at five o'clock in
the morning or at eleven in the evening—the attitude was said to have
changed:

> When we discussed this together, around the flyer or the petition, the
> women did not feel isolated anymore; they dared to tell about things they
> had never entrusted to anyone, memories that were so suppressed that it
> remained only a tenacious fear of men. By talking about it, the WOMEN
> STARTED TO REBEL. [Underlining and capitalization in original][21]

In an optimistic manner, the paper reported that many of the working-
class women signed the first petition of their lives after the meeting,
but many of them continued to think that it was "too difficult" to
participate in a public campaign and would limit their activities to
group discussions. The fact that just speaking of rape was perceived as a
rebellion among women outside the hard-core women's liberation movement speaks volumes about the taboo surrounding rape and thus how
groundbreaking the campaign against rape actually was. When Women
in Struggle explained the causes of rape, they emphasized, as did many

---

[19] "Femmes violées, ne nous taisons plus!" [Raped Women, Let Us Not Be Silent
Anymore!], *Femmes travailleuses en lutte*, no. 7, October–November 1975, p. 20.

[20] "Un procès, une campagne..." [A Trial, a Campaign...], *Femmes travailleuses en
lutte*, no. 7, October–November 1975, p. 21.

[21] Ibid.

others on the left, "sexual misery"—a misery caused by the dominance of the bourgeoisie. An article entitled "Condemning Rape Is Condemning the Rottenness of this Society" described how "sexual misery" led men to sometimes behave like "beasts," in that those with money "bought a whore," while those with no money raped women because it was free.[22] In this way a parallel was drawn between rape and prostitution, and the bourgeoisie was seen as responsible for the "rottenness." According to this perspective, relationships of dominance permeated the whole of society: the bourgeoisie dominated the working class, and men dominated women. These relationships of dominance were explained primarily as financial. Because men earn more than women, women are valued merely as disposable objects to be used. Women in Struggle believed that all forms of dominance were due to the bourgeoisie and led, among other things, to men raping women:

> Rape is a daily risk for women because the bourgeoisie imposes on workers an existence in which time to live is banished, because they make lots of money by exploiting the sexual frustrations of workers through porn films and prostitution. But also because one tries to force women to be passive, dominated, treated as objects that cannot or should not have other desires than to satisfy others, especially men's sexual desires. (...)
>
> NOW WE'VE HAD ENOUGH! We demand that rape be recognized by the judicial system, even if the sexual misery is a mitigating circumstance. [Emphasis in original][23]

"The sexual misery" was thus a "mitigating circumstance" for men to rape. But at the same time, it was not so mitigating that rape should not be reported. This presented a difficult dilemma concerning the relationship between personal responsibility and more or less deterministic structures for which the bourgeoisie was responsible, a dilemma that also

---

[22] "Dénoncer le viol, c'est dénoncer la pourriture de cette société" [To Denounce Rape Is to Denounce the Rottenness of this Society], *Femmes travailleuses en lutte*, no. 7, October–November 1975, p. 22. See also "Prostituées des femmes comme nous" [Prostitutes Are Women Like Us], *Femmes travailleuses en lutte*, no. 7, October–November 1975, p. 12.

[23] "Femmes violées, ne nous taisons plus!" [Raped Women, Let Us Not Be Silent Anymore!], *Femmes travailleuses en lutte*, no. 7, October–November 1975, p. 21.

troubled others on the left. Because rapists were seen as victims of structures and sexual misery, they could not be held fully accountable for their actions:

> Of course, we don't want miserable types who are not responsible for the view on women that has been put into their heads, to be oppressed. But by invoking the judiciary, WE PRIMARILY REJECT THE SILENCE AND THE ISOLATION OF SHAME: We demand our RIGHT to make decisions regarding our bodies. [Emphasis in original][24]

The solution to the dilemma of using the bourgeois judicial system was to use it as a kind of speaker's platform to break the silence and shame related to rape. Although Women in Struggle believed that "the bourgeoisie will take advantage of our rebellion to confirm the idea that rape is a problem of law and order," they supported the women who reported it and used the judiciary because it was "the first rebellion." Of greatest importance, however, was to lead a "real collective struggle." This was about collecting evidence from raped women, demonstrating outside courtrooms, creating solidarity among women, and learning self-defense. The purpose was to convince working-class women and men that women make decisions about their own bodies; that "when a woman says no, it is not yes, but no."[25]

The fact that Women in Struggle supported the use of the judicial apparatus at the same time as they were opposed in principle to imprisonment and accountability for rapists, can be interpreted as a compromise directed toward the political environment in which they were associated on the revolutionary left. For example, the revolutionary newspaper *Libération* asked: "Who dares today to say that the prison environment helps a man, imprisoned with other men, to change his perception of women? Does it not rather preserve his attitudes?"[26] One did not believe that imprisonment could change attitudes, or that the threat of imprisonment could deter potential rapists. In *Rouge*, the weekly newspaper of

---

[24] "Le procès de Marseille..." [The Process in Marseille], *Femmes travailleuses en lutte*, no. 7, October–November 1975, p. 22.

[25] "VIOL est-ce que la loi défend les femmes?" [RAPE: Does the Law Defend Women?], *Femmes travailleuses en Lutte*, no. 11, 1976, p. 23.

[26] *Libération*, 16 April 1976, quoted in Mossuz-Lavau 1991, p. 208.

the Trotskyist party *Ligue communiste révolutionnaire*, LCR (The Revolutionary Communist League) which was politically close to Women in Struggle, it was written:

> In the longer term, we prefer rapists not to be responsible in front of bourgeois courts, but in front of workers' meetings, women and men gathered together, in neighborhoods or in factories. When one can mobilize for such meetings to condemn rape, women will have no need to resort to the courts.[27]

It is likely that Women in Struggle's compromise on using the judicial system as a speaker's platform was the result of the Marxist women wanting to avoid stepping on their male comrades' toes unnecessarily. For revolutionary feminists, however, this was not a widespread concern. According to the League for Women's Rights, LDF, of which Simone de Beauvoir was the leader, the main problem with the judicial system was not that it was dominated by the bourgeoisie, but that it was male-dominated and acted as a "sex court." A symptom of this male dominance was the fact that rape was not taken seriously, and that the word of the accused was considered more trustworthy than that of the victim. The majority of judges and jury members were men, and they were unable to understand the woman's situation because she was seen as "the other," according to the LDF. Despite these shortcomings, however, the LDF encouraged rape victims to use the judicial system.[28]

A post written by an anonymous "group of female lawyers and non-lawyers" in *Libération* in 1976 illustrates how difficult it was to get the left to agree on the necessity of reporting rape. They pointed out that, in order to legitimize the reporting of rape, "the judicial struggle has been used in revolutionary combat"—for example, to condemn French war crimes during the Algerian war, without meeting any opposition by those on the left. They claimed that "rapists shall no longer have a left-wing alibi about 'the sexual misery,' because rape means misogyny in action."[29]

[27] *Rouge*, 10 December 1976, quoted in ibid.

[28] "Le viol" [Rape], *Les Nouvelles féministes*, no. 1, December 1974, p. 13.

[29] Groupe des femmes avocates et non-avocates: "La lutte juridique a été utilisé dans le combat révolutionnaire" [The Judicial Struggle Has Been Used in Revolutionary Combat], *Libération*, 26–27 June 1976, p. 9.

Clashes Over Rape in the May 1st Rally

During the spring of 1976, the campaign against rape intensified and was brought into the public discourse in France. The case of Anne and Araceli had mobilized the MLF, and during the spring several rape cases were dealt with in the Correctional Tribunal. There, activists demonstrated outside the court demanding that the cases be considered felonies and thus transferred to the Assize Court. And on several occasions they succeeded in their demands. One example was the much-publicized case of a high school student, Véronique, who had been raped by a man on her way home from school. On April 26, 1976, the case was litigated in the Correctional Tribunal in Paris. Outside, women protested and claimed that the case should be taken to the Assize Court. The judges—who, incidentally, were all men—agreed unanimously with this claim and forwarded the case to the higher court.[30]

The fact that in many cases the protesters succeeded in their demands was perceived as a major victory and led to a new euphoria among members of the MLF, who had experienced a certain downturn after the initial enthusiasm had faded by 1974.[31] For instance, women activists decided to engage in more protests against rape by, for the first time, leading an MLF contingent in the labor movement's rally of May 1st. The MLF's presence was approved in advance by the CGT, the principal trade union in France, which was affiliated with the Soviet-oriented Communist Party PCF, at this time the largest party on the left.[32] But when more than a thousand women were to enter their assigned place in the march, the CGT guards claimed that the agreement had not been "respected." They contended that the MLF slogans were not the "normal worker's slogans" that the management of CGT said they had agreed to. The main slogan of the MLF was "Oppressed Women, Exploited Women, Let's Take the Fight into Our Own Hands," and colorful banners and posters proclaimed "Down with Rape!"; "When a Woman Says No, It Is Not Yes, It Is No!"; "Rape from the Left, Rape from the Right, Same Fight"; and

---

[30] Collectif national pour les droits des femmes: "Chronologie: 'Féminisme et lutte de classes'" [Chronology: "Feminism and Class Struggle"], http://collectifdroitsdesfemmes. org/spip.php?article245. Consulted 20 June 2017.

[31] Picq 1993, p. 237.

[32] Until the election for the National Assembly in 1978, PCF membership was steadily increasing, with more than half a million members and just over 20% support. Zancarini-Fournel 2008d, pp. 672–674.

"A Woman Without a Man Is Like a Fish Without a Bicycle."[33] In line with the MLF demonstration style, many of the women were costumed, carried balloons, danced and sang, and shouted slogans such as "Yes Dad, Yes Boss, Yes Dear, We Are Tired of It!" They also brought a small truck carrying children on the loading platform.

The CGT guards refused to allow the women to join the march, and after a few hours of futile negotiations, impatient women sought to march anyway. At that point, hundreds of guards formed three ranks to prevent them from entering. They began with sexist insults about "whores," "sluts," "you haven't got enough dick," and "do you want me to pull down my pants?" Even the children on the truck were told that they were "bastards" who had no business being there. The women responded by calling the guards "Stalinist phallocrats" and "fascists," and shouting "No Socialism Without Women's Liberation!" Everything quickly spun out of control; the guards knocked and kicked women, tore up their posters and banners, and tried to overturn the truck carrying the children. The women formed chains and refused to give up. Several of them were injured, and some fainted and had to be taken away from the rally. Among the women were members of the CGT who tore up their membership cards and shouted that they were ashamed to belong to the union. Passersby were also angry, and the competing union CFDT welcomed the MLF contingent into its segment of the march. Similar episodes occurred in other cities, including Toulouse and Rouen.

The CGT county leadership in the Paris region did not disapprove of the conduct of the guards. Their position, as stated in a CGT circular after the incident, was that the women's section had to be stopped because the slogans on rape were not agreed to in advance.[34] CGT leadership

---

[33] The description of the events is based on "Après le 1er mai... Lettre de la coordination des groupes femmes à la direction de la CGT" [After 1 May... Letter from the Coordinator of Women's Groups to the CGT Leaders], *Femmes travailleuses en lutte*, no. 10, June 1976, p. 9; "La C.G.T. et les femmes" [The CGT and Women], *Libération*, 3 May 1976, p. 8; "Débats" [Debates], *L'Information des femmes*, no. 7, 1976, pp. 14–17; *Les Pétroleuses*, no. 6, 1976, pp. 19–21; Picq 1993, pp. 237–238; and the circular of the CGT trade union of the Paris Region, printed in *Femmes travailleuses en lutte*, no. 10, June 1976, p. 10, *L'Information des femmes*, no. 7, 1976, pp. 16–17, and *Libération*, 15–16 May 1976, p. 5.

[34] Circular from the CGT of the Paris region, printed in *Femmes travailleuses en lutte*, no. 10, June 1976, p. 10; *L'Information des femmes*, no. 7, 1976, pp. 16–17; *Libération*, 15–16 May 1976, p. 5.

did not deny that the guards had used obscene invective, or that they had engaged in violence, but this was excused by the provocation of the women's slogans and behavior. Moreover, the circular pointed out that homosexuals, lesbians, and anarchists who used slogans that had nothing to do with class struggle and labor demands had followed the MLF section. The CGT reported that this group had included "naked women, lesbians on display and general provocative behavior." The presence of these groups thus legitimized the violent reaction. The guards felt they were attacked and took offense at being called "Stalinist phallocrats" and "fascists" and thus thought it was entirely reasonable to defend themselves. As the circular stated, "The comrade guards" only wanted to get the women to "respect the character of the march."[35] Within the MLF, the incident was viewed as proof of sexism on the part of the communist labor movement. Previously, Women in Struggle had not addressed sexism and gender conflicts in that movement. Now, however, as the behavior of the CGT guards on May 1st caused the class-struggle feminists to feel angry and disappointed, they began to vehemently criticize the CGT leadership.[36] According to them, the guards of the CGT went mad because the leadership of the union had not accepted the slogans against rape. The fact that the communists did not take rape seriously had already been exposed in a widely discussed (among feminists) article in the PCF party organ *L'Humanité* in the fall of 1975.[37] The article held that it was a "grotesque and ridiculous exaggeration" and an expression of a "failing sense of humor" that the 23-year-old nurse Cathérine had reported Michel for raping her when she came to his place for a drink. Instead of rejecting his advances, she should have understood what he was expecting. When Michel beat up and raped Cathérine, it was because he had expected to get what he "implicitly had been promised." Instead of three months in prison, he should have received a small fine of 10 Francs for "lighter violence." The article concluded with the following admonition: "Certainly one should not beat a woman, not even with a flower. But

[35] Ibid.

[36] "CGT, quelle place pour les femmes?" [CGT, What Place for Women?], *Femmes travailleuses en lutte*, no. 10, June 1976, p. 8.

[37] The article is printed in "Le sexisme de '*L'Humanité*.' L'engrenage de la justice" [The Sexism of '*L'Humanité*': The Gearing Up of Justice], *Libération*, 18–19 October 1975, p. 4; and "La galanterie vue par '*L'Humanité*'" [The Gallantry Seen by '*L'Humanité*'], *Les Nouvelles féministes*, no. 4–5, 1975, pp. 22–23.

when the bird flies into the gape of the big ugly wolf, it cannot complain about some scratches."[38]

Feminists interpreted the tumult of the May 1st rally as a gender struggle, but the incident can also be understood as a confrontation between different political cultures.[39] The CGT recruited its activists on the basis of class affiliation as workers, and they made their demands for improvements in working life in a respectable manner. When they participated in marches, they went arm in arm in disciplined ranks. The feminists, the anarchists, and the homosexuals that the CGT guards did not allow to join the march represented the new social movements that flourished with the 1968 revolt. They mobilized on the basis of identities other than class, such as sexuality and disobedience to authority. Their provocative slogans and carnival-like forms of demonstration could seem alien to workmen who regarded politics as a serious matter and not an occasion for festivity. The CGT leadership did not interpret the conduct of the guards as a display of sexist attitudes, but rather as a response to the newcomers' mocking the labor movement. Thus they felt justified in tearing up the banners and beating up those who carried them.[40] Further, the CGT leadership believed that the entire scene was a conspiracy against the CGT orchestrated by the competing union CFDT in collaboration with the socialist party PSU. That fear was not entirely unfounded, because at this time the CGT's supreme position was threatened by the growth of this union.[41]

---

[38] Ibid.

[39] Tarrow 1998, p. 103.

[40] Patrick Fonvieille: "'Faiblesse de ceux d'en face'" [Weakness of Those on the Other Side], *Libération*, 10 May 1976, p. 2; A.B.: "Ras l'bol" [Fed Up], *Libération*, 10 May 1976, p. 2.

[41] CFDT was originally a Christian union that connected with the socialist party PSU in the 1960s. The PSU was established in 1960 as an alternative leftist party between the social democrats in SFIO and the communists in the PCF. During the general strike of 1968, the CFDT gained increased support among activists from the new social movements on the far left. The CFDT also led a more feminist policy than the CGT. About the PSU and 1968, see Duclert, Vincent (2008): "Le PSU, une rénovation politique manquée?" [PSU, a Missed Political Renovation?], in P. Artières and M. Zancarini-Fournel (eds.), pp. 152–157. About the feminist policies of CFDT, see Jenson, Jane (1996): "Representations of Difference: The Varieties of French Feminism", in M. Threlfall (ed.): *Mapping the Women's Movement: Feminist Politics and Social Transformation in the North*. London: Verso, p. 84; and Chaperon, Sylvie (1995): "La radicalisation des mouvements féminins français de 1960 à 1970" [The Radicalization of the French Feminist Movements from

Although irreconcilability marked the first reaction after the confrontation between communists and feminists on May 1, 1976, the events led to a debate about women's place in the labor movement and, as we shall see later in the chapter, to a change in the communist movement's women's policy.

"Ten Hours Against Rape"

Encouraged by the fact that the mobilization against rape had lent fresh energy to the women's struggle, activists from different branches of the MLF decided, for the first time in four years, to hold a joint gathering. About 3000–4000 women attended the mass meeting "Ten Hours against Rape" [*Dix heures contre le viol*] at the Mutualité in Paris on June 26, 1976. The event resembled the Days to condemn crimes against women that was held at the same location in 1972 (see Chapter 2), except that this time it was a women-only event, and rape was the single topic of discussion. The meeting has historical significance in that it created the manifesto "When a Woman Says No, It Is Not Yes, It Is No!" which has since become a canonical MLF text.[42]

Despite the unpleasant topic of rape, a festive atmosphere characterized the gathering. The conference hall was decorated according to the aesthetic sense of the women activists, with flowers, balloons and Indian fabrics, and there was music and dance. The media referred to the event

1960 to 1970], *Vingtième Siècle. Revue d'histoire*, vol. 48, no. 1, pp. 61–74. About the cautious strategy of the CGT in 1968, see Dreyfus, Michel (1995): *Histoire de la CGT. Cent ans de syndicalisme en France* [The History of CGT: One Hundred Years of Syndicalism in France]. Bruxelles: Éditions Complexe, pp. 267–283; Pennetier, Claude (2008): "PCF et CGT face à 68" [PCF and CGT Facing 68], in P. Artières and M. Zancarini-Fournel (eds.), pp. 336–347. See also Zancarini-Fournel, Michelle (2008b): "L'épicentre" [The Epicenter], in P. Artières and M. Zancarini-Fournel (eds.), pp. 209–269. About CGT's behavior toward young Maoist contenders in the 1960s and early 1970s, see Bourseiller 1996, pp. 99–145.

[42] "Quand une femme dit non, ce n'est pas oui, c'est non!" See also the websites "A dire d'elles. Il y a 35 ans, le manifeste féministe contre le viol" [To Say about Them: 35 Years Ago, the Feminist Manifesto against Rape], http://sandrine70.wordpress.com/2011/09/25/il-y-a-35-ans-le-manifeste-feministe-contre-le-viol/; Oooutils féministes, "Manifeste féministe contre le viol, 1976, France" [Feminist Manifesto against Rape, 1976, France], http://oooutilsfeministes.wordpress.com/2012/02/28/manifeste-feministe-contre-le-viol-1976-france. The manifesto is also printed in its entirety in Bernheim, Kandel, Picq, and Ringart (eds.) 2009, pp. 250–252.

as a "party against rape," or even as a "rape party."[43] The planning and implementation of the gathering occurred "without organization," management, or control, according to the feminist journalist Martine Storti, who described the event as the product of a movement rather than of an organization.[44] The festivities, the chaos, the dancing, the quarrels, and the lack of discipline annoyed the class-struggle feminists, while others were just happy to be together and thrilled that they had agreed on a common manifesto against rape.

Even in a chaired meeting, discussion is difficult when there are 3000–4000 people in the same room. Only the most outspoken were said to have approached the microphone, and the level of aggression was high. The most intense disagreement was between class-struggle feminists, who explained rape as the manifestation of "sexual misery," and the revolutionary feminists, who emphasized men's property rights and power over women's bodies. There were also highly contentious discussions about whether it was right to report rape to the police or not, and about how to combat rape. Some revolutionary feminists argued that women should carry firearms to defend themselves against rape. The disagreements about this were interrupted by music and dance. When the party was over around midnight and the 1000 women who had stayed until then exited to the street, they experienced a bit of a contrast from the community of women indoors. Outside they were met by the police and angry men passing by who called them "whores" and hurled other sexist insults at them. A woman who responded to a policeman's comments about her breasts by calling him a fascist was kicked in the crotch. "Then we were no longer three thousand," Martine Storti wrote. "The party was over and the street was as it used to be; it did not belong to us."[45]

The "Ten Hours against Rape" event produced, as mentioned, the manifesto "When a Woman Says No, It Is Not Yes, It Is No!" The manifesto was written collectively at general meetings prior to the gathering

[43] "'10 heures sur le viol'. samedi 26 juin à Paris" ['10 Hours on Rape': Saturday, 26 June in Paris], *l'Information des femmes*, no. 8–9, July–August 1976, p. 23; Martine Storti: "Une fête contre le viol" [A Party against Rape], *Libération*, 28 June 1976, p. 9.

[44] Martine Storti: "Dans la mouvance d'une mobilisation" [In the Movement of a Mobilization], *Libération*, 26–27 June 1976, p. 9.

[45] Martine Storti: "Une fête contre le viol" [A Party Against Rape], *Libération*, 28 June 1976, p. 9.

and presents a radical feminist analysis of rape. (The class-struggle feminists did not support the manifesto for ideological reasons.[46]) It includes six points that describe what rape *is not*: (1) rape is not a fairy tale; (2) rape is not a coincidence; (3) rape is not punished as a crime against women; (4) rape is not a law of nature; (5) rape is neither a desire nor a pleasure for women; and (6) rape is not a fate. In the manifesto, rape is presented as an everyday fact that can occur anywhere and at any time of day or night, and which women continually live in fear of. Rape is explained structurally, as the outcome of patriarchy and myths created to legitimize women's subordination. The denunciation of rape as a "law of nature" indicates that the feminists framed rape as a cultural phenomenon, and they believed that the exploitation of women's bodies was the basis of the patriarchal society. To legitimize this exploitation, the manifesto states, patriarchy produces the myth of an unruly and uncontrolled male sexuality and a correspondingly passive, masochistic female sexuality. This myth helps to justify the "imperialism of male sexuality" that allows men—and some women—to believe that women consciously or unconsciously want to be raped, or, in other words, that a rape is not a rape.

The manifesto's framing of rape is mainly a situational description of what the problem is about, rather than a list of suggested strategies for bringing an end to rape, beyond that women must stand together behind the demand that rape be taken seriously in the judicial system and in society at large. It is a woeful description of reality, but at the same time it brings hope because it insists that the misery is culturally created and can thus be changed politically.

International Tribunal on Crimes Against Women

In 1976, the fight against rape went international. A few months before the mass meeting against rape in Paris, the International Tribunal on Crimes against Women in Brussels drew over 2000 women from 40 countries and from all continents.[47] The March 1976 tribunal was intended to be an antiauthoritarian feminist, grassroots revolt, unlike the United

---

[46] Bernheim et al. (eds.) 2009, pp. 250–252.

[47] Russell, Diana E.H., and Nicole Van de Ven (1976): *Crimes Against Women: Proceedings of the International Tribunal.* Milbrae, CA: Les Femmes, p. xiii. Besides the story of the event itself, this book contains all 108 testimonies, transcribed and translated into

Nations' International Women's Year 1975, which was perceived as organized by male society in order to "confuse women," as Simone de Beauvoir put it.[48] The slogan of the International Tribunal was "*Sisterhood is powerful! International sisterhood is more powerful!*" referring to the fact that women everywhere are subordinate to men economically, ideologically, socially, and politically, and thus share common interests across borders. As was typical of the 1970s feminists, the goal was to break down hierarchies. There were no experts, but the women themselves were to share experiences of abuse through personal testimony. By sharing experiences, women were expected to become politicized and motivated to struggle against oppression.[49]

The definition of "crimes" was similar to that of the French feminists—namely, "all man-made forms of women's oppression."[50] This definition included rape and physical abuse, but also forced motherhood, forced sterilization, brutality of women giving birth, harassment of unmarried

English, as well as solutions that were prepared by various workshops. The idea of an international tribunal on crimes against women was hatched during the international week at the Women's Camp on Femø in Denmark in August 1974, which the Danish Red Stockings Movement had arranged every summer beginning in 1971. The idea was to create an alternative to the "male conference model." There were conflicts during the event: among other things, the chairpersons were dismissed because some of the activists thought they were authoritarian. There were also quarrels about whether male journalists were allowed inside, and at one point there was a bomb scare. In addition, at the tribunal, the French feminist Annie interrupted the meeting to warn that Psych et Po was about to pull off a coup in MLF. Annie took the microphone on the podium and shouted that feminists were prevented from presenting their views because the media had begun to relate to Antoinette Fouque as spokesperson for the entire movement. Other women came up to the podium to argue with Annie and to remove the microphone, but she didn't give up. Finally, the microphone was turned off, but Annie continued. The audience was divided into those for and those against Annie. Some saw her as aggressive, others as a victim of aggression. The incident caused the internal conflicts in the French women's movement to become internationally known, and contributed to the characterization of it as plagued by a particularly high level of dissension. Russell and Van de Ven 1976, pp. 6 and 287; Jenson 1996, p. 77; Mazur 1996, p. 81.

[48] Simone de Beauvoir in *Nouvel Observateur*, 1 March 1976, quoted in Russell and Van de Ven 1976, p. xiii.

[49] Russell and Van de Ven 1976, p. xv.

[50] Op. cit., p. 219. See also the booklet by Gerd Brantenberg et al. (eds.) (1976): *Forbrytelser mot kvinner. Internasjonalt tribunal i Brussel 4.–8. mars 1976* [Crimes Against Women: International Tribunal in Brussels 4–8 March 1976]. Oslo: Kvinnehuset, Tribunalgruppa, p. 2. The Norwegian participants were largely members of the New Feminists associated with the Women's House in Oslo.

mothers and persecution of lesbians, economic crimes, pornography and prostitution, and the "double oppression" of women from the Third World, religious minorities, and immigrant women. Violence against women was the tribunal's most prominent topic, with a total of 36 "witnesses" who spoke of rape, battering, forced incarceration in mental hospitals and in marriage, femicide (murder of women), female genital mutilation, torture of women for political ends, and the brutal treatment of women in prison.

Prior to the International Tribunal, women's groups in each country had been encouraged to form national groups to raise consciousness about crimes against women in their countries and abroad and, on the basis of feedback from women and women's groups, decide which three or four crimes women from their country should testify about.[51] In France, feminists from the League for Women's Rights, LDF, took the lead in the national tribunal group. French women also dominated the section on rape, which illustrates how important the fight against rape had become in the MLF at this time. Of the nine witnesses who spoke about rape at the International Tribunal, five of them recalled rapes they had been subjected to in France, and how they had not been taken seriously by the judicial system.[52] Among the witnesses were Anne and Araceli, who told about their case and called for international support for the upcoming trial in the Assize Court. They wanted it to be a "show trial" and a "political" trial that would reflect women's solidarity and draw the most attention possible to men's attitudes toward women.[53] (Of course, at the time they did not know that it would be more than two years before their case would be heard by the Assize Court in Aix-en-Provence.)

For the book *Crimes against Women: Proceedings of the International Tribunal*, edited by Diana Russell and Nicole Van de Ven, French feminists wrote the introduction to the testimonies of rape. In line with their analysis, rape was explained as a class crime carried out by men as a group against women as a group. Rape was not understood as a means of sexual

---

[51] Op. cit., pp. 220–221.

[52] Russell and Van de Ven 1976, pp. 111–120. Belgians Anne and Araceli were considered French "witnesses," as the rape had taken place in France. One of the nine witnesses who talked about rape was from Norway. Unlike the others, she did not talk about her own experience as a rape victim, but about her research on how the Norwegian judicial system did not take rape seriously.

[53] Op. cit., p. 119.

satisfaction, but as a means of power that men use against women, as torture and terror, with the purpose of breaking down women's resistance and annihilating them as human beings.[54] The analysis of rape as a terror tactic against women is reminiscent of the theories of the American feminist Susan Brownmiller, who, in her book *Against Our Will* from 1975, claimed that while not all men rape women, all men benefit by those who do. In other words, rape is a "terrorist tactic used by some men, but serving to perpetuate the power of all men over women."[55] Thus, rape was not framed as individual sexual deviations, but as a patriarchal social system. In the tribunal book, French feminists situated rape in the context of other institutions and social phenomena to which they were opposed:

> Through rape, a man wants to subjugate and humiliate the woman, and if possible to make her participate in her own subjugation and her own humiliation. These are the same goals sought by the structures of the patriarchal society: the nuclear family, economic exploitation, class hierarchy, authoritarian religion, militarism, control of our reproductive functions, the sexist system of education, prostitution, pornography, and sexual permissiveness disguised as liberation. As long as these structures persist, we will continue to be raped.[56]

Because rape was perceived as the basis of patriarchal structures, the fight against it became fundamental to the struggle for women's liberation.

Strategies for Combating Rape

The public activism against rape made it necessary to take a stand on the question of strategies for combating rape. In the MLF, there was initial disagreement as to whether it was right to report rape to the police, but most of the activists came around to the belief that it was. The question of imprisonment for rapists was highly controversial, however, and various alternatives to imprisonment were proposed.

In their testimony at the International Tribunal, Anne and Araceli suggested that an alternative to imprisonment was to report the names of

[54] Op. cit., pp. 110–111.
[55] Op. cit., p. 127.
[56] Op. cit., p. 111.

rapists to the press, as well as to force rapists to pay maximum damages which, in turn, should be used for shelters and legal aid for battered women and rape victims.[57] Such sanctions would, according to Anne and Araceli, embarrass the rapists and make them reflect on their "pseudo-virility" and "pseudo-potency"—"since prison is unlikely to affect these attitudes at all."[58] Anne and Aracelis's most important strategy, however, was to promote "women's solidarity," wherein women stood together and supported each other in rape cases. The publication of rapists' names as an alternative to imprisonment was also proposed by the Women in Struggle.[59] Recommendations on how such publication could take place involved painting the rapists' names on the walls of their homes, putting up posters in the neighborhood and handing out flyers: "Or, why not women's courts in the markets and in the shopping centers?"[60] However, some feminists raised objections to the publication of rapists' names because it directed too much attention to individuals and thus did not lead to social change. Moreover, it could affect the rapist's wife and children, with whom one had to be in solidarity.

The French Tribunal group's analysis of rape as a "class crime" was radical, but its proposals were pragmatic and feasible within the existing social order. Measures that were proposed were reporting rape and following the case to the end, reforming rape legislation, implementing gender equality measures to get more women into the police and the judiciary, and setting up crisis centers for rape victims.

Arming of Women?

A more drastic suggestion was that women arm themselves with automatic weapons to defend against rape. The revolutionary feminist Annie Cohen suggested this tactic in a *Libération* debate piece the same day the

---

[57] Op. cit., p. 119.

[58] Op. cit., p. 120.

[59] "La commission 'viol, violence' au stage du 15 oct" [The Commission on "Rape, Violence" at the Training Session of 15 October]. *Femmes travailleuses en lutte*, no. 15, 1977, p. 5.

[60] "viol et justice" [Rape and Justice], *Femmes travailleuses en lutte*, n.s. 1 (1978), pp. 12–13.

mass meeting "Ten Hours against Rape" took place.[61] Three years earlier, Cohen had written that revolutionary men expected women to be raped "in the name of the revolution."[62] Now her tone was further sharpened:

> The war is on-going and we have not declared it. Now it is up to us to defend ourselves and respond to it, for my part, with violence. For all other weapons have been used, all persuasion has been carried out; all tricks have been used to calm the beast and to mitigate the morbid and acute desires of these men (...).
>
> With the prevailing situation in this country, I say that to fight rape, against the death which men are able to inflict upon us, we must arm ourselves with automatic weapons to defend ourselves and to live.[63]

The state of war that Cohen described in the opinion piece was thus a sex war that men had initiated against women, with rape as the weapon, and which women were now urged to defend themselves against. In the piece, Cohen raised several issues related to women's relationship to violence:

> How should women regain the force of life without revenge and without justice? What humiliated people haven't posed the question of their relation to violence?
>
> Rape is the act that summarizes all hatred and contempt for women. Can we answer it with indifference or with love? Can we forget the traces after the rape and the suffering that the men have left on our bodies? Can we remain silent about this desire for righteous revenge?
>
> We are attacked, we are beaten, we are raped, humiliated, despised. We cannot just cry about all this misery, but must fight violently against those who use the violence. And alas, there is no miracle, but violence is ruled by violence (...).
>
> How long can men, in all their impunity, be able to trample on our lives without fear of their lives? How long can men beat their wives to blood without risking having to pay for it?

---

[61] Annie Cohen: "Le port d'armes automatique pour nous défendre et pour vivre" [The Carrying of Automatic Weapons to Defend Us and to Live], *Libération*, 26 June 1976, p. 8. This was one of five debates in this issue of *Libération* that discussed rape from different perspectives.

[62] Annie Cohen: "Au nom de la révolution" [In the Name of the Revolution], *Libération*, 8 November 1973, p. 8.

[63] Ibid.

The answer to these rhetorical questions was that women had to arm themselves with automatic weapons to "gain the freedom to conquer the fear." This was a controversial solution that led to heated discussions at the "Ten Hours against Rape" event. The class-struggle feminists' main contention was that they opposed individual solutions and believed that society as a whole needed to undergo a fundamental change.[64] Subsequently, Gisèle Halimi, the feminist lawyer for Anne and Araceli, wrote that violent revenge was a "terrible mistake" for the feminist movement. It was, in her opinion, a "barbaric practice" that would lead to a breakdown in civilization and a return to the "law of the jungle."[65]

The revolutionary feminist Anne Sugier, who also supported the use of violence, argued that feminists who opposed violence were cowards because they knew that the fight against rape would become popular in the mass media only if "we clarify that we will not imitate men."[66] Commenting on the discussion about violence, she claimed that it was precisely women's violence against men that was to be avoided:

> To understand all the nasty quarrels between feminists about violence, one must keep in mind that women's violence is completely accepted if it serves a group of men. Women have always used violence within the framework of men's struggles: women who placed bombs for the FLN in Algeria, female terrorists in Ireland, Israel, Palestine, and Russian nihilists.... In history there is more than one Charlotte Corday (...). It is thus not women's violence as such that is fundamentally opposed, but violence in the service of a feminist movement. It is women's violence against men that one wants to avoid at all costs. Although women daily are victims of men's violence.[67]

It is uncertain whether the revolutionary feminists' suggestion to arm women with guns was meant literally, or whether it was a provocation to get people to take rape seriously and to make them reflect on taboos related to women's exercise of violence against men. Although Annie Cohen's rhetoric was warlike, she also argued that raped women

[64] "'10 heures sur le viol' samedi 26 juin à Paris" ["10 Hours on Rape": Saturday, 26 June in Paris], *l'Information des femmes*, no. 8–9, July–August 1976, pp. 22–23.

[65] Halimi, Gisele (1978): "Le crime" [The Crime], in *Viol. Le procès d'Aix* [Rape: The Process in Aix]. Paris: Gallimard, p. 15.

[66] de Pisan and Tristan 1977, p. 255.

[67] Ibid.

should use the judicial system: "All other crimes are punished today, so why not rape? You have to stop living in utopia. We are not in the People's Republic of China after the Cultural Revolution," she wrote.[68] The proposal that women arm themselves with automatic weapons to combat rape did not catch on in the MLF.

THE ANTI-PORNOGRAPHY STRUGGLE TAKES OFF IN NORWAY

In the fall of 1977, the anti-pornography campaign became a "big issue" in Norway. Pornography was burned in public, and there were rallies, petitions, and lots of newspaper coverage. Pornography was discussed on television and on the radio, and the newspapers followed up with tabloid reporting about confrontations between porn dealers and anti-porn campaigners. Women's organizations that normally avoided each other began to cooperate in the fight against pornography, and dozens of nationwide organizations eventually joined the anti-pornography movement. While the Women's Front had not previously prioritized actions against the porn industry, this now became one of the organization's most pressing issues.

Sex War at the Holmenkollen Line

The campaign began at the metro, specifically the Holmenkollen Line (*Holmenkolbanen*) in Oslo.[69] At this metro line, two summer replacement conductors, 22-year-old Liv Alming and 29-year-old Rannveig Snortheim, were suspended from their jobs after being accused by management of engaging in a protest action involving advertising posters for the "men's magazine" *Nye Alle Menn* (New All Men). Several conductors, whose job was to walk around the cars and sell tickets to passengers, had torn down advertising posters that were hanging in the cars. The posters showed Ingeborg Sørensen, "Norway's Miss Europe," with naked

---

[68] Annie Cohen, *Libération*, 26 June 1976, p. 8.

[69] Korsvik, Trine Rogg (2016): "Jentene på Holmenkolbanen: Pornokamp og 'AKP-bråk' i fagbevegelsen på 1970-tallet" [The Girls at the Holmenkollen Line: Porn Struggle and 'AKP Noise' in the Trade Union Movement Since the 1970s], *Arbeiderhistorie 2016*, pp. 163–185.

torso, "portrayed as a typical sexual object."[70] It was remarkable that the two young women were accused of being solely responsible for the action, as approximately thirty conductors had taken part in it. Some men had also participated, but several other male employees eagerly protected the advertising posters. When the posters were taken down, new ones were hung up, even in places where they were not supposed to hang, such as in the staff rooms and in the men's bathrooms. The women who removed the posters were scolded as man haters, hysterics, and criminals.[71] According to the chairman of the Service Association (*Betjeningsforeningen*, the conductors' union), the battle over the posters created "war-like conditions" at the Holmenkollen Line. To the tabloid newspaper *VG*, he stated: "This is not to be joked about. It almost loosens the fists and creates everything but a good atmosphere among the employees"[72] (Fig. 3.2).

The action against the advertising posters of the "men's magazine" was collective and spontaneous, but the young summer replacements Liv and Rannveig were held responsible for the action. They had, in fact, continued to tear down posters after the others had stopped and were thus reported to management by the deputy chairman of the Service Association. Management sent the two women home from work on the grounds that the Holmenkollen Line was overstaffed, despite the fact that the company constantly advertised for new conductors. The two women were dismissed without pay. Liv Alming and Rannveig Snortheim tried to gain the support of union officials to no avail. The deputy chairman of the Service Association, who had reported the two women to management, said that he had never experienced "similar contempt for the orders of the superiors."[73] The chairman of the Service Association said that the action was "meaningless," because a "group of women cannot just take the law into their own hands," and the trade union could not take responsibility for "their behavior."[74] Later, the chairman of the union reported

[70] Haukaa 1982, p. 141.

[71] *Arbeiderbladet*, 4 August 1977, p. 8; *Klassekampen*, 6 August 1977, p. 8; Inger Anne Olsen: "'Er'u perrvers du'a, som ikke liker nakne kvinnfolk?'" ["Are You a Pervert Who Doesn't Like Naked Womenfolk?'], *Sirene*, no. 9–10, 1977, p. 26.

[72] *VG*, 3 August 1977, p. 9.

[73] *Arbeiderbladet*, 5 August 1977, p. 2.

[74] *VG*, 3 August 1977, p. 9.

Fig. 3.2 The Holmenkollen Line (*Holmenkolbanen*) at Majorstua station in Oslo. In August 1977, Liv Alming and Rannveig Snortheim were suspended from their summer job as ticket-sellers at the Holmenkollen Line because management held them responsible for a protest action against advertising posters for the "men's magazine" *Nye Alle Menn*. The incident triggered the women's movement to take action against pornography (Photo: Unknown @ Oslo byarkiv)

Liv and Rannveig for defamation after anarchists had created a parody of the *Nye Alle Menn* ad in which the chairman of the union was presented as "model boy" next to a photo of a naked man with erect penis, and posted it around in the city. Liv and Rannveig, who had nothing to do with the anarchists' stunt, were questioned at the Victoria Terrace police station, but the case was dropped.[75]

In looking back, Liv Alming reports that she and Rannveig were "personally pissed" by the view of women represented by the *Nye Alle Menn* poster.[76] She recounts that on the Holmenkollen Line there was a lot of "everyday sexism," including older men pinching young female

[75] Interview with Liv Alming, Oslo, 16 April 2012.

[76] Ibid.

employees on the butt and the like. When some of these men began to put up the posters everywhere, the girls became even angrier and refused to end the action. That they were deemed responsible was because they refused to give in, according to Alming, who also thinks it might have been due to the fact that Rannveig was openly lesbian, which was not widely accepted in this period. At the same time, the case was marked by political controversies in Oslo Tramways (*Oslo Sporveier*) between members of the social-democrat Labor Party and the Worker's Communist Party (Marxist-Leninists), the AKP (m-l). Among the union officials who had pushed for the dismissal of Liv and Rannveig, members of the Labor Party predominated. These officials perceived the demolition action as part of the general "AKP noise" in the workplace, although neither Liv nor Rannveig were Marxist-Leninists. This controversy caused the case to attract the interest of both the Labor Party and the AKP (m-l) party press. While the newspaper of the Labor Party, *Arbeiderbladet*, used the case to attack the "AKP faction" in Oslo Tramways, the Marxist-Leninist newspaper *Klassekampen* used it to discredit shop stewards from the Labor Party in the trade unions.[77] Parliamentary elections were coming up in September 1977, and the intense coverage of the case, particularly in *Klassekampen*, made it known to a larger audience. The Labor Party—the governing party at this time—had been scheduled to promote a law prohibiting sex-discriminatory advertising, and *Klassekampen* and the Marxist-Leninist movement actively used the Holmenkollen Line case to show that this was merely an empty election promise. According to the Marxist-Leninists, the case served as a major example of the "hypocrisy" of the Labor Party when it came to the disconnect between the party's official criticism of advertising that was discriminatory toward women and the party members' actual practices in the workplace. The "bosses" of the unions and the Labor Party had not supported Liv and Rannveig; on the contrary, they had reported them to management. *Klassekampen* claimed that these steps carried out the Labor Party's "policy in action." According to the newspaper, although the Labor Party presented itself as an "equality party," in practice it was "a women's discrimination party" and even a "porn party."[78] During the

---

[77] *Arbeiderbladet*, 4 August 1977, p. 8; *Arbeiderbladet*, 5 August 1977, p. 2; *Arbeiderbladet*, 6 August 1977, p. 4; *Arbeiderbladet*, 18 August 1977, p. 3; *Arbeiderbladet*, 1 September 1977; *Arbeiderbladet*, 2 September 1977, p. 6.

[78] Editorial in *Klassekampen*, 15 August 1977, p. 2.

autumn of 1977, *Klassekampen* worked as a virtual campaign organ in support of Liv and Rannveig and in the fight against pornography.[79]

Not surprisingly, the Women's Front, which at this time was dominated by Marxist-Leninists, shared *Klassekampen*'s analysis that the Holmenkollen Line case was about political contradictions that transcended gender conflicts. They emphasized unity among worker activists against management and the "bosses" of the union, and Liv and Rannveig were featured as role models in the fight against "the sale of the female body."[80] The New Feminists, on the other hand, presented the conflict as a sex war and as proof that the "sex struggle runs across the class struggle." Because male workers had defended the advertising posters, they had made an "open alliance with the financial interests of the corporation and advertising companies." Thus, their class affiliation was of less importance than their power as men, according to an article in *Feministen*, the journal of the New Feminists.[81] The Holmenkollen Line case was seen as a manifestation of the power struggle between the sexes—specifically, about women's right to make decisions concerning their own bodies and their own life situations without being "subject to men's games of power"—as stated by three New Feminists in an article in the independent feminist journal *KjerringRåd*.[82] The male employees on the Holmenkollen Line had felt threatened by the women's protest, and by defending their power as men, they defended capital interests as well. This fact facilitated the creation of divisions within the working class in its struggle against capitalism, according to the New Feminists.

[79] *Klassekampen*, 4 August 1977, last page; *Klassekampen*, 5 August 1977, p. 8; *Klassekampen*, 6 August 1977, p. 8; *Klassekampen*, 8 August 1977, p. 8; *Klassekampen*, 9 August 1977, p. 1; *Klassekampen*, 10 August 1977, p. 1; "Holmenkollbaneaksjon på gatene," *Klassekampen*, 11 August 1977, p. 1; *Klassekampen*, 13 August 1977, pp. 4–5; *Klassekampen*, 16 August 1977, p. 8; *Klassekampen*, 9 September 1977, p. 4; *Klassekampen*, 15 September 1977, p. 8; *Klassekampen*, 17 September 1977, p. 1; *Klassekampen*, 27 September 1977, p. 1; *Klassekampen*, 11 October 1977, pp. 4–5; *Klassekampen*, 18 October 1977, p. 4; *Klassekampen*, 22 October 1977, p. 1; *Klassekampen*, 7 November 1977, p. 4; *Klassekampen*, 21 November 1977, p. 5; *Klassekampen*, 24 November 1977, pp. 4–5.

[80] *Kvinnefront*, no. 4, 1977, p. 4.

[81] Anne Lise: "Kvinnediskriminerende reklame på Holmenkollbana" [Women's Discriminatory Advertising on the Holmenkollen Line], *Feministen*, no. 7, September 1977, pp. 20–21.

[82] Elisabeth Bjørk, Inge Ås, and Anne Lise Nestande: "Kvinneforkjempere straffes med yrkesforbud" [Women Activists Are Punished with Work Ban], *KjerringRåd*, no. 1, 1978, p. 27.

Feminist Action in Support of Liv and Rannveig

Liv and Rannveig were not passive victims. Although they were not part of any particular women's group, they knew people in the feminist movement whom they contacted with the purpose of initiating a campaign to get back their jobs and to bring an end to women-discriminatory advertising. Soon, a meeting was called, the first joint event the women's organizations in Oslo had had in two years, thanks to disputes related to the Women's Front's leadership having been taken over by Marxist-Leninists. The Cooperation Committee that was set up for Liv and Rannveig was comprised of representatives from the new women's liberation movement organizations such as the New Feminists, the Women's Front, Bread and Roses, and the Lesbian Movement, as well as representatives of established women's organizations such as the Oslo Association for Women's Rights and the Norwegian Women's Federation. The aim of the action was twofold: to nurture broad public condemnation of women-oppressive advertising and pornography, and to get Liv and Rannveig reinstated at the Holmenkollen Line. The primary importance of the latter was that it would create precedents for other women to protest against the oppression of women in the workplace without running the risk of getting fired. Liv and Rannveig were themselves driving forces in this work.[83]

Signatures and money were collected for the support campaign. According to the lesbian magazine *Lavendelexpressen*, people "queued up to support the action," and the two suspended young women received "tremendous support among the people."[84] One of those who supported Liv and Rannveig was the Municipal Commissioner and chairman of the Oslo Tramways, Jon Erlien, from the Labor Party. To the party's newspaper *Arbeiderbladet* he stated that he respected people who feel offended by sex-discriminatory advertising and had "sympathy for women reacting to the poster."[85] This support was symbolically important, but it was not up to him to decide about the employment of Liv and Rannveig. The management of Oslo Tramways refused to reinstate the two women on

---

[83] *Klassekampen*, 8 August 1977, p. 8; Anne Lise, *Feministen*, no. 7, September 1977, p. 20.

[84] "Støtt aksjonen på Holmenkollbanen!" [Support the Action at the Holmenkollen Line!], *Lavendelexpressen* no. 3 (1977) [no page number].

[85] *Arbeiderbladet*, 4 August 1977, p. 8. See also *Arbeiderbladet*, 18 August 1977, p. 3.

the grounds that such action would anger the union committee of shop stewards who didn't want them there. As stated by the CEO of Oslo Tramway, it was important to respect corporate democracy.[86]

The first rally in support of Liv and Rannveig was held on August 12th by the Music Pavilion at the parade street Karl Johan. Some 100 people attended, holding banners that read, for example, "We Lend Our Full Support to the Action on the Holmenkollen Line against Women-Discriminatory Advertising," and Rannveig made a speech.[87] The following week, representatives from the Cooperation Committee for Liv and Rannveig submitted a letter to the board of Oslo Tramways, which was to hold a meeting wherein the case was to be handled.[88] The letter encouraged the board to oppose women-discriminatory advertising and to reinstate Liv and Rannveig.[89] While the meeting was in progress, a handful of members of the Women's Front and the New Feminists demonstrated outside the Tramway House with placards and slogans. This demonstration was conducted despite the fact that it had been voted down by the majority in the Cooperation Committee, something that led to a bitter dispute concerning what means of action were the most effective. This was just one of many upsetting conflicts for the Cooperation Committee.

The contradictions revolved around what demands were to be presented and what strategies and forms of action were to be pursued. While representatives of the "old" women's movement wanted to limit cooperation to the matters of women-discriminatory advertising and Liv and Rannveig's employment on the Holmenkollen Line, the younger generation wanted to expand the case to a fight against the porn industry. Liv and Rannveig agreed on this point, and the latter spoke at several

---

[86] Quote from a letter by the CEO of Oslo Sporveier Ove Skaug to Rannveig's lawyer, referred to in "HKB-saken" [The HKB Case], *Feministen*, no. 1, 1978, p. 11.

[87] *VG*, 12 August 1977, p. 17.

[88] *Klassekampen*, 15 September 1977, p. 8.

[89] "To the board of Oslo Sporveier A/S," letter of 17 August 1977, signed by Norsk Kvinneforbund (Norwegian Women's Federation), Oslo Kvinnesaksforening (The Oslo chapter of the Norwegian Association for Women's Rights), Kvinnefronten (Women's Front), Brød og Roser (Bread and Roses), Økofeministene (Eco Feminists), Kontor-gruppa i Nyfeministene (the Office Group of the New Feminists), Anarkogruppa i Lesbisk Bevegelse (The Anarko Group of the Lesbian Movement), Kvinneverkstedet Sfinxa (The Women's Workshop Sfinxa), referred to in *Lavendelexpressen*, no. 3 (1977) [no page numbers].

anti-porn rallies.[90] Members of both the New Feminists and the Women's Front agreed that it was reprehensible to make money from products that express contempt for women. At this time, the Women's Front's opposition to pornography was essentially confined to this argument, while the New Feminists insisted on highlighting the fact that pornography was a manifestation of patriarchy: "Pornography plays on, is conditioned by, and reinforces the hatred of women, the disdain of women, and a crippled male sexuality," as espoused by some New Feminists.[91] The New Feminists more directly attacked men's "crippled" sexuality and hatred of women, which, in their view, could not be dismissed as strictly a result of financial conditions. For them, patriarchy was a basic social system that preceded and interacted with capitalism, a system that made it possible to profit from pornography. They argued that this perspective should be stressed in all contexts where pornography was discussed. But insisting that the fight against pornography had to be conducted as an attack on patriarchy could conflict with other activists' attempts to show the "breadth" of the opposition to pornography, and such disagreements caused numerous political quarrels.[92]

A further challenge for the collaborative effort against pornography revolved around the Marxist-Leninist movement. Within the New Feminists, some of the most active members formed the so-called Anti-Porn Group in order to work in a more targeted manner against pornography. This group cooperated with members of the Women's Front who were adherents of the Worker's Communist Party (Marxist-Leninists), the AKP (m-l). Their strategy was one of militancy. Instead of "polite inquiries and courteous behavior," they wanted "action from below," as claimed by Liv Finstad of the Anti-Porn Group: "The activists walk around streets and places, gathering support and signatures, discuss with people, and thus

---

[90] *Kvinnefront*, no. 4, 1977, p. 4; Gyda: "Holmenkollbane-saka: en av mange politiske oppsigelser av kvinner" [The Holmenkollen Line Case, One of Many Political Dismissals of Women], *Feministen*, no. 7, 1977, pp. 31–32.

[91] Lise, Pia og Sidsel: "Pornodemonstrasjon—NF's politikk på pornografi" [Porn Demonstration—NF's Policy on Pornography], *Feministen*, no. 10, 1977, p. 9.

[92] Ingvild: "Kjære Kirsten og andre medsøstre" [Dear Kirsten and Other Fellow Sisters], *Feministen*, no. 10, 1977, p. 15; Ada and Marianne: "Referat fra siste fellesmøte" [Minutes from Last Joint Meeting], *Feministen*, no. 10, 1977, p. 3; Kirsten N: "Om valg av representanter" [On the Election of Representatives], *Feministen*, no. 10, 1977, p. 12.

put pressure on the responsible authorities."[93] To achieve this goal, the strategy was to recruit as many women as possible for various actions "to raise consciousness and to learn to fight the oppression of women." In Liv Finstad's opinion, the "feminist activist principle" was that "action is the best propaganda." She viewed the Holmenkollen Line case as "part of a revolutionary women's struggle that will not end when Liv and Rannveig eventually get back their jobs, but only when patriarchy is abolished."[94] This would occur, she stated, when "hundreds of thousands of women's actions flow together in a wide and invincible flood wave."[95] One of the actions Finstad welcomed was porn burnings, a form of action that was introduced by members of the Women's Front.

Other members of the New Feminists were suspicious of the motives of the Women's Front and feared that they were using the Holmenkollen Line case and the anti-porn actions to strengthen their own organization and, by extension, the Worker's Communist Party (Marxist-Leninists). During the fall of 1977 and winter of 1978, tensions escalated within the New Feminists between those who advocated cooperating with the Women's Front and those who opposed it. Members of the New Feminists who experienced cooperation with members of the Women's Front as an "exclusively positive" encounter, not least because the anti-porn struggle also recruited women who usually did not identify with the women's liberation movement, were perceived as renegades. The factional struggles eroded the solidarity within the New Feminists: "We all know that the personal is political, but we are working full speed to make the political personal," a member wrote in the organization's internal journal.[96] The contradictions within the New Feminists in regard to cooperation with the Women's Front culminated in the decision reached

---

[93] Liv Finstad: "Mer om holmenkollbanesaka: om samarbeid og retningslinjer for aksjonering" [More about the Holmenkollen Line Case: About Cooperation and Guidelines for Action], *Feministen*, no. 7, 1977, p. 25.

[94] Liv Finstad: "Hva kan vi lære av HKB-saka? Føljetongen fortsetter" [What Can We Learn from the HKB Case? The Serial Continues], *Feministen*, no. 1, 1978, p. 9.

[95] Liv Finstad: "Mer om holmenkollbanesaka. Om samarbeid og retningslinjer for aksjonering" [More About the Holmenkollen Line Case: About Cooperation and Guidelines for Action], *Feministen*, no. 7, 1977, p. 28.

[96] Kirsten N.: "Om valg av representanter" [On the Election of Representatives], *Feministen*, no. 10, 1977, p. 10. See also Ingvild: "Kjære Kirsten og andre medsøstre" [Dear Kirsten and Other Fellow Sisters], *Feministen*, no. 10, 1977, p. 15; "Referat fra fellesmøtet" [Minutes from the Joint Meeting], *Feministen*, no. 2, 1978, p. 3; and

at the New Feminists' joint meeting in May 1978 to exclude the two who had been the most active in the Anti-Porn Group.[97]

The exclusions led to a decline in the level of activity of the New Feminists. The internal journal was published less frequently, and, unlike before, it was characterized by consensus and the absence of debate. The journal no longer reported on any political actions in the name of the New Feminists. Thus, the Holmenkollen Line case and the fight against pornography did not lead to a resurgence of the New Feminists. On the contrary, they more or less disappeared from the public scene.[98] For its part, the Women's Front profited from the mobilization against pornography and recruited hundreds of new members. In just over four months—from their summer camp to the national convention in November 1977—their membership increased from 2700 to 3500.[99]

Økofeministene [The Eco Feminists]: "Liv Finstad—Norges forhåpentligvis eneste stalinistiske feminist" [Liv Finstad—Norway's Hopefully only Stalinist Feminist], *Feministen*, no. 2, 1978.

[97] "Referat fra fellesmøtet 11/5-78" [Minutes from the Joint Meeting 11 May 1978], *Feministen*, no. 4, 1978. See also Haukaa 1982, p. 142.

[98] The problem of inactivity had for several years been the subject of discussion in the New Feminists' internal journal. There, members rebuked each other for being irresponsible, lacking self-discipline, and being "politically lazy" because they chose cinema rather than attending meetings. It was claimed that members of the New Feminists slipped away from the organization and joined organizations and parties where they could "do something." Those who were excluded in the spring of 1978 claimed that the New Feminists had been characterized by a "stiffened, introverted style" with a low level of activity and with recruitment problems. See, e.g., "Om å melde seg inn i politiske partier" [About Joining Political Parties], *Feministen*, no. 3, 1975; Hege Hallset: "Et debattinnlegg om organisasjonsformen vår og forholdet til andre politiske grupperinger" [A Debate About Our Organizational Form and the Relationship to Other Political Groups], *Oslofeministen*, no. 8, 1975; "Referat fra fellesmøte 6. November" [Minutes from the Joint Meeting on 6 November], *Oslofeministen*, no. 10, 1975; "Contact seminar in Fredrikstad—impression" [Contact Seminar in Fredrikstad—Impressions], *Oslofeministen*, no. 10, 1975; Ingvild Gaasemyr, Marit Nørve, Siri Nørve, and Kristina Kjærheim: "Eller er det så inspirerende å jobbe i bevisstgjøringsgruppe" [Or Is It So Inspiring to Work in the Consciousness-Raising Group], *Oslofeministen*, no. 15, 1976; "Abortaksjonen" [The Abortion Action], *Oslofeministen*, no. 16, 1976; Liv Finstad: "Et lite gjennomtenkt eksklusjonsforslag" [A Little-Considered Suggestion for Exclusion], *Feministen*, no. 4, 1978.

[99] *Klassekampen*, 29 November 1977, p. 8; Nyhamar, Solveig: "'Bak slagordene'. Hvor ble det av kvinnekampen?" [Behind the Slogans: Where Did the Women's Struggle Go?], *Kvinnejournalen*, no. 1, 1983, p. 36. See also Rønning, Ole Martin (2005): "Kvinnekamp, imperialisme og monopolkapital. Kvinnefronten i Norge og ml-bevegelsen 1972–1982" [Women's Struggle, Imperialism and Monopoly Capital. The Women's Front

For action-oriented women who wanted to fight the porn industry, the Women's Front offered a wealth of activities. There were demonstrations, meetings, stands with flyer distribution, the collecting of signatures and money, and door-to-door visits to enlist new activists. For the toughest ones, militant action against porn dealers became an exhilarating form of protest.

"Let the Thousand Porn Fires Burn!"

The first public porn burning took place in the working-class district of Grünerløkka in Oslo on Saturday, August 27, 1977. The porn magazines were taken from Six Shop, run by Magne Severinsen, the porn dealer mentioned in the previous chapter. "Let the Thousand Porn Fires Burn!" was the headline of the flyer that was handed out to passersby, and people stopped and applauded the fire.[100] One of the young women who participated in the action reported in the Marxist-Leninist newspaper *Klassekampen*:

> Some girls were inside the store, where the porn was lying around openly and filled their arms with magazines and booklets. The clerk was rather perplexed—shouting that this was most rude, and "damn feminist girls" (…)
>
> The magazines were carried out to a nearby place and it became a great porn fire with yelling of slogans, speeches, and distribution of flyers. The clerk likely had problems in reporting the theft of illegal magazines, because we didn't get a glimpse of the police despite the fire burning vigorously for about half an hour. Finally, we cleaned up nicely, put the ashes in a trash bag that we placed in front of the door of the porn shop—as thanks for the loan and an expression of what we thought about the filth. The action was successful. People were hanging out of the windows. Many people got to know what happened and supported us. The reactions around the fire were unequivocal: "This was really nice—we have to do this every Saturday!" (…)
>
> It is important to continue protesting, and I encourage everyone to take action against all forms of women-discrimination whether it comes to

---

in Norway and the Marxist-Leninist Movement 1972–1982], *Arbeiderhistorie*, Oslo: Arbeiderbevegelsens Arkiv og Bibliotek.

[100] *Kvinnefront*, no. 5–6, 1977, p. 6.

advertising posters for *Nye Alle Menn*—or to "rob" pornography shops and make book burnings.[101]

This militant action was thus considered "successful" and blessed with popular support, and as a suitable form of action that could be carried out every Saturday without interference from the police or others. This proved not to be the case, however. One month later, when members of the Women's Front, the New Feminists, and others engaged in an action against the porn shop K. Lund in Rådhusgata in Oslo city center, tensions escalated, because the porn dealers had prepared themselves. As approximately one dozen girls seized porn magazines in the shop, they were attacked by a "guard corps" accompanied by a German shepherd dog. Some male passersby interfered to protect the girls, and one of them was arrested. Running away with the "guard corps" at their heels, the girls got away with trash bags filled with porn magazines and films that they set afire at the square of the Oslo University at Blindern in front of some 200 people. The porn dealer K. Lund stated to the newspaper *VG* that he would probably report the group for theft.[102]

With his threatening "guard corps," K. Lund appeared to be a more confrontational type of porn dealer than Severinsen of the Six Shop. So did Leif Hagen, who now appeared on the Norwegian public scene. Hagen told the newspaper *Dagbladet* how he and other porn dealers had agreed to help each other take on the Women's Front with the assistance of 15 to 20 men and three German shepherds. The "guard corps" had already been in action against the girls who had attacked the shop of K. Lund and, on another occasion, had prevented the activists from entering Hagen's porn shop. "In this business, we don't handle people with silk gloves," Hagen said, and warned: "We have completely free hands and don't have to take into account what the police must take."[103] He assured the readers that this was "not an empty threat".

Hagen's threat of violence did not cause the actions to be halted; on the contrary, it encouraged the protesters to intensify their actions, including standing outside porn shops handing out flyers and collecting signatures and money. The money was used to pay for an ad posted

[101] *Klassekampen*, 3 August 1977, p. 5. A similar article was published in *Kvinnefront*, no. 4, 1977, p. 5.

[102] *VG*, 22 September 1977, p. 18; *Klassekampen*, 23 September 1977, p. 8.

[103] *Dagbladet*, 24 September 1977, p. 8.

on the so-called "porn page" of the Saturday edition of the newspaper *Dagbladet*, which contained weekly ads for pornography and prostitution masked as personal ads. The anti-porn ad, decorated with woman-power symbols (clenched fist in a Venus sign), was a petition that people were encouraged to sign, saying, "Fight against the rotten business of the porn profiteers! No to women as merchandise! Ban all porn! Join the struggle!"[104] The ad stated that in just four days, members of the Women's Front and the New Feminists had collected 8179 signatures in support of the petition. The same ad was published on the "porn page" every Saturday throughout the autumn of 1977, garnering a steadily increasing number of signatures.

Standing in front of porn shops and distributing flyers and collecting money and signatures turned out to be risky. Because the presence of the activists scared away potential customers and thus hindered the trade, the "guard corps" of the porn dealers threatened to beat up the activists and took photos of them. On one occasion, a girl who attempted to take a camera from the guard corps was knocked down.[105] At first, the direct confrontations with the porn dealers failed to scare off the activists; they did, however, lead to a further escalation of the actions. October 6, 1977, was an exceptionally energetic protest day. An action against Six Shop led to a series of events in Oslo that were duly covered by the paper *Klassekampen*.[106] It all began with a raid of Six Shop on Grünerløkka by 20 to 30 anti-porn activists. While some activists restrained the owner, Severinsen, others robbed the shop of all its magazines and films. These were taken to Egertorget Square in Oslo city center, where 250 people watched as the porn was burned. Meanwhile, a dozen police cars carrying 40 officers arrived. Though they had difficulty distinguishing between spectators and activists, they nevertheless arrested two girls.

After the burning, the activists proceeded to the Holmenkollen Line, where they tore down advertising posters for the "men's magazine" *Express* that had been posted in the cars. The day before, when a girl who had torn down one such poster had been physically attacked by an angry conductor, one hundred passengers spontaneously rallied to her defense.

---

[104] *Dagbladet*, 8 October 1977, p. 28.

[105] *Klassekampen*, 8 October 1977, pp. 4–5; *Klassekampen*, 22 October 1977, p. 5; *Klassekampen*, 22 October 1977, p. 4.

[106] *Klassekampen*, 8 October 1977, pp. 1, 4–5, and 8. The action is also mentioned in *VG*, 11 October 1977, p. 40.

After the activists tore down the *Express* poster ads on the Holmenkollen Line, they continued to the police station at Victoria Terrace, where they shouted slogans until the two girls who had been arrested during the porn burnings at Egertorget were released. Then the protesters went on to the parliament building with banners calling for a ban on pornography, with slogans such as "No to the Sale of Women—Fight against the Porn Mafia!" According to *Klassekampen*, there were some 100 people outside the police station, but as random passersby joined the rally they became "300–400 in an enthusiastic and militant protest march" to the parliament building. Here the march was disbanded when the police arrived. Those who were not yet tired of campaigning continued on to the Birkelunden at Grünerløkka, where they painted slogans on the walls of the shop of porn dealer Trygve Thorsen (see Chapter 2). According to *Klassekampen*, such actions would escalate until pornography was banned.

After five or six forays against porn shops, members of the Women's Front and the New Feminist Liv Finstad held a press conference at which they announced that the porn burnings would continue. Unni Rustad of the Women's Front, who had recently been arrested during an anti-porn raid, said that the cause of the actions was that "porn goes against women as autonomous individuals," which she placed in the context of women being "second-rate in the working life."[107] The strategy for combating pornography outlined in the press conference was primarily to continue the porn burnings. At the same time, the activists put forth a more legal-oriented strategy. The Women's Front wanted to report the porn shop Nortrade in the working-class district Tøyen in Oslo for selling illegal pornography, including "toddler porn." In the longer term, the Women's Front wanted a legal ban on pornography, in the same way that racial discrimination was prohibited by law. Turid Øvrebø, from the Women's Front at the University of Oslo, said that the goal was to criminalize the sale of the female body: "Pimping is criminalized and we see no difference between these two things," she said.[108] The argument was that several of those who ran porn shops in Oslo were also convicted of pimping, including "Porn-Thorsen," who had been convicted six or seven times for pimping. Thus, the Women's Front had begun to see pornography in

[107] *Dagbladet*, 18 October 1977, p. 7; *Klassekampen*, 19 October 1977, p. 16.
[108] *VG*, 18 October 1977 p. 13.

connection with prostitution, a viewpoint that became more prevalent as the activists gained further knowledge of this business.

Porn burnings as a form of action spread to other Norwegian cities, including Bergen, Kristiansand, Tromsø, and Trondheim. The reactions of the police and magazine dealers varied. In Trondheim the response was particularly dramatic. Three girls who had attempted to empty the magazine shop "Blad-Madsen" of porn magazines to be burned in public, were captured by guards and locked up in the shop, and then arrested. When protesters outside the police station chanted "Release the Girls," the police were said to have threatened them with dogs if they did not leave. In addition, the police refused to accept the activists' report of the sale of illegal pornography.[109]

In the city of Skien in Telemark County, the militant anti-porn actions took on a somewhat different character, as they were directed against a sex club that Trygve Thorsen, the previously mentioned convicted pimp, attempted to establish in the town in the summer of 1977. The concept of the sex club included porn films and striptease shows, and the customers were offered "intimate massages" in the back room by scantily clad women from Denmark and Jamaica. Establishments of this sort were usually shut down by the police after a short time and the owners convicted of pimping.[110] When Thorsen attempted to launch the sex club "VIP Biliard Club" in Skien, he was faced with local opposition. At the same time as the Holmenkollen Line case was going on in Oslo, protest actions were carried out against the planned sex club in Skien. The "Action Against the VIP Club," which included the Women's Front and the Red Electoral Alliance Party (Rød Valgallianse, RV, which was connected to the Marxist-Leninist movement), led a resolute struggle against the sex club. Because in several cases the demonstrations led to blows between protesters and people from the sex club, the case received

---

[109] *Klassekampen*, 25 October 1977, p. 2. See also *VG*, 17 October 1977, p. 9; and *Dagbladet*, 29 October 1977, p. 8.

[110] Århelle 1981, pp. 30–32. Thorsen was sentenced in 1976 on the pimp clause because he had taken two-thirds of the payment that the sex club hostesses had received to sell their services at his establishment Club Blue Heaven. *Dagbladet*, 13 August 1977, p. 28; *VG*, 16 October 1977, p. 17. About the (short-lived) sex clubs in Oslo during the 1970s, see Høigård, Cecilie, and Liv Finstad (1986): *Bakgater. Om prostitusjon, penger og kjærlighet* [Backstreets: About Prostitution, Money and Love]. Oslo: Pax Forlag, pp. 257–269. For a view of the sex clubs as seen from the inside, see Fjeld-Pedersen 1976.

much media attention.[111] When in November 1977 Thorsen abandoned his attempt to open the club and sent the Danish sex club hostesses back home, he said to the paper *VG* that the demonstrations had ruined his business.[112]

Why Porn Burnings?

Burning porn in public was a risky form of protest. Activists experienced persecution, threats, capture, and beatings at the hands of the porn dealer's "guard corps," as well as arrest by the police. One might ask why members of the Women's Front, who for the most part preferred forms of action "appealing to the masses," chose to promote this form of militant direct action.

According to the Women's Front's Unni Rustad, the purpose of the porn burnings was to "direct the spotlight to those who get more and more fat wallets by selling women" and to "protest against the degrading view of women that these people profit from." As she explained to *Klassekampen*:

> Some argue that our actions are illegal. We will ask: Who are the criminals? Are they those who live by oppressing women, or are they all those women who are now revolting against the oppression? We, in the Women's Front, have experienced that the porn burnings have received tremendous support.[113]

Thus, the anti-porn activists considered themselves above the law because their motive for combating women's oppression was morally superior to the money interests of those who sold pornography. This was justified by reference to the many people who supported the porn burnings.

[111] *Klassekampen*, 22 August 1977, p. 5; *Klassekampen*, 5 September 1977, p. 1; *Klassekampen*, 20 September 1977, p. 3; *Klassekampen*, 5 October 1977, p. 3; *VG*, 11 October 1977, p. 7; *Dagbladet*, 17 October 1977, p. 18; *Klassekampen*, 20 October 1977, p. 3; *Klassekampen*, 10 October 1977.

[112] *VG*, 10 November 1977, p. 6.

[113] *Klassekampen*, 7 November 1977, pp. 4–5.

In interviews some 30 years after the porn burnings took place, several activists who partook in these militant protests claimed that they themselves had invented this form of protest.[114] Their motivation was anger, and they wanted to destroy the porn shops and terrorize those who owned them. Also, they thought the actions were hard-hitting, exciting, and fun. Most of the activists were affiliated with the Worker's Communist Party (Marxist-Leninists), the AKP (m-l). But within the party's leadership, including chairman Pål Steigan, several are said to have disapproved of the porn-burning activities, even though they saw in the anti-porn campaign the potential for building a front movement (Fig. 3.3).[115] The participants of the secret action group that worked specifically with sabotage against porn shops were not part of the leadership of the AKP (m-l). According to one of the activists in the secret action group, they were "tough guys who gave a damn and had lived a life" and often came from the east-side, working-class district of Oslo.[116]

Rather than being spontaneous, these acts of sabotage against the porn shops were carefully prepared to avoid the perpetrators' being caught. The typical tactic was that three men first entered the store one by one, pretending to be customers. At a scheduled time, five to ten women entered the shop with large trash bags that they filled with porn magazines, while the men held onto those who were behind the counter to prevent them from triggering the alarm. Outside, guards were scattered around the quarter. In the early phase of such actions, it had happened that girls had been trapped inside the porn store and were threatened with being beaten and cut up, so the activists eventually became more vigilant and placed guards at the front door. After filling the trash bags, the activists would go to a square where the magazines were publicly burned, and would deliver a speech explaining why they were campaigning against

---

[114] Interview with "Anne" and "Kari"; Liv Finstad; Sissa Lindqvist.

[115] A front movement or front organization in this context means an organization that is, in reality, controlled by another organization in order to recruit members to it. This tactic has been common within the communist movement, but also within the CIA. There are many examples of how communist parties have initiated interest organizations that focus on individual issues (such as peace), where communist ideology is not stated. The purpose is to attract members who do not share the party's views. A front organization is different from a united front, where different political groups join together for a common goal.

[116] Interview with Sissa Lindqvist.

Fig. 3.3 Mobilizing poster for the 1st of May rally of the Worker's Communist Party (Marxist-Leninists) in 1978, declaring "Away with Porn" and "Unity on the Basis of Class Struggle!". Marxist-Leninists saw in the anti-porn campaign the potential for building a front movement (*Source* AKP-ml/pdf-arkivet.no)

pornography. However, sometimes the activists would be arrested before they could reach the square.[117]

The relationship between the activists and the police was one of ambiguity. In some cases, the police defended the porn dealers and arrested the activists, who were fined for vandalism and theft. Other police officers showed more sympathy toward the anti-porn actions because they sometimes uncovered porn dealers who sold illegal pornography, which allowed the police to eventually raid the shops. Unni Rustad, on the other hand, writes about how she, when questioned by a police officer after a porn burning, was warned that "the people we were now challenging were dangerous and that we should beware."[118]

The danger attached to carrying out the porn burnings caused the activists to eventually abandon this method of protest. The environment of the porn shops turned out to be more gangster-like than the activists had imagined. Despite many security measures, the activists were not masked, and they were photographed several times by the shop owners and the "guard corps" who then established their identities. Anti-porn campaigners were pursued and received letters in which they were threatened with torture, rape, and murder.[119] These letters were commonly accompanied by images from sadistic porn magazines. As a result, the activists switched to another strategy: filling the keyholes of the stores with the powerful glue Aralditt at night and spray-painting slogans on the walls.

Mixed Reactions to Porn Burnings

The anti-porn activists justified their burning of the porn stores' goods by claiming that they wanted to hurt the porn dealers financially while attracting attention to their own cause. The symbolism of the porn burnings, which might have been reminiscent of book burnings and ritual purification, does not seem to have occurred to the activists. Others, however, did make such associations. For example, in an editorial entitled "Book Burnings" in *Arbeiderbladet*, it was stated:

---

[117] Interview with "Anne" and "Kari"; Liv Finstad; Sissa Lindqvist.

[118] Rustad 2007.

[119] Interview with "Anne" and "Kari"; Liv Finstad; Sissa Lindqvist; Rustad 2007.

We have no particular sympathy for dealers of porn magazines. Nevertheless, we find it is going too far when some women's groups take the law
into their own hands and make raids on the dealers' premises—for eventually to burn up their catch. It tastes of book burnings, and the [historical]
traces are frightening.[120]

Thus, *Arbeiderbladet*, in finding it frightening that women's groups took
the law into their own hands and burned pornography, implicitly drew
parallels between them and the Nazis in Germany during the interwar
period. The act of burning printed material that one finds repellent is
explosive, and the activists did not have control over how such action
would be interpreted by the outside world.[121] As political communication, porn burnings could be interpreted in ways other than simply
protesting the oppression of women. Besides its obvious association with
book burnings, the act of burning pornography was interpreted as a
manifestation of puritanism and an authoritarian ideology. The tabloid
newspaper *VG* represented this view and, in an editorial, claimed that the
activists' "porn-guerrilla crusade" was "an inferior variety of the women's
struggle for equality and against male dominance."[122] "We are at the
beginning of something that can become quite dangerous," the newspaper held, expressing fear of the combination of "left-wing people with
experience from violent demonstrations" and "'the vigilantes' of the porn-
profiteers."[123] *VG* argued that the police had to intervene to stop the
"vandalism" and seems to have interpreted the porn burnings as the seed
of a Norwegian variant of left-wing terrorism, which in this period was
taking place in Europe.

Although this form of "guerrilla warfare" was controversial, the anti-
porn activists claimed that it was widely supported among ordinary
people. They were surprised by passersby who stopped to applaud the
porn burnings, and by how easy it was to collect signatures against
pornography. Now they were being supported by "old ladies" who otherwise wanted the women's rights movement to "go where the pepper

---

[120] Editorial in *Arbeiderbladet*, 11 October 1977, p. 4.

[121] Rowbotham 1990, p. 249.

[122] Editorial in *VG*, 10 October 1977, p. 2.

[123] Ibid.

grows."[124] The fact of reacting to hard-core pornography with disgust required no particular ideological explanation, nor did it presume the support of other typical demands of the women's movement, such as abortion on demand or free day care for all children. The militant anti-porn actions also received unexpected support from established politicians. For example, the leader of the Labor Party Women's Secretariat, Aud Blegen Svindland, stated that: "Personally, I don't see anything negative in the fire burning of the Women's Front. They focus on problems that are certainly not to be joked with."[125] She viewed pornography as "the result of a sexually hostile culture" and believed that sexual enlightenment and openness were necessary tools for changing attitudes.

Porn Struggle in the Media

Sex and violence sell. In the media, the porn struggle was used for creating sensational tabloid reports taking a variety of viewpoints. Liberal tabloid newspapers such as *VG* and *Dagbladet* frolicked in headlines such as "Porn Battle," "'The Porn Guerrilla' Meets Resistance: The Sex Shops Form Fierce Guard Corps," "'Porn Women' with Bodyguards," "Wild Sex Fight," "Porn and Fist Fight," "The Porn War Increasingly Harder," and "I'm Not an Impotent Money Piglet."[126] The Marxist-Leninist newspaper *Klassekampen* took a different tack. For example, "The Girls at the Holmenkollen Line: Obvious Right to Take Action against the Sale of the Female Body," "Porn Dealer in Oslo Chased Girls with Truncheon," and "Young Girl at Grünerløkka: Porn-Thorsen Threatened my Life!".[127]

The social-democrat newspaper *Arbeiderbladet*, on the other hand, initiated a campaign to get the police to intervene against child pornography, but police officials claimed that they did not have the

---

[124] Ingvild: "Kjære Kirsten og andre medsøstre" [Dear Kirsten and Other Fellow Sisters], *Feministen*, no. 10, 1977, p. 15. See also *Kvinnefront*, no. 5–6, 1977, p. 6; and Rustad 2007.

[125] *Dagbladet*, 11 October 1977, p. 24.

[126] *VG*, 22 September 1977, p. 18; *Dagbladet*, 24 September 1977, p. 8; *VG*, 11 October 1977, p. 7; *VG*, 12 October 1977, pp. 1 and 22; *Dagbladet*, 13 October 1977, p. 14.

[127] *Klassekampen*, 6 August 1977, p. 8; *Klassekampen*, 13 August 1977, pp. 4–5; *Klassekampen*, 6 October 1977, p. 3; *Klassekampen*, 23 November 1977, p. 6.

legal authority to do so.[128] The triggering event of the *Arbeiderbladet* campaign was the publication of an article on children's sexuality by sexologist Thore Langfeldt in the soft-porn magazine *Lek*, illustrated with photographs of the genitals of nude little girls. The sexologist had told *Arbeiderbladet* that child pornography was part of sexual liberation and was thus neither wrong nor harmful, and that the condemnation of sexual relations between children and adults was due to "sexual hostility." [129] According to Langfeldt's view, many children enjoyed having sex with adults. It was the "condemnation of society" that was "unfortunate."[130] *Arbeiderbladet* claimed that Langfeldt's statements could be perceived as encouraging child molestation.[131] This was rejected by the sexologist, who claimed in *VG* that he was a "victim of a stream of rumors from women activists and other groups."[132] The campaign of *Arbeiderbladet* led to the fall of Langfeldt's status as an expert on sexuality in many milieus, and also to a heightened awareness of the existence of child pornography in broader circles. Until then, many people did not know that it existed, and in the long run, the debate led to an increase in police activity targeted at against child pornography.

As a result of the porn burnings, pornography became a topic of debate on TV. At a time when Norway had only a single TV channel that "everyone" watched, the programs of the government-owned Norwegian Broadcasting Corporation (NRK) had a huge impact on the public debate. When pornography was debated on the popular TV discussion forum "*På sparket*" (On the Fly), it made front-page headlines in the newspapers and triggered a flood of readers' posts.[133] The content of

---

[128] *Arbeiderbladet*, 31 August 1977.

[129] *Arbeiderbladet*, 2 September 1977. At this time, Langfeldt is said to have been affiliated with the Norwegian Working Group for Pedophilia (NAFP), also known as Pedophile Working Group, according to the group's own history. The group was established in 1974 and disappeared in the early 1980s after pedophilia was condemned by most, including by Langfeldt. According to the history of this group, it should "illuminate the emotional and sexual bonds between young people and adults and be a forum for all debate on children and sexuality," "Historien om NAFP" [History of NAFP], http://www.pedofili.info/Nafp.htm. Consulted 8 August 2017.

[130] Thore Langfeldt: "Har barn seksualitet" [Do Children Have Sexuality], *Arbeiderbladet*, 27 September 1977.

[131] *Arbeiderbladet*, 10 October 1977.

[132] *VG*, 20 October 1977, p. 6.

[133] *VG*, 20 October 1977, p. 1; *Dagbladet*, 21 October 1977, p. 1.

these posts indicates that many people had become aware, for the first time, of what pornography was about, and that others were critical of the anti-porn campaign. The "discovery" of the porn industry was also reflected in the newspapers, which began to devote more attention to what *VG* referred to as "raw porn," something that an editorial in its pages claimed that women had "every reason to protest."[134]

In an October 1977 edition of the above-mentioned NRK discussion program "På sparket," anti-porn activists and porn dealers met for a fight. It was here that "TV-Norway" got to meet for the first time Unni Rustad and Leif Hagen, the two people who in the following years came to respectively personify the anti-porn movement and the porn industry in Norway.[135] Rustad attacked Hagen for making money on the degrading of women and argued for prohibition in order to "drive the porn dealers underground and to make it more difficult for them to spread their contempt for women."[136] Women's own actions were, however, most important, Rustad argued, and warned that the porn burnings would continue. Hagen did not conceal his involvement in the porn industry solely to make money, and said he hoped Rustad and her "likeminded [allies] in the AKP" would continue with the porn burnings because they provided good advertising and increased sales.[137] With the organization of the "guard corps" fresh in their memories, the Women's Front did not believe Hagen. "You probably have noticed as well as we have that your empire is about to collapse," their magazine stated after the program.[138]

The debate panel of the TV program was broadly representative. Besides Rustad and Hagen, the panel included Rannveig Snortheim from the Holmenkollen Line and representatives of the women's organizations Norwegian Association for Women's Rights (*Norsk Kvinnesaksforening, NKF*), Center Women (*Senterkvinnene*), and Bread and Roses (*Brød og*

---

[134] Editorial in *VG*, 22 October 1977, p. 2.

[135] *VG*, 20 October 1977, pp. 1 and 5.

[136] *Klassekampen*, 22 October 1977, p. 2.

[137] *VG*, 20 October 1977, p. 5; *Dagbladet*, 21 October 1977, p. 1; *Dagbladet*, 21 October 1977, p. 8.

[138] *Kvinnefront*, no. 5–6, 1977, p. 1.

Roser), as well as the editor of the sex and crime magazine *Kriminaljour-nalen*, Ernst Polezynski, and the sexologist Thore Langfeldt.[139] Unlike Hagen, Polezynski argued that his motive for publishing the violent porn magazine wasn't money: rather, he claimed to be involved in a "mission" to help people with sexual problems.[140] In this regard he was supported by the sexologist Langfeldt, who argued that pornography played an important part in helping "sexual minorities" such as pedophiles and homosexuals. The representative of the Norwegian Association for Women's Rights (NKF) disagreed with the Women's Front's porn burnings, as well as their demand for a ban on pornography, which they thought would "create a black market." Instead of a ban on pornography, it was necessary to change "the upbringing of the man who makes him so helpless or emotionally cold that he can enjoy porn at all." At the same time, NKF wanted a ban on women-discriminatory advertising and a modernized pornography law in which phrases such as "human dignity and equality" would replace "obscenity and chastity." Thus the NKF explained the incidence of pornography as a result of upbringing, and not, as the Women's Front believed, of economic conditions in which women were particularly exploited, or—as the New Feminists held—of patriarchy. These different ways of framing pornography posed challenges when the women's organizations attempted to cooperate politically against pornography, as we will soon see.

A few days after the TV debate program "*På sparket,*" pornography was debated in the Students' Society (*Studentersamfundet*) in Oslo. Based on the minutes of the meeting published in *Klassekampen*, it seems that this was almost an anti-porn revival meeting.[141] The keynote speakers were Turid Øvrebø from the Women's Front at the University of Oslo and the sexologist Thore Langfeldt. According to *Klassekampen*, the latter received little support for his view that the resistance against pornography was driven by sexual hostility, and that the Women's Front's methods of resistance mirrored fascism. Øvrebø denied that the resistance to pornography was due to puritanism; on the contrary, she declared that puritanism was the cause of pornography: "Porn, like the church in the

---

[139] The following quotations are from *VG*, 20 October 1977, p. 5; *VG*, 20 October 1977, p. 5; *Klassekampen*, 22 October 1977, p. 2.

[140] *VG*, 20 October 1977, p. 5.

[141] *Klassekampen*, 24 October 1977, p. 2.

Middle Ages, portrays the woman as a body without soul and brains. Porn is part of the same oppression that Kåre Kristiansen and Bergfrid Fjose [two leading Christian conservative politicians from the Christian Democratic Party] stand for," she said, and argued for sex education.

The Students' Society voted to join the anti-porn rally, which was to be held on November 5, 1977. At this rally, 1200 people marched from the University Square (*Universitetsplassen*) in the city center to Grønland Square, with banners proclaiming "Yes to Sexual Education—No to Porn" and "No to the State's Porn Sales—Porn out of Narvesen."[142] After the march, some of the protesters gathered in front of the porn shop Nortrade at Tøyen, where they unfurled a banner saying "Yes to Lesbian Love—No to Pornographic Exploitation." Several residents in the district joined in the action.[143]

The Women's Joint Action Against Pornography

While the pornography debate raged during the autumn of 1977, the women's section of the agrarian Center Party, the Center Women (*Senterkvinnene*), initiated an action against pornography that crossed political lines. Representatives from 26 women's organizations participated in the kickoff meeting, including some of the political parties' women's sections or committees. An action committee was set up at the meeting consisting of representatives of the Women's Front, the New Feminists, the Norwegian Housewives' Association (*Norges Husmorforbund*), the Norwegian Association for Female Agronomists (*Norges kvinnelige agronomlag*), the YWCA of Norway, the Norwegian Women's Public Health Association (*Norske Kvinners Sanitetsforening*), the Center Women (*Senterkvinnene*), and the Women's Committee of the Socialist Left Party SV. Anna Louise Beer, from the umbrella organization the Norwegian National Women's Council (*Norske Kvinners Nasjonalråd*) was elected leader of the action committee.[144]

---

[142] Narvesen is a Norwegian nationwide chain of newsagents/convenience stores with outlets all over the country. Through The Norwegian State Railways NSB, the Norwegian state owned 41% of the shares, and the rest were owned by the private foundation Fritt Ord [Free Speech].

[143] *Klassekampen*, 7 November 1977, pp. 4–5.

[144] *Dagbladet*, 22 October 1977, p. 32; *Klassekampen*, 27 October 1977, p. 1.

The Women's Joint Action against Pornography was met with skepticism. An editorial in *VG* stated that "the unholy alliance between the Marxist-Leninists of the Women's Front and the women of the Center Party and the Christian Democratic Party "gives off a burning smell."[145] This characteristic is typical of how many liberals initially perceived the initiative. Within the women's liberation movement, it was controversial to cooperate with Christians against pornography because of their alleged puritanism.

However, when the action committee of the Women's Joint Action against Pornography was formally established in November 1977, the controversies didn't revolve around puritanism. According to internal minutes by the representative of the New Feminists, the controversy was more about different perceptions of gender, which coincided with generational differences. The older women, who were not part of the women's liberation movement, wanted to emphasize "the human cause," because pornography is also degrading to men, while the younger women made it clear that it was the oppression of women that they wanted to target.[146] The younger women also wanted to include slogans about pornography's exploitation of lesbians, while the elderly were "unenthusiastic about lesbianism."[147] Generational differences were also reflected in the style of debate. While the younger ones were accustomed to fierce political discussions, the older women were reluctant to cause conflict. At the same time, according to the minutes of the New Feminists, the older women showed a "fierce respect" for the young ones and their competence regarding the pornography issue, a matter that the seniors had not previously discussed.

The Women's Front focused heavily on building the Women's Joint Action against Pornography into a mass movement. A euphoric article in their magazine *Kvinnefront* that fall offered the following report:

> The fight against the porn industry is raging at full speed. Porn burnings are flaring up in more and more places in the country; the porn shops are painted with "No to the Sale of Women," sex clubs and striptease

---

[145] Editorial in *VG*, 2 November 1977, p. 2.

[146] Ulla: "Noen refleksjoner og betraktninger omkring referatet og vår deltakelse i denne aksjonen" [Some Reflections and Considerations about the Minutes and Our Participation in this Action], *Feministen*, no. 10, 1977, p. 24.

[147] Ibid. For example, in this period the Norwegian Association for Women's Rights, NKF, believed that lesbians' situation did not "concern" the association. Lønnå 1996, pp. 276–277.

shows are faced with actions and struggles, women-oppressive commercial posters are torn down, discussions run hot everywhere, 28 organizations are joining the Centre Women's action against pornography, the TV, newspapers, and radio have recorded what is happening—the women are on the offensive![148]

Because the Women's Front had a high level of activity and prioritized the building of the Women's Joint Action against Pornography into a mass movement, most of their proposed statements were accepted when the political platform of the initiative was adopted in February 1978. The platform was shared by the organizations that joined in the action, although they could also front their own policies. The shared statements were as follows:

1. Speculative use of the female body is a devaluation of women as human beings
2. No to the sale of the female body
3. Prohibition in the Marketing Act or the Gender Equality Act against women's discriminatory advertising and advertising for porn
4. Yes to sex education, No to porn
5. Stop the sale of semi-pornographic magazines through Narvesen
6. Stop the sale of semi-pornographic magazines through grocery stores
7. Real enforcement of the ban on hardcore porn
8. Simplified language in the law and facilitation of enforcement of the prohibition of porn
9. No to porn's exploitation of lesbians and other minorities[149]

The Women's Front thus succeeded in its effort to make the Women's Joint Action frame pornography as a women-oriented—rather than a gender-neutral—political issue, including a lesbian perspective. There were no "puritan" statements, as for it, for example, demanded sex education.

---

[148] *Kvinnefront*, no. 5–6, 1977, p. 5.

[149] Reproduced in "'Gjør kvinnenes fellesaksjon mot porno til en stor bevegelse!'" [Make the Women's Joint Action Against Pornography a Great Movement!], *Vi er mange*, no. 5–6, 1978, p. 8; and in "Nei til salg av kvinner. Et debatthefte om porno fra Kvinnefronten" [No to the Sale of Women: A Debate Booklet on Porn from the Women's Front], 1978, p. 27.

The political platform could probably have had a stronger feminist perspective if not for the fact that the New Feminists had withdrawn from the Joint Action because they didn't want to cooperate with Christians. The Norwegian Association for Women's Rights had also withdrawn because they could advocate for neither "the sexual hostility of the Christian Democratic Party nor the activist style of the Women's Front, where book burning was one of the methods."[150] This was a perception of the Joint Action shared by other skeptics. Thus, in 1978, the Joint Action consisted of 22 nationwide organizations: The Women's Front, the Center Women, Bread and Roses, the Norwegian Housewives' Association, the Norwegian National Women's Council, the Norwegian Association for Female Agronomists, the YWCA of Norway, the Norwegian Women's Federation, the Norwegian Agrarian Women's Association (*Norges Bondekvinnelag*), the Norwegian Farmers and Small Farmers Union's Women (*Norsk Bonde-og Småbrukalags kvinner*), the Norwegian Nurses Organization (*Norsk Sykepleierforbund*), the Norwegian Association for Female Academics (*Norske Kvinnelige Akademikeres Landsforbund*), the Oslo Association of Business Women (*Oslo Kvinnelige Handelstands Forening*), Singles' National Association (*Ensliges Landsforbund*), Christian Women's Rights Association (*Kristent Kvinnesaksforbund*), Female Teachers' Mission Federation (*Lærerinnenes Misjonsforbund*), Women's Federation of the Methodist Church (*Metodistkirkens Kvinneforbund*), Norwegian Girl Scouts Association (*Norsk Speidepikeforbund*), and the White Ribbon (*Det Hvite Bånd*). In addition, the liberal New People's Party (*Det Nye Folkepartiet*) and the women's committees of the Christian Democratic Party and the Liberal Party enlisted in the Joint Action.[151]

Although Christian organizations did not make up a majority of the Joint Action, their participation nevertheless alarmed those who feared the "mighty puritan forces of our country," as the editor of the feminist magazine *Sirene*, IdaLou Larsen, put it. Pornography should not be fought with "prohibitions and puritan sexual anxiety," she held, and

---

[150] Lønnå 1996, p. 277. Norwegian Association for Women's Rights (NKF) member Else Michelet was sent to the foundation meeting with "instructions not to involve NKF in this."

[151] *Kvinnefront*, no. 4, 1978, p. 9; "Nei til salg av kvinner. Et debatthefte om porno fra Kvinnefronten" [No to the Sale of Women: A Debate Booklet on Porn from the Women's Front], p. 25.

instead of burning porn magazines one should "take them home and discuss them with our men."[152] The Women's Front had a pragmatic attitude toward working with Christians. They insisted on distinguishing between Christian leaders, such as conservative bishops and politicians, and "grass roots Christian women" who "fight for women's demands and who are themselves against the leadership of the church," as was claimed in a debate booklet on pornography.[153] Instead of "labelling people" like "the Christians," it was considered acceptable to work with people on single issues, even if one disagreed with them on other matters. Cooperating with Christians against pornography was not essentially different from working with them against an unfair dismissal, according to the booklet. The Women's Front argued that possible puritanism could be avoided by targeting the fight against the porn industry's profiteering on the female body and by promoting sex education and erotic literature as alternatives.

The aim of the Women's Joint Action against Pornography was to create a broad popular movement against pornography, and its grassroots orientation was reflected in its choices of action. In local communities, action groups were formed. They held discussion meetings and set up stands outside stores where pornography was sold—for example, Narvesen kiosks, where they distributed flyers and collected signatures in support of the Joint Action's claims. Also, a significant part of its activities involved raising money, since Joint Action received no government funding.

The Joint Action relied on volunteer work. There were no employees, and only in 1984 did it get its own office and telephone.[154] The action strategies were public education and mobilization to put pressure on the shops to make them stop selling pornography and to request of municipal authorities that pornography not be sold on municipal grounds. Moreover, after the introduction of the law banning sex-discriminatory

---

[152] *Sirene*, no. 11–12, 1977, p. 8.

[153] "Nei til salg av kvinner. Et debatthefte om porno fra Kvinnefronten" [No to the Sale of Women. A Debate Booklet on Porn from the Women's Front], p. 29.

[154] Note from the archive of the Joint Action, 27 January 1984. "Til pressekonferansen. Innledning og litt om vårt ståsted pr. i dag" [To the Press Conference: Introduction and a Little About Our Point of View per. Today]. FA D-0001 Administrative Archive 1981–1985, ABA. See also FA D-0003 Administrative Archive 1984 and FA D-0005 Administrative Archive 1985, ABA.

Fig. 3.4 Porn dealer Leif Hagen. Facsimile from *Kvinnejournalen*, no. 5–6, 1982

advertising as part of the Marketing Act of 1979, much effort was expended on reporting pornography ads to the Consumer Ombudsman as a violation of the Marketing Act. In 1979, activists collected 42,000 signatures in support of the claims of the Joint Action as described above.[155] An important reason why the group received such substantial support was the fact that, again, attention had been directed to the "porn king" Leif Hagen (Fig. 3.4). In January 1979, the police raided Hagen's two shops and warehouse in Oslo in what was at the time the largest porn seizure in Norwegian history: 16 tons of pornography, including 98,000 photo magazines and 18,000 films.[156] The following day, the shops were re-stocked, and the police carried out a second raid. On November 26,

[155] Karlsen 1991, p. 14.

[156] In the magistrate's court, the prosecuting authorities demanded that Hagen be detained for 14 days to prevent him from escaping the country, but his defense lawyer, Tor Erling Staff, ensured that he was released on a promise to report. Tessem and Wiedswang 1984, pp. 56–58.

1979, Norway's highest penalty in a pornography case up until that time was imposed when Hagen was sentenced to six months' unconditional imprisonment, fined one million Crones, and banned from trading for five years.

Leif Hagen: The perfect enemy

The "Porn King" Leif Hagen was Norway's largest wholesaler of pornography in the 1970s.[157] He was repeatedly convicted of selling illegal pornography and did not even hide his past as a thief.[158] In 1976, Hagen launched *Aktuell Rapport*, which surpassed other Norwegian porn magazines regarding the number of photographs of sprawling women. The magazine also boasted contact ads in which explicit sexual wishes were stated, and included pages of ads for the product selection of Hagen's mail-order company, L. Hagen Import, which offered illegal hard-core pornography that one could receive discreetly through the mail. In his editorial column in *Aktuell Rapport*, Hagen issued coarse-grained statements about well-known feminist anti-porn activists such as Unni Rustad and Liv Finstad.

After the seizure of 16 tons of pornography in 1979, Hagen was deprived of the right to pursue business for five years, but he did not give in. From prison, he reorganized his companies so that he was no longer the majority shareholder, and took the title of "consultant." He continued to publish *Aktuell Rapport*. In addition, he expanded his

---

[157] In 1977, Hagen stated that the store alone had an annual turnover of NOK 3 million. In addition, he had revenues from mail-order sales and magazines that were sold through Narvesen, where the state owned 41% of the shares through the Norwegian public rail company NSB. Tessem and Wiedswang 1984, p. 12.

[158] Tessem and Wiedswang 1984, p. 56. Unless otherwise stated, the following information about Hagen's business has been obtained from this source, in particular pp. 48, 56–58.

business abroad by publishing Danish and Swedish editions of *Aktuell Rapport* and opening a major porn shop in Stockholm.

The police suspected that Hagen, despite the fact that he had been deprived of the right to trade, was in reality the majority shareholder and controlled an estimated ten different companies. In November 1982, the police once more undertook a gigantic porn seizure at L. Hagen Import, so large that the confiscated material filled three vacant prison cells. However, it was only after the debate on pornography flared up again in 1983 that the public prosecutor brought charges against Hagen for illegal business activities.[159] Later, he was also convicted of dealing in illegal pornography.

In 1983, Hagen estimated that his market share of the Norwegian porn business was 70%, and that his companies had annual revenues of close to NOK 150 million, with 30 employees in Scandinavia.[160] 85% of the pornography was sold through his mail-order company, L. Hagen Import AS.

Leif Hagen and the Women's Front met in court in August 1983. A member of the Women's Front, Bente Volder, had reported Hagen for defamation after he referred to her in an editorial in *Aktuell Rapport* as a "terrorist," "bitch," and "intellectual whore" who "belonged to a minority group of schizophrenic women with some wretched soft men backing them up."[161] The reason why Hagen characterized Volder as such was her involvement in porn burnings in the city of Ålesund on the west coast, which had resulted in her receiving a wrist-slap penalty—a conditional fine of only NOK 200.

Despite persistent attempts by Hagen's attorney, Tor Erling Staff, to have his client acquitted, Volder and the Women's Front won the case. Hagen's comments in *Aktuell Rapport* were found to be baseless, and he was ordered to pay the Women's Front NOK 20,000 in compensation, money that would be used in the fight against pornography.

---

[159] *VG*, 7 October 1983, p. 7; *Klassekampen*, 8 October 1983, p. 1; *Klassekampen*, 16 November 1983, p. 2.

[160] Tessem and Wiedswang 1984, p. 95.

[161] On this trial, see *Kvinnejournalen* no. 5–6, 1982, p. 37; *Arbeiderbladet*, 10 August 1983, p. 3; *Klassekampen*, 16 August 1983, p. 2; *Dagbladet*, 17 August 1983, p. 8; *Arbeiderbladet*, 31 August 1983.

For the anti-porn movement, Leif Hagen was the perfect enemy. His many convictions for selling illegal pornography and the vulgar, gangster style he cultivated in the media made him seem like a villain.[162] With Hagen as its public face, the porn industry appeared not as a contributor to sexual freedom and pleasure, but as a nefarious and speculative enterprise.

After several convictions for illegal business activity during the 1980s, Leif Hagen emigrated to Sweden, where he continued his business in the porn industry.

The Women's Front Becomes More "Feminist"

Since its founding in 1972, the Women's Front had given priority to economic demands such as women's right to work, free day care, and "a living wage" as essential to women's liberation.[163] Following the anti-porn campaign, however, some heated internal discussions took place within the Women's Front. Members criticized the organization for not adequately addressing sexual oppression of women in fear of "stepping on men's feet" and "splitting the working class struggle."[164] Several of them argued that not all aspects of women's oppression could be ascribed to capitalism's drive for financial profit, pointing to issues such as the banning of abortion and the battering and rape of women. Some activists argued that there was an "ideology" behind the oppression that held that women are created to serve the needs of men. Feminists would call this patriarchy, but members of the Women's Front would not go that far. Nevertheless, they became more "feminist" than before, in the sense that they began to include explanations other than purely economic ones in

[162] See, e.g., the series of articles entitled "My Life with the Porn King," published in *Dagbladet* from 16 to 20 April 1983. Here, Hagen's ex-wife told about her cohabitation with the "Porn King." The introduction to the series stated: "It's about how he created a money machine out of commercial sex, and about how she prostituted herself during her first few years with Leif Hagen." The article presented an image of Hagen as a cynical, money-hungry megalomaniac without scruples.

[163] Rustad, Unni (2010): "Spredte minner fra kampen mot porno" [Scattered Memories from the Struggle Against Porn], *Gnist Marxistisk tidsskrift*, no.1.

[164] *Vi er mange*, no. 5, 1977, p. 21. This debate continued until 1979. See, e.g., the internal journal *Vi er mange* no. 9–10, 1978, and 11, 1979, as well as *Kvinnefront*, no. 4, 1979, p. 30.

explaining the oppression of women. The main driver of this change was the fact that members began studying, discussing, and analyzing pornography, which hitherto was a relatively unknown world to most of them.

In 1978, the Women's Front published a booklet on pornography.[165] The following quote is representative of how the organization framed pornography in the years to come:

Why is the Women's Front against porn?

The porn profiteers make women a commodity that can get them cash.

All qualities that characterize a human being—work ability, thoughts and opinions—are gone. Back is a body that men can use to satisfy their desires and then throw away. A piece of meat men can use to satisfy their own needs, a body that can be replaced by an inflatable sex-doll, or a plastic head with the vagina in the mouth, that's the women in porn. "This doll has all the qualities a woman can have," a porn dealer advertised.

We can decorate advertising posters—we can be folded out on the middle pages—we can be used in a new variation together with dogs and pigs. We are an applicable thing to use. If you are young and pretty, you are highly valuable to the porn industry. If you start to get wrinkles and sagging muscles, you sink in value, but you may still be *used*—it is still possible to make money off of you. For in porn, the offer varies: little girls of 30 kilos or women of 150 kilos. Big breasts or small breasts? The porn dealers pick out the item—either presented in gorgeous nature, as in *Lek*, or drowned in alcohol and drugs at a dirty hotel room in Bangkok.

In no other context is it so clearly and unambiguously established that women are inferior.[166]

---

[165] "Nei til salg av kvinner. Et debatthefte om porno fra Kvinnefronten" [No to the Sale of Women: A Debate Booklet on Porn from the Women's Front] (1978). The booklet is a practical guide for people who want to fight pornography and includes, among other things, analyses of pornography, accounts of the economic conditions in the industry, a list of typical arguments for pornography with counter-arguments, and concrete "manuals" for how to combat pornography, whether targeting a local hardcore store, Narvesen, or mail-order companies. The booklet is said to have sold very well, according to the enthusiastic article "It's Easy to Sell Anti-porn Booklets!" in *Vi er mange*, no. 2, 1979.

[166] "Nei til salg av kvinner. Et debatthefte om porno fra Kvinnefronten" [No to the Sale of Women: A Debate Booklet on Porn from the Women's Front], 1978, p. 3.

Actions as Learning Processes

The outwardly extending actions against rape and pornography gener-
ated important learning processes with the development of new theories,
demands, and strategies. The actions attracted attention and drew potential allies and adversaries into the open. In both France and Norway, it
was striking that men with positions in the traditional labor unions were
among the first "enemies" that women activists met when they began
their struggle. These men did not believe that sexual abuse of women
had anything to do with labor struggles, and reacted strongly to the
load-mouthed women they encountered. In Norway, however, it was the
pornography dealers with their "bodyguards" who stood out as the main
enemies of the anti-porn activists. These were "good" enemies to deal
with, as they emerged as cynical criminals driven by money interests.

Theory Development

The politicization of sexual exploitation and violence against women led
to the development of theories regarding these issues. For women activists
associated with Marxist-Leninist parties, the issue caused them to direct
their attention to oppression mechanisms other than purely economic
ones. They became more independent of the political doctrines of the
parties in the sense that, to a larger extent than previously, they challenged
men's views regarding women, including within the labor movement. The
French class-struggle feminists showed bravery in challenging their male
comrades and advocated the use of the "bourgeois" legal system in rape
cases. Nevertheless, neither the French class-struggle feminists nor the
Norwegian Women's Front publicly confronted men on the basis of sex,
because they were deeply concerned about not creating divisions in the
working class. For them, class conflicts were more important than gender
conflicts, and it was important to recruit men in the fight for women's
liberation.

Radical feminists were not reluctant to confront individual men, as
they believed that these men were the beneficiaries of patriarchal exploitation. The French revolutionary feminists were more productive than the
Norwegian New Feminists in the area of theory development. According
to the French revolutionary feminists, rape was a "class crime" that men
as a class perpetrated against women as a class in order to keep them
down. Rape was understood as the foundation of patriarchal exploitation,

that is, men's control over women's bodies and sexuality was viewed as the basis for all other structures of women's oppression, whether they be the nuclear family, religion, prostitution, the military, or the educational system. Thus, the fight against rape was fundamental. The French revolutionary feminists' analysis of rape gained worldwide attention in connection with the International Tribunal on Crimes Against Women in Brussels in 1976, during which they dominated the session on rape. The tribunal was a breakthrough in the fight against violence against women and led to its becoming an important issue in the transnational women's movement. In the aftermath of the event, crisis centers for abused and raped women were established in several countries, including Norway, and a number of books and articles were written about rape and other forms of sexual violence. In addition, an international petition was circulated against clitoridectomy.[167] The fact that women from so many countries met to discuss women's problems implied that they learned from each other, and that ideas and forms of action were being spread across borders. The analyses of violence against women were thus increasingly transnational.

The revolutionary feminist analyses of rape were radical, though Annie Cohen's appeal for the arming of women to defend themselves against rape was still an exception. In addition to advocating that women act in solidarity with each other, the solutions were first and foremost proposed within the framework of the law. The most prominent strategy was that women who had been raped were encouraged to report to the police and pursue the case right up to the Assize Court. This was an approach that all of the different factions of the MLF eventually agreed upon. The rationale for using the courts was not that one wanted to put rapists in prison, but that it would help break the silence and shame surrounding rape. It was about acknowledging raped women as victims and rapists as abusers, with the ultimate goal that women would stop being victims when men stopped raping.

---

[167] Brantenberg et al. (eds.) 1976, p. 40.

Challenging Cooperation

The campaigns against rape and pornography led to increased cooperation in the women's liberation movement. On the one hand, the mobilizations resulted in renewed fervor in the movement, but cooperation between different groups was generally challenging and conflict-ridden. The different factions of the women's liberation movement framed the issues in different ways, and there were disagreements about how the problems should be defined and how they should be addressed. In France, the dispute in the MLF was specifically about explaining rape as a result of "the sexual misery" created by the bourgeoisie, or as a manifestation of men's ownership and control of women's bodies. The disagreements over the analysis were so strong that any committed cooperation became difficult. Nevertheless, women with different political affiliations demonstrated together outside courts where rape cases were being tried. Any formal cooperation with organizations outside the MLF was rejected.

The Norwegian women's movement was far more pragmatic in terms of cooperation, including with women's organizations that were politically remote. For action-oriented feminist activists, it was challenging to collaborate with "bureaucratic"-oriented members of the Norwegian Association for Women's Rights, but the greatest challenge concerned cooperation with Marxist-Leninists and Christians. While the Marxist-Leninist dominated Women's Front held the pragmatic view that one could cooperate with anyone who agreed that pornography was something "filthy," the New Feminists and other left-wing groups rejected cooperation with "bourgeois" Christians in this matter. Further, they feared that the Worker's Communist Party (Marxist-Leninists), the AKP (m-l), was using the anti-pornography campaign to bolster its own movement.

For any political movement, it is essential to clarify whether it is appropriate to cooperate in specific cases with people and organizations with whom one disagrees on other issues. In the 1970s, the French left, including the MLF, was strongly characterized by a principle of purity—one that dictated against contaminating the revolutionary political purity with erroneous ideology and analysis.[168] The "all or nothing" strategy was successful in gaining attention, but it led to the MLF eventually

---

[168] Picq, Françoise (1991): "A French Feminism," in D. Haase-Dubosc et al. (eds.), p. 39.

becoming politically isolated. This sequence of events had a parallel with the Norwegian New Feminists, who lost momentum when the anti-porn campaign became too broad. However, the pragmatism of the Women's Front proved to be a successful strategy as well as a valuable recruiting tool, since they were the ones who took the lead in the anti-porn movement in Norway.

Changes in Attitudes

These mobilizations led to changes in attitudes. In France, judges and jury members agreed with the MLF's demand that rape should be handled as a felony in the Assize Court and not as a misdemeanor in the Correctional Tribunal. The violent behavior of the CGT guards on May 1, 1976, had confirmed feminists' assertion of sexism in the labor movement. However, the incident contributed to attitude changes in the CGT. One year after the tumult, the CGT held a national women's conference whose aim was to describe, analyze, and distance themselves from the exploitation of working women. The attitude toward women's issues was said to have changed drastically, according to class-struggle feminists, who wrote that the conference was characterized by free-wheeling discussions about the necessity of ending "phallocratic attitudes" in the labor movement.[169] After the conference, the CGT's women's committee was revitalized and began to engage in the campaign against rape, including by protesting outside courts along with MLF activists. At the same time, CGT's newspapers actively supported the campaign. For example, *Lutte ouvrière* declared that rape had to be considered "a horrific crime, unworthy of civilized people, and condemned by all."[170]

The Communist Party PCF changed as well. From being overtly hostile to the new women's liberation movement's demands to free

---

[169] Storti 2010, pp. 136–137. From the article "Sixième conférence sur les femmes salariées: La CGT à l'heure des femmes" [Sixth Conference on Women Employees: The CGT at the Time of Women], *Libération*, 16 May 1977; "La CGT à l'heure du féminisme" [The CGT at the Time of Feminism], *Femmes travailleuses en lutte*, no. 14, June 1977.

[170] *Lutte ouvrière*, 13 November 1976, quoted in Mossuz-Lavau 1991, p. 197. The CGT's women's journal *Antoinette* evolved into an increasingly feminist newspaper, but at one point the criticism of the labor union movement went too far. In 1982, CGT decided to close the newspaper. *Le temps des femmes*, no. 17, 1982.

women from the roles of mother and sex object, the PCF took up feminist issues and presented itself in the autumn of 1976 as the "Women's
Liberation Party." Feminists were not convinced and saw the change as
a ruse to recruit women to the party.[171] Meanwhile, the PCF showed a
growing understanding of rape as a problem. Female party spokespersons
engaged in the campaign against rape, and the party newspaper *L'Humanité* followed the lead of those in charge. The sardonic tone of the
1975 article on Cathérine "playing with fire and being surprised when
she gets burned" was gone. Though in 1977 the Sunday edition of the
newspaper published an interview with a woman who had been raped,
feminists of the MLF doubted the sincerity of the PCF's commitment and
suspected the party of using the campaign against rape to "take over" the
women's fight.[172] In the MLF, it was common to suspect that other political movements that took up feminist demands were in fact trying to "take
over" the authentic women's struggle. When women from the communist
Union des femmes françaises (UFF), in collaboration with other women's
organizations, initiated a joint action against rape—the *Collectif féministe
contre le viol* (Feminist Community against Rape) of 1977—there was
no mention of it in any of the MLF's publications.[173] However, while
there existed no formalized cooperation between MLF and the traditional
women's movement on this issue, this action showed that the feminist
framing of rape had spread to new environments.

In Norway, porn burnings were a particularly effective means of initiating debate. Whether supporting porn burnings was an appropriate tactic
or not, there could be no argument that this form of action brought
considerably greater attention to the cause than did peaceful demonstrations and the writing of opinion pieces for the newspapers. It was
a form of action that compelled one to take a stand and that allowed
the activists to spread their message that pornography was oppressive
to women. As social movement researcher Sidney Tarrow has pointed
out, such disruptive forms of contention are powerful, but there are also
challenges associated with them. They are difficult to maintain over long

[171] Storti 2010, p. 99. From the article "Le parti de la libération de la femme" [The
Party of Women's Liberation], *Libération*, 13–14, November 1976.

[172] Excerpts from the interview in *l'Huma-Dimanche* are published in *Femmes
Travailleuses en Lutte*, no. 15, November 1977, p. 7.

[173] In retrospect, however, the initiative of UFF was commented on in Fouque et al.
(eds.) 2008, p. 210.

periods of time because they depend on the activists having a high degree of commitment and willingness to take risks.[174] Eventually, the anti-porn activists abandoned porn burnings because the countermeasures enacted by the porn dealers made them too dangerous. But Leif Hagen and other porn dealers' undisguised threats of retaliatory violence through the media served to lend legitimacy to the actions of the protesters. The public came to view the dealers as members of a criminal industry that did not shy away from gangster-like methods. The aura of criminality was amplified by the porn shops' selection of products that included illegal violence pornography, "toddler pornography," and pornography that showed women engaging in sexual intercourse with animals. This sort of pornography was shunned by most people. Thus, in the view of many, the anti-porn activists—who, unlike the porn dealers, were not driven by money interests—inhabited the moral high ground. However, an exception to the general opposition to hard-core pornography was the sexologist Thore Langfeldt, who publicly argued that this form of pornography could be of help to sexual minorities such as pedophiles. His view failed to gain public acceptance, and as a result of the debates, the police began to intervene against this type of pornography.

The year 1977 represented the peak of "men's magazines" in Norway.[175] According to official figures, 8 million copies of Norwegian and 1.4 million foreign porn magazines were sold in Norway—a country with a population of 4 million—in 1977. The competition between Norwegian and foreign publishers was fierce, and the intense marketing of the magazines, which included pictures of half-naked girls in newspapers and on public transport posters, made them more visible to the public eye than before. This angered many people. With the porn debate in the autumn of 1977 came new voices that began to oppose the growing industry, among them members of the Fruit and Tobacco Dealers' National Federation (*Frukt- og Tobakkhandlernes Landsforening*), who protested against their obligation to sell pornography. They received their magazine stock from the partly state-owned Narvesen company, and now they began negotiations with the magazine distributor about the possibility of refusing to sell pornography.[176] Some of the roughest

---

[174] Tarrow 1998, p. 98.

[175] Tessem and Wiedswang 1984, p. 99.

[176] *VG*, 28 October 1977, p. 19.

magazines were removed from window exhibitions. According to an opinion survey published by *Dagbladet* in January 1978, 53 percent of the respondents supported a prohibition on pornography, an increase from 50 percent in 1976. *Dagbladet* interpreted this as "a natural consequence of the flourishing of the porn debate after the Women's Front's bonfires. New issues have been included, such as discrimination against women and a greed-driven desire for profit."[177]

The Women Who Spoke up

In both Norway and France, the first street actions against pornography and rape were triggered by the fact that specific women had experienced various forms of abuse, spoken up, and initiated campaigns on their own behalf in collaboration with activists of the women's liberation movement.

Things turned out better for Liv and Rannveig than for Anne and Araceli. In the fall of 1977, Liv and Rannveig were granted salaries during their suspension, and after applying several times, they were given jobs in Oslo Public Transportation in early 1978, although not on the Holmenkollen Line, as they had wished, but on the Blue City Tram.[178] Even union officials managed to prevent them from being hired on the Holmenkollen Line, their case was not entirely without victory. During the autumn of 1977, the Oslo City Council unanimously adopted a recommendation to Oslo Public Transportation that women-discriminatory advertising in public transportation should not be posted.[179]

Anne and Araceli fared worse. Almost four years after the rape, they struggled with nightmares, anxiety, and depression, and became dependent on sleeping pills and anti-anxiety medicine. They considered suicide, and feared revenge from the rapists. Their physician, who documented

---

[177] Cited in "Porno er kvinneundertrykking" [Porn Is Women's Oppression], *Kvinnefront*, no. 1, 1978, p. 15. The study is also referred to in the Marxist-Leninist journal *Røde Fane*, no. 2, 1978, pp. 35–36; and in Tessem and Wiedswang 1984, p. 76.

[178] Anne Lise: "Holmenkollbanesaka" [The Holmenkollen Line Case], *Feministen*, no. 2, 1978 [no page numbers]; interview with Liv Alming, who relates how she continued working on the Blue City Tram until retirement, while Rannveig Snortheim left Oslo Public Transportation to pursue her studies, later becoming a physiotherapist.

[179] Elisabeth and Anne Lise: "Liv Finstad på ville veier!" [Liv Finstad on the Wrong Track!], *Feministen*, no. 10, 1977, p. 41.

these events, stated that it is not unusual for post-rape trauma to last for several years.[180] The young women referred to themselves as "living dead." When their case came up in the Assize Court in Aix-en-Provence in 1978 (to be discussed in more detail in the next chapter), Anne's mother testified that the two had been human wrecks over the past four years: "They die little by little, and I die with them…".[181]

---

[180] "Témoins de l'accusation" [Prosecution Witnesses], *Viol. Le procès d'Aix*, p. 111.

[181] "Les témoins d'Anne et d'Araceli (suite)" [The Witnesses of Anne and Araceli (continued)], *Viol. Le procès d'Aix*, p. 268.

CHAPTER 4

Success and Criticism of the Campaigns Against Rape and Pornography

The women's movements' mobilizations against rape in France and pornography in Norway led to changes in public opinion. By the late 1970s, political elites and the judicial system had begun to take the sexual exploitation of women more seriously, as manifest in legal reforms of the 1980s. However, the success of the campaigns was compromised by accusations that the women's movements were totalitarian, puritan, and hateful toward men. Moreover, the introduction of more progressive laws against rape and pornography led to a decrease in feminist political activity in these areas.

The year 1978 marked a breakthrough for the campaign against rape in France. By then it was no longer taboo to talk about rape, and, according to *Libération*'s feminist journalist Martine Storti, media coverage had shifted from "silence to cacophony."[1] Women's magazines such as *Marie Claire* and *Elle* reported on rape, as did the communist labor union CGT's women's journal, *Antoinette*. Radio and TV offered discussion programs about rape, and the movie *L'Amour violé* (Raped Love) scored a notable screen success.[2] The movie, which was pedagogically constructed, revolved around issues that had emerged in the

---

[1] M.S.: "La presse, la 'révolution des mœurs' et le viol" [The Press, the "Morality Revolution" and Rape], *Libération*, 5 May 1978, p. 5.

[2] According to Mossuz-Lavau, rape was discussed for the first time on French television during the debate program "Le dossier de l'écran" [The Dossier of the Screen]

© The Author(s) 2021

T. R. Korsvik, *Politicizing Rape and Pornography,*
Citizenship, Gender and Diversity,
https://doi.org/10.1007/978-3-030-55639-6_4

campaign against rape, including psychological trauma and the use of the judicial system. It tells the story of the young nurse Nicole, who is raped by four men one evening while she is out driving her moped. Seriously traumatized, she experiences a series of emotions: silence, fear, shame, and suicidal thoughts. After talking with her friends and her boyfriend, she rebels. While a friend urges her to report the rape, her boyfriend is against it "because prison doesn't change anything." Nevertheless, she reports it and eventually wins the case.

In May 1978, the case of Anne and Araceli was settled in the Assize Court of Aix-en-Provence, an event that was duly covered by the national media. The key question raised by the case was whether rape had occurred, or whether it was an instance of seduction that had "gone a bit too far." The case was symbolically important because it challenged cultural notions about the "erotic game" wherein "the woman says no, but means yes" and gives in after some "persuasion." According to historian Georges Vigarello, psychological traumas were discussed in a way never before heard in a French court and revolved around the fact that a terrified person might forego resistance and "let" herself be raped—that is, "consent" to the rape. In addition, the psychological consequences of rape were discussed for the first time. The case of Anne and Araceli went beyond their individual rape case and concerned women's liberation from the "male society."[3] At the time of the trial, several French politicians introduced bills designed to modernize rape legislation. The new law was adopted in 1980.

In Norway, the campaign against pornography received a significant boost in the fall of 1983 when a TV documentary on the Norwegian Broadcasting Corporation (NRK) featuring anti-porn activist Unni Rustad from the Women's Front displaying and analyzing pornography, shocked viewers and made front-page headlines in the major national newspapers.[4] That same evening, people who were disturbed by what they

---

in October 1977. Invited guests were Gisèle Halimi, the lawyer representing Anne and Araceli, two raped women, and a German rapist who had voluntarily undergone a surgical operation. Mossuz-Lavau 1991, p. 195. The movie *L'Amour violé* [Raped Love] was directed by Yannick Bellon and premiered in January 1978. Martine Storti: "Le viol au cinéma (*L'Amour violé*, de Yannick Bellon) [Rape in the Movies (*Raped Love* by Yannick Bellon)], *Libération*, 11 November 1978, reprinted in Storti 2010, pp. 232–234.

[3] Vigarello 1998, p. 249.

[4] See, e.g., the headline "TV PORN WAKES NORWAY," *VG*, 7 October 1983, p. 1.

had seen on TV called the NRK and the Women's Front, saying that they wanted to do something to help stop pornography. Over the following days, newspapers overflowed with readers' posts against pornography, and the Joint Action against Pornography received a large number of letters from people who wanted to lend a hand in stopping pornography. Soon after, more organizations and parties joined the Joint Action, and new anti-porn groups cropped up all across the country. By the end of 1983, the Joint Action comprised nearly 40 national organizations. Politicians quickly joined the movement. On the day after the broadcast of the TV documentary featuring Rustad, the young MP of the Labor Party, Sissel Rønbeck, questioned the Minister of Justice as to what the government might do to combat pornography.

Over the following months the porn debate raged in the media. The police, along with Narvesen, the nationwide chain of newsagents partly owned by the state, issued statements about what could be done to outlaw hard-core pornography. Immediately after the TV documentary, the Women's Front initiated a petition that collected almost 50,000 signatures in support of establishing porn-free municipalities, that is, places where pornography could not be sold on public property. A number of municipalities in the country adopted such policy. The political debates in the wake of the 1983 TV documentary resulted in pornography becoming a national political issue and fueled the adoption of a new pornography law in 1985.

Though the TV documentary with Unni Rustad marked a breakthrough for the anti-porn campaign, progress had been made earlier. Early in 1983, for example, the Children's Ombudsman Målfrid Grude Flekkøy had asked the Ministry of Justice to intervene against Narvesen's distribution of child pornography, and in April of that year the group "Menfolk against Porn" was launched on the island of Dønna in Northern Norway.[5] Soon after, other "Menfolk against Porn" groups were established, including in Oslo and in Bamble in Telemark County. During the

---

[5] A press release from Menfolk against Porn in *Kvinnejournalen*, no. 5–6, 1983, p. 20, reads: "We have been silent for years as an alibi for the porn industry. Porn presents us as emotionally cold, brutal and cynical. We have uncontrollable desires that drive us to violence and sexual abuse of women and children. No means are too rough to sexually satisfy us. Now we say stop!" See also the articles "Bamble Men against Porn" in *Klassekampen*, 16 November 1983, p. 6, and "Men against Porn" in *Arbeiderbladet*, 24 November 1983.

election campaign of 1983, the fight against pornography was a political issue for the Red Electoral Alliance Party (Rød Valgallianse, RV) and in August of that year, Bente Volder, the Women's Front activist, won her libel suit against the porn dealer Leif Hagen, who in an editorial in *Aktuell Rapport* had characterized her as a "terrorist," "bitch," and "intellectual whore" (see Chapter 3). Other court cases awaited Hagen, and in the fall of 1983 he moved to Sweden because he was no longer allowed to do business in Norway. Meanwhile, the porn industry was in decline in Norway. After peaking in 1977, the volume of pornography had fallen by almost half by 1982.[6] In October 1984, the newsagent company Narvesen stated that "men's magazines" had experienced a sharp decline in sales. The major decline affected Leif Hagen's *Aktuell Rapport*, which, according to *Dagbladet*, had cut its sales figures from 50,000 to 25,000 copies per issue. Narvesen attributed the decline to the anti-porn activists' efforts.[7]

Although 1983 was an exceptional year in the anti-porn struggle, the breakthrough can be said to have begun a few years earlier. In 1981, the Joint Action against Pornography had reorganized, allowing the participation of gender-mixed organizations and electing Unni Rustad from the Women's Front as its leader, replacing the more conservative Anna Louise Beer from the Norwegian National Women's Council. The mission of the Joint Action was broadened to include combating prostitution, a response to feminist researchers' having exposed the fluid connection between pornography and prostitution. The new Joint Action against Pornography and Prostitution decided to advocate the criminalization of purchasing sex. At the same time, the anti-porn campaigners became increasingly aware of the more violent aspects of pornography and emphasized how it promoted sexual abuse. Meanwhile, some opponents of pornography sought alternative, non-repressive erotic depictions. But when, in the summer of 1983, the Women's Front's journal was launched as "a magazine to make you horny," there were mixed reactions.

---

[6] Tessem and Wiedswang 1984, p. 100. The sales of porn magazines dropped from 9.4 million copies (of which 8 million were Norwegian publications) in 1977 to 5.26 million copies (of which 4.6 million were Norwegian) in 1982. The decline may have been due to the fact that more people took a stand against pornography, but may also be a result of the upsurge in the sale of VHS video players around 1980, causing porn print users to switch over to porn movies.

[7] *Dagbladet*, 18 October 1984, p. 11.

The French and Norwegian women activists responded differently to the success of their resolute struggles. In Norway, the activists were generally happy that their framing of the anti-porn struggle as a fight against women's oppression and for sexual liberation had gained acceptance in wider public circles. In France, on the other hand, many activists felt uneasy that so many actors outside the MLF, including representatives of the judicial system, had begun to portray rape as a crime against women and as a serious societal problem. They feared that they had walked into a "trap," that their campaign had been "taken over" by their adversaries and had helped to strengthen reactionary institutions. This perception was also shared by political groups on the far left. In Norway, the women's liberation movement was accused of promoting a bogus image of women as helpless victims and men as predators. As a consequence, the reaction to the success of the anti-porn movement engendered a fierce public debate about the women's movement's alleged hatred of men as a driving force in their mobilization. Although there were some dissimilarities in the criticisms lodged against the Norwegian and French feminist activists, the various critiques shared the logic that the fight against the sexual abuse of women was authoritarian and rendered men's sexuality suspect.

The Settlement of Anne and Araceli's Case in the Assize Court

The rape case of Anne and Araceli was dealt with in the Assize Court in Aix-en-Provence on May 2–3, 1978. From the very beginning, the trial was characterized by tension and aggression.[8] MLF activists had mobilized for the case for almost four years, and there was an impassioned atmosphere among the demonstrators who had gathered outside the courthouse to show their support for Anne and Araceli. The tense situation was triggered by the fact that just a few days earlier, a girl had who had been raped committed suicide after the judiciary refused to believe her,[9] and it was not clear whether Anne and Araceli would be

---

[8] The account of the trial and the events surrounding it are based on Choisir (1978), *Viol. Le Procès d'Aix* [Rape: The Process in Aix] and the following national newspapers: *Le Figaro*, 3 May 1978 and 5 May 1978, p. 5; *Le Monde*, 4 May 1978, p. 9; *L'Humanité*, 3 May 1978, p. 12; 4 May 1978, p. 12; and 5 May 1978, p. 5; *Libération*, 3 May 1978, p. 8; 4 May 1978, p. 5; and 5 May 1978, p. 5.

[9] *Libération*, 4 May 1978, p. 1.

believed. The crowd waiting for Anne and Araceli, their family, and their lawyers was made up of supportive protesters, including activists from the MLF, labor unions, and human rights organizations, as well as journalists, curious bystanders, and even a number of friends of the three defendants.[10] Shouted slogans and insults reverberated within the walls. The Palace of Justice was blocked off, angering the protesters supportive of the plaintiffs because, while police officers let the defendants' friends enter the building, they kept Anne and Araceli's supporters outside, waving banners and shouting slogans. Some young women tried to break through the barriers, but with no success. Thus, on the first day of the trial, the audience inside the courtroom consisted mainly of supporters of the defendants, something that troubled Anne and Araceli.[11]

A Political Trial

This was just the first of a series of controversies that arose during the trial. Anne and Araceli had wanted the trial to be used as a means to highlight rape as a societal problem and had therefore summoned eleven famous "solidarity witnesses" to talk on the subject during the trial. Using trials as a political platform with well-known witnesses, a strategy known as *procès-tribune*, was a concept that had been used several times in France—for example, during the Algerian war—to shed light on war crimes committed by the French Army.[12] Gisèle Halimi, the assistant attorney for Anne and Araceli, had successfully used this strategy at the Bobigny trial in 1972,

---

[10] The demonstration was supported by the political parties PCF and PS, the labor unions CGT, CFDT, and the teachers union FEN, as well as and the human rights organization Ligue des Droits de l'Homme. *Libération*, 29–30 April and 1 May 1978, p. 5.

[11] "Audience du matin" [Morning Audience], *Viol. Le procès d'Aix*, pp. 37–39.

[12] In 1960, President de Gaulle rushed through a decree to amend the procedural regulations to prevent future litigation from being used as a political platform. In the so-called Jeanson trial of that year, a number of famous people, including Jean-Paul Sartre and Simone de Beauvoir, testified about the French army's use of torture in Algeria, demanded that French forces withdraw, and provided active support to the FLN. The procedural regulations of 1960 prohibited persons who were not directly involved from testifying in court unless they were experts or could say something about the personality and morale of those involved. In the Aix trial of 1978, the judge referred to these procedural rules when he interrupted the "solidarity witnesses." Halimi had also been a legal adviser to the FLN and in 1961 was the defender of the terrorism-charged woman Djamila Boupacha, who became a symbol of the resistance to French torture. In 1962

when she succeeded in securing the acquittal of a 16-year-old girl accused of having had an illegal abortion.[13] The list of Anne and Araceli's "solidarity witnesses" was impressive and also revealed that the two Belgian women had a far more pragmatic attitude toward alliance partners than was typical of the various factions of the MLF, who did not want to cooperate with people who did not share their viewpoint on patriarchy. Two of the witnesses were professors of medicine, three were award-winning authors, and six were female politicians who spanned the entire political spectrum from the far left (Trotskyites) to conservative (Gaullists). Four of the witnesses were also highly decorated war heroes from the French resistance—*La Résistance*—during World War II.[14]

she and Simone de Beauvoir published the book *Djamila Boupacha* (Gallimard). Halimi 1978, pp. 9–28.

[13] Halimi 1978, pp. 13 and 21. Furthermore, in 1977, Halimi was the assistant attorney in another rape case, which she made a "*procès-tribune*." The case was about the village girl Violette, who had been raped by four former classmates. When Violette reported the rape, she was ostracized from her native village and fired from her job. From the villagers' point of view, the real "scandal" was not the rape, but that Violette had made it public, saying that she would pursue the case right to the Assize Court. During the trial, activists from Choisir and local women's groups in Pau, as well as activists from the leftist political parties LCR and PS, demonstrated outside the courthouse. Halimi wanted to make the point that gang rape was equivalent to fascist mass psychology. Martine Storti: "Le procès d'un viol collectif aux Assises de Pau: 'Des filles comme vous, on n'en veut pas ici'" [The Trial of a Gang Rape in the Assize Court in Pau: 'Girls Like You, We Do not Want Them Here'], *Libération*, 18 February 1977. Reprinted in Storti 2010, pp. 170–172. See also Halimi 1978, p. 21.

[14] Anne and Araceli had personally contacted the solidarity witnesses—for example, by showing up in the National Assembly and presenting their case. Of the six female politicians, five were deputies of the National Assembly. At the time (1978) there were only 21 female deputies in the French National Assembly; thus these five women represented the elite of female politicians of the country. The five deputies on Anne and Araceli's list of solidarity witnesses were: Gisèle Moreau from the Central Committee of the Communist Party PCF, where she was responsible for women's issues; Marie Jacq from the Socialist Party PS; Hélène Mistoffe from the Gaullist Party RPR; and Louise Moreau from President Valéry Giscard d'Estaing's center-right party UDF. Moreau was a veteran of WW2, had been awarded the Cross of War (*Croix de Guerre*), and was an officer in the Legion of Honor (*Légion d'honneur*) and the French Resistance, *la Résistance*. The fifth deputy was the Gaullist Florence d'Harcourt, former leader of the Gaullist women's organization Femmes-Avenir. In addition, the list of female politicians included Arlette Laguiller, the Secretary General of the Trotskyist Party *Lutte Ouvrière*, and the only female presidential candidate in 1974. Her party promoted a socialist-feminist program. Laguiller was summoned as a witness because she was politically close to those who opposed the use of the judicial system. Other solidarity witnesses included the trio of Pierre Emmanuel,

Using the judicial system as a political tool to shed light on societal problems was by no means without controversy. In the Assize Court in Aix-en-Provence, the judge and defense lawyers were worried that the "celebrity witnesses" would influence the jury and thus threaten the legal protection of the defendants, who were entitled to a fair trial.[15] The judge had received a number of letters and telegrams from France and abroad (including from Norway) demanding justice and punishment. He grumbled that people had tried to influence him and quickly made it clear that the trial was not to be used as a platform for a general discussion about rape. Its purpose was to determine whether the three defendants had actually committed rape, and the judge warned that he would not tolerate any "useless digression"[16]—a refusal that he reinforced as soon as the "solidarity witnesses" began to speak in general terms about rape as a societal problem. Shocked at having been dismissed from the witness box, the celebrities held a spontaneous press conference during which they raged against having been dismissed by the "rude" judge.[17]

Several violent incidents took place inside and outside the courthouse during the trial. Friends of the defendants physically attacked women from *Choisir*, the association headed by Gisèle Halimi, the assistant attorney for Anne and Araceli. They were pushed, scolded, and spat on, and a female journalist was slapped. Halimi was constantly threatened with death and, at some point, was punched in the face. Only then did the police intervene. The whole scene was recorded by TV cameras and broadcast on the evening news. Eventually, the drama surrounding the trial in Aix became

Armand Lanoux, and Françoise Mallet-Joris. Emmanuel was a former member of the council of the French-language *Académie Française* and famous for his poetry on resistance during the occupation. Lanoux was a former member of the *la Résistance*, a knight in the Legion of Honor, a recipient of the Cross of War, and a member of the *Haut Comité de la langue française* (High Committee of the French Language) and the literary organization Académie Goncourt. Also, the feminist author Mallet-Joris was a member of the Académie Goncourt. The two professors of medicine were gynecologist Pierre Vellay and neonatalist Alexandre Minkowski. Both were highly decorated heroes from *la Résistance*. Minkowski had also been tortured by the Gestapo during WW2.

[15] "Audition des témoins d'Anne et Araceli (suite)" ["Hearing of the Witnesses of Anne and Araceli (continued)"], *Viol. Le procès d'Aix*, p. 231.

[16] "Mardi 2 mai 1978" [Tuesday, 2 May 1978], *Viol. Le procès d'Aix*, pp. 41–42.

[17] Afterward, however, the solidarity witnesses' written testimonies were published in Choisir's book on the trial, *Viol. Le procès d'Aix*, p. 231.

an iconic narrative in the French women's liberation movement, highlighting how feminists were physically attacked by brutal men when they tried to protest against rape.[18] However, the defense attorneys were also badly treated. Every time they exited the courthouse, they were hissed at by protesters and rebuked as rapists. Prior to the trial, Anne and Araceli and their assistant attorneys had received a number of threatening letters, but the defense lawyers had also received hate mail addressed to "the three bastards defending the three rapists from Morgiou."[19] During the trial, hundreds of women outside the Palace of Justice shouted slogans against rape with such fervor that one could barely hear what was being said inside the court.

Rape—Or a Communication Problem Between Different Cultures?

The question of guilt that was to be settled in court was whether rape had taken place or whether the incident was merely an attempt at seduction that had gone wrong. Or, as the prosecutor expressed it:

> Was this summer night in Morgiou, as the young women say, a terrible drama and an ordeal for them, or was it, as the accused claim, a conspiracy that was subsequently hatched by a lesbian couple to take revenge on the three men who were responsible for the two women having betrayed one other, which they eventually regretted?[20]

The prosecutor believed that the three men were guilty of rape. The defense attorneys, on the other hand, demanded the acquittal of their clients on the grounds that the case was about a "misunderstood encounter" between two cultural worlds—between two "free" women from the north and three proletarian southern men.[21] The questions to be

---

[18] See, e.g., "Procès d'Aix contre le viol" [Trial in Aix against Rape], 8 mars info. http://8mars.info/proces-d-aix-et-attaques-antifeministes?lang=fr; "1978," elles cheminèrent, http://caminare.free.fr/1978.htm; "Le procès d'Anne et d'Aracelli [sic]," *Choisir*, no. 101, November 2007, p. 22. http://www.choisirlacausedesfemmes.org/uploads/documents/Choisir_N101_Retrospective.pdf.

[19] "Les plaidoires pour les Accusés" [The Pleas for the Accused], *Viol. Le procès d'Aix*, p. 373.

[20] "Le réquisitoire" [The Indictment], *Viol. Le procès d'Aix*, p. 357.

[21] "Les plaidoires pour les Accusés" [The Pleas for the Accused], *Viol. Le procès d'Aix*, p. 373.

answered in court were: Did the three men believe that the women's rejection, which included Anne's hitting one of them on the head with a hammer, was part of a "game"? Was it true that the women, as they claimed, had given up the fight because they were terrified? Did Anne and Araceli pretend to struggle against a trauma they had in fact fabricated? The question of what "consent" entails was central to the attorneys' arguments and was subject to very lengthy questioning directed at Anne and Araceli, who, naturally, felt they were being labeled as suspicious.

The defense attorneys' main argument for acquittal was that the incident was not rape; rather, it was simply a "communication problem" between two different "cultures" involving social class and region. The proletarian background of the three defendants and their witnesses stood in stark contrast to Anne and Araceli's list of "solidarity witnesses" who were drawn from the ranks of professors, politicians, and cultural elites. The defense's main argument was that the trial was a "clash of two worlds," between a "proletarian Mediterranean culture" and "the 16ième arrondissement" (that is, the wealthy district of Paris).[22] Although Anne and Araceli lived in Belgium and worked as a teacher and as a kindergarten assistant, respectively, the status of their celebrity witnesses seems to have worked against them. Halimi, their assistant attorney, pushed back against the class argument, insisting that rape has nothing to do with class conditions: "There is rape in all classes, within the same class, and between one class and another."[23] The defense attorneys argued that their clients were "coarse and rude" and "simple souls from Provence" who did not understand "subtleties or girls' psychology."[24] But their strategy of using the defendants' cultural background as an extenuating circumstance backfired, as the supporters of Anne and Araceli replied that rape was obviously accepted in the "male-chauvinist" Mediterranean culture.[25]

---

[22] Only one of the three defense attorneys, Petrilli's lawyer Michel Tubiana, allowed Choisir to publish his defense speech in the book on the trial. "La Défense a choisi... l'absence" [The Defense Chose ... Absence], *Viol. Le procès d'Aix*, p. 371.

[23] "Plaidoires des avocats d'Anne et d'Araceli (Maître Agnès Fichot et Maître Gisèle Halimi)" [Pleadings of Anne and Araceli's Lawyers (Master Agnes Fichot and Master Gisèle Halimi)], *Viol. Le procès d'Aix*, p. 336.

[24] "Les plaidoires pour les accusés" [The Pleas for the Accused], *Viol. Le procès d'Aix*, p. 387.

[25] *Le Monde*, 4 May 1978, p. 9; *Le Figaro*, 5 May 1978, p. 5; *L'Humanité*, 3 May 1978, p. 12.

The Three Defendants and Their Credibility

Guy Roger, Albert Mouglalis, and Serge Petrilli, the three defendants, appeared to be ordinary working-class young men. At the time of the rape, they were 29, 24, and 22 years old, respectively. The three helped a local fisherman in Morgiou, who, at the trial, testified that they were hardworking, splendid chaps. All were in relationships with women, and none of them had been previously convicted or had serious psychological problems. The seven witnesses for the defendants included relatives and former colleagues, all of whom testified that they were "brave boys" and that it was impossible that they had done the things they were charged with.[26]

Serge Petrilli, who, unlike the two others, was not from Marseille, but from the suburbs of Paris, was essentially unemployed at the time of the rape. He was doing unauthorized fishing in Morgiou, dwelled in a cabin with friends, and lived a "bohemian life." According to the testimony of an expert psychiatrist, he was a "braggart" and a "rude."[27] Despite the fact that Petrilli was considered sane, the psychiatrist found that he was in fact mentally unstable and quick-tempered, with a tendency to act in a violent manner. His entire family was "overexcited," according to the psychiatrist. (To some extent this was confirmed during the trial, when Petrilli's Italian father was twice ejected from the courtroom because he was crying, screaming, and sobbing.) The psychiatrist concluded that Petrilli lacked emotional control, but that the other two had nothing in particular wrong with them.[28]

All three defendants claimed to have been surprised to be charged with rape. They had just tried to hook up with the girls, they said, and when Guy Roger "insisted a little," Anne gave him a blow to the head with the hammer. The fact that he punched her in the face was just a reflex. When he returned to the tent after washing the blood from his head, he said that the girls had changed and were now "in the game."[29] The three defendants were united in their claim that they had been reported because the girls—both lesbians—had conspired to take revenge.[30]

[26] "Témoins des accusés" [Witnesses for the Accused], *Viol. Le procès d'Aix*, pp. 77–90.

[27] Serge Petrilli, *Viol. Le procès d'Aix*, pp. 57–68.

[28] Guy Roger, *Viol. Le procès d'Aix*, p. 75.

[29] Op. cit., pp. 69–75.

[30] Serge Petrilli, *Viol. Le procès d'Aix*, p. 198.

Fig. 4.1 Caricature of the three rapists in Morgiou, saying: "It's a misunderstanding… we thought… they were consenting." Facsimile from *Femmes travailleuses en lutte*, no. 7, 1975 (*Source* Drawing by unknown artist)

The credibility of the three defendants was weakened by the fact that they had changed their explanations since the initial police interrogations and the preliminary judicial investigation to the point where their stories were now identical.[31] In the initial interrogations, Roger and Mouglalis had admitted that the purpose of "hooking up" was to carry out a "punitive expedition" to "scare" the girls who had rudely rejected Petrilli. They had also admitted to having sexually assaulted the girls to make them "pay" for the hammer blow to the head that Roger had received. But four years later, they claimed it had actually been a pleasant night. Another factor that damaged their credibility was that Petrilli had initially denied any knowledge of the case and had even concocted a false alibi. He had admitted the sexual contact only after his comrades had confessed to the police[32] (Fig. 4.1).

The Question of "Consent"

The defense claimed that there was no evidence that Anne and Araceli had resisted the sexual contact, and that they had behaved in a way that led the three men to believe that they actually consented. Moreover, the defense

---

[31] Interrogation of Albert Mouglalis, Guy Roger, and Serge Petrilli, *Viol. Le procès d'Aix*, pp. 175–200.

[32] Ibid.

argued that Anne and Araceli probably simulated the trauma or, alternatively, that the idea of possible trauma might have been reinforced by all the attention given to the case.[33] This argument was rejected by Anne and Araceli's doctor, who said that, on the contrary, the attention had served as reassurance and encouragement, and that as a result the women felt understood and not alone.[34] According to Araceli, the support of the women's liberation movement had served as a kind of therapy and had helped them tremendously.

The issue of trauma and consent was the focus of intense questioning of the women.[35] Anne and Araceli repeatedly stated that the reason they had not resisted more forcefully was that they were in shock and terrified because the men threatened to cut their throats, cut them up in pieces, and throw them into the sea. The prosecutors' witnesses, including the gendarme who had received the initial report the morning after the fatal night, confirmed that the two had been in shock and were having difficulty speaking and expressing themselves.[36] The doctor who had examined them assured the courtroom that the women had been beaten with fists and eventually struggled with depression, lack of appetite, and nightmares.[37]

In court, assistant attorney Halimi emphasized that to give in when one is terrified and exhausted is not the same as "consent."[38] Several of Anne and Araceli's witnesses, including those who had experienced torture at the hands of the Gestapo during World War II, drew parallels between rape and torture, and in her closing argument, Halimi rhetorically asked: "Who would say that a person who breaks down after torture is consenting?" When "heroes spoke after torture," did it mean that they

---

[33] "Témoins de l'accusation" [Witnesses for the Prosecution], *Viol. Le procès d'Aix*, pp. 111–113.

[34] "Les témoins d'Anne et d'Araceli (suite)" [The Witnesses of Anne and Araceli (continued)], *Viol. Le procès d'Aix*, p. 265.

[35] The transcripts of the explanations show that the interrogation of Anne and Araceli totaled 53 pages, while the interrogation of the three defendants totaled 23 pages. *Viol. Le procès d'Aix*, pp. 119–200.

[36] "Témoins de l'accusation" [Witnesses for the Prosecution], *Viol. Le procès d'Aix*, pp. 91–93.

[37] Op. cit., p. 108.

[38] Araceli Castellano, *Viol. Le procès d'Aix*, p. 171.

"consented" to the tactics of the executioners?[39] The framing of rape as torture was gender neutral and involved a humanitarian principle of not accepting the violation of human dignity. However, the gender-specificity of rape was highlighted by Halimi and several prosecution witnesses who emphasized that rape means the destruction of woman's identity: women are raped because they are women, just as fascists deny and want to subjugate others because they are Jews or Arabs, Halimi asserted.[40] Anne and Araceli's witnesses all described rape as a crime against women, but not necessarily based on a feminist analysis of patriarchy. Several of them emphasized humanist values, and some of the conservative witnesses pointed out that combating rape was about defending the family and the love between man and woman. Feminists such as *Libération* journalist Martine Storti lamented the "humanistic and moralistic" way in which some of the witnesses had described rape.[41] She shared the opinion of many other French feminists in criticizing the goal of a broad campaign against rape: the mobilization had to be based on correct political analyses about rape as connected to patriarchal society.

The Verdict

In his ruling, the prosecutor sentenced Petrilli to a minimum of seven years in prison and the other two defendants to six years for gang rape. He was convinced that Anne and Araceli had been raped and that they had abandoned their resistance in order to satisfy the men so that they would leave. The fact that they had immediately reported the rape indicated their honesty and sincerity, he argued in court. By contrast, Petrilli had lied four times, admitting the sexual contact only after his alibi was debunked and his friends had confessed to the charges. The prosecutor held that Petrilli's motive for raping the two women was revenge, because they had rejected him and thus wounded his male pride.[42]

The indictment shows that the MLF's analysis of rape had, to a certain degree, gained acceptance in broader circles. The prosecutor stressed that

---

[39] "Plaidoires des avocats d'Anne et d'Araceli (Maître Agnès Fichot et Maître Gisèle Halimi)" [Pleadings of Anne and Araceli's Lawyers (Master Agnes Fichot and Master Gisèle Halimi)], *Viol. Le procès d'Aix*, p. 330.

[40] Op. cit., p. 335.

[41] *Libération*, 5 May 1978, p. 5.

[42] "Le réquisitoire" [The Indictment], *Viol. Le procès d'Aix*, p. 359.

it was necessary to confront men's attitudes, "which today are called phallocratic," and said that he supported "the movement in support of victims of sexual abuse."[43] Thanks to the latter, the prosecutor maintained, rape victims were now less afraid to report rape, and he emphasized that this coincided with the principles of the judiciary: those who are guilty of rape are "abominable villains, criminals, in the same way as those who assault or kill with rogue purposes."[44] But the fact that the prosecutor endorsed the efforts of the women's liberation movement was not well received by many feminists, as we shall soon see.

The jury was not entirely convinced by the prosecutor's argument. The three defendants were not found guilty of gang rape. Only Petrilli was convicted of rape, while Roger and Mouglalis were convicted of attempted rape. The sentences handed down were six and four years in prison, respectively.[45]

Mixed Reactions to the Verdict

There was no great rejoicing in the MLF over the verdict in the Morgiou case. Some feminists were disappointed that the men were not convicted of gang rape; others thought the sentence too severe.[46] In contrast, the conservative newspaper Le Figaro described the trial as the start of a "new era" and "a small step toward a new consciousness."[47] Anne and Araceli's distinguished witnesses, including conservative politicians, revered professors, and award-winning authors, certainly helped to make Le Figaro lend its support to the campaign against rape. But the leftist newspaper Libération was deeply disappointed by the verdict. In an interview, Petrilli's defense lawyer, Michel Tubiana, said that this was a victory not for the cause of women, but for the desire for punishment and suppression.[48] The trial had served as a "judicial exorcism" in which the cultural conflict that, in his view, was the basis of the rape, was made into a "gigantic purification of society." According to the lawyer, what "touches upon the

---

[43] Op. cit., p. 352.

[44] Op. cit., p. 355.

[45] "Le verdict" [The Verdict], Viol. Le procès d'Aix, pp. 391–392.

[46] L'Humanité, 5 May 1978.

[47] Le Figaro, 5 May 1978, p. 5; Le Figaro, 6 May 1978, p. 7.

[48] Libération, 5 May 1978, p. 5.

mysterious continent of sexuality" should not be punished in the Assize Court, and the security of women will not be improved by dramatizing lawsuits and initiating legal campaigns. In *Libération*, the prevailing attitude was now that the women's struggle had fallen into a trap by invoking the legal system.

A few days after the verdict in Aix-en-Provence, opposition to using the legal system in rape cases was expressed in a very noticeable and dramatic way. A "commando group" consisting of eight women who called themselves "*Les bombeuses à chapeau*"[49] attacked Psych et Po's bookstore in Paris. Masked and armed with razor blades and iron bars, they looted the store, overturned bookshelves, threw plants on the floor, spray-painted walls and books, cut the telephone line, and threw tear gas cannisters. Outside, a group of men stood waiting and ensured that no one tracked them down.[50] A statement on behalf of the commando group, published in *Libération*, declared that the rape case in Aix was the reason for the attack on the bookstore. In "a grotesque way," the feminists had not wanted to give in on the rape case: "We accuse them of inconsistency for invoking (…) a rotten justice system that they themselves do not acknowledge [and of] a morbid thoughtlessness for all the years of prison time that they have given the men."[51] The group stated that it would fight along with men against the state, the capital, the "cops," and the "gauchistes" (i.e., the organized political left).

The commando group threatened more violence. A week later, Psych et Po's bookstore was hit by shotgun fire during the night. A statement in *Libération* declared that the shooting was a reaction to the campaign of lies that followed the previous action. The group had not used razor blades, the statement ironically declared.[52] The identity of "*Les bombeuses à chapeau*" is uncertain, but they were probably connected to

---

[49] Lisa Greenwald suggests a rough translation would be "The Classy Taggers." Greenwald, Lisa (2019): *Daughters of 1968: Redefining French Feminism and the Women's Liberation Movement*. Lincoln, NE: University of Nebraska Press, p. 221.

[50] *Libération*, 13–15 May 1978, p. 5.

[51] Ibid.

[52] *Libération*, 19 May 1978, p. 6.

the "autonomous" group that, at this time, had begun to make themselves known: for instance, by initiating violent street riots on May 1, 1978.[53]

All of the different MLF factions distanced themselves from the commando group's attacks on Psych et Po's bookstore.[54] But the feeling that the campaign against rape was a dead end spread among feminist advocates who had been active in the mobilization. The paradox of why many people on the left found it more difficult to make use of the legal system in rape cases than in other cases—for example, against racist violence—will be further discussed later in this chapter.

A New Rape Law

Around the time of the trial in Aix in May 1978, a number of draft bills on a new rape law were submitted to the Senate. The first bill to "protect women against rape" was submitted on April 20, 1978, by the independent senator Brigitte Gros, who belonged to the left-wing majority.[55] In her draft bill to the Senate, Gros proposed to establish a "Central Office for the Protection of the Woman" under the Ministry of Internal Affairs, which, on a national level, could initiate and coordinate research on and punishment for the abuse of women. In addition, she proposed the establishment of rape victim reception centers and suggested that every police district employ a female police officer to deal with rape cases. Gros' proposal also suggested that the deliberation and disposition of rape cases should last no longer than three months, and that the names of rapists should be published in newspapers and in places reserved for public announcements.

A month after the trial in Aix-en-Provence, more bills were submitted to the Senate. All of them highlighted the change in attitude toward rape

---

[53] *Le Monde*, 3 May 1978, p. 40. The pillage of Psych et Po's bookstore is featured in the Wikipedia article on the autonomous movement in France. "Mouvement autonome en France" [The Autonomous Movement in France], https://fr.wikipedia.org/wiki/Mouvement_ autonome_en_France. Consulted 6 November 2019.

[54] Feminists who—despite the conflicts with Psych et Po—strongly distanced themselves from the attack on their bookstore pointed out the irony that "Les bombeuses à chapeau" who had mistaken their target as Psych et Po was the only group in the MLF that *did not* label themselves feminists. *Libération*, 16 May 1978, p. 5.

[55] Mossuz-Lavau 1991, p. 217.

that had recently taken place, noting that the law had to be adjusted to reflect public opinion. In the various draft bills, rape was defined as a societal problem that had to be combated because it was incompatible with the ideals of freedom and gender equality and, as a felony, had to be dealt with in the Assize Court.[56] The bill submitted by the Socialist Party's group in the Senate proposed a new definition of rape: "Any sexual act committed against the will of a woman or a man, whether the lack of consent is due to physical violence or other forms of coercion or surprise, constitutes the felony of rape."[57] This definition of rape was much broader than that of rape as forced vaginal penetration of a woman who was not the wife of the perpetrator. The Socialist Party also proposed reducing the penalty for rape from a prison sentence of 10–20 years to one of 5–10 years, and to ensure that there were female magistrates and police officers to receive the reports. It would no longer be necessary for the rape victims to make complaints; instead, all organizations whose purpose was to defend women's rights could act as plaintiffs. Also, it was stated that in rape trials, it was up to the victims to decide whether or not to hear the case behind closed doors. Moreover, the Socialist Party's bill proposed the introduction of sex education in schools that would include information about the rights of victims of sexual violence.

Following a late-night debate in the Senate on June 27–28, 1978, the Socialist Party's bill was unanimously adopted with some changes. In the French bicameral system, it often takes some time to adopt laws, and it was almost two years before the National Assembly dealt with the new rape law on April 11, 1980.[58] After reaching a compromise, the law was unanimously adopted, and the decision was confirmed by the National Assembly on November 19, 1980. The new law defined rape as follows: "Any act of sexual penetration, of any nature whatsoever,

[56]Vigarello 1998, p. 251.

[57] "Toute relation sexuelle obtenue contre la volonté d'une femme ou d'un homme, soit que le défaut de consentement résulte de violences physiques soit qu'il résulte de tout autre moyen de contrainte ou de surprise, constitue le crime de viol." Mossuz-Lavau 1991, p. 217.

[58]Three different bills were discussed in the National Assembly in 1980. Two of the bills were presented by the two former "solidarity witnesses" for Anne and Araceli in the Aix trial in 1978: the Gaullist Florence d'Harcourt and the Communist Party's Gisèle Moreau. The third bill was presented by François Mitterrand of the Socialist Party. The bills were largely identical to those that had been submitted to the Senate two years earlier.

committed on the person by another, by violence, coercion or surprise, constitutes rape."[59] This definition was narrower than that of the Senate, as it restricted rape to penetration. Other types of sexual abuse continued to be defined as "indecent assault" (*attentat à la pudeur*). However, the new law recognized that both men and women could be victims of rape, and that rape could occur within marriage.

The Senate had voted for lowering the penalty for rape, but because of the conservative majority in the National Assembly in 1980, the penalty remained as before. Rape was to be punished by a 10–20 year prison sentence, including possible preventive detention in light of aggravating circumstances—for example, if the victim was under the age of 15, or the rapist was an authority figure, or if the rape was particularly violent.[60] Both conservatives and leftists agreed that rape should be treated as a felony against a woman's dignity, against her person, and no longer against "the honor of the family."[61] Their main political difference involved the sentencing: conservatives lobbied for higher penalties, while the left wanted to lower them. There were also political differences as to how to explain rape. Several right-wing parliamentarians argued that the cause of rape was the destruction of traditional society and the concurrent weakening of institutions such as the family and the Church.[62] In other words, rape was explained as a new phenomenon that had not existed in the traditional farming community, and was the result of moral decay. The position of the socialists and communists was starkly different, as they argued that rape was a holdover from ancient times, when women were considered the property of men. The way to put an end to rape was therefore to modernize society, to advance women's liberation and equality, and—for the communists—to create a classless society. The communists also emphasized how the porn industry facilitated rape.

---

[59] In original: "Tout acte de pénétration sexuelle, de quelque nature qu'il soit, commis sur la personne d'autrui, par la violence, contrainte ou surprise, constitue un viol." Vigarello 1998, p. 255.

[60] Op. cit., pp. 224–225.

[61] Mossuz-Lavau 1991, p. 221.

[62] Op. cit., pp. 221–222.

Little Enthusiasm for the New Rape Law

Within the women's liberation movement, there was relative silence about the new rape law in 1980. Little commentary is found in the feminist publications, and it appears that no demonstrations took place. The lack of political mobilization may have been related to the fact that the parliamentary debate on April 11 took place during the Easter holidays. (At least that was the explanation given by the feminist newspaper of the Trotskyist party LCR, *Cahiers du féminisme*, as to why there had been no mobilization for any demonstration.[63]) Another reason why there is not much information about the new rape law to be found in the feminist publications is that most of them had ceased to exist by that time. In France, the general decline of the 1970s women's movement was reinforced by the by the fact that in 1979 Psych et Po had patented the name "women's liberation movement" and the abbreviation MLF as a trademark and as an association (see Chapter 1). In 1980, other groups were no longer allowed to say that they belonged to the MLF, a restriction that paralyzed the movement and the activists.

Cahiers du féminisme expressed little enthusiasm for the new rape law. The publication criticized it for not being feminist enough and regarded it a tool to ensure respect for law and order. The newspaper recognized the new definition of rape as a form of progress, but interpreted the primary aim of the modernized law as a means to "restore the state's authority" over women. According to *Cahiers du féminisme*, this was a general feature of all laws that are indirect products of collective mobilization:

> In a deformed way, the new rape law takes up some of the demands that were forwarded in the struggles. But as all laws that have been drafted and adopted within the framework of bourgeois institutions, it is designed to restore and engender new respect for peace and order and bourgeois morality.[64]

Cahiers du féminisme did not believe that the law would change anything for women or that it would result in fewer rapes. To bring about change, collective women's mobilization was needed, similar to that which started

---

[63] Claire Bataille: "Viol: une loi nouvelle pour assurer leur ordre" [Rape: A New Law to Ensure Their Order], *Cahiers du féminisme*, no. 14, 1980, pp. 14–17.

[64] Op. cit., p. 15.

with Anne and Araceli's "courageous decision." According to the Trot-skyist feminists, it was the collective mobilization of women that had helped to change attitudes, not the politicians.

Such a grass roots mobilization against rape was less present in 1980 than it had been in the 1970s. The decline was general for most protest movements rooted in the 1968 revolt, but the French MLF was in a particular state of crisis due to Psych et Po's extraordinary patenting. Adding to the decline in the mobilization against rape was the fact that many feminists struggled with guilt because of the severe punishments handed down in rape cases, i.e., up to 20 years' imprisonment. At the same time, there was indeed grass roots activism taking place, though it was less visible than street demonstrations and newspaper debates. In 1977, for example, the *Collectif femmes contre le viol* (Women's Community against Rape) was established by feminists engaged in solidarity work with and for raped women.[65] Here, women victims of rape could meet someone to talk to and to get legal and medical assistance. In several French cities, such crisis shelters were formed, inspired by solidarity with the victims, and run by volunteers.

The lack of grass roots activism against rape in 1980 can also be seen as a result of the success of the campaign in getting broad acceptance for its views. It had simply become commonplace to take a stand against rape, and the feminist framing of rape as a serious societal problem had "won over" French public opinion.

THE JOINT ACTION AGAINST PORNOGRAPHY AND PROSTITUTION

In Norway, the feminist anti-pornography campaign evolved into a broad popular movement. By the mid-1980s, the Joint Action against Pornography and Prostitution included almost 40 organizations repre-senting almost half a million people, ranging from the Norwegian Agrarian Women's Association (*Norges bondekvinnelag*) to Lesbian Activists, and included Christian groups, feminist self-defense groups, labor unions, and social democratic and liberal youth organizations. The

---

[65] "Femmes contre le viol, solidarité" [Women against Rape, Solidarity], *Le Temps des femmes*, no. 2, 1978, p. 18.

broad alliance of the movement had historical parallels with the mobilization against Norwegian membership in the European Communities (EC, predecessor of the EU) in 1972. As in the anti-EC struggle, urban leftist radicals formed an alliance with rural people's movements at the periphery of Norway in a united struggle against a common enemy, despite their ideological and political disagreement on other issues.[66]

Fight Against Prostitution

In 1981, the Women's Joint Action against Pornography, which had been formed in 1977, broadened its scope and took the name the Joint Action against Pornography and Prostitution. That year, the much-discussed report "Prostitution in Oslo" was published, based on the work that the so-called Oslo Project had been engaged in since 1979.[67] The Oslo Project combined research on prostitution with measures of assistance to underage prostitutes. The three employees, among them Liv Finstad, the former activist of the New Feminists (who by 1981 was a member of the Women's Front), combined research, social work, and political activism to fight prostitution. The Oslo Project cooperated with the Joint Action, which adopted the former's policy recommendations. In the report "Prostitution in Oslo," which detailed the experiences after the Oslo Project was completed in 1981, the connection between pornography and prostitution was highlighted. It was pointed out that pornography helped to promote prostitution, which the authors defined as violence

[66] Furre 1991, pp. 344–347.

[67] Finstad, Liv, Lita Fougner, and Vivi-Lill Holter (1981): "Oslo-prosjektet. Erfaringer fra to års forsøksarbeid blant barne- og ungdomsprostituerte i Oslo 1979–1981" [The Oslo Project. Experiences from Two Years of Experiental Work among Child and Youth Prostitutes in Oslo 1979–1981]. Barnevernskontoret i Oslo [Oslo Child Protection Office], 28 September 1981. See also Finstad, Liv, Lita Fougner, and Vivi-Lill Holter (1982): *Prostitusjon i Oslo* [Prostitution in Oslo]. Oslo: Pax Forlag. After the publication of this book, Liv Finstad and Cecilie Høigård received funding from the Norwegian Research Council to do further research on the prostitution scene in Oslo. Their research produced the groundbreaking book *Bakgater: Om prostitusjon, penger og kjærlighet* [Backstreets. Prostitution, Money, and Love], published by Pax Forlag in 1986 and later translated into several languages, including English (Pennsylvania State University Press, 1992). Prior to this research-based book, Finstad and Høigård had helped edit the autobiography of the young woman Ida Halvorsen (a pseudonym), *Hard asfalt* [Hard Asphalt] (Pax Forlag, 1982). This was the first autobiography about prostitution and the drug scene in Norway; it was made into a film in 1986. Interview with Liv Finstad 11 June 2010.

against women. Liv Finstad from the project team declared to the journal of the Women's Front that the fight against prostitution needed to become a primary focus of the women's liberation movement.[68]

In the spring of 1981, women activists carried out the first of several spectacular actions targeting sex purchasers. The participants would walk in pairs as "prostitutes" in Oslo's "red-light district." When a customer stopped his car, one of the women would negotiate the transaction. When it was confirmed that the driver indeed wanted to buy sex, she would give a sign to the other, who then painted "Whore Customer" (*horekunde*, a new Norwegian word for "John") on his car using a template and a spray box. The action aroused tremendous attention. The newspaper *Klassekampen*, whose photographer was involved in the action by capturing what was going on, used the sensational front-page headline "Whore Customers Hunted in Oslo" (Fig. 4.2). The activists said that their intention was to scare men from buying sexual services.[69] These actions targeted at Johns were controversial but helped to focus attention on the sex buyers, a group that until then had received little scrutiny. In addition, they triggered a public debate on criminalizing the purchase of sex.[70] As the Joint Action against Pornography expanded to include the fight against prostitution, its list of demands (as detailed in the previous

---

[68] "Prostitusjon et samfunnsproblem—ikke en privatsak" [Prostitution Is a Societal Problem—Not a Private Matter], *Kvinnefront*, no. 4, 1980, p. 16.

[69] *Klassekampen*, 11 April 1981, p. 1. See also *Aftenposten* (evening edition), 11 April 1981, p. 2. In an interview with the journal of the Women's Front, the activists of the Action Group against Porn and Prostitution [*Aksjonsgruppa mot porno og prostitusjon*] said that their motivation for the actions against the Johns was frustration over "too much talk and too little action" in the women's movement. In addition to scaring the Johns, the actions were intended to raise awareness, and they said that one had to "be a little drastic to be heard." They argued that their best weapon was that they possessed the element of surprise. Sigrun Johnstad: "Horekunden kan være hvem som helst" [The John May Be Anyone], *Kvinnejournalen*, no. 1, 1983, p. 15.

[70] For more details on the activism against Johns, see Korsvik 2013, pp. 474–478 and Korsvik 2014, pp. 11–43. In interviews, former activists of the Action Group against Porn and Prostitution tell about how several of them had participated in porn burnings and thus had gained experience from audacious and carefully planned forms of action. The Action Group Against Porn and Prostitution consisted of a dedicated core of activists who acted anonymously and with strict safety instructions and thorough planning. Some of them were members of the Women's Front and/or AKP (m-l); others had no organizational affiliation. Most of them were young, and a few of the most active in the beginning were young girls under the care of child welfare. Interview with Vigdis Vollset, 1 April 2009, and with "Anne" and "Kari," 9 June 2009.

Horekunder

jages i Oslo

HOREKUNDE sto det malt på flere biler som kjørte hjem fra kjøttmarkedet i Oslo sentrum torsdag kveld. Nå skal ingen som kjøper tjenester fra prostituerte føle seg trygge lenger. Aksjonsgruppa mot porno og prostitusjon gjennomførte en vellykka aksjon i sentrum.

De vil gjennomføre nye aksjoner mot kundene der de minst venter det, og når de minst venter det.

MIDTSIDENE

Fig. 4.2   Facsimile from *Klassekampen* April 11, 1981, front-page headlined "Whore customers hunted in Oslo." The ingress reads: "WHORE CUSTOMER was painted on several cars that drove home from the meat market in downtown Oslo on Thursday evening. From now on, nobody who buys services from prostitutes can feel safe anymore. The Action Group against Porn and Prostitution carried out a successful action downtown. They will take new actions against the customers where they least expect it, and when they least expect it" (Photo: Ola Sæther © *Klassekampen* [Reprinted with permission])

chapter), was supplemented by claims for banning the purchase of sexual services, enforcing the ban on pimping, improving measures of support for prostitutes, as well as calling for more research on the prostitution scene.[71] The Joint Action also demanded an end to "sex tourism" to countries like Thailand and the Philippines, an activity that was promoted in articles and advertisements in porn magazines, including Leif Hagen's *Aktuell Rapport*, which even attempted to act as a tour operator for "sex tourists."[72]

A Broad Popular Movement

When the Women's Joint Action against Pornography was initiated in 1977, liberals and feminists had been skeptical about the alliance between conservative Christian women and militant Marxist-Leninists. However, only a few years later, the Joint Action against Pornography and Prostitution became a popular movement that involved hundreds of activists who, though spanning different political, social, and geographical affiliations, managed to come together to promote a common cause. The Women's Front succeeded in making its framing of pornography as "sales of women" as hegemonic in the Joint Action, because it was the best-prepared and most well-organized in the decisive start-up phase when the political basis for the action was formulated. The Women's Front saw in the Joint Action the potential for a broad women's revolution, and in 1981 its member Unni Rustad became leader of the action. Rustad was far more militant and was thus profiled more extensively than her rather conservative predecessor from the Norwegian National Women's Council (*Norske Kvinners Nasjonalråd*). The Joint Action was based on voluntary grass roots activities that, for the most part, took place in local communities. The broad cooperation required political compromises. Younger radical women put forward the political agenda, and older and more conservatively minded women agreed to claims that were most likely distant from them in the first place, including "Yes to Sexual Education" and "No to Porn's Use of Lesbians and Other Minorities."

---

[71] Published in Rustad 2010.

[72] "Sexreiser til Thailand. Intervju med en av deltakerne" [Sex Tours to Thailand. Interview with One of the Participants]. Ukeslutt, radio program, the Norwegian Broadcasting Corporation, 2 December 1977.

Membership Organizations in the Joint Action Against Pornography and Prostitution After 1983[73]

1. Center Women (*Senterkvinnene*)
2. Center Youth (*Senterungdommen*)
3. Christian Democratic Party (*Kristelig Folkeparti, KrF*)
4. Christian Democratic Party's Women's Association (*Kristelig Folkepartis Kvinner*)
5. Christian Feminist Forum (*Kristent Kvinnesaksforum*)
6. Ergon
7. Inner Mission Society's Department of Children and Youth (*Barne- og ungdomsavdelingen i Indremisjonsselskapet*)
8. Legal Aid for Women (*Juridisk rådgivning for kvinner*; JURK)
9. Lesbian Activists (*Lesbiske Aktivister*)
10. Liberal Party's Women's Association (*Norges Venstrekvinnelag*)
11. Liberal People's Party's Youth (*Det Liberale Folkepartis Ungdom*)
12. Liberal People's Party (*Det Liberale Folkepartiet*, DLF)
13. Menfolk against Porn (*Mannfolk mot porno*)
14. Methodist Church Youth Federation (*Metodistkirkens Ungdomsforbund*)
15. National Union of Norwegian Nursing Students (*Landslaget for Norske Sykepleierstudenter*)
16. National Union of Norwegian Teaching Students (*Landslaget for Norske Lærarstudentar*)
17. New Feminists (*Nyfeministene*)
18. Norwegian Agrarian Women's Association (*Norges Bondekvinnelag*)
19. Norwegian Association for Women's Rights (*Norsk kvinnesaks- forening, NKF*)
20. Norwegian Catholic Layman Council (*Norsk Katolsk Legmannsråd*)
21. Norwegian Christian Youth Association (*Norges Kristelige Ungdomsforbund* [including the YMCA and YWCA])
22. Norwegian Communist Student's Union (*Norges Kommunistiske Studentforbund, NKS*)
23. Norwegian Conservative Party's Women's Association (*Høyrekvinnenes Landsforbund*)
24. Norwegian Housewives' Association (*Norges Husmorforbund*)
25. Norwegian National Women's Council (*Norske Kvinners Nasjon- alråd, NKN*)
26. Norwegian Rural Youth (*Norges Bygdeungdomslag*)
27. Norwegian Teachers' Union (*Norsk Lærerlag*)
28. Red Youth (*Rød Ungdom, RU*)[74]

29. Socialist Left Party (*Sosialistisk Venstreparti, SV*)
30. Socialist Youth (*Sosialistisk Ungdom, SU*)
31. Students against Porn (*Studenter mot porno*)[75]
32. Woman's Christian Temperance Union (WCTU) / The White Ribbon (*Hvite Bånd*)
33. Women in Struggle (*Kvinner i kamp* [feminist self-defense])
34. Women's Front (*Kvinnefronten*)
35. Worker's Communist Party (Marxist-Leninists) (*AKP (m-l)*)
36. Workers' Youth League (*Arbeidernes ungdomsfylking, AUF* [the youth organization of the Labor Party])
37. Young Christian Democrats (*Kristelig Folkepartis Ungdom, KrFU*)
38. Young Liberals of Norway (*Unge Venstre*)

As of 1977, neither the New Feminists nor the Norwegian Association for Women's Rights had wanted to take part in the Joint Action. But in the early 1980s they teamed up with other organizations that had previously been skeptical about cooperating with "puritans" in the Worker's Communist Party (Marxist-Leninists), the AKP (m-l), and Christians, as the Socialist Left Party SV.[76] Several factors made the cooperation easier. First, by the early 1980s, the political climate on the left had become less conflict-ridden, thanks to the decline of the Marxist-Leninist movement, and the adoption of abortion on demand in 1978 had diminished the fear of Christians' political influence. Also of significance were changes in the women's liberation movement, which by the early 1980s had become more oriented toward working on concrete matters and less concerned with "honing the ideological differences," as Runa Haukaa formulated it.[77] The shift from believing in revolutionary utopias toward a more

---

[73] It is not clear exactly when each of these organizations joined. The list of organizations in the archives of the Joint Action is not dated, but is probably from ca. 1985. Rustad (2010) mentions the same organizations.

[74] In 1983, the male members of the RU collectively joined Men against Porn. FA D-0001 Administrative Archive 1981–1985, ABA.

[75] Students against Porn was initiated by the Women's Front chapter at the University of Oslo. *Klassekampen*, 19 October 1983, p. 17.

[76] The Norwegian Association for Women's Rights joined in 1983. Lønnå 1996, pp. 277–278.

[77] Haukaa 1982, p. 144.

utility-oriented pragmatism was characteristic of the entire political left in the early 1980s. The fact that more organizations joined the Joint Action and that new anti-porn groups such as Menfolk against Porn and Students against Porn were established, also reflected the change in public opinion and the more favorable debate climate for the anti-porn activists. Many people were particularly upset by pornography that featured violence, children, and animals. The sweeping police confiscations of pornography in Leif Hagen's shops and warehouse in 1979 helped to stamp the porn industry as a criminal enterprise. As the police and judicial authorities began to intervene more actively against porn dealers, many law-abiding citizens found it more legitimate to oppose pornography than when activists "took the law into their own hands" and burned pornography in public. An additional factor was the 1979 law prohibiting sex-discriminatory advertising, which likely sensitized more people to take a stand against the portrayal of women as "sex objects," as was typical of the so-called men's magazines. Finally, the activism of the Joint Action was widely seen to be more respectable than that of the porn-burning militants.

The style of the Joint Action was grass roots oriented and community based, but from 1981 onward, the group entered into stronger alliances with the political elite. That year saw the election of a new Minister of Justice, Mona Røkke, a feminist of the Conservative Party, who engaged more actively against pornography than had her predecessors from the Labor Party. Røkke was responsive to the demands of the Joint Action and invited its members to meetings. In addition, she granted the police the authority to close down porn shops following raids to prevent the porn dealers from re-stocking the shelves the next day.[78] Beginning in 1983, several political parties joined the Joint Action; eventually, only the far-right Progress Party (*Fremskrittspartiet, FrP*) and the Soviet-loyal Communist Party of Norway (*Norges Kommunistiske Parti, NKP*) were not in some way affiliated with the Joint Action, either with the entire party organization, its women's section, or the youth party organization (see fact box).

Of course, any decision among the various organizations to affiliate with the Joint Action did not take place without discussion. For example, in the Socialist Left Party SV, which, as mentioned, had refused to join the

[78] Minutes from a meeting with the member organizations, 25 November 1981, FA D-0001 Administrative Archive 1981–1985, ABA.

campaign in 1977, the question was highly controversial. In the SV, the principal advocates for the party's increased involvement in the anti-porn struggle were female politicians active in the party's Women's Committee, including its leader, Kirsti Nøst, as well as Tora Houg and the MP Kjell-bjørg Lunde. These three women had drafted a recommendation for the SV to vote to work collectively with the Joint Action in order to unite against pornography, "a mass industry that promotes a humiliating view of women and men."[79] In the SV, however, hostility toward the Joint Action persisted. When the National Board of the party met on October 1–2, 1983, to deal with the issue of affiliating with the Joint Action, 15 voted yes and a substantial minority of 9 voted no.[80] The most outspoken opponent of the SV affiliating with the Joint Action was the party veteran Finn Gustavsen, formerly MP and leader of the party, and at the time a member of the SV's main board and a contributor to the party newspaper *Ny Tid*. He argued that the anti-porn struggle was foolish and that porno-graphy was not a problem: "Swedish comrades yawn if you raise the porn question. Danish comrades get debris in the eye. Norwegian comrades let it overshadow the atomic bomb," he wrote in *Ny Tid*.[81] According to Gustavsen, the Joint Action consisted of Marxist-Leninists, housewives, and Christian puritans, all of whom he found it inappropriate to cooperate with. He believed that the Worker's Communist Party (Marxist-Leninists) was spearheading all of it: "Its specific new-moralism—with its effect of contagion on the entire left—coincides with the dark pietism of the Chris-tian Democratic Party and a lesbian ideology that characterizes parts of a largely reduced women's liberation movement," he commented after SV's national board's decision to partake in the Joint Action.[82] It was evident that the "new moralism" had "contaminated" several of Gustavsen's party comrades—for example, city council member Per Eggum Mauseth, who,

---

[79] *Klassekampen*, 5 October 1983, p. 9.

[80] SV's affiliation with the Joint Action came with a reservation to the demand that "Purchasing sexual services must be prohibited by law," as a majority of the National Board did not want to take a stand, despite the fact that party leader Theo Koritzinsky and the principal board were in favor of criminalizing sex purchases. *Ny Tid*, no. 38, 1983, p. 6; and *Klassekampen*, 5 October 1983, p. 9.

[81] Quoted in Tessem and Wiedswang 1984, p. 137.

[82] Finn Gustavsen: "Pornodebatten—en avsporing" [The Porn Debate—A Derailment], post in *Arbeiderbladet*, 3 November 1983.

that same autumn, was promoting an interpellation to Mayor Albert Nordengen about Oslo as a porn-free city.[83]

The fact that political parties and large organizations joined the Joint Action served as an important recognition of the anti-porn struggle, but most of the activities took place in local communities. The activity level of the local groups increased after the organizational changes of 1981 and escalated after the airing of the TV documentary with the leader of the Joint Action, Unni Rustad, in 1983.

The TV Documentary "the Struggle Against Porn"

The purpose of the documentary "The Struggle Against Porn" (*Kampen mot porno*), aired by the Norwegian Broadcasting Corporation (NRK) on October 5, 1983, was not to present a nuanced picture of pornography, but to inspire a struggle. It was produced by NRK journalist Ellen Aanesen, a member of the Women's Front who was active in the anti-porn struggle. Unni Rustad was the primary subject of the documentary, which followed her around the country as she presented her anti-pornography slideshow and met with local activists. But others were also interviewed, including police officers who reported an increase in the confiscation of coarse pornography from sexual offenders. The documentary shocked and "awakened" Norway, according to the newspaper *VG*.[84] According to *Arbeiderbladet*: "After this documentary, it will be more difficult to gain an understanding of the view that pornography prevents abuse: they will be forced to think again."[85]

Reaction to the documentary was immediate. The same evening, the NRK and the Women's Front were flooded with calls from shocked people. The following day, the young MP of the Labor Party, Sissel Rønbeck, submitted an interpellation to Minister of Justice Mona Røkke about prohibiting pornography that exploits women and children. Rønbeck cited reports from the police, crisis shelters for abused women, and child welfare workers that victims of violence and rape reported having been subjected to increasing violence directly inspired by violent

---

[83] *Aftenposten*, 2 November 1983, p. 7.

[84] *VG*, 7 October 1983, p. 1. I am grateful to Ellen Aanesen and NRK for providing me with a copy of the documentary.

[85] *Arbeiderbladet*, 6 October 1983. See also *Aftenposten*, 6 October 1983, p. 4; *Klassekampen*, 7 October 1983; *Arbeiderbladet*, 7 October 1983, p. 3; and *VG*, 7 October 1983 p. 6.

pornography.[86] The police officers also reacted quickly by stating that they would give priority to the investigation of illegal pornography—including the huge porn seizure from L. Hagen Import of 1982, which remained untouched pending investigation and was stored in three vacant cells at Oslo police headquarters. The police attributed this change in policy to the fact that they were increasingly finding porn magazines and films in connection with cases of sexual abuse.[87] The documentary also evoked reactions from both the employees and management of the newsagent company Narvesen.[88] Because Narvesen was partly owned by the government through the Norwegian State Railways NSB, the Minister of Transport and Communications, Johan J. Jacobsen of the Center Party, said that he would investigate how the government might regulate Narvensen's assortment of magazines.[89] Just a week after these initiatives, Narvesen decided to stop the distribution of Leif Hagen's *Aktuell Rapport* because of advertisements discriminatory to women, a decision that was approved by the employees' union. Two issues of the magazine were left undistributed, causing a financial loss to *Aktuell Rapport* of about NOK 2 million.[90]

---

[86] In her interpellation, Rønbeck asked what the Ministry of Justice would do to (1) halt the sale of pornography through Norwegian mail-order companies, (2) halt advertising by foreign mail-order companies that were peddling pornography in Norway, and (3) halt the sale of pornography in kiosks and grocery stores. She also asked if the ministry would tighten penal regulations for importing, printing, distributing, and selling pornography. At the same time, she urged Labor Party representatives in local councils to launch the fight against pornography locally. Other MPs had also had their "eyes opened" by the documentary. The parliamentary leader of the Socialist Left Party SV, Hanna Kvanmo, said that the documentary had "made a deep impact on the Storting" and declared that "now is the time for a ban." *Aftenposten*, 10 October 1983, p. 3. See also *VG*, 7 October 1983 p. 6; *Arbeiderbladet*, 7 October 1983, p. 3; and *Dagbladet*, 7 October 1983, p. 48.

[87] *Arbeiderbladet*, 7 October 1983, p. 3; *Dagbladet*, 7 October 1983, pp. 42–43; *VG*, 7 October 1983, p. 6; *Arbeiderbladet*, 8 October 1983, p. 8.

[88] *Aftenposten* (evening edition), 6 October 1983, p. 1; *Arbeiderbladet*, 8 October 1983, p. 8.

[89] *VG*, 8 October 1983, p. 8. See also *VG*, 1 December 1983, p. 6.

[90] *Klassekampen*, 17 October 1983, p. 7; *Arbeiderbladet*, 17 October 1983; *Aftenposten*, 17 October 1983; *Klassekampen*, 17 October 1983, p. 1; *Klassekampen*, 22 October 1983, p. 11. The subsequent issues of the magazine contained only advertisments for the mail-order assortment of children's cartoons. *Arbeiderbladet*, 3 November 1983, p. 3.

Striking while the iron was hot, the Women's Front used the Joint Action to launch a nationwide petition campaign against pornography. The demands were: "Porn-free cities and villages. Porn out of Narvesen, kiosks, gas stations and grocery stores. Advertising bans on porn ads. Simpler rules on seizure of porn."[91] After two months of campaigning, Unni Rustad handed over 46,700 signatures to Minister of Justice Mona Røkke.[92] Meanwhile, several stores, including cooperatives, had stopped selling pornography, and several newspapers terminated their advertising agreements with "men's magazines."[93] Moreover, several municipalities opted to be porn-free, including Vefsn, Harstad, and Molde, as well as 12 out of 13 municipalities in the district of Romerike.[94] The archives of the Joint Action bear witness to the tremendous impact of the TV documentary cited above. In the weeks after its airing, hundreds of letters flowed into the organization's mailbox. They included requests for lectures and other anti-porn material, questions about how to form a local anti-porn group, and pure "fan mail."[95] The letters offered evidence of the extent to which the documentary had shocked and frightened people, many of whom wrote that they feared the future and the increasing violence in society. Many expressed thanks to Unni Rustad for "opening their eyes." A number of local anti-porn groups across the country were formed on the heels of the documentary. Sometimes they were initiated by local Agrarian Women's Associations or members of the Marxist-Leninist movement, at other times by individuals, mostly young women and girls. The movement was wide-ranging—for example, in Northern Norway, local anti-porn groups were established in rural communities such as Bardufoss, Borkenes, Isfjorden, Karasjok, Meløy, and Storsteinnes. Around the country, the groups took on local names, such as "North Dales Folks against Porn" (*Norddøler mot porno*) in Otta in the Gudbrand Valley, and, in the southern city of Kristiansand, "The Kristiansand Action

---

[91] *Dagbladet*, 11 October 1983, p. 13; *Klassekampen*, 12 October 1983, p. 9; *Nationen*, 14 October 1983; *Klassekampen*, 22 October 1983, p. 11.

[92] *Klassekampen*, 17 December 1983, p. 23.

[93] *Aftenposten*, 11 October 1983; *Arbeiderbladet*, 17 October 1983; *Aftenposten*, 17 October 1983.

[94] *Klassekampen*, 9 November 1983.

[95] FA D-0001 Administrative Archive 1981–1985 and D-0002 Administrative Archive 1983–1991, ABA.

against Porn" (*Kristiansand-aksjonen mot porno*, abbreviated KAMP, literally meaning "struggle" in Norwegian).[96]

Popular Education Against Pornography

Popular education and grass roots mobilization against pornography were typical strategies of the Joint Action. The activists would organize stands outside local stores from which they distributed flyers, brochures, and posters, sold anti-porn material, and collected signatures and money for the Joint Action. They wrote letters to the newspapers and drafted collections of arguments against pornography for people to use in preparation for discussions.[97] Sometimes they organized national action weeks in which groups across the country handed out roses and stickers with "Praise for a porn-free neighborhood" to kiosks and shops that did not sell pornography. The so-called Narvesen Card Campaign involved selling pre-stamped postcards addressed to the Narvesen company's headquarters, saying: "Respect women's human dignity; stop selling and distributing porn." Twenty-five thousand cards were reported to have been sold.[98]

Popular education comprised a significant part of the Joint Action's undertaking. The group published brochures and arranged an unknown number of study circles. The book *Porno*, which was written by a group of anti-porn activists (mostly from the Women's Front) and released by the publishing house Friundervisningen (Popular Education) in 1982, was used as study material in anti-porn groups.[99] The most important items

---

[96] FA D-0001 Administrative Archive 1981–1985, ABA.

[97] Minutes from a meeting with the member organizations, 25 November 1981, FA D-0001 Administrative Archive 1981–1985, ABA.

[98] Karlsen 1991, p. 19.

[99] Volder, Bente, Adelheid Hommelvoll, Helen Vogt, Ulf Pettersen, Frøydis Eidheim, Unni Rustad, Marianne Sætre, and Elisabeth Bjørk (1982): *Porno* [Porn]. 2nd edition. Oslo: Friundervisningen Forlag. The booklet provides analyses of the content of porn, the financial interests behind the industry, the current legal provisions regulating it, and practical advice on how to combat it. The revenues on the sales of the booklet went to the Joint Action against Pornography and Prostitution. Later in the 1980s, the Joint Action published brochures that were distributed to schools, with titles such as "Yes to Eroticism—No to Porn" and "Sex Roles, Violence, Pornography, Prostitution," in which the famous soccer player Erik Solér was interviewed about why boys should engage in the fight against porn and prostitution. FA Z-0002 Reference Material 1977–1997, ABA.

in Joint Action's educational arsenal, however, were the so-called porn lectures, by Unni Rustad referred to as the organization's "most important weapon" in the war against the porn industry.[100] In 1982, Rustad and other activists began to offer what would become an ongoing lecture tour on porn. The concept was to use "porn against porn," that is, to show slides of photos and text from pornography that was currently on the market, and to provide a feminist political analysis of the content. One of the aims of the porn lectures was to encourage the establishment of local anti-porn groups. Although Unni Rustad became famous throughout Norway for her porn lectures, those talks were also presented by a number of other (usually young) women. In 1983, 20 copies of the porn slide show were in circulation, and there were long waiting lists to have them presented.[101] The women received no fees for the porn lectures other than having their travel expenses covered by those who had invited them to come.

How many times these porn slide show lectures were offered to different audiences is not known, but there were undoubtedly several hundred presentations. In connection with the TV documentary "The Struggle against Porn" of October 1983 (cited earlier), in which Rustad presented part of the lecture to an evidently shocked audience at Oslo Teachers' College, Rustad told *VG* that she had presented the slide show somewhere between 100 and 150 times.[102] The TV documentary served as a marketing tool for the porn slide show lectures and led to an increased demand for them. The porn lectures were presented in public settings around the country, for all sorts of organizations, groups and associations, in schools, adult education institutions, colleges and universities, in leisure youth clubs, in municipal councils and in prisons, for workers on oil platforms, and for drug addicts in rehab facilities, as well as in military camps. In looking back on her experience of presenting anti-porn lectures to soldiers in military camps, Unni Rustad recalled:

> In the military camps, which received porn magazines for free from Leif Hagen, there was often a gang sitting in the back who had had some beers and were ready to take on that bitch.

[100] Rustad 2010.

[101] Note from a press conference, 27 January 1984. FA D-0003 Administrative Archive 1984, ABA.

[102] *VG*, 5 October 1983, p. 46.

Everywhere we came, it was quiet after a few minutes. We never had problems with unrest or lack of interest.

In the military camps you could say: I bet it's easier to throw out a comment about how you got yourself laid than to say that you're longing for your girlfriend, not to talk about how difficult it is to say you're in love with another boy. And who can you tell that you're fairly lonely or have complexes because your dick is too small?

Who decides the style here?

The male role described in porn, is it something for you?[103]

According to Rustad, she did not experience ridicule or mockery when she gave the anti-porn lectures, either in military camps or elsewhere. On the contrary, she harbors warm memories from the lecture tours. The sympathetic reception they were met with is confirmed by a lesser-known anti-porn activist, who says that she was genuinely surprised to meet so many men who were truly engaged in combating pornography.[104] She found meeting people through the anti-porn lectures to be rewarding, but recalls her discomfort in getting into the content of pornography, which included porn movies that allegedly contained authentic rapes, torture, and murder of women.

One reason why the anti-porn lectures were successful was the form in which they were presented. Instead of instructing in a distanced academic style, the comments were delivered in informal terms, sometimes mixed with humor. Rustad writes:

When we gave a lecture, we showed slides of the usual fold-out pictures that were typical of all the so-called "men's magazines" that were sold everywhere. We asked people to look at the image of the woman who was posing, and then we asked: Do you think she has a sense of humor? What do you think she voted for in the last election? Do you think she likes classical music?

It never struck the audience the wrong way; many people started laughing only at the thought. So effective are the porn images in removing these women from the ordinary human community that it is ridiculous to imagine that they are like the rest of us.[105]

[103] Rustad 2010.

[104] Interview with Liv Jakobsen, Nesodden, 10 February 2013.

[105] Rustad 2007.

The idea behind the porn lectures was to welcome people with generosity and friendliness and to make them think about sexuality and the contempt shown toward women in pornography. The aim was to make people organize to fight the porn industry. According to Rustad, they succeeded in this goal:

> The fight against porn and prostitution became a movement that changed people. I got a lot of evidence of that—I became the face that many people recognized; people came to me wherever I was. Many of them were men. The porn struggle changed my life, a man I recently met said to me—for the first time, I started to ask myself about what had shaped my sexuality.[106]

Although the struggle against pornography was supported by many people, those who formed a local action group and stood up in front of the store with anti-porn material also encountered resistance. According to Torill Enger Karlsen, anti-porn activism could be a stigmatizing experience. In small villages where everybody knew each other, women who participated in anti-porn groups were labeled bitches, man haters, and communists, and children were bullied at school because of their mothers' involvement in the movement.[107] Furthermore, studying pornography could be stressful. The anti-porn activists did not limit their scrutiny to the usual "men's magazines," but also examined hard-core porn. As in other political mobilizations, it was necessary to acquire knowledge about the target of the struggle, but this meant that the emotional life of the anti-porn activists was visited on by pornographic images and stories of sexual abuse. The fact that the activists risked having their own sex lives ruined made the anti-porn struggle particularly personal in a way that differed from most other political struggles and that created a persistent dilemma.

Pornography as Violence Against Women

As the anti-porn activists gathered knowledge about pornography, they became increasingly aware of its violent content. A 1981 article in the

---

[106] Ibid.
[107] Karlsen 1991, p. 15.

Women's Front's journal entitled "The Violent Society of the 80s: Are Women to Be Hanged on Meat Hooks?" stated:

> The porn magazines become rougher, with stronger elements of sadism. The latest disgusting feature in this field is video films in which women are raped, abused, mutilated, killed. There are people trying to make big money from such films—and there is actually a market for them.
>
> Are women fair game? Why is violence against women so widespread? Is there a connection, a common denominator in that women are punched by their husbands and murdered behind the profiteers' film cameras? Is violence against women accepted as punishment in our society—and for what kind of crime? Are we as women accepting this violence—to some extent? Is there anything we can do to stop it—or should we watch as the snowball just rolls on? Is it that all men are potential violators? Or why is the path from anger to violence so short in many men?[108]

The fact that by the early 1980s the topic of violence had become a more prominent issue in the women's liberation movement's framing of pornography, was hardly the result of a general increase in violence against women, but rather of a greater awareness of the existence of sexual violence. As discussed in Chapter 1, from the second half of the 1970s on, a transnational trend of the women's liberation movement was to pay increasing attention to sexual abuse and violence against women and children.

The framing of pornography as violence against women included both the direct violence that was shown in hard-core magazines and movies—which the opponents of pornography claimed was steadily increasing—and a more subtle or symbolic form of violence. This was a furtherance of the understanding of violence that implied that "making the woman an object, an object of use is, in itself, an act of violence," as stated in the booklet *Porno*.[109] This framing of pornography as violence against women was inspired by U.S. feminists' analyses as they appeared in the

---

[108] Berit Morland: "80 åras voldssamfunn. Skal kvinner henge på kjøttkrokene?" [The Violent Society of the 80s. Are Women to Be Hanged on Meat Hooks?], *Kvinnefront*, no. 1, 1981, p. 1.

[109] "Søkelys på loven" [Spotlight on the Law], *Porno* 1982, p. 79.

1980 anthology *Take Back the Night: Women on Pornography.*[110] The U.S. influence is also apparent in the feminist journal *KjerringRåd*, which in 1982 published a double issue on sexual violence. Here, pornography was interpreted as a caricature of already-existing power relationships between women and men, and as a reaction to the women's liberation movement:

> The new women's liberation movement's redefinition [of sexuality] has meant a problematization of the traditional gender equality ideology: women no longer want to comply with the principles of male sexuality and become like men, but develop their own sexuality on women's own terms.
>
> Pornography must be seen as a reaction to these demands of women. It symbolizes the reconquest of lost domination. The explanation for its spread and development can be found partly in men's social-psychological [sic], and partly in capitalist market forces.
>
> The consciousness-raising of women, within and outside the women's liberation movement, has meant that women's claims toward men in the sexual area have become clearer, and women's needs have proved to be very different from men's. Men's lack of consciousness-raising and therefore reference to traditional sexuality, along with the capitalist market forces, constitute two necessary conditions for pornography, and the escalation of violence. (…)[M]en fantasize about a power relationship that is about to

---

[110]Lederer, Laura (ed.) (1980): *Take Back the Night. Women on Pornography.* New York: William Morrow. The anthology collected articles by 33 women, including prominent U.S. feminists Alice Walker, Marge Piercy, Adrienne Rich, Audre Lorde, Gloria Steinem, Andrea Dworkin, Diana E.H. Russell, Robin Morgan, and Susan Brownmiller. Another important source of inspiration for Norwegian anti-porn activists was Andrea Dworkin (1981): *Pornography—Men Possessing Women.* London: The Women's Press. The understanding of all pornography as violent was also put forward by people who did not necessarily have a feminist rationale, such as the Norwegian poet Stein Mehren. In the newspaper *Aftenposten*, he published a long article entitled "Pornography as Confession and Imagination," which argued that pornography is always violence against the human, "both with the producer, the depicted victim, and the viewing public." In Mehren's view, pornography functioned as the "soul police" by penetrating the imagination to open it up and to manipulate it, thus exploiting the fantasies, because "fantasies are fantasies because they are secret." Mehren, Stein: "Pornografi som betroelse og fantasi" [Pornography as Confession and Imagination], *Aftenposten*, 2 November 1983, p. 6. This was the first of four parts that together made up the article.

disappear. Pornography is an expression of this, and it also plays on these feelings.[111]

In Chapter 3, we saw that French feminists also interpreted violent pornography as a reaction to women's liberation in their 1975 campaign against the film *Story of O*. Interestingly, this interpretation was confirmed by stakeholders and actors in the porn industry, albeit along slightly different lines. In a 1981 Canadian documentary about the industry, *Not a Love Story*, porn producer David S. Wells stated that the increase in gross violence in pornography was the "fault" of the women's liberation movement, because many men now felt their masculinity to be threatened. "Men won't be equal to women, it's that simple," he stated.[112]

In their 1984 book on pornography in Norway, journalists Liv Berit Tessem and Kjetil Wiedswang claimed that the genre had not become more violent in the early 1980s. They had studied the development of the pornography market in Norway from the 1970s onward, and found that it had become increasingly violent during the 1970s but, in fact, had become less violent in the 1980s. The reason for this, they argued, was that the police, in response to the women's liberation movement, had begun to direct their attention toward pornography and—to a greater extent than ever before— intervened against pornography involving violence, children, and animals. [113] According to Tessem and Wiedswang, the anti-porn activists who claimed that violence in pornography was steadily increasing were basing their analyses on American pornography. What's more, they had propagandistic motives: by displaying hard-core pornography that offended a vast majority of the people and claiming that it was becoming increasingly offensive, the opponents of pornography garnered more support and sympathy. However, when the anti-porn activists argued that violence and exploitation were increasing, it was not necessarily deliberate manipulation on their part. On the contrary, it might well have been because they perceived this to be a matter of accepted fact. It was only in the 1980s that they began to systematically

---

[111] Brita Gulli and Karin Tilrem: "Porno—reaksjon på kvinnefrigjøring" [Porn—Reaction to Women's Liberation], *KjerringRåd*, no. 3–4, 1982, p. 15.

[112] *Kvinnejournalen*, no. 5–6, 1983, pp. 5 and 8. Clips from the interview with the porn producer were also featured in Ellen Aanesen's TV documentary with Rustad that aired on NRK on 5 October 1983.

[113] Tessem and Wiedswang 1984, pp. 97–98.

study pornography. Although the incidence of violence may have diminished since 1980, one still did not have to look hard to find pornography with such content.

Does Pornography Have an Impact?

According to the opponents of pornography, both men and women were influenced by pornography, but in different ways. Boys and men learned to view women as objects to be used, and pornography, in its worst form, could inspire them to commit sexual abuse. Girls and women, on their part, learned that their mission was to satisfy men and to accept being abused. According to the booklet *Porno*:

> Porn presents violence against women as something sexual. Men who find their sex life boring, are advised to try violence. They are often encouraged to tie up their female partner and start experimenting with whips and gags. [...] Porn promotes the idea that women want it that way, that women's NO should not be taken seriously. Some people actually believe that women like to be raped, beaten, and humiliated. Porn underpins these ideas by writing about women who get horny by rape and mistreatment.[114]

The issue of the impact of pornography was controversial among experts. While some claimed that pornography had no impact on people's sexuality or could even prevent abuse, others maintained that pornography inspired people to engage in sexual abuse. The different positions reflected different psychological approaches.[115] There was a tendency for psychoanalytically inspired approaches to sexuality to have a more positive view of pornography, one deriving from a belief that it might work as a path into the unconscious, stimulate the imagination in the area of the forbidden, and satisfy the drives. Based on this *katharsis* theory, violent pornography could serve to prevent sexual crimes by enabling the potential perpetrator to find an outlet for his fantasies through a magazine or a movie instead of abusing real people.

Conversely, learning theoretical perspectives—or behavioral perspectives— emphasized how people learn response patterns from external

[114]Volder et al. 1982, p. 15.

[115] Gulbrandsen, Holøs, and Bertelsen 1984, pp. 14, 25–30.

stimuli, that is, through observation of other people's behavior, including in images and movies. According to this perspective, frequent exposure to violent pornography leads to the normalization of the connection between sex and violence. A U.S. study of college students' reactions to pornography that was often cited by Norwegian opponents of pornography showed that those who had been heavily exposed to violent pornography began to identify with the rapist in the movie and to look down on the victim. After the experiment, half of the test subjects were said to have confirmed that they would like to rape someone if they knew that they would not be caught.[116] In the 1980s, this type of human experiment was considered unethical, and it was out of the question to repeat it. However, among the opponents of pornography, a learning theoretical—or behavioristic—perspective on the impact of pornography was prevalent.

The argument that pornography inspired abuse was, as stated earlier, promoted both by the police and by crisis shelters for battered and abused women. Several women who came to the shelters said that their male partners had forced them into sexual acts after using pornography, and the crisis shelter movement thus publicly condemned pornography.[117] An additional source that was used to reinforce the argument, came from women with experience from prostitution who told about how sex buyers carried porn magazines with them and wanted to try out what they had seen there. In addition, former porn models said that the production of porn involved rapes and other forms of abuse, and that the boundary between prostitution and porn production was murky.[118] On the heels

---

[116] This experiment is also featured in *Take Back the Night*. For a review of various U.S. research studies on porn, see Bronstein 2011, esp. pp. 70–71, 226, and 276.

[117] Tessem and Wiedswang 1984, p. 78; Rustad 2010.

[118] Finstad et al. 1982. See also, e.g., the article entitled "En tidligere prostituert: 'Drømmen min er å ta knekken på pornospekulantene'" [A Former Prostitute: "My Dream is to Crack the Porn Profiteers"], *Kvinnefront*, no. 4, 1978, p. 5. Several former prostitutes and porn models were in contact with the Women's Front, the most well-known of them being the American Linda Boreman, aka Linda Lovelace, world famous from the porn movie *Deep Throat* (1972), in which she played a woman whose clitoris was in her throat and had orgasms from sucking men. Boreman was in Norway on several occasions and befriended members of the Women's Front. In the 1970s, Linda Lovelace had appeared as a happy porn star, but in 1980 she published the autobiography *Ordeal* (published in Norwegian translation in 1981 as *Marerittet* [the Nightmare]), in which she told of the violence and coercion she had been subjected to in the porn industry. After attempts to escape, she got out of the porn business and became an anti-porn

of the much-discussed TV documentary of 1983, the learning theoretical perspective that people—especially young people—mimic what they see in movies prevailed in the media.[119]

The Women's Front Attempts to Make Erotica

By 1983, the question of whether it was possible to produce non-oppressive erotic images was widely discussed in women's liberation movement circles. The debates were inspired by the book *I lyst og last. Seksuelle bilder før og nå* (In Vice and Pleasure: Sexual Images Before and Now), authored by Hans Nestius, the chair of the Swedish Association for Sexuality Education (RFSU), and published in Norwegian in 1983. Using the slogan "Death to pornography—long live the erotic image!" Nestius wanted to show the difference between pornography and erotica.[120] In 1983, the Joint Action's political program replaced the demand "Yes to Sexual Education, No to Porn" with "Yes to Erotica, No to Porn." The reason for the change was probably that "sexual education" carried a dull and boring connotation, and that the anti-porn activists wanted to appear fresh, modern, and fond of sex. Inspired by Nestius, the Women's Front strove to show non-oppressive erotica. The summer issue of their journal *Kvinnejournalen* in 1983 was launched as "a magazine to make you

activist. She saw it as her job to dispel the myth that she had been a happy porn star, later traveling around and speaking about the porn industry and how women are harmed by porn. See "'Linda Lovelace'—det var ikke meg!" [Linda Lovelace—It Was Not Me!], *Kvinnejournalen*, no. 1, 1982, pp. 28–30; Rustad 2007; and Bronstein 2011, pp. 74–75 and 257–263.

[119] As the VHS home video player became more widespread in the 1980s, there were many discussions as to whether children were harmed by "video violence." In 1985, the book *Vold på skjermen* [Violence on Screen], written by Danish author J. Bruun Pedersen, was published in Norwegian, with a foreword by the Children's Ombudsman Målfrid Grude Flekkøy. An authority in the field in Norway was child psychologist Magne Raundalen, who was frequently interviewed about how children were harmed by video violence, and how some of them had to undergo long-term treatment as a result of "shock experiences". See, e.g., *Dagbladet*, 10 January 1985, p. 1, and *VG*, 2 February 1985, p. 1.

[120] Nestius, Hans (1983): *Lyst og last. Seksuelle bilder før og nå* [In Vice and Pleasure: Sexual Images Before and Now]. Oslo: Pax Forlag.

horny."[121] In a radio interview for the Norwegian Broadcasting Corporation (NRK), two members of the editorial team that had produced the erotica edition said that their motivation was to show that they were not puritans, and that one should not be ashamed to be horny. In this way, they hoped to create a magazine with erotic images and texts that were not oppressive but "cheerful and exciting," that showed reciprocity and sensuality without the woman being depicted as an object.[122]

Thus, in 1983, the Women's Front had become eager to show that they were not puritan or disapproving of sex. As in the 1970s, they argued that they were against pornography because it played on puritan prejudices against sexuality—for example, when writing about "dirty fantasies" and "sinful girls." However, the new approach of the Women's Front involved defining the difference between an erotic and a pornographic image. According to Unni Rustad, the difference was not about "how many people are in the picture, whether they are naked or whether genitalia are displayed in full view." It was the "attitude" and the power relationship between women and men that determined whether an image was pornographic and oppressive, or erotic and making the viewer "horny and happy."[123] But who was to decide if the "attitude" behind an image was to make the spectator "horny and happy" or if it was about oppressive power and objectification? Many men probably got both horny and happy by ogling porn models in the typical "men's magazines,"

---

[121] *Kvinnejournalen*, no. 5–6, 1983. An important source of inspiration was Nestius's book. Like the U.S. feminist Gloria Steinem, he argued that it was not the degree of nudity that defined pornography and erotica, but the *message* behind it. See also Steinem, Gloria (1980): "Erotica and Pornography: A Clear and Present Difference," in L. Lederer (ed.): *Take Back the Night. Women on Pornography.* New York: William Morrow.

[122] "Er det forskjell på erotikk og pornografi? Intervju med May Jacobsen og Solveig Skaare fra Kvinejournalen" [Is There a Difference between Erotica and Pornography? Interview with May Jacobsen and Solveig Skaare from the Kvinnejournalen]. The Norwegian Broadcasting Corporation NRK's radio show Ukeslutt, 11 June 1983.

[123] Rustad, Unni (1983): "Porno er dop for redde menn" [Porn Is a Drug for Scared Men], in B. Bjerck et al. (eds.): *Mannfolk! 13 innlegg om mannshat i kvinnebevegelsen* [Menfolk! 13 Posts on Man Hatred in the Women's Movement]. Oslo: Pax Forlag, p. 70. *Sirene* editor IdaLou Larsen problematized Nestius's assertion that the *attitude* or *purpose* of the person making the images decides whether an image is pornographic or erotic, and argued that even the noblest intentions could lead to a dubious product. She asked rhetorically: Should a state erotic monopoly led by people like Unni Rustad be introduced to approve the erotic images? IdaLou Larsen: "Erotikk med heftighet, varme og nytelse" [Erotica with Passion, Affection, and Pleasure], *Sirene*, no. 5, 1983, p. 29. Emphasis in original.

even though the opponents of pornography did not. Multiple interpretations of a sexual image are possible and distinguishing between erotic and pornographic images was probably easier in theory than in practice. The responses to *Kvinnejournalen*'s "magazine to get you horny" illustrate this problem. Although the issue sold exceptionally well, the readers' posts in the subsequent issues suggest that many of them found the content embarrassing. What the editorial team considered "cheerful and exciting" erotic images were for others pornography.

The attempt to depict non-oppressive erotica was not repeated by *Kvinnejournalen*. Instead, others resumed the effort, in particular the social policy journal *Hverdag*, which in 1984 launched *Cupido*—"the magazine for horniness and joy." According to one of its founders, Terje Gammelsrud, the magazine's producers wished to create an erotic publication that would appeal to both women and men, one "without the banal boasting, the unimaginable clichés and the oppressive sex roles. We wanted to convey erotic texts that could make us horny without at the same time getting an embarrassed taste in the mouth."[124] The Joint Action's working committee welcomed *Cupido* and wrote that it was "admirable to challenge the monopoly of the porn industry in the magazine market" and to show sexuality without coldness and degradation—in other words, without shame.[125] However, after studying the magazine, the Women's Front came to the conclusion that it had not met its objectives, though there was disagreement about this within the organization. The discussions about whether *Cupido* was pornography or erotica continued into the 1990s.[126]

New Law on Pornography in 1985

In January 1985, the 1983 documentary on pornography with Unni Rustad was rebroadcast by the NRK. Public debates and anti-porn actions followed. Two issues of *Aktuell Rapport* were halted by the Narvesen

---

[124] Gammelsrud, Terje: "Cupido—hvordan det begynte" [Cupido—How It Started], *Cupido*, 28 October 2014 (updated 2019), 2019.

[125] Press release from the Joint Action's Working Committee, 16 May 1984, Administrative Archive, D-0002 ABA.

[126] For an account of these discussions, see, e.g., Stø, Ane and Asta Håland (2013): "A Grassroots Story," in T.R. Korsvik and A. Stø (eds.), *The Nordic Model*. Feminist Group Ottar, pp. 15–29.

company because they contained illegal ads for hard-core pornography. The Joint Action experienced a large increase in people wanting to participate in its campaign against pornography, and the activities increased in local communities.[127] The attention directed toward Narvesen also led to militant actions against Narvesen kiosks, such as porn burning in the small town of Førde on the west coast, and spray-painting actions in Bergen. Rustad said that although the Joint Action did not encourage criminal activities, she understood that people were angry.[128]

At this point, several politicians wanted to put in place a new pornography law as soon as possible.[129] The legislation was originally proposed as a private bill by the Labor Party MP Helen Bøsterud, but the preparatory work was insufficient. Among other things, the bill was not sent on ordinary consultation rounds, and it was not clear how central concepts in the bill were to be interpreted. The lack of preparation was criticized by both the Joint Action and by prominent law professors such as Johannes Andenæs and Andres Bratholm.[130]

The new pornography law was passed by Parliament on April 25, 1985, with the following language:

> With fines or with imprisonment for up to 2 years, or with both, will be punished:

---

[127] *Klassekampen*, 11 January 1985, p. 3; *Dagbladet*, 12 January 1985, p. 8; *Vårt Land*, 19 January 1985, p. 15; *Klassekampen*, 25 January 1985, p. 17.

[128] *Aftenposten*, 6 January 1985; *Arbeiderbladet*, 10 January 1985, p. 9; and 16 January 1985, p. 2; *Dagbladet*, 6 January 1985, p. 8; 12 January 1985, p. 8; and 21 January 1985, p. 8; *Klassekampen*, 9 January 1985, p. 9; 11 January 1985, p. 3; 17 January 1985, p. 19; 22 January 1985, p. 14; and 25 January 1985, p. 17; *Vårt Land*, 19 January 1985, p. 15; *VG*, 22 January 1985. On February 2, 1985, Narvesen published a full-page advertisement in several of the country's largest newspapers entitled "Skal bålbrennere få bestemme?" [Are Fire Burners to Decide?]. The ad argued that Narvesen would not be pressured by activists to exercise censorship, and that the politicians were to decide what Norwegians should read. See, e.g., last page of *Dagbladet*, 2 February 1985.

[129] *VG*, 10 January 1985, p. 6; *Arbeiderbladet*, 10 January 1985, p. 9; 12 January 1985, p. 4; and 17 January 1985, p. 7; *Dagbladet*, 19 January 1985 (part 2), p. 9.

[130] Private Bill Amending Section 211 b of the Criminal Code from Helen Bøsterud, Ragna Berget Jørgensen, and Åge Hovengen to the Presidency, 17 January 1984. Ellen Aanesen's archive. Interview with Torill Dahl, Joint Action Against Pornography and Prostitution in *Arbeiderbladet*, 26 April 1985; Enger, Lill Kristin (2007): "Straffbar pornografi—Har jussen endret seg i takt med samfunnet?" [Criminal Pornography—Has Law Changed According to Societal Changes?], Master's thesis, Faculty of Law, University of Oslo, p. 33.

a. anyone who holds public lectures or arranges public performances or exhibits of obscene content or pornographic content,
b. anyone who publishes, makes available for sale or rent or otherwise seeks to distribute obscene or pornographic writings, images, films, videograms or the like,
c. anyone who offers obscene or pornographic writings, images, films, videograms and the like to people under the age of 18.

With obscene or pornographic depictions, this clause refers to sexual depictions that are offensive or in other ways are likely to seem degrading or dehumanizing, including sexual depictions utilizing children, animals, violence, coercion and sadism. Complicity is punished in the same way.

With fines or imprisonment for up to 6 months, or both, will be punished anyone who, by negligence, makes any such act as mentioned in this clause.

Similarly, the proprietor or superior who intentionally or negligently fails to prevent the action being undertaken as mentioned in this clause.

At sentencing, aggravating emphasis is placed on whether the obscene or pornographic depictions include the utilizing of children, animals, violence, coercion and sadism.[131]

---

[131] Cited in Enger 2007, pp. 35–36. In Norwegian: Med bøter eller med fengsel inntil 2 år eller med begge deler straffes:
    a. den som holder offentlig foredrag eller istandbringer offentlig forestilling eller utstilling av utuktig eller pornografisk innhold,
    b. den som utgir, frambyr til salg eller leie eller på annen måte søker å utbre utuktige eller pornografiske skrifter, bilder, film, videogram eller lignende,
    c. den som overlater utuktige eller pornografiske skrifter, bilder, film, videogram og liknende til personer under 18 år.
    Med utuktige eller pornografiske skildringer menes i denne paragraf kjønnslige skildringer som virker støtende eller på annen måte er egnet til å virke menneskelig nedverdigende eller forråe ende, herunder kjønnslige skildringer med bruk av barn, dyr, vold, tvang og sadisme.
    Medvirkning straffes på samme måte.
    Med bøter eller fengsel inntil 6 måneder eller begge deler straffes den som av uaktsomhet foretar noen sådan handling som nevnt i denne paragraf.
    På samme måte straffes den innehaver eller overordnet som forsettlig eller uaktsomt unnlater å hindre at det i en virksomhet blir foretatt handling som nevnt i denne paragraf.
    Ved straffeutmålingen legges det i skjerpende retning vekt på om de utuktige eller pornografiske skildringer omfatter bruk av barn, dyr, vold, tvang og sadisme.

What essentially distinguished the new law from the old one (from 1902) was the definition of pornography as "offensive" and "degrading or dehumanizing" and the specific mention of "sexual depictions using children, animals, violence, coercion and sadism." Thus, the amendment was a codification of current practice, which banned this type of pornography. However, what was defined as "offensive", "degrading or dehumanizing" was ambiguous. The definition of punishable pornography became a so-called legal standard reflecting "the current prevailing morality and jurisprudence in society." It was "the perception of most people, based on an average consideration" that should be the basis for the assessment.[132]

The opponents of pornography interpreted the new law as a victory. In the parliamentary debate, the Joint Action and Unni Rustad received recognition for having brought up the issue, and the anti-porn activists optimistically interpreted the new wording of the law as validating the fight against all pornography.[133] However, it was up to the courts to decide the merit of each case, and it would soon become clear that their assessment of what was "offensive", "degrading", and "dehumanizing" was not the same as that of the anti-porn activists. When they reported pornography with reference to the new law, the cases were almost always dropped by the police. In 1986, the Joint Action reported about fifty violations of the new pornography law, and all of them were quashed.[134]

In the wake of the legislation, Torill Dahl of the anti-porn committee of the Women's Front was quoted as saying that "this is not a law to stop the porn industry, but to stop us."[135] The law was thus interpreted as a means by which politicians undercut the engagement of the popular anti-porn movement. This was an interpretation similar to that of the French Trotskyist feminists' response to the new rape law in 1980. However, it is unlikely that the Labor Party MPs Sissel Rønbeck and Helen Bøsterud's efforts against pornography were not sincere, or that they had a hidden

---

[132] Op. cit., pp. 32 and 57.

[133] *Klassekampen*, 26 April 1985, p. 2; Women's Front National Board: "Gratulerer med ny lov!" [Congratulations on the New Law!], *Klassekampen*, 3 May 1985, p. 15.

[134] FA D-0004 Administrative Archive 1984–1988, ABA.

[135] Rustad 2010.

agenda to weaken the women's struggle. Nonetheless, the Joint Action's archives bear witness to a clear decline in grass-roots activity after the law was passed. The days of the Joint Action as a popular movement were over.[136]

CRITICISM OF THE CAMPAIGNS AGAINST RAPE AND PORNOGRAPHY

The campaigns against rape and pornography succeeded in changing attitudes and laws, but for the women's liberation movement, the success was mixed. The struggles came with a cost. Not only was it discouraging to witness the sexual abuse that was going on; it also affected the image of the feminist activists. While French media at the beginning of the 1970s portrayed feminists as "Amazons with hats and boots," the campaign against rape resulted in a more frequent characterization of them as puritans.[137] Of course, feminist activists with a self-image as rebels in a subversive struggle were more likely to relate to the image of warlike Amazons than of puritans.

This unintended consequence of the fight against sexualized violence had its parallels in Norway. Since the anti-porn campaign began in the late 1970s, the activists had been accused of being totalitarian puritans. In the 1980s, an additional allegation gained popularity—namely, that hatred of men was the driving force behind the women's liberation movement's struggle against sexual exploitation and violence against women. In Norway, the so-called man-hater debate raged in the media in 1983. In its aftermath, an anthology on man-hating in the women's movement was issued by Pax publishing house, and the country's most popular feminist magazine, *Sirene*, was closed down.[138] However, it is unclear whether the accusations of man-hating weakened the women's movement.

---

[136]From 1986 onward, the Joint Action received significantly fewer letters than before. That same year, Rustad quit her leadership position, and the Joint Action was transformed from being an action movement to becoming an association with personal memberships. The association was professionalized, and in 1988 most local groups were gone. From then on, the activities of the Joint Action primarily involved preparing information for use in schools. FA D-0004 Administrative Archive 1984–1988, ABA.

[137]Issorel 2000, p. 129.

[138]There were several reasons for the closing down of *Sirene*, including financial problems over time. For a detailed history of *Sirene*, see Lindtner, Synnøve Skarsbø (2013):

Was the Campaign Against Rape a "Dead End"?

In France in 1978, Algerian immigrant Lakhdar Setti was sentenced to 20 years in prison by the Assize Court in Beauvais for a series of rapes. In response to the verdict, *Libération* journalist Martine Storti declared: "Today, our struggle against rape, which has been carried out seriously and thoughtfully, is at a dead end."[139] In the article, she related with emotion how feminists who were present at the trial, including the assistant attorneys for the rape victims, cried out in shock when the severe punishment was announced. They felt that it was unfair and that they could no longer continue the fight against rape: The campaign against rape had been abused to strengthen the institutions. "In a way, it was also against me that the verdict was directed," Storti regretfully maintained.

As the MLF succeeded in advancing its framing of rape as a societal problem that had to be taken seriously, criticism from the far left intensified. *Libération* expressed concern that the campaign against rape served as an alibi for oppression that helped legitimize right-wing "security propaganda" and strengthened authoritarian institutions. A number of articles argued that the struggle against rape had become a dead end, thanks to the severe penalties being handed down, and that the women's liberation movement had walked into a trap.[140] The newspaper claimed that the public had now arrived at a point at which any woman, through her sole testimony, could send an innocent man to prison. In addition, the

"Over disk som varmt hvetebrød—Sirene og den norske populærfeminismen" [Over the Counter as Hot Wheat Bread—Sirene and Norwegian Popular Feminism], in H. Danielsen (ed.): *Da det personlige ble politisk. Den nye kvinne- og mannsbevegelsen på 1970-tallet* [When the Personal Became Political. The New Women's and Men's Movement in the 1970s]. Oslo: Scandinavian Academic Press/Spartacus Forlag, pp. 103–151; Lindtner, Synnøve Skarsbø (2014): "Som en frisk vind gjennom stuen" – Kvinnebladet Sirene (1973–1983) og det utvidete politikkbegrepet ["A Spanking Breeze through the Living Room" The Feminist Magazine Sirene (1973–1983) and the Broadened Notion of Politics]. Ph.D. thesis, University of Bergen; Lindtner, Synnøve Skarsbø (2015): "Instead of Burning those Magazines, Maybe We Should Bring Them Home and Discuss Them with Our Husbands?". The Feminist Magazine Sirene's Critiques of the Politics of the Norwegian Organized Women's Movement, *Ethnologia Scandinavica. A Journal for Nordic Ethnology*, pp. 158–171.

[139] Martine Storti: "Vingt ans, c'est pas possible" [Twenty Years—It's Not Possible], *Libération*, 24 February 1978. Reprinted in Storti 2010, pp. 240–241.

[140] *Libération*, 29–30 April and 1 May 1978, p. 5; *Libération*, 3 May 1978, p. 8; *Libération*, 4 May 1978, p. 5, and *Libération*, 12 May 1978, p. 7.

paper printed sympathetic interviews with convicted rapists.[141] *Libération* did not see it as a victory that the judicial system had embraced the MLF's demands, including by showing greater respect for the victims and being less inclined to treat them as "guilty." The problem was that sending people to prison was deeply reactionary and oppressive. According to *Libération*, one could not rule out that the death penalty by guillotine would be the next step in the acceleration of harsh sentences in rape cases.[142]

The women's solidarity that characterized the campaign against rape was breaking up, and the growing severity of penalties caused conflicts among feminists, including among feminist lawyers.[143] After the verdict in the Setti case, the assistant attorneys for the rape victims stated that the campaign against rape was a failure driven by hatred, and that they, in the future, would refuse to represent women who had been raped by immigrants.[144] Lawyer Gisèle Halimi and her association Choisir criticized this position because of its implicit premise that immigrants were especially inclined to rape. Choisir had conducted an investigation that showed that only one of 126 rapists in France was an immigrant. According to Halimi, the self-proclaimed radicals who, through their "care" for immigrants actually helped to spread racism, were the ones who had fallen into a trap regarding rape.[145]

Alternatives to Imprisonment?

As an alternative to prison, the assistant attorneys for the victims from the Setti case suggested that offenders ought to pay financial compensation to rape victims, because money "is the least bad of the symbols of

[141] *Libération*, 29–30 April and 1 May 1978, p. 5. See also *Libération*, 17 May 1978.

[142] *Libération*, 4 May 1978, p. 5. On September 10, 1977, Tunisian immigrant Hamida Djandoubi was executed by guillotine in Marseille for torturing and killing his ex-girlfriend. This was the last time the death sentence was used in France, but people couldn't know this at the time, since the death penalty was not abolished by the Socialist government until 1981.

[143] Mossuz-Lavau 1991, p. 213.

[144] Monique Antoine, Colette Auger, and Josyane Moutet: "Contre le viol, la prison?" [Against Rape, Prison?], *Le Nouvel Observateur*, 29 May 1978, p. 67.

[145] "Plaidoires des avocats d'Anne et d'Araceli (Maître Agnès Fichot et Maître Gisèle Halimi)" [Pleadings of Anne and Araceli's Lawyers (Master Agnes Fichot and Master Gisèle Halimi)], *Viol. Le procès d'Aix*, p. 338.

oppression."[146] The logic was that a monetary payment from the rapist means that the rape victim takes back the body as a commodity, so that the rape is understood not as violence but as an exchange. The proposal to replace imprisonment with financial compensation for rape victims, a new approach, received little support in the MLF.[147] Women in Struggle (*Femmes en Lutte*) deemed the proposal a device to turn women into a commodity—that the rapist should pay cash for the sex he had stolen.[148] Gisèle Halimi held that the proposal of financial compensation was an insult to all raped women: "To equate a raped woman with a forced prostitute is simply dishonorable."[149] Moreover, it was a dangerous proposal, she argued, because the problem in rape cases is often a lack of evidence. If reporting rape led to the award of a large sum of money, the credibility of rape victims would be weakened. Moreover, the proposal was not particularly beneficial to the immigrants whom the lawyers wanted to defend: Should they pay with their social security allowance? Halimi rhetorically asked.

In the discussions on punishment and imprisonment, no one in the MLF or on the left recommended psychotherapy for rapists. One reason was that rape, to some extent, was understood not as an individual act but rather as a product of society, whether the patriarchy or the bourgeoisie were to blame. Therefore, the logic was that the whole of society must change, not just the individual rapist. At this time, Halimi was relatively alone among feminists on the left in promoting the idea that the threat of imprisonment could actually help to change societal attitudes toward rape, by sending a message that society did not tolerate sexual assault. Halimi claimed that rape was perhaps the only crime against which punishment could actually help. This was in contrast to, for example, theft or political offenses, where imprisonment worked in a counterproductive way. Halimi's reasoning was this: If a man steals because he is poor and is put in prison, he will come out even poorer and with a record and will therefore steal again. A political prisoner will be strengthened in his political convictions by being imprisoned. Halimi maintained that

---

[146] Antoine, Auger, and Moutet, *Le Nouvel Observateur*, 29 May 1978, p. 67.

[147] Mossuz-Lavau 1991, p. 214.

[148] "Viol et justice" [Rape and Justice], *Femmes travailleuses en lutte*, 1 nouvelle série [1978], pp. 12–13.

[149] Halimi 1978, p. 17.

rape was different because it is part of the culture that men have always raped women, and it is therefore not perceived as a serious problem. This might change if rape were punished as a felony, Halimi stated in court in Aix-en-Provence.[150]

Why the Controversy Over Using the Judicial System in Rape Cases?

One might ask why so many left-wing radicals couldn't accept the use of the legal system in rape cases. The same radicals demanded penalties against racially motivated violence and against employers' abuse of workers. In 1972, for example, they demanded that the Assize Court convict the policeman who had killed the immigrant Mohammed Diab at the police station. The Assize Court was also called on to convict a security guard who shot and killed the Maoist Pierre Overney during a strike at Renault factory in 1972.[151] The funeral marchers demanding justice for the murdered Overney numbered more than 200,000, including the philosophers Michel Foucault and Jean-Paul Sartre, and formed a 7-kilometer long procession to the Père-Lachaise cemetery in Paris in 1972.[152] When women demonstrated outside the courthouse in Aix-en-Provence to demand justice for Anne and Araceli in 1978, *Libération* characterized the demonstration as "unsustainable and disgusting."[153] The newspaper would hardly have used the same language to describe a similar show of support for an immigrant who had been beaten up by a fascist. Thus, the condemnation of institutions, punishments, and imprisonment by the left-wing radicals was inconsistent, tending to depend upon who had committed the crime, and who was the victim. If the crime were carried out by a racist or a loyal defender of the capital and targeted an immigrant or anti-capitalist activist, it was different from a politically

---

[150] "Plaidoires des avocats d'Anne et d'Araceli (Maître Agnès Fichot et Maître Gisèle Halimi)" [Pleadings of Anne and Araceli's Lawyers (Master Agnes Fichot and Master Gisèle Halimi)], *Viol. Le procès d'Aix*, p. 341.

[151] The security guard who killed Overney was killed on 23 March 1977 by members of the NAPAP group (Noyaux armés pour l'autonomie populaire) [Armed Groups for Popular Autonomy]. Bourseiller 1996.

[152] Artières, Philippe (2008): "Pierre Overney, le militant ouvrier assassiné" [Pierre Overney, the Assassinated Worker Activist], in Artières and Zancarini-Fournel (eds.), pp. 550–551.

[153] *Libération*, 4 May 1978, p. 5.

ambiguous crime such as rape, where the perpetrator might be a frustrated man in "sexual misery." While one wishes not to extend the comparison too far, it can be observed with fairness that there are historical parallels to the traditional jurisprudence in rape cases where the "quality" of the victim and the perpetrator was a decisive factor in whether or not a case was pursued (see Chapter 2). However, for the left-wing radicals of the 1970s, class affiliation was measured using different criteria than during the *ancien régime*, and a victim of fascist political violence was considered more "valuable" than a victim of sexual violence.

The criticisms lodged against the campaign against rape must also be understood in light of the sexual revolution and gender relations. Historian Christine Bard argues that the anger directed at the feminist campaign against rape was provoked by its opposition to the prevailing view of a successful sexual revolution. When feminists pointed out that removing "guilt and shame" from sexual life by praising prostitution, pornography, and even rape, would not cause power and dominance to disappear from sexuality, it was like throwing a cobblestone into the sexual liberal pond.[154] As mentioned above, one of the defense lawyers in the rape case of Anne and Araceli told *Libération* that what touches "upon the mysterious continent of sexuality" should not be punished in the Assize Court. This view was also advocated by the prominent intellectual Michel Foucault, who argued that matters related to sexual life should not be governed by law. While a member of a government-appointed commission to revise the Criminal Code, Foucault argued that rape should be decriminalized as a *sexual* offense. It was only the *violence* in rape that was to be punished because sexuality, in his opinion, had nothing to do with the penal code.[155] A similar view was put forward by Benoîte Groult, editor of the feminist *F magazine*, a startup of 1978. She held that, in principle, there was no difference between getting raped and being punched in the face. It was time to "desacralize the vagina," because a "real liberation" implied "trivializing the genitals."[156] By no longer

---

[154] Bard, Christine (1999): "Les antiféminismes de la deuxième vague" [The Anti-Feminisms of the Second Wave], in C. Bard (ed.), *Un siècle d'antiféminisme* [A Century of Anti-feminism]. Paris: Fayard, pp. 301–328.

[155] See Macey, David (1993): *The Lives of Michel Foucault*. New York: Pantheon, p. 283.

[156] Benoîte Groult: "Le prix d'une femme" [The Prize of a Woman], *F magazine*, no. 4, April 1978.

understanding the genitals as a symbol of the whole being, rape victims could avoid being traumatized for the rest of their lives, according to Groult.

At the core of the sexual revolution was the idea that sexuality was a natural, positive force that had been suppressed for many years, and was now to be released by removing all barriers and restrictions. For example, in the 1970s, many radicals, including Foucault, advocated the elimination of the sexual minimum age—that is, authorizing the legalization of sexual intercourse between adults and children.[157] From the early days of the women's liberation movement, feminists pointed out that unequal power relations persisted in sexual relationships despite the removal of some of the restrictions, but this position that was far from generally accepted. Drawing attention to unequal power relations in the domain of sexuality by, for example, protesting against sexual abuse could easily be perceived as being against sex. In order to legitimize the idea that sexual abuse must be taken seriously by people on the left, feminist activists used various strategies, including comparing rape with racist violence, fascist torture, or imperialist warfare. The above-mentioned reactions to the campaign against rape show that the feminist activists only partially succeeded in this strategy.

What Georges Vigarello has referred to as the "relative tolerance" of rape remained prevalent in the 1970s. Indeed, a culturally diffuse boundary between what was perceived as rape and what was considered part of the "erotic game" persisted. Gisèle Halimi emphasized the "normality" of rape when explaining why it was not taken seriously:

---

[157] In 1977, 69 well-known French personalities signed a petition demanding the removal of the minimum age for sexual activity and the legalization of sex between children and adults. The petition was triggered by a case in which three men were charged with sexual abuse of children under the age of 14, documented by photographs. Among the signatories of the petition to decriminalize sex between children and adults were intellectuals such as Michel Foucault, Roland Barthes, Gilles Deleuze, Louis Aragon, Philippe Gavi, André Glucksmann, Guy Hocquenghem, Jean-François Lyotard, Jean-Paul Sartre, and a number of well-known psychiatrists and doctors, including the founder of Doctors Without Borders, Bernard Kouchner. Feminists such as Simone de Beauvoir and Christiane Rochefort also signed the petition, but later claimed that they did not know what they had signed, because at this time they signed so many petitions and manifestos that they had lost track of them. *Le Monde*, 1 January 1977. See also "Quelques pétitions ou lettres ouvertes pas sans équivoque" [Some Unclear Petitions or Open Letters]. Consulted 15 November 2019.

If unemployment and misery create the thief, if accident or passion creates the killer, if oppression creates the political "offender," it is the *normal* life that creates the rapist. A normality that obscures the deformed faults, and mutilates the relations we have with each other.[158]

The difference between what was considered rape and the "erotic game," wherein the woman submits to the man's conquest, was only measured in degrees: "rape is a dramatic and intolerable caricature of the sexual relations," according to Halimi.[159]

The "Man Hatred Debate" in Norway

The exposure of the violence that occurred in pornography, in prostitution, and behind closed doors in private homes, lent a new solemnity to the women's movement. Sexual abuse, torture, and humiliation were even less suitable to joke about than calls for abortion on demand, the right to employment, and free day care for children. In addition, the women's movement's attention to men's violence and sexual abuse of women faced pushback. Opponents interpreted it as an expression of suspicion of men and male sexuality, and of viewing women as helpless victims. Among the strongest critics of the mobilization against men's violence and abuse of women were former New Feminist, Nina Karin Monsen and IdaLou Larsen, the editor of the feminist magazine *Sirene*. Several others soon joined in the criticism.

During the spring of 1983, the so-called *Sirene* debate raged in the columns of the newspaper *Dagbladet*, following an article by *Sirene*'s editor IdaLou Larsen in which she argued that hatred of men was the driving force in the fight against pornography, rape, sexual harassment, and incest.[160] Leading feminist activists thus accused *Sirene* of betraying the women's movement, while Larsen defended herself by pointing out

[158] Halimi 1978, p. 19.

[159] Op. cit., p. 22.

[160] The debate was triggered after IdaLou Larsen, in *Sirene*, no. 8, 1982, published the editorial "Om mus og elefanter" [About Mice and Elephants], in which she criticized the women's movement for addressing sexual harassment that she thought was just flirting. The editorial was followed by subsequent articles in which she criticized the feminist anti-porn movement. The controversy peaked after her editorial in *Sirene*, no. 2, 1983 entitled "Og forøvrig ... bør vi komme mannshatet til livs" [And by the Way ... We Should End the Man Hatred], in which she argued that this phrase would thereafter be mentioned in

that the magazine was independent of any organization. On April 12, 1983, the *Sirene* editors, who by then included only Larsen and Gerd Korbøl, were summoned to a meeting at the Women's House in Oslo, where 31 representatives from various women's organizations accused them of not recognizing that women's oppression existed and must be combated.[161] The meeting revealed that the organized part of the women's liberation movement sympathized with the criticism of *Sirene*, as the representatives included members of the Oslo Association for Women's Rights, the New Feminists, Bread and Roses, the Lesbian Movement, the Norwegian Women's Federation, the Women's Front, and the Oslo Trade Union Women's Movement. The debate led to a drastic decline in *Sirene*'s circulation figures, and during the summer of 1983 the magazine was shut down.[162]

In the last issue of *Sirene*, an article by Larsen and Korbøl entitled "We Accuse" identified several well-known feminists as being responsible for having delivered the magazine's "death blow," because the *Sirene* editors did not share their views that "hatred of women permeates today's patriarchal society" and that "pornography is the ideology of this [patriarchal] society which thus accepts and encourages rape and other brutal abuses against women."[163] The accusation stated that the designated feminists were spokespersons for a "man-hating theory" that "views male sexuality as a threat to women's physical and mental integrity." They characterized this as "a 'lesbian' theory, whether or not those who advocate it are lesbians." According to Larsen and Korbøl, this "man hating" and "lesbian" theory might have "extremely unfortunate consequences," such as making women suspicious of men's sexuality and triggering aggression in men who felt unjustly accused. Moreover, they argued that it was "unfortunate" that the women's movement used its resources to combat pornography and prostitution "while neglecting other, more important tasks."

IdaLou Larsen elaborated on her criticism of an increase in man hatred in an article in the anthology *Mannfolk! 13 innlegg om mannshat i*

every issue of the magazine. In the same issue of *Sirene*, Larsen ridiculed a feminist book about incest as an exaggeration and an expression of man hatred.

[161] Gerd Korbøl and IdaLou Larsen: "Det som skjedde, slik vi ser det" [What Happened, as We See It], *Sirene*, no. 3, 1983, p. 3.

[162] See also Lindtner 2013, 2014, and 2015.

[163] "Vi anklager" [We Accuse], *Sirene*, no. 5, 1983, p. 2.

kvinnekampen (Menfolk! 13 Contributions about Man Hatred in the Women's Struggle). The anthology was published by the Pax publishing house in the autumn of 1983 with help from the New Feminist Birgit Bjerck. Larsen made it clear that it was the feminists' demand for unilateral criminalization of the Johns in prostitution (and not the prostitutes) that had triggered her conclusion of man hatred in the women's movement: "In a society where the man is the executioner and the woman the victim, it is obvious that the John is a criminal, while the prostitute is always helpless and irresponsible," according to Larsen.[164] The demand to criminalize the Johns also led former New Feminist Nina Karin Monsen to conclude that the women's movement had developed a hatred of men. The term "John" (or "whore customer," as was the new Norwegian expression introduced by feminists) showed clear evidence of man hatred, she said in an interview in *Arbeiderbladet*, adding that not to support the criminalization of the prostitutes was to deprive them of legal standing.[165]

Activists in the women's movement clearly believed that Larsen and Monsen were wrong, and that hatred of men was not at all the driving force in the fight; rather, it was a righteous anger over women's oppression. The anthology *Mannfolk!* (Menfolk!) was, with the exception of Larsen's article, an apologia for this view, in which activists from different parts of the women's movement illumined the topic of man hatred from different perspectives. For example, Unni Rustad, in her chapter on the anti-porn struggle, argued that "it requires faith in men to fight against

[164] Larsen, IdaLou (1983): "Kjetterske tanker om samfunnets kvinnehat" [Heretical Thoughts on Society's Hate of Women], in B. Bjerck et al. (eds.), *Mannfolk! 13 innlegg om mannshat i kvinnekampen* [Menfolk! 13 Contributions about Man Hatred in the Women's Struggle]. Oslo: Pax Forlag, p. 32. In addition to Larsen, contributors to the anthology were feminists and/or activists in the women's movement, including Birgit Bjerck, Liv Finstad, Cecilie Høigård, Edel Hildre, Unni Rustad, Solveig Nyhamar, Gerd Brantenberg, Sigrun Hoel, Astrid Brekken, Else Michelet, Myklebust, Margit Glomm, and Grethe Rønneberg. The variety of topics covered in the anthology included views on men inside and outside the Norwegian women's movement; prostitution and how the Johns reflect the male role and how prostituted women despise men; the anti-porn struggle; the media debate that took place after a woman was acquitted of murdering her abusive husband; lesbian women and their relationships with men; gender quotas that favor men; the experiences of victims of incest; the game of flirtation; feminist self-defense; sexual harassment in the workplace; and men's attempts to curb women's mobilization within the labor unions.

[165] *Arbeiderbladet*, 9 November 1983, p. 2.

porn. In many ways, the struggle is a statement of trust. Had we believed that men are as perverse and oblivious as porn tells us, we would have given up a long time ago."[166] Rustad didn't believe that the way to go was to feel pity for men and comfort them, as IdaLou Larsen had suggested in an interview in the men's magazine *Vi Menn* in which she had declared "I love men." According to Rustad, "we must not treat men as children or under-developed creatures or fragile people who can't bear to be challenged. Far too many men respond to women's challenges by clinging to a male role that is increasingly on a collision course with the emerging new women's role." She believed that men could handle the challenge and fight along with women against "those who dig the trenches deeper between women and men"—namely, the porn industry.[167]

The rise in accusations of man hatred in the early 1980s was hardly a result of an increased loathing of men in the women's movement.[168] It was rather a reaction to feminist researchers' and activists' success in exposing men's sexual abuse and violence against women—a topic that had previously been little discussed. The attention paid to the more brutal aspects of male sexuality and men's view of women could, on the one hand, trigger problematic feelings toward men in some women. On the other hand, the focus on men's violence and abuse could be interpreted as a criticism of all men. Interestingly, the demand for the criminalization of the purchase of sex from prostitutes was emphasized by IdaLou Larsen and Nina Karin Monsen as evidence of the hatred of men in the women's movement. They reacted to the fact that feminist activists with a gender-political agenda placed the responsibility for prostitution on the sex buyers—not, as was usual, characterizing prostitution as primarily a social phenomenon related to poverty. Furthermore, when feminist activists claimed that the John was an "ordinary man," the statement was

[166] Rustad 1983, p. 63.

[167] Op. cit., p. 74.

[168] In her chapter in the *Menfolk!* anthology, Bjerck relates how, for example, the manifesto of the Women's Activists, a group that Nina Karin Monsen joined in the early 1970s, was far harsher in its criticism of "the man" than was commonplace in the women's movement later on. Also, in the 1970s, *Sirene* had been perceived as hateful toward men, especially by members of the Women Front, who criticized the magazine for attacking individual men rather than the capitalist system. Bjerck 1983, pp. 9–10.

misinterpreted to mean that all ordinary men are Johns, even if the feminist researcher Liv Finstad repeatedly pointed out that "ordinary men" didn't signify that "all men are Johns," but that the John is not "special, different, deviant, but boringly normal."[169]

The criticism directed at the anti-porn activists heightened after the success of the TV documentary "The Struggle against Porn" featuring Unni Rustad in October 1983. Several well-known male commentators were unhappy about the success of the documentary. Clearly inspired by Larsen and Monsen's allegations that the struggle against pornography was motivated by "man hatred" and "lesbian" theory, those commentators intensified their disapproval of the mobilization against pornography by attributing derogatory characteristics to the anti-porn activists. In addition to labeling them as man haters, terrorists, female chauvinists, puritans, and authoritarian Stalinists, they likened them to the Mafia and to the Ayatollah Khomeini in Iran. The detractors hailed from a variety of political and professional backgrounds and received much media attention. For example, the liberal journalist Arvid Weber Skjærpe published an article in *Dagbladet* about how Unni Rustad and her "Khomeini gang" in the Joint Action were "more dangerous to society than the pornography they want to ban":

> The porn debate shows that the female chauvinists have made progress in their fight against men's fantasy life. Are we really to be guided by those who, for years, have talked degradingly about the family and its ability to foster "whole relationships" between human beings? [...] We begin to see the outlines of the lesbian ideology, in which the woman is attributed "*Aryan*" characteristics, against the man's "*Jewish*" [characteristics], where the "male pig's" desires, fantasies, dreams, and behavior must be state regulated in order not to disturb the women chauvinists' image of the place of the man and the woman.[170]

While Skjærpe viewed "the lesbian ideology" as a variant of Nazism, the criticism put forward by sexologist Berthold Grünfeld took a milder form. In an article for the conservative newspaper *Aftenposten*, he claimed that

---

[169] Liv Finstad: "Kvinnen på en pidestall?" [The Woman on a Pedestal?], *Klassekampen*, 28 November 1983, p. 4.

[170] Arvid Weber Skjærpe: "Om mus og menn" [Of Mice and Men], *Dagbladet*, 23 October 1983, p. 4. Italics in original.

feminist activists exaggerated the increase in sexual violence, explaining that:

> One cannot escape the feeling that there is an intense man hatred and disdain of men behind it [...] It can almost seem that generations' accumulated bitterness, hatred, and despair is all of a sudden focused in a raging frontal attack on male hegemony in the form of its perversion, the sexual violence.[171]

Grünfeld thereby explained the resistance to pornography in psychological terms, namely, as an "intense man hatred" attributable to accumulated rage. The claim that the women's movement was driven by hatred of men was also upheld by men on the political left. Author and journalist Bjørn Nilsen, who was affiliated with the Marxist-Leninist movement, said in an interview with the tabloid newspaper *VG* that "The small core of progressive girls who just keep talking and writing about violence, incest and male pigs helps to create attitudes about the man that today is killing relationships and exuberance."[172] Nilsen had previously supported the women's movement, but now he thought that "progressive men" were becoming increasingly less enthusiastic about "the women's rights mafia's entrenched mindset." He spoke up for men's sex lives and said that women had to accept that men are "thinking, horny rabbits."

Finn Gustavsen, from the Socialist Left Party SV, insisted in various media that the women's movement was poisoned by hatred of men. In this "hysterical climate," "dynamic men" become "muttering, silent eunuchs," he worriedly stated in an article in *Arbeiderbladet*.[173] Gustavsen also believed that the anti-porn struggle "delves into the depths of the worst in the Norwegian people's soul, permanently injured as it is after centuries of religious oppression." According to him, Norwegians were "number two after the Ayatollah Khomeini" when it came to being puritan. At the same time, however, he believed that most people realized

---

[171] Berthold Grünfeld: "Seksuelle overgrep og vold mot kvinner og barn" [Sexual Abuse and Violence Against Women and Children], *Aftenposten*, 15 October 1983, p. 2.

[172] *VG*, 6 October 1983, p. 37.

[173] Finn Gustavsen: "Pornodebatten—en avsporing" [The Porn Debate—A Derailment], *Arbeiderbladet*, 3 November 1983.

that "it is foolish to spend so much time on this while the atomic bomb and economic crises are constantly threatening."[174]

While Oslo's city council was discussing the Socialist Left Party's interpellation of Oslo as a "porn-free city" on November 9, 1983, worry over the success of the anti-porn movement was simultaneously being voiced by right-wing parties. The representative of the far-right Progress Party, Peter N. Myhre, warned that the anti-porn movement was a "Stalinist threat to democracy." Anders Melteig, from the Conservative Party, expressed concern that the left had become puritan: "A woman's breast is no longer a genital organ. It is only a point to attract as much tanning as possible. If a man accidently directs his gaze at this breast, he is called a male pig," he was quoted as having said in the city council debate.[175]

The fear that the fight against pornography was motivated by totalitarian attitudes was also voiced by Leif Hagen's defense attorney, Tor Erling Staff: "I do not hesitate to say that we find the terrorist's attitudes among the activist women," he said to *Aftenposten*. The newspaper had appointed Staff as "person of the week" after he had met strong opposition for having said in a TV debate that "women can often enjoy sexual intercourse when it appears to be done with coercion," and that both violent and child pornography should be sold freely.[176] In Staff's view, this type of pornography had the greatest "justification" because "deviant groups" needed it to "relieve the pressure."[177] Staff was supported by Ketil Lund, a lawyer colleague who, in an article in *Dagbladet*, claimed

---

[174] *Dagbladet*, 12 November 1983, pp. 8–9.

[175] *Klassekampen*, 11 November 1983. The interpellation of Oslo as a porn-free city did not get a majority.

[176] *Aftenposten*, 29 October 1983. See also *Dagbladet*, 22 October 1983, p. 9. After the TV debate, Staff had the entrance to his office painted with slogans like "Castrate Staff" and "Porn Lover." In *Dagbladet*, he claimed that the Women's Front had done it. Although the Women's Front stated that they understood that people could be provoked, they did not support the action and demanded that Staff's accusations be dismissed. If not, they would bring the case to the Lawyers' Association. *Dagbladet*, 24 October 1983, p. 9; *Klassekampen*, 25 October 1983, p. 2; *Aftenposten*, 25 October 1983, p. 10.

[177] *Aftenposten*, 29 October 1983. In an interview in *Arbeiderbladet*, Staff said that hardcore porn and child porn should be considered therapeutic items and sold by prescription through monopolies. *Arbeiderbladet*, 25 October 1983.

that the resistance to pornography was an expression of totalitarian attitudes in Norway, and the degree of openness to pornography indicated
the degree of liberty in a society.[178]

DID THE CRITICISM HARM THE WOMEN'S MOVEMENTS?

Did the accusations of being authoritarian, totalitarian, hateful, and anti-
sex negatively affect the women's movement? The answer is complicated,
but it is clear that the allegations against the French MLF for having
helped strengthen oppressive institutions hit harder than did the charges
of man hatred lodged against the Norwegian women's movement. There
are obvious differences between rape and pornography as criminal cases.
While rape may be perpetrated by a man with problems, making big
money from producing and selling pornography is a calculated financial
activity. For radical activists, it was harder to accept that an immigrant or
other "man of the people" received 20 years behind bars for rape than
that a capitalist like Leif Hagen was sentenced to fines and deprived of
the right to do business because of selling violent pornography.

At the same time, it was evident that the French MLF had already
managed to harm itself. Because the movement refused to cooperate with
other movements or groups that did not share all of its political stances, it
had become isolated even before it had succeeded in gaining acceptance
for its framing of rape as a serious crime. The final blow was Psych et Po's
legal and commercial patenting of the "Women's Liberation Movement"
and "MLF" as a trademark and association in 1979.

In Norway, feminist activists of the day felt that the accusations of man
hatred, which featured prominently in the media, damaged the anti-porn
struggle, and they went to great lengths to defend themselves against
the charges.[179] At the same time, the allegations showed the importance
of the issue and can be taken as evidence that the women's movement
had succeeded in placing the sexual abuse of women on the agenda.
Moreover, the man hatred accusations, which also came from the left,
brought new actors to the scene, individuals who had otherwise issued
no public opinion about the anti-porn fight, but chose to defend the

---

[178] Ketil Lund: "Totalitære signaler" [Totalitarian Signals], *Dagbladet*, 28 October
1983.

[179] See also Lønnå 1996, pp. 278–281.

anti-porn activists. Many of those who came to the rescue were men who challenged the male role and men's relationship to pornography, women, and sexuality. Several men took to self-criticism for being too passive and made sincere attempts to understand how women felt offended by pornography in a way that had not previously been part of the porn debate. Typical of this new engagement was an article by Rolf Berg, columnist and member of the Socialist Left Party, who criticized liberal men who clearly distanced themselves from racism but fell silent when it came to expressions of contempt toward women. Berg argued that it should be established by law that such disrespect of women in words and image should be banned in the same way as racism was forbidden: "Because it *is* indeed contempt of women. [...] We men may have the imagination to envisage how we would thrive with male genitals dangling from the magazine counters, and boy's butts aloft in the store windows."[180]

Journalist Arne Wam, who was married to Labor MP Sissel Rønbeck and, in the 1980s, became the head of the government-appointed Committee on the Role of Men (1986–1991), analyzed men's relationship to pornography in several articles in *Arbeiderbladet*. Here he claimed that behind all the theoretical discussions about freedom of speech and tolerance, the true rationale for justifying "the degradation and exploitation of women and children" was that pornography was a "tool for men's ejaculation."[181] Several readers noted that men had to endure criticism for their attitudes toward pornography, including "Geirulf from Bergen," who in a letter to *Klassekampen* wrote that "the problem is not that we men are required to understand the relationship between porn, violence against women, and the male culture. The problem is rather that we realize this to a very small extent, and that we rarely fight against the view toward women that characterizes our environment."[182]

[180] Rolf Berg: "Gutte-liberalismen" [Boy-Liberalism], *Arbeiderbladet*, 5 November 1983, p. 14.

[181] Arne Wam: "Om menn, sex og porno: Idealer, myter—og virkelighet" [On Men, Sex, and Porn: Ideals, Myths—Reality], *Arbeiderbladet*, 6 December 1983, p. 16.

[182] Geirulf: "Kvinnekamp og kanindebatt" [Women's Struggle and Rabbit Debate], *Klassekampen*, 7 November 1983. See also Jahn Arne Olsen: "Gustavsens 'tause evnukker'" [Gustavsen's "Silent Eunuchs"], *Klassekampen*, 5 November 1983, p. 19. The anti-porn movement also became part of popular culture. The rocker Stig Nilsson and his band Stig Pig wanted to use rock to "get rid of porn pigs." With the album "Stakkars lille mann" [Poor Little Man], he plunged into the porn debate: "Porn pigs and other

In the debates, parallels were often drawn between the views of women in pornography and racism: "[In the men's magazines] it is pervasive that women are holes. [...] Women are men's servants, and in this capacity they have only one task in life: to make it comfortable for the man. The parallel to racist attitudes is clear: People with different skin color and women are both portrayed as individuals of lesser value than their masters," a man wrote in a reader's post to *Arbeiderbladet*.[183]

While French feminists were deeply divided in their view of punishment for rape and disagreed on whether it was something to celebrate that the judiciary had begun to take rape seriously, Norwegian feminist activists in fact became more united as a result of the criticism. In response to a storm of accusations of man-hating in the media in the fall of 1983, various women's organizations made a collective "Petition against the Smearing of Women." The appeal, which was unanimously approved and signed by 26 women's and feminist organizations and forums, stated that: "When women poke around in men's privileges and fight for equality and liberation, accusations of man hatred emerge. Such accusations have been directed at the women's movement at regular intervals over the last century." The charges of man hatred were interpreted as a backlash:

> [The backlash] is an attempt to cast suspicion on the women's struggle in general and lesbians in particular. A conspiracy theory is constructed which states that lesbians work with women's issues because they hate men and want other women to do so, too. The women's movement will not be split according to criteria of sexual orientation. The place of lesbians in the women's movement is indisputable, necessary, and desirable.[184]

men without attitude must not trample on and soil society. My new album is meant as a powerful kick against the male brutes," he told *Arbeiderbladet*, 5 November 1983, p. 24.

[183] Jan Rokne: "Kvinnediskriminering rasisme" [Discrimination against Women Racism], *Arbeiderbladet*, 22 November 1983.

[184] "Opprop mot kvinnehets" [Petition against the Smearing of Women], *Klassekampen*, 29 November 1983, p. 14. The petition was signed by Legal Aid for Women (*Juridisk rådgivning for kvinner*, *JURK*), Lesbian Feminists (*Lesbiske Feminister*), Lesbian Mothers' Group (*Lesbisk mødregruppe*), Literary Women's Forum (*Tverrlitterært kvinneforum*), Norwegian Women's Federation (*Norsk kvinneforbund*), Students against Porn (*Studenter mot porno*), the Association of Female Lawyers (*Kvinnelige juristers forening*), the Crisis Center (*Krisesenteret*), the female journalist network *Engebretbevegelsen* (Engebret movement), the feminist radio *RadiOrakel*, the Joint Action against Pornography and Prostitution (*Fellesaksjonen mot pornografi og prostitusjon*), the journal *KjerringRåd*,

In Norway, such a statement signed by so many women's and feminist organizations would hardly have been possible without the cooperation that was channeled through the Joint Action against Pornography and Prostitution. Further, it was unusual for lesbians to be so loudly defended in public. Thus, an outgrowth of the accusations of man hatred was the strengthening of the position of lesbians in the women's movement.

Libération's Martine Storti had been among the feminists who felt guilty that the campaign against rape had helped to strengthen the institutions. In hindsight, however, she believes that she and other feminists were wrong.[185] She explains that the guilt that they felt at the time was due to the pressure and arrogance of those who said, "what were we saying." Thirty years after the campaign against rape, she wrote that instead of feeling guilty, feminists should have felt courageous. According to Storti, they were brave when they led a fight against rape—an ancient fear of women—and brave when they recognized the ambiguity of the fight.

the journal *Kvinnejournalen*, the lesbian workshop *Sfinxa*, the New Feminists (*Nyfeministene*), the Oslo Trade Union's Women's Movement (*Oslo Faglige Kvinnebevegelse*), the Oslo Women's Rights Association (*Oslo Kvinnesaksforening*), the Support Movement for Prostitutes (Støttebevegelsen for prostituerte), the Women's Front (*Kvinnefronten*), the Women's Group in AHF [Action Group for Gay Liberation] (*Kvinnegruppa i AHF [Aksjonsgruppa for homofil frigjøring]*), the Women's Group in DNF-48 (Gay Liberation Group) (*Kvinnegruppa i DNF-48*), the Women's Judiciary (*Kvinneretten*), the Women's Rights Group at the Faculty of Law (*Kvinnesaksgruppa ved Juridisk fakultet*), Women in Struggle (*Kvinner i kamp*), Women in Male Occupations (*Kvinner i mannsyrker, KiM*), and the Women's Political Planning Forum (*Kvinnepolitisk planforum*).

[185] Storti 2010, pp. 196–197.

CHAPTER 5

Politicizing Rape and Pornography—What Now?

Fighting sexual exploitation and violence against women was by no means unique to the 1970s women's movements in France and Norway. In various forms, feminist mobilizations against sexual abuse took place in many countries, and still do. Combating violence against women is one of the goals of the United Nations, as pledged in The Convention on the Elimination of all Forms of Discrimination Against Women (CEDAW) of 1979, which many countries have ratified.[1] However, this recognition does not imply that governments prioritize and allocate substantial resources to combating violence against women, and to include the fight against pornography as part of this effort is rare. For example, the UN's declarations and recommendations designed to combat violence against women make no mention of pornography, nor do all feminists embrace the old 1970s slogan that "Pornography is the theory, and rape is the practice." Several feminists think that pornography can be sexually liberating, and today there is also "feminist porn" on the market.

In this concluding chapter, we start by discussing why the 1970s feminist mobilization against sexual exploitation and violence against women

---

[1] Convention on the Elimination of All Forms of Discrimination against Women, New York, 18 December 1979, http://www.ohchr.org/EN/ProfessionalInterest/Pages/CEDAW.aspx. The fight against violence directed at women receives special mention in the UN's General Recommendations 12 and 19 and in the UN Declaration on the Elimination of Violence against Women from 1993.

© The Author(s) 2021
T. R. Korsvik, *Politicizing Rape and Pornography*,
Citizenship, Gender and Diversity,
https://doi.org/10.1007/978-3-030-55639-6_5

was primarily expressed as a fight against rape in France and against pornography in Norway. Was rape indeed a more serious problem in France, while pornography was perceived as the larger threat in Norway? Were there any particular features of each country's movement that led it to engage in these specific issues? What impact did the media coverage, as well as the mobilization of allies and opponents, have on lending urgency to the issues in the respective countries?

The mobilizations against sexual exploitation and violence against women served as learning experiences and led to changes in societal attitudes. How can this relative success be explained, and what effect did the mobilizations have in the long run? To answer these questions, we jump ahead to the 2010s for a look at how the successors of 1970s feminist activists in France and Norway frame rape and pornography as gender-political issues. What are the similarities and differences between today's feminist organizations in the two countries when it comes to these concerns? How have the organizations and their policies changed in 40 years? The chapter concludes with a discussion of continuing dilemmas related to gender-political mobilization against sexual exploitation and violence against women.

Why Was the Fight Against Sexual Exploitation and Violence Against Women Conveyed Differently in France and Norway?

In the 1970s, the struggle against sexual exploitation and violence against women was carried out in many countries through active feminist movements. Actions against representations of women as "sex objects" could be violent. In 1970, for example, five British women were arrested on suspicion of having detonated a bomb under one of the BBC's TV cars in connection with protests against the Miss World competition. Feminist activists stormed the stage of the Royal Albert Hall, where the competition was taking place, and tossed stink bombs and smoke bombs.[2] In Stockholm in 1973, some thirty women from the feminist Group 8 (*Grupp 8*) invaded a porn club waving posters saying "Refuse the Humiliation—Crush the Capital's Porn Industry" and singing the song "We Will Not Be Bought, We Will Not Be Sold. MEAT MEAT MEAT!" In 1975,

[2] Rowbotham 1990, pp. 247–248.

lesbian women campaigned against a porn club in Stockholm, arguing that pornography distorts lesbianism by presenting it as a pleasure to men. They interrupted a performance by flashing the banner "Stop Humiliating Lesbian Women."[3] That same year, two West German feminists initiated an action in which they, along with 13 other women, chased a man who had raped them through the streets of Paris, and painted "Here lives a rapist" on his house.[4] In West Germany, feminists carried out militant actions against porn cinemas, sex shops, and peep shows.[5]

In Paris, there were also actions against the porn industry, as when some 20 women in 1978 attacked several porn stores and porn cinemas on the Rue de la Gaité, smashing windows and spray-painting slogans against rape, "fascist masculinity," and the sale of women's bodies. They issued a statement saying that they wanted to use more violent methods because they were tired of how the porn industry was exploiting the female body.[6]

What characterized the movement in Norway was not that feminists fought against pornography, but that their campaigns were exceptionally widespread and served to make the Joint Action against Pornography and Prostitution a popular, broad-based movement in the 1980s.

What distinguished the feminist movement in Norway was thus not the commitment to fight pornography, but that the campaign became exceptionally widespread, serving to make the Joint Action against Pornography and Prostitution a broad-based mass movement in the 1980s. What distinguished the movement in France, by contrast, was that the fight against rape dominated the political agenda of the MLF from its very inception in 1970. Why was this so? Four factors can help to explain why the fight against rape became more prominent for the MLF than for the 1970s women's movement in Norway, and why the anti-porn struggle became more important for the Norwegian movement

---

[3] Isaksson 2007, pp. 87–89.

[4] *Libération*, 31 October 1975, pp. 1 and 6.

[5] Bergman 2002, pp. 112–113.

[6] "Femmes" [Women], *Libération*, 13–15 May 1978, p. 5. The statement was signed "women from the movement," but it is unknown who they were. According to the Wikipedia article on the autonomous movement in France, on March 8, 1978, 300 women sacked and partially destroyed several porn stores and a porn cinema on the Rue Saint-Denis. Mouvement autonome en France, https://fr.wikipedia.org/wiki/Mouvement_autonome_en_France. Consulted 29 November 2019.

than for the French. The first factor concerns the perception of rape and pornography as political problems, and the second has to do with the characteristics of the women's movements in France and Norway. The third factor relates to the importance of media coverage in highlighting these issues, while the fourth deals with the mobilization of enemies and supporters.

Was Rape Seen as a More Serious Problem in France and Pornography as More of a Concern in Norway?

One explanation for why the fight against rape gained such prominence in France is simply that rape was experienced as a more serious problem there than in Norway. The study of 1970s French women's political publications reveals that women were constantly subjected to sexual harassment and rape, while the same issues are hardly mentioned in their Norwegian counterparts. It is impossible to quantify whether there were actually more rapes in France than in Norway, as official figures for these crimes do not exist. One must therefore seek answers in other ways than through quantification. Historian Georges Vigarello has pointed out the historical "relative tolerance" for rape in France—as long as the victims were not children, virgins, or married women, and unless the rape had been carried out with extreme brutality.[7] Although such tolerance for rape gradually decreased from the nineteenth century onward, we have seen that the MLF activists spent a great deal of energy in their attempts to build consensus that rape of "free" women was indeed a serious problem by, for example, comparing rape to fascism or imperialist warfare.

Vigarello offers no explanation as to why rape was historically so tolerated in France. However, Swedish historian Jonas Liliequist claims that since Antiquity, the traditional ideal of masculinity in the Mediterranean has been linked to sexual potency and assertiveness.[8] Similarly,

---

[7] Vigarello 1998, p. 7.

[8] Liliequist, Jonas (1999): "Från niding till sprätt: En studie i det svenska omanlighetsbegreppets historia från vikingtid til sent 1700-tal" [From Villain to Fop: A Study in the History of the Swedish Concept of Unmanliness from the Viking Age to the Late Eighteenth Century], in Borggren, Anne-Marie (ed.): Manligt och omanligt i ett historisk perspektiv [Manly and Unmanly in Historical Perspective]. Stockholm: Forskningsrådsnämnden, report 99:4.

according to Liliequist, the Nordic ideal of masculinity has been associated with bravery and strength rather than sexual insistence. Although the whole of France cannot, strictly speaking, be defined as part of the Mediterranean, one should not overlook the fact that this historic ideal of masculinity can help explain the highly charged notion of men's sexual "insistence" toward rejecting women as part of the "erotic game" still prevalent in the 1970s. This notion was rarely referred to in Norway during the same period, except in "men's magazines." When renowned lawyer Alf Nordhus, in a 1977 article in one such magazine, *Nye Alle Menn*, claimed that a drunk girl who gets into a car with a group of young men and embraces one of them invites rape, he faced savage criticism in the Norwegian mainstream media.[9] The fact that Norwegian activists did not take up the fight against rape to the same degree as their French companions might be attributable to the fact that they did not consider the cultural acceptance of rape to be an equally serious problem. Consequently, they directed their energy at addressing another issue that challenged the notion of women as "sex objects"—namely, pornography.

In any case, evidence suggests that pornography was perceived as a bigger problem in Norway than in France. In the second half of the 1970s, pornography was much more visible in the Norwegian public space than before. The "men's magazine" *Nye Alle Menn* was launched in 1975, *Aktuell Rapport* in 1976, and *Express* in 1977, the peak year for circulation figures of porn magazines. The competition among these "men's magazines" led to aggressive marketing campaigns. Never before had the public space, including subways, been adorned with billboards for magazines that combined images of naked women with photo-reports of bloody axe-slayings. People were simply not accustomed to being confronted with such ads, and many of them responded with disgust. At about the same time, the French sex and crime magazine *Détective* began to advertise stories of sexual murders and rapes on posters outside newsagents, prompting reactions both from the women's liberation movement and from the government. In response, the government intervened by banning ads for *Détective* and forbidding the sale of it to minors, causing the demise of the magazine.[10]

---

[9] *VG*, 21 September 1977; *VG*, 19 November 1977; *Klassekampen*, 21 November 1977; *Dagbladet*, 23 November 1977.

[10] Storti 2010, p. 197.

The situation was somewhat different in regard to pornography that was less visible in the public space. Historically, France had been the "homeland" of pornography. From the eighteenth century on, French authors were the major producers of pornographic literature, a genre that was considered politically and socially subversive.[11] In the 1970s, pornography still carried a subversive image in France. Parts of the "alternative" press often published photographs, drawings, and texts containing explicit sexual content, and were continuously prosecuted by the government for violating censorship legislation.[12] In 1972, the MLF journal *Le Torchon Brûle* was actually convicted of violating the law on pornography for having printed a French translation of the American radical feminist text "The Power of the Cunt", which included an illustration of a female genitalia.[13]

Thus, the practice of the French censorship legislation was more stringent than that of Norway. In addition, the pornography on the Norwegian market in the 1970s was to a small extent linked to the politically subversive. There was no domestic tradition of pornography in the same way as in France. It was a product imported from abroad, beginning in the 1950s as part of a mass culture export from the United States, and later from Denmark, Sweden, and West Germany as well. Even those who opposed banning pornography didn't consider it subversive, but simply a commercial product.

Distinctive Features of Women's Movements in France and Norway

The fact that the women's liberation movements in the two countries placed differing emphases on the fight against rape and pornography can also be seen as an expression of distinctive features of the respective movements. The standard work on the history of ideas in Norway,

---

[11] Kraakman, Dorelies (1999): "Pornography in Western European Cultures," in Eder, Franz X., Gert Hekma, and Lesley A. Hall (eds.): *Sexual Cultures in Europe: Themes in Sexuality*. Manchester: Manchester University Press, p. 107.

[12] Guisnel 2008.

[13] *Le Torchon Brûle* no. 2, 1972. The case is discussed in *Le Torchon Brûle* no. 4, 1972. Two women who had worked with the magazine were reported, but as the magazine was made collectively, 165 women signed a letter sent to the judge claiming that they had been involved in writing the article.

Norsk idéhistorie, states that the Norwegian women's liberation movement's resistance to pornography was grounded in the notion that it "presented itself in a more puritanical version" than, for example, the Danish movement.[14] As mentioned in Chapter 1, the Danish Red Stockings Movement (*Rødstrømpebevægelsen*) hardly addressed pornography as a political issue. In this respect, however, it was the Danish movement, not the Norwegian, that differed from women's liberation movements in other Western countries. Further, in countries other than Norway, feminist activists were considered "puritanical" when they questioned power structures in heterosexual relations. The labeling of puritanism was a feature not only of anti-porn activism but also of feminist mobilization against rape, as shown in Chapter 4.

A more fruitful approach than discussing which women's movements were the most or the least puritanical is to compare the way in which the various movements raised political issues. The French MLF activists, to a much greater extent than their Norwegian counterparts, used personal testimonies of painful experiences—including rape—as the starting point of policy development, whether in written form or speeches at public meetings. This form of confession, which was also widespread in the U.S. radical feminist movement, can be understood as an expression of a Catholic cultural influence that was not present to the same degree in the traditionally Lutheran Norway. Blending with the revolutionary and intellectual style of the MLF, activists typically delved deeply into problems and analyzed and theorized them. An examination of the texts that were produced by the Norwegian women's liberation movement texts bears witness to a more practical and pragmatic way of addressing political issues. Few activists wrote about the intimate details of their own sex lives or other taboo topics. However, a presentation by the New Feminists in 1976 shows that problems in the private sphere, including sexuality and intimate relationships were (at least initially) topics of discussion in the consciousness-raising groups. The following sample is illustrative of this point:

> We were really brutal toward each other. For example, we took rounds on the topic of masturbation after quite a short time. Then, each one had to say something about the subject, and we gave each other homework

---

[14] Hompland 2003, p. 284.

for the next meeting. After such a strong start, we thought we could talk about almost anything, and we didn't have to [avoid] difficult topics.[15]

As this member of the New Feminists reported, it could be challenging to participate in consciousness-raising groups, which were neither the equivalent of group therapy nor a tool for individual liberation, but were intended to serve as a political process. Their purpose was to find out how the oppression of women worked in practice, so as to be more capable of rebelling against it. However, the way in which such consciousness-raising was to take place within the groups adhered to certain guidelines. For instance, everyone was required to say something and to respect others' statements.

In France, the attempt to organize consciousness-raising groups failed. In the standard historical work on the MLF, Françoise Picq claims that the American consciousness groups' formalism did not fit well with the "French mentality" and the dominant political culture of the period following May 1968.[16] The women could not refrain from contradicting and shouting at each other and ridiculing the views of those with alternative opinions—all of which were basic violations of the principles of the consciousness-raising group.[17] However, they were not afraid to talk and write about taboo topics based on their own experiences of abuse. In public, Norwegian women activists generally kept their discourse to a less personal and passionate level. An example that illustrates the difference between how French and Norwegian women activists addressed political issues, can be seen in their appearance as witnesses at the International Tribunal Against Crimes Against Women in Brussels in 1976. The five French witnesses (including Belgians Anne and Araceli) all told in detail about rapes they had personally been subjected to, while the one Norwegian witness in the section on rape talked about her investigation of the treatment of rape cases in the judicial system.[18]

[15] New Feminists in Oslo [1976]: "Bevisstgjøring" [Consciousness-Raising], *Kvinnenes eget verk, Oslofeministene okt. 1976. En presentasjon* [The Women's Own Creations, Oslo Feminists, Oct. 1976. A Presentation], p. 22.

[16] Picq 1993, pp. 122–124.

[17] *Le Torchon Brûle* no. 4, 1972, and no. 5, 1973.

[18] Russell and Van de Ven 1976.

Another aspect of these movements that led to the above-mentioned issues receiving different emphasis regards the importance of specific individuals. In both cases, the issues became "big" only after the fight took on the faces of the persons involved. In France, Anne and Araceli personified the campaign against rape; in Norway, the fight against pornography gained importance after Liv and Rannveig were dismissed from the Holmenkollen metro line in Oslo for having torn down promotional posters for a men's magazine. In both cases, the women were victims, though not at all the passive type. They even initiated support campaigns for themselves and against the sexual oppression of women in general, with strong support from their friends in the women's liberation movement. In Norway, however, Unni Rustad came to personify the anti-porn movement in the early 1980s. Her charismatic, generous, and straightforward character, along with her unremitting willpower, attracted the attention of both supporters and opponents, catapulting her to the status of a national celebrity.

The Importance of Media Coverage

The fact that Unni Rustad became a national celebrity, reflects the strong media interest in the anti-porn struggle in Norway. The struggle would never have become that "big" if it had not been for periods of intense media coverage first triggered by the spectacular porn burnings in 1977 and, successively, by the TV documentary "The Struggle against Porn" in 1983 and its rebroadcast in 1985. Rustad relates how, at times, she was telephoned daily by journalists who wanted to get the opinion of the Women's Front on pornography and prostitution. According to her, "It became possible for women to raise our voices; our opinions dominated in the public space; we set the premises; and we had the power to define the problem—at least part of the time."[19]

When French feminists took action against pornography, they received almost no press coverage at all, except for minor notices in the newspaper *Libération*. Of course, media coverage is essential to maintaining the activists' willingness to take on a risky project like attacking porn stores. Thus, the French media's lack of interest in MLF activities regarding pornography helps to explain why this issue did not become as prominent

---

[19] Rustad 2010.

for the movement. On the other hand, the French media devoted much attention to the campaign against rape. As we have seen, in reporting rape cases, the French media published the names of both defendants and rape victims, information that was withheld in the Norwegian media coverage of rape cases. In Norway, the media didn't inform the public in advance about rape trials, and feminist activists were thus not encouraged to protest outside the courts.

The Importance of Clearly Defined Enemies and Alliances

In order to be successful, it is essential for social movements to have clearly defined enemies. The Norwegian women's liberation movement benefited greatly from having the porn dealer and magazine owner Leif Hagen, a gangster-like personification of the Norwegian porn industry, as one of its main enemies. The MLF was less fortunate with respect to clearly defined enemies in their mobilization against both pornography and rape. In France, there was no representative of the porn industry of the caliber of Leif Hagen. The public defenders of pornography were instead intellectual, left-wing radicals such as Serge July, the editor of *Libération*. When feminists launched a campaign against the porn magazine *Détective* in 1978, July argued: "It is forbidden to forbid, also for feminists," referring to a famous 1968 slogan.[20] With their anti-authoritarian ideals and sexual liberation projects, the so-called "pornophiles" on the left were tougher adversaries for feminists to relate to than the vulgar and convicted "Porno-Hagen." The advantage of having such a clearly defined enemy, evidently helped to make the anti-porn struggle a big issue in Norway.

In the MLF campaign against rape, individual rapists were not designated as enemies. Rather, the enemies were society, patriarchal structures, and, for the class-struggle feminists, the "bourgeoisie." Given such abstract enemies, it can be difficult to identify the best target of attack. One strategy was to make the courts symbols of patriarchal and bourgeois power. By protesting outside courthouses where rape trials took place, the campaigners wanted to show solidarity with the victims. The problem was that this tactic could also be interpreted as a campaign for punishment. The vague identification of the enemy was probably instrumental

---

[20] Storti 2010, p. 197.

in causing many feminists to judge the campaign against rape a failure once it had gained traction in the political elite and the judicial system. However, not all feminists agreed that the campaign was unsuccessful, since rape began to be taken more seriously as a social problem. Simone de Beauvoir was among those who criticized feminists who suffered from conscience pangs because of the conviction of rapists. She argued that reforms strengthening the position of women was "a path to revolution."[21] Once rape was condemned as a crime, society signaled that this ancient threat to women was no longer acceptable.

Supporters and alliance partners are crucial to the success of social movements, but in the MLF there was widespread concern about the alliances becoming too broad. When, despite this attitude, the movement received support from groups that were politically aloof from them—for example, Soviet-oriented Communists, right-wing Gaullists, and liberal humanists—it was not generally appreciated by MLF activists. Acceptance was easier to handle for the Norwegian women's movement, which generally valued allies. Initially, however, some feminists opposed cooperating with Christians against pornography, but this changed once the latter, through their adherence to the Joint Action against Pornography and Prostitution, adopted feminist and anti-capitalist arguments. One reason why the fight against pornography was so successful, was that it gained widespread support and that the activists of the women's liberation movement appreciated such acknowledgment. Anti-porn activists who collected petition signatures felt it was far easier to get the approval of so-called "ordinary" women for the fight against pornography, than it was for calls for abortion on demand and free day care for all children. The success of the Joint Action, which eventually garnered the backing of almost 40 organizations from virtually every corner of Norwegian civil society, provides evidence of the great support to be gained from "ordinary" people (Fig. 5.1). To oppose pornography required no particular ideological or theoretical justification; it was sufficient to react with disgust and think of it as "filthy" and to feel personally offended and angered by it. In addition, the fact that the porn industry was rife with criminal activity gave the anti-porn movement a moral advantage.

The combination of these four dimensions—to repeat, the experience that rape and pornography were serious problems, the character of the

21 de Beauvoir 1977, p. 11.

Fig. 5.1 Text: In Norway, the alliance against pornography was broad. Here are leaders of the Oslo chapter of the Women's Joint Action against Pornography. From the left: Unni Rustad of the Women's Front, Olaug Storløkken from the Center Women, and Åse Bollmann from the Norwegian National Women's Council. The photo is taken during a so-called confrontation meeting the Women's Joint Action organized in *Folkets Hus* (People's House) in Oslo November 21, 1978, to which "Porn Hagen" refused the invitation (Photo: Unknown ©The Norwegian Labour Movement Archives and Library [Arbark] [Reprinted with permission])

women's liberation movement, the media coverage, and the importance of enemies and alliances—worked hand in hand to make the fight against rape more prominent in France, and the anti-porn struggle more vital in Norway.

Breakthrough

The women's liberation movement's mobilization against sexual abuse and the exploitation of women led to changes in attitudes. The public debates on gender roles and sexuality also included the voices of men who confronted what they perceived as negative aspects of the male role, including the myth that men have uncontrollable sexual urges that women have the duty to satisfy. In France, the "wall of silence" about rape was broken. It became commonplace for rape victims to tell about the abuse they had been subjected to, and even to report it to the police. Following the passage of new laws on rape from 1980 to 1987, the number of reports thereof almost doubled: while 1886 rapes were reported in 1980, the number had risen to 3196 by 1987.[22] According to political scientist Janine Mossuz-Lavau, the police and the courts treated rape victims with greater respect than before. Further, the traumas they struggled with following rape were widely recognized by society in general, and the government developed health services for rape victims and initiated campaigns against rape. It became less common for rapists to claim that rape was intended as a joke.

In Norway, the anti-porn struggle made it more acceptable among leftists of both sexes to say that they were against pornography, even though voices were still being raised in criticism of the anti-porn movement as puritan. However, the voices that condemned pornography with phrases such as "Away with the pornography plague, love is pure" and "Norway—remember Sodom and Gomorrah" were no longer audible in public. The feminists' framing of pornography as oppressive to women had become the quintessential message of the resistance against pornography, even in environments that had traditionally not assigned women's liberation great importance. Unlike in the United States, where Christian conservatives during the Ronald Reagan era of the 1980s were on the verge of taking over the anti-porn movement while simultaneously opposing abortion and gay rights, leftist feminist activists retained control over the Norwegian anti-porn movement.[23] Thus, organizations that were affiliated with the Joint Action, including the Norwegian Agrarian Women's Association and various Christian women's organizations, adopted a feminist stance toward pornography. In addition to the basic slogan of "No to the Sale of Women," the Joint Action demanded Yes to sex education and erotica, and "No to porn's exploitation of lesbians and other minorities."

[22] Mossuz-Lavau 1991, p. 225.

[23] On "The Feminist Sex Wars" in the United States in the 1980s, see Bronstein 2011, pp. 294–308.

These changes in attitude in both France and Norway—all the result of the women's liberation movement's campaign—demonstrate how the struggles served as learning processes not only for the activists themselves, but also for broader segments of society.

The breakthrough for the women's liberation movement's framing of sexual exploitation and violence against women as serious societal problems, was made possible by political conditions that were favorable to new feminist demands. By the second half of the 1970s, the women's liberation movement was well established, had human resources at its disposal in the form of activists who had accumulated considerable political experience and organizational skills, and had established a collective identity as women activists. Another important factor in this breakthrough was that the main issue of the 1970s women's liberation movements—the fight for the right to abortion on demand—had led to more liberal abortion laws. The principle of a woman's right to make decisions about her own body, which underpins the claim for abortion on demand, could easily be transferred to the fight against sexual exploitation. In other words, the right to choose whether or not to bear a child is not fundamentally different from the right to choose whether or not to have sex.

State Feminism in Norway and France

After several years of political mobilization, the women's liberation movement's framing of discrimination against women as structurally and culturally conditional and thus susceptible to political change, was recognized by large segments of society, including the political elite. In Norway, the early 1980s were the heyday of "state feminism" in the sense that the government listened to and institutionalized women's organizations' demands "from below," including gender quotas in government bodies and affordable child care facilities.[24] Women's organizations were linked to the government through the Norwegian Equality Council, which in turn increased their funding. Later, the Equality Council was shut down, and the funding of women's organizations decreased. According to political scientist Beatrice Halsaa, women's organizations' space to maneuver weakened from the end of the 1980s onward. Paradoxically, as the gender equality policy was institutionalized, the government tended

[24] Skjeie 2013, pp. 29–43.

to perceive women's organizations less as political stakeholders.[25] Talking about "women's interests" became less legitimate as gender equality policies moved in a gender-neutral direction. Simultaneously, the authorities increased the funding of organizations of ethnic minorities and LGBT organizations, and—from the 2000s on—to gender equality work aimed at men which was institutionalized through the foundation REFORM, the Resource Center for Men.[26]

In France, following 25 years of right-wing governments, François Mitterrand and the socialists came to power in 1981. A new Ministry for Women's Rights was created under the leadership of the socialist and feminist Yvette Roudy. The ministry represented a new form of French state feminism with which feminist associations such as Choisir and the League for Women's Rights (*Ligue du droit des femmes*, LDF) cooperated. Roudy succeeded in instituting gender equality reforms, including the introduction of contraception guidance, continuing education opportunities for women who wanted to enter male-dominated professions, and covering the costs of abortions funded by the Social Security Administration. (Previously, women had had to pay for abortions.)[27] Roudy also lobbied for the adoption of an anti-sexist law, one of the LDF's main demands, but failed to gain sufficient parliamentary support for it.[28] As the Ministry for Women's Rights' budget was very modest, there developed a rivalry among women's organizations over funding.

Loosely organized feminists were skeptical of the new "state feminism" in the belief that it would harm the true women's struggle. Their anarchist methods had worked better when the "enemy" was in power, according to researcher Claire Duchen.[29] However, their uncompromising style isolated them politically well before the Mitterrand presidential term.[30]

---

[25] Halsaa, Beatrice (2013): "Muligheter for mobilisering: stat og kvinnebevegelse" [Opportunities for Mobilization: State and Women's Movement], in B. Bråten and C. Thun (eds.): *Krysningspunkter. Likestillingspolitikk i det flerkulturelle Norge* [Intersections. Gender Equality Policy in Multicultural Norway]. Oslo: Akademika forlag, p. 74.

[26] Op. cit., p. 66.

[27] Duchen 1986, p. 128.

[28] Picq 2008.

[29] Duchen 1986, pp. 138–139.

[30] Picq 1991, p. 39.

The organizations that proved viable when the utopian post-1968 movements faded in the late 1970s, were precisely those that were *organizations*, such as LDF and Choisir, and not the loosely organized groupings that were vulnerable to fluctuations in activity level. The French form of state feminism made the feminist landscape generally more "organized" than it was in the 1970s, meaning that the groups were registered as associations with elected boards and political programs.

SUCCESS WITH A BITTER AFTERTASTE

Women's organizations demanded legal reforms to bolster the fight against rape and pornography. French feminists demanded an anti-sexist law that defined rape as a crime against women, while Norwegian anti-porn activists sought an amendment that banned women-discriminatory pornography. Although laws were introduced, they were not framed according to the wishes of the movements. The new laws were compromises that had been formulated in gender-neutral terms. Thus, some activists interpreted the amendments as attempts to pacify women and halt their collective mobilization. It may seem conspiratorial to doubt the sincerity of the mainly female politicians who championed the legislative changes in Norway and France. However, it is evident that the women's political mobilizations against pornography and rape declined after the new laws were passed. This was particularly apparent in Norway.

Indeed, following the introduction of the new law on pornography in 1985, the activity level of the Joint Action significantly decreased. There were periods when the porn debates flared up again in the media, as in 1989, when the Women's Front in Stavanger organized the much-visited mobile exhibition "Porn and Myths." In 1997, the Joint Action decided at its annual meeting to mark its 20th anniversary by closing down the organization. Apart from Legal Aid for Women (*Juridisk rådgivning for kvinner*, JURK), no organizations from the radical part of the women's movement remained to represent the working committee of the Joint Action, which consisted of the Norwegian Teachers' Association (*Norsk Lærerlag*), the Christian Democratic Party's Women's Association (*Kristelig folkepartis Kvinner*), the Christian Democratic Party's Youth

(*Kristelig Folkepartis Ungdom*), the Center Youth (*Senterungdommen*), and independents.[31]

The reason for the decline in anti-porn activism after the new porn law was enacted in 1985, was more complex than simply that the law provided a calming effect. On the one hand, the radical wing of the women's liberation movement was considerably weakened in the late 1980s. On the other, it turned out that the new pornography law did not lead to a significant change in legal practice. When activists reported pornography that they believed violated the law, the reports were most often dismissed by the police, a circumstance that served to demotivate those who thought that the law could be used to combat all pornography. Also, the anti-porn struggle had inflicted personal costs. Former activists have stated that they simply could not bear to study pornography any longer, because it ruined their own emotional and sexual lives. Thus, they opted either to work on other political issues or to become politically passive. Even though the new law was not intended to have a pacifying effect, it certainly underscored the fact that the anti-porn struggle was entering another phase.

RAPE AND PORNOGRAPHY
AS GENDER-POLITICAL ISSUES IN THE 2010S

The mobilization of the women's liberation movement failed to bring an end to either rape or pornography. There exist no valid figures to indicate whether or not the number of rapes has increased since 1980. In France, the government estimates that about 86,000 women are raped each year.[32] Less than 10 percent of the rapes are reported to the police, and only two percent of rapists are convicted. In Norway, a government-appointed committee in 2008 estimated that between 8000 and 16,000 rapes and rape attempts occur each year.[33] Figures from Statistics Norway

---

[31] FA D-0004 Administrative Archive 1984–1988, ABA.

[32] Présentation Collectif Féministe Contre le Viol [Feminist Collective Presentation Against Rape], https://cfcv.asso.fr/. The information that follows is from this brochure.

[33] NOU 2008: 4. *Fra ord til handling* [Norwegian Official Report 2008: 4. From Words to Action]. Referenced in Kruse, Anja Emilie, John-Filip Strandmoen, and Kristin Skjørten (2013): *Menn som har begått voldtekt—en kunnskapsstatus* [Men Who Have Committed Rape—*The State of Knowledge*]. Oslo: Nasjonalt kunnskapssenter om vold og

showed that, in 2011, there were 1213 rape reports. Of these, 108, or just below nine percent, resulted in sentencing. According to a report from the Norwegian center for violence and traumatic stress studies (NKVTS), between 10 and 15 percent of Norwegian women, and between one and three percent of Norwegian men, have experienced rape or serious sexual trauma during their lifetimes. In most cases, the abusers are men who know the person they are abusing. The report concluded that the high number of dismissed rape reports and the low rate of prosecution and conviction in rape cases, indicate that the claims of many rape victims are not believed by the police and the judicial system.[34]

There is no doubt that the sheer amount of pornography has increased since the 1980s. Indeed, sales of so-called men's magazines dropped drastically in the years when the anti-porn struggle raged most intensely in Norway. But the decline may also be attributed to the fact that porn users switched from printed material to porn movies once private video players became widespread in the 1980s. With the advent of the Internet in the 1990s, pornography gained a new channel of diffusion and became more easily accessible than ever. In 2006, researchers found that, worldwide, there were 4.2 million online porn sites, pulling in a total of $97 billion in revenue per year. This change in technology also brought with it magazines and analogue movies, including the roughly 11,000 porn movies produced in Hollywood each year.[35]

French and Norwegian Feminists of the 2010s

More than four decades after feminists placed sexual exploitation and violence against women on the gender-political agenda, how did their successors in the 2010s relate to these issues? How did feminist organizations in France and Norway frame rape and pornography in the 2010s, and what strategies did they pursue? What were the differences and similarities between the French and Norwegian feminist organizations

traumatisk stress (Norwegian Center for Violence and Taumatic Stress Studies) (NKVTS), p. 30.

[34] Kruse, Strandmoen, and Skjørten, 2013, p. 121.

[35] Johnson, Jennifer A. (2011): "Mapping the Feminist Political Economy of the Online Commercial Pornography Industry: A Network Approach," *International Journal of Media and Cultural Politics*, vol. 7, no. 2.

regarding these matters? And how had the movements changed since the 1970s and 1980s?

Far more people labelled themselves as feminists in the 2010s than in the 1970s, and it would be too comprehensive to enumerate all the variations of feminism across the feminist landscape in France and Norway, not least because much feminist activity is online and through social media. Moreover, France, which has more than ten times the population of Norway, has many more feminist organizations than does Norway, and dozens of these work specifically against sexual exploitation and violence toward women. To find out what the successors of the 1970s feminist movement think and do in this policy area, three French and two Norwegian feminist organizations were selected for examination for this study. They were not chosen because they were representative of all feminists in their respective countries, but because they were particularly politically dedicated and organized in fighting sexualized oppression and violence against women, if in different ways. The three French organizations chosen were *Osez le féminisme!* (Dare Feminism!, abbreviated OLF), *Collectif Féministe Contre le Viol* (Feminist Community Against Rape, or CFCV), and *Le Mouvement du Nid* (The Nest Movement). The two Norwegian organizations selected were *Kvinnefronten* (The Women's Front) and *Kvinnegruppa Ottar* (The Feminist Group Ottar).

First, a very brief summary of these groups' foundings. *Osez le féminisme!*, OLF, was formed by a new generation of feminists in 2009 and counted 26 local chapters by 2017. *Collectif Féministe Contre le Viol*, CFCV, was established in 1985 after several women had been raped at metro stations and other public places in the Paris region, without any passersby intervening. On March 8, 1986, with financial support from the Ministry of Women's Rights, CFCV launched a free hotline for rape victims. Since then, the CFCV has collected more than 50,000 testimonies from victims of sexual violence.[36] *Le Mouvement du Nid* is a support center for prostitutes working to bring to the public eye the violence of prostitution. The Norwegian Women's Front has, as we have seen in previous chapters, been a key women's political actor in Norway

---

[36] Ninety-six percent of these are from girls and women, and in 99% of cases the abuser is a man. Half of the cases now concern victims who are minors. *Présentation Collectif Féministe Contre le Viol* [Feminist Collective Against Rape], https://cfcv.asso.fr/le-collectif-feministe-contre-le-viol-cfcv/. In Chapter 3 we saw that in 1977 an action group against rape with the same name was created.

250 T. R. KORSVIK

since the 1970s. The Feminist Group Ottar was formed in 1991 by dissenters from the Women's Front who thought the organization had become too passive in the anti-porn struggle, among other things.[37]

The information on these organizations was collected differently. In the case of the OLF, the CFCV, and the Women's Front, their elected boards responded collectively by e-mail. The spokesperson for *Le Mouvement du Nid* was Claudine Legardinier, a feminist journalist and activist who works for the organization. She responded by e-mail, while the leader of the Feminist Group Ottar, Ane Stø, was interviewed in person.[38] It can be noted that all the interviewed representatives were too young to have participated in the 1970s women's movement.

The activists from the five feminist organizations were asked about the position of rape and pornography in their politics, and how they understand and explain these phenomena. They were also asked about the strategies they use to ensure that their policies achieve results, and whether it is difficult or easy to obtain support for them.

In contrast to the 1970s and the 1980s, the French and Norwegian feminist organizations had become more similar in the 2010s in terms of the way they organized themselves and how they framed sexual exploitation and violence against women. French feminist associations of the 2010s resembled the Norwegian organizations more than they did in the 1970s, insofar as they were more tightly organized and more focused on cooperation and alliances with other groups. But there were also differences, one of which relates to the position of rape and pornography as political matters. While the fight against rape was already fundamental to French feminist organizations in the early 1970s, it was not until much later that it achieved a similar prominence for Norwegian feminists. By the 2010s, however, there were recurring campaigns and demonstrations calling for women's legal protection in rape cases, as well as Internet campaigns urging women and girls to come forward to relate abuses

---

[37] Korsvik, Trine Rogg (2006): "Historien om Kvinnegruppa Ottar" [History of the Feminist Group Ottar], *Ottar* nos. 2–3.

[38] E-mail from Eléonore Stévenin-Morguet, former spokesperson for the OLF, 6 September 2017; email from Alison Boyer, CFCV office assistant, 3 August 2017; e-mail from Cathrine Linn Kristiansen, member of the Kvinnefronten national council 15 August 2017; e-mail from Claudine Legardinier, 31 June 2017; interview with Ane Stø, 23 June 2017. See also the organizations' websites: http://osezlefeminisme.fr; http://www.cfcv.asso.fr; http://www.kvinnefronten.no; http://www.mouvementdunid.org; http://kvinnegruppaottar.no.

they had been subjected to, including *#jegharopplevd* (#I have experienced), *morketall.no* (hidden statistics.no) by the Women's Front, and the transnational #metoo campaign.[39]

In 2016, the so-called Hemsedal case led to major protests in several Norwegian cities.[40] The case involved an 18-year-old girl who, in a drugged state at a holiday resort in the Hemsedal mountains, had been subjected to sexual abuse by three adult men who had filmed the event. The girl reported the rape, but the three men claimed they thought she had consented, and were eventually acquitted. In a "first" for the Norwegian experience, the girl, Andrea Voll Voldum, told her story in the media and even published the names of the three men on Facebook. The case received massive media coverage, and in January 2017, Andrea and another young victim of rape, June Holm, established a foundation called *Vi Tror deg* (We Believe You).[41] Although modern internet technology helped to spread the message, the campaign of Andrea and June bear a striking similarity to the way in which the fight against rape became a major issue in France after Anne and Araceli told their story and launched a campaign against rape.

In terms of pornography, the situation is somewhat the opposite. In Norway, feminist activists have been mobilizing against pornography continuously since the late 1970s, albeit with varying intensity. The activists from the Women's Front and the Feminist Group Ottar who were interviewed were very conscious of the historic anti-porn struggle, which peaked in the 1980s, and voiced their pride in continuing that struggle. The French activists, for their part, claimed that it is only recently that they have prioritized the fight against pornography, viewing it as an extension of their attempt to combat prostitution.

---

[39] https://twitter.com/hashtag/jegharopplevd; http://www.morketall.no.

[40] The case received massive media coverage. See, for example, "Andrea (21) om demonstrasjonene: Blitt større enn jeg hadde trodd" [Andrea (21) About the Demonstrations: Became Bigger Than I Thought], NRK, 8 August 2016; https://www.nrk.no/norge/demonstrasjoner-mot-voldtekts- frikjennelse-1.13078384. Consulted 15 January 2018.

[41] http://www.vitrordeg.com/.

The Framing of Rape and Pornography

In the 2010s, French and Norwegian feminist organizations shared a relatively similar framing of rape and pornography. Activists from both countries claimed that rape and pornography are interconnected and explained these phenomena as manifestations of a patriarchal culture in which women are degraded and subordinated because of their sex. Both French and Norwegian activists emphasized cultural aspects rather than characteristics of the individual abusers. They used terms such as "rape culture," "porn culture," and "pornification of the culture."[42] According to the OLF, rape culture revolves around what is called a "continuum of violence," which includes sexist jokes, everyday sexism, sexual violence, sexual harassment, domestic violence, and feminicide, that is, the murder of girls and women around the world because of their sex.[43] With regard to pornography, OLF described it as a "pornographic system" and a "system of oppression." Both the Norwegian and French feminist organizations were inspired by British-American sociologist and radical feminist Gail Dines's analyzes of "porn culture." Dines emphasizes the violence that women in the porn industry are exposed to, describing how the eroticization of violence has consequences for the sex lives of both porn users and their partners.[44]

Another shared feature of the French and Norwegian feminist activists was their emphasis on the connections between pornography and prostitution. This framing was also apparent in the 1970s and 1980s, but met with greater acceptance in the 2010s due to the fact that, in recent years, Norwegian and French feminist organizations had campaigned for the criminalization of the Johns in prostitution—but not of those who sell sex. In Norway, this demand was made by the women's movement as

---

[42] See the articles "La culture du viol" [The Culture of Rape], https://feministo clic.olf.site/la-culture-du-viol/; "L'érotisation du viol et de son impact psychotrauma-tique, primée aux Césars" [The Eroticization of Rape and Its Psycho-Traumatic Impact, Awarded to the Cesars], https://feministoclic.olf.site/lerotisation-viol-de-impact-psycho traumatique-primee-aux-cesars/; "Rocco et les médias: une histoire de fascination" [Rocco and the Media: A Story of Fascination], https://feministoclic.olf.site/rocco-medias-his toire-de-fascination/.

[43] "Les féminicides dans le monde: un système" [Feminicides Worldwide: A System], https://feministoclic.olf.site/les-feminicides-dans- le-monde-un-systeme/.

[44] Dines, Gail (2010): *Pornland: How Porn Has Hijacked Our Sexuality*. Boston: Beacon Press.

early as in 1980, as we saw in Chapter 4. In France, the feminist mobilization to criminalize the Johns began only in the 2000s. In 1999, Sweden became the first country to introduce a prostitution law that criminalized clients and not those who sell sex. In 2008, the Norwegian parliament passed a similar law, to take effect in 2009. A comparable prostitution law, which took effect immediately, was adopted by the French National Assembly in April 2016. This law is more far-reaching than the Norwegian one, as it not only prohibits the purchase of sexual acts, but also involves improving support schemes for prostitutes, strengthening sex education among youth, and mandating awareness courses for sentenced clients on the harmful effects of prostitution.[45] In both countries, pimping, defined as making money from the prostitution of others, has been prohibited for many years—unlike, for example, in Germany.

The connection between pornography and prostitution described by the interviewed feminist activists is related to cultural and economic conditions. According to Claudine Legardinier, pornography and prostitution are both symbols of patriarchy and means of maintaining sexist and racist hierarchies that promote the message that women should remain submissive. Both the Norwegian and French activists emphasized that pornography and prostitution are major capitalist industries that profit financially from others engaging in sex acts: "Porn is prostitution in front of the camera," Ane Stø stated. Legardinier held that pornography does not become fiction even if it is filmed; on the contrary, the filming entails the multiplication of the act of prostitution, through unlimited distribution. For 30 years, Legardinier took testimony from women with experience in prostitution, several of whom had also acted in porn movies. According to Lergardinier, women who have engaged in porn movie-making report experiencing even more violence than do women in prostitution, including gang rapes and torture. Legardinier maintained that the two industries feed each other in the sense that the prostitution clients are inspired by pornography, which she regards as propaganda for rape. According to a study by the Feminist Community

---

[45] In contrast to the term "purchase of sexual services" used in Norway, the French prostitution law uses the term "achat d'acte sexuel" [purchase of a sexual act]. Loi n° 2016-444 du 13 avril 2016 visant à renforcer la lutte contre le système prostitutionnel et à accompagner les personnes prostituées [Law no. 2016-444 of 13 April 2016 to Strengthen the Fight against the Prostitution System and to Support Prostituted Persons]. Légifrance, https://www.legifrance.gouv.fr/affichTexte.do?cidTexte=JORFTEXT0000323 96046&categorieLien=cid.

Against Rape, CFCV, many of the victims of abuse that the organization has been in contact with have told about how pornography played a part in the acts of abuse inflicted on them. Watching a porn movie could trigger such abuse, or the abuse was filmed and eventually became available online.[46]

Strategies and Forms of Protest

There were frequent feminist campaigns against rape in France and Norway in the 2010s, including street protests, participation in public debates, and Internet campaigns. One of the first campaigns of the OLF following its establishment in 2009 was targeted at rape, and was pursued in collaboration with other feminist organizations, including the CFCV. The campaign "Rape: Shame Must Switch Sides" (*Viol: la honte doit changer de camp*) received a great deal of media attention. In 2016, the OLF launched a campaign against abusers, #StopAggressors (*#StopAgresseurs*).[47] In Norway, the online campaign of the Women's Front, "I am a hidden statistic—morketall.no" (*Jeg er et mørketall—morketall.no*) has collected and published anonymous reports from victims of abuse. The Women's Front, like the Feminist Group Ottar and other feminist organizations, advocates amending existing rape legislation by introducing "active consent." That is, instead of defining rape as a perpetrator's use of violence or threats to coerce a victim into providing sex, or abusing a person who is "unconscious or for other reasons unable to oppose the act," rape ought to be defined as sex without consent. Hence, the perpetrator must prove that there was consent, rather than the victim having to prove that there was not.[48]

In terms of strategies for combating rape and pornography, there were certain differences between the French and Norwegian feminist activists. The French seemed to be more concerned with the importance of changing the language than the Norwegians, who in turn were

---

[46]"Le système pornographique dans la stratégie des agresseurs" [The Pornographic System in the Strategy of the Aggressors], Collectif Féministe contre le Viol, 2016.

[47]www.contreleviol.fr; http://osezlefeminisme.fr/osez-le-feminisme-lance-la-campagne-stopagresseurs/.

[48]Schultze-Florey, Sunniva: "Derfor trenger vi lov om samtykke" [That Is Why We Need a Law of Consent], Feministisk Initiativ, November 2, 2016, https://www.femini stiskinitiativ.no/blog/2016/11/02/derfor-trenger-lov-samtykke/.

more concerned with changing the legislation. Language is power, and the OLF had, for example, carried out a campaign in which they challenged euphemisms for abuse, including replacing the saying "he is fond of women," with "he is an abuser." To make visible men's violence against women, they insisted on using the term "male violence" rather than "violence against women" because they felt that the latter term renders the perpetrators invisible. Regarding pornography, the OLF called it "the pornographic system," while *Le Mouvement du Nid* labeled it "filmed prostitution" or "filmed sexual exploitation."

The French activists prioritized changing the language to make the oppression visible. Although Gail Dines's concept of "porn culture" was adopted by the Norwegian activists, they seemed less concerned with linguistic changes than with legislation. The Feminist Group Ottar did advocate, for example, for the introduction of a law regarding online porn blockers. Porn blockers would require those who want to watch pornography to take deliberate action to get to see it—for example, contacting the Internet Service Provider and requesting access to porn sites. Ane Stø held that online porn blockers could harm the financial interests of the porn industry.

An important difference between the Norwegian and the French feminist organizations, as mentioned earlier, is that it was only after the introduction of the law banning the purchase of sexual acts, in 2016, that French feminists began campaigning against pornography. According to Claudine Legardinier, they would never succeed in getting the new prostitution laws adopted if they were running a parallel struggle against pornography. Since 2016, however, all three French feminist organizations interviewed for this book have begun to focus on this policy area. In the summer of 2016, the OLF put out its first press release against pornography in connection with the launch of a porn version of PokémonGo by the porn company Jacquie et Michel, in which the challenge is to rape women.[49] Since then, the OLF has published several articles critical of pornography on its website. However, the representative of the OLF claimed that the organization was aware that it had not yet devised an effective strategy for gaining maximum attention in the fight

---

[49] "'Niquez les toutes': le viol, un jeu d'enfants pour Jacquie et Michel" ["Fuck Them All": Rape, a Children's Game for Jacquie and Michel], OLF, http://osezlefeminisme.fr/niquez-les-toutes-le-viol-un-jeu-denfants-pour-jacquie-et-michel/.

against pornography. The OLF wanted to establish closer cooperation with feminists outside of France.

Regarding the question of Legardinier's experience in addressing the fight against pornography as a feminist issue—in particular, whether it is hard or easy to gain support—she answered that she didn't know much about such support, but that she considered it a chore to bring on board the more than 40 feminist organizations they partnered with against prostitution.[50] Despite admitting the difficulties of combating pornography, she was cautiously optimistic. She felt that it was easier to campaign against pornography nowadays than it was 10–20 years ago, because feminists have developed "solid analyzes of prostitution." Although the group's strategies were poorly developed at the time of the interview in 2017, *Le Mouvement du Nid* had clear objectives. It aimed at supporting victims of pornographic violence, ending abuses that occurred on porn movie sets, and conducting awareness-raising activities, including the education of young people through sex education and gender equality courses. The prostitution legislation of 2016 included in its objectives the teaching of students—from secondary school to higher education—about sexual violence, the dangers of prostitution, and the rights of victims of abuse. Legardinier claimed that *Le Mouvement du Nid* wanted to use this law to strengthen its sex education program in schools.

According to Stø, the anti-porn struggle was weak at the time of her interview. Nevertheless, she talked about alliances internationally and nationally. The Feminist Group Ottar collaborated with American and British feminists through the *Stop Porn Culture* network and also planned closer cooperation with Swedish feminists. Ottar had hosted several anti-porn conferences and, like the Women's Front, had produced informational material on pornography, primarily aimed at youth. The strategy that Ottar devised to combat pornography was to emphasize its harmful effects on children and adolescents—in other words, the strategy that had gained prominence in Norway back in the 1950s (cf. Chapter 2). Stø recognized that this strategy was a signal that feminists were on the defensive regarding the porn issue because the porn industry and "porn culture" had become stronger than before. At the same time, she held that the appropriate strategy was to start from the concern that pornography

---

[50] For an overview of the 46 partners in the fight against prostitution, see Nos partenaires [Our Partners], http://www.mouvementdunid.org/Nos-partenaires.

was affecting children's and young people's view on sex, and that pornography had consequences for public health and society. Further, Stø believed that the campaigns against rape could serve to bring greater attention to pornography. She pointed out that in several of the gang rape cases referred to in the media, the sexual abuses had been filmed, a circumstance she thought reflected an inspiration from pornography. Yet, she maintained that the old slogan that "pornography is the theory, and rape is the practice" was "too categorical," and thus Ottar had abandoned it. Stø was concerned that the strategy for fighting pornography must be to set limits on what may be regarded as legitimate profit-making enterprises and to campaign against "porn culture" and the porn industry, rather than against the individual porn user. She believed in the necessity of consciousness-raising work regarding the negative aspects of the porn industry, including how porn actors are physically and mentally destroyed, even though their participation is "voluntary."

Although there were differences in the political strategies of the French and Norwegian feminist organizations interviewed for this book, there were nonetheless commonalities, such as the belief that the prostitution laws ought to have consequences for pornography legislation. Because it is forbidden in both countries to make money on the prostitution of others, the activists argued that this legislation could be applied to the porn industry.

Impact and Resistance

When feminist activists related their experiences in fighting rape and pornography, their reports could be characterized as mixed. They all expressed a feeling of having been listened to, especially with respect to violence against women as a societal problem. According to the representative of the Women's Front, the women's movement had achieved "many victories," including the fact that violence is no longer seen as a private matter, that its work for crisis shelters for abused women and support centers against incest is recognized, and that the Sex Purchase Act "sets limits on what society accepts."

The representative of the OLF held that the organization was recognized by, for example, being represented on the French Council for Gender Equality (*Haut Conseil à l'Égalité entre les femmes et les hommes*), a "state feminist" institution that had no parallel in Norway. In addition, an OLF member served as deputy head of *Centre Hubertine Auclert*, a gender equality center for the Paris region Île-de-France. The organization was satisfied with its high media visibility and claimed to have succeeded in getting the term "rape culture" used in broad circles outside the feminist movement.

At the same time, both the French and Norwegian feminists complained about the attitudes toward victims of sexual violence. It was still a problem that girls and women who had been raped were regarded as accomplices in what they had been exposed to, as revealed in the focus on their behavior or clothing as explanations for rape. Both French and Norwegian feminists claimed that rape was not being taken seriously enough either by the police or the judiciary. According to the Women's Front, the lack of men actively engaged in the struggle to change men's attitudes toward women and sexual violence was a problem. They also viewed it as a problem that neither the political parties nor male politicians "stand on the barricades of women's legal security."

Publicizing the fight against pornography met with challenges in both countries. According to Ane Stø, it was easier to garner sympathy concerning "trafficking, cynical pimps, and exploitation of poor women from Eastern Europe" than for the fight against pornography, because the latter often tended to revolve around "people's sex lives, tastes, and preferences." Stø regretted that the anti-porn struggle wasn't more robust, but believed the problem was first and foremost a question of resources. With limited financial means and no employees, the Feminist Group Ottar had to make hard choices when prioritizing the struggles it intended to pursue. A few years earlier, Ottar had initiated the campaign *Stopp pornokulturen* (Stop Porn Culture), which had some success in the media, but it didn't have the resources to run two organizations.[51] Stø pointed to a survey in Norway showing that 65% of the respondents were against pornography. "More people are against pornography than you'd think," she said.

Legardinier and Stø both held that powerful moneyed interests were the main enemy in the fight against pornography. Legardinier claimed that although more and more people had become aware of the abuses by the porn industry and the negative effects of pornography, "it is a protected industry." According to her, the French intellectual environment is very concerned with freedom of speech and fear of censorship, which made it

---

[51] Stopp Pornokulturen [Stop Porn Culture], http://stopp-pornokulturen.no/.

difficult to take action against pornography. Stø also emphasized that the current situation was significantly more challenging than in the 1980s, given that most pornography can be found online rather than available in the form of magazines and films in kiosks and grocery stores. It is more difficult to act against pornography on the Internet, and also easier for those who are not interested to avoid online porn. Stø argued that it was easier back in the 1980s when Leif Hagen personified the porn industry; today, however, "porn moguls sit abroad and are more intangible." To attack them requires hackers, but there are not as many opponents to porn among them, she reasoned. However, she vowed that she would happily resort to civil disobedience in the fight against the porn industry.

Another obstacle in the anti-porn struggle, as held by Stø, was the difficulty in criticizing what people perceive as private acts affecting individuals' sex lives. Further, more women in the 2010s declared their support for pornography, talking about their porn use, and even producing pornography. Stø had no illusions about the possibility of making "feminist porn." She said she had seen examples of it and considered it "just as violent and sexist as mainstream porn," the only difference being that women are directing it. Stø thought a general societal problem that served to make the anti-porn struggle more difficult, was that people today are "paralyzed and less willing to sacrifice anything for the cause." In the 1980s, people more firmly believed that they could change social conditions through organizing. Today, Stø believes that people, including feminists, have become "more conformist and afraid of being outed."

OLD AND NEW CHALLENGES

Several of the issues related to the difficulty in addressing sexual abuse and pornography was also discussed in the 1970s and 1980s. However, the feminist activists interviewed in 2017 seemed to care less than their predecessors about defending themselves against allegations of puritanism, authoritarianism, and man hating. Nevertheless, politicizing sexuality and imposing restrictions on it can still be understood as expressions of exactly this. Attention to sexual abuse can also be interpreted as seeing women as eternal victims and all men as abusers. The desire to place restrictions on pornography is frequently seen as an attack on freedom of speech.

Puritanism and Totalitarian Ideology

Resistance to pornography has often been seen as a manifestation of a puritan view of sexuality. The argument is that pornography can be liberating because it removes taboos surrounding sexuality. When radical women activists in the 1970s began to protest women's role as objects of pleasure in pornographic images, many liberals interpreted the movement as being against sex, not as a struggle for another non-oppressive woman-liberating sexuality.[52] Since the feminist anti-porn fight began in Norway in the 1970s, a battle has raged over the concept of puritanism. Opponents of porn have argued that they are not puritans; on the contrary, it is pornography that is a "trueborn child of puritanism. Of a sexually hostile culture that has banished the erotic portrayal to the porn ghetto [...] [spreading] millennials-old attitudes on sexuality as a forbidden, sinful, and shameful part of our lives," as stated in the Women's Front's "magazine to make you horny" in the summer of 1983.[53]

By 2017, the interpretation of the fight against rape as an expression of puritanism had begun to seem peculiar. Back in the 1970s, however, it was not uncommon in France for women activists to be seen as puritan when they began their fight against rape. Historian Christine Bard explains this as a reaction on the part of sexual liberals who saw the campaign against rape as an attack on what they thought was a successful sexual revolution. One of the slogans of 1968 was "enjoy without restriction," and the general belief was that sexuality would be liberated as a positive force if all restrictions were removed.[54] When women demanded the right to refuse sexual advances—in other words, to restrict men's sexual behavior—some men reacted negatively. According to Bard, many men simply became angry when feminists pointed out that power relations and domination continued to exist between the sexes despite the sexual revolution. In addition, when feminists wanted to use the judicial system to end rape, it was, in the view of many sexual liberals, not just an expression of puritanism, but also of a totalitarian ideology.

An interesting parallel between France and Norway is the position taken by sexologists in these debates. In both countries, sexologists have

---

[52] Rowbotham 1990.

[53] I.W.: "Solidaritet i kampen mot skammens industri" [Solidarity in the Fight Against the Industry of Shame], *Kvinnejournalen* no. 5–6, 1983, p. 8.

[54] Bard 1999, pp. 301–328.

been very critical of the women's movement's mobilizations against sexual exploitation. In the 1970s, for example, the well-known French sexologist Michel Meignant stated that women have a subconscious desire to be raped.[55] In Norway, sexologist Thore Langfeldt characterized the resistance to pornography as an expression of "sexual hostility," while his colleague Berthold Grünfeld claimed it was based on "intense man-hatred."[56] In both countries, sexologists in the 1970s advocated decriminalizing adults' sexual intercourse with children.[57] The criticisms by sexologists of the way that the women's liberation movement was politicizing sexual abuse, may be seen as an expression of these professionals' self-image as defenders of sexual freedom and opponents of restrictions on sexuality. But the criticism may also be interpreted as a manifestation of psychology and psychiatry as traditionally male-dominated disciplines that took men as the norm, a theory proposed by Norwegian psychologist Hanne Haavind.[58]

Man Hatred

When female activists have politicized men's sexual exploitation of women, they have not only been accused of being puritan and totalitarian, but also of being hateful. The accusation of being motivated by is obviously intended to delegitimize their cause. By portraying the activists as irrational, one doesn't need to take the issue seriously. Especially in Norway, when the anti-porn campaign gained momentum in 1983, the criticism of feminist activists as man haters was intense in the media.

---

[55] Quoted in Storti 2010, p. 115.

[56] *Klassekampen*, 24 October 1977, p. 2; Berthold Grünfeld: "Seksuelle overgrep og vold mot kvinner og barn" [Sexual Abuse and Violence Against Women and Children], *Aftenposten*, 15 October 1983, p. 2. See also Langfeldt, Thore (2005): *Erotikk og fundamentalisme. Fra Mesopotamia til Kvinnefronten* [Eroticism and Fundamentalism. From Mesopotamia to the Women's Front]. Oslo: Universitetsforlaget, p. 117.

[57] Thore Langfeldt: "Har barn seksualitet" [Do Children Have Sexuality], *Arbeiderbladet*, 27 September 1977; "Quelques pétitions ou lettres ouvertes pas sans équivoque" [Some Unclear Petitions or Open Letters], https://web.archive.org/web/20050404190912/; http://www.decadi.com/dignaction/Fpetit.html.

[58] Haavind, Hanne (1998): "Understanding Women in the Psychological Mode: The Challenge from the Experience of Nordic Women," in D. von der Fehr, A.G. Jónasdóttir, and B. Rosenbeck (eds.): *Is There a Nordic Feminism?* London and New York: Routledge, pp. 243–271.

Swedish sociologist Carin Holmberg, who has analyzed a number of statements in the media about feminists' alleged man hatred, points out that only female feminists are referred to as man haters. Male feminists, who, for example, oppose pornography, are not similarly accused.[59] Holmberg shows that castration—the fear of the "dick pliers"—is often mentioned in connection with feminists' alleged hatred of men. She argues that the link between castration and the women's struggle is part of society's collective subconscious, which revolves around men's fear of losing privileges associated with their sex. On a more symbolic level, castration anxiety can be understood as a fear that women no longer want to have sex with men, which leads to anxiety about being sexually rejected, Holmberg claims.[60] The Norwegian socialist politician Finn Gustavsen's fear that the anti-porn struggle had created a climate in which "dynamic men" were turned into "muttering silent eunuchs" clearly illustrates this castration anxiety.[61] That the anti-porn fight was an attack on masculinity was perhaps the most important counter-argument in the Norwegian pornography debates. In 1977, for example, the famous lawyer Alf Nordhus claimed that he regretted that men supported the women's fight against pornography and rape: "These must be men who accept their function as peaceful domestic pets in a home under female domination. Then I react as a man," he said in an interview with the newspaper *VG*.[62]

Women as Victims and Men as Abusers

Since the women's liberation movements began to draw attention to men's violence and sexual abuse of women, critics have held that this viewpoint leads to women being seen as passive victims and all men as abusers. This criticism has also been voiced by women who identify—or have identified in the past—as feminists.[63]

[59] Holmberg, Carin (1996): *Det kallas manshat. En bok om feminism* [It Is Called Man Hatred. A Book on Feminism]. Göteborg: Anamma Böcker AB, p. 53.

[60] Op. cit., p. 55.

[61] Finn Gustavsen: "Pornodebatten—en avsporing" [The Porn Debate—A Derailment], *Arbeiderbladet*, 3 November 1983.

[62] *VG*, 19 November 1977, p. 18.

[63] Picq 2008.

In 1983, Birgit Bjerck, a member of the New Feminists, wrote about how, in the early 1970s, the New Feminists had not regarded women as victims.[64] The focus at that time was on women's strength and how women, through collective struggle, empowered each other. Back then, they lacked knowledge about sexual abuse and the maltreatment of women. Once feminists established crisis shelters for battered and raped women in the late 1970s, the revelation of the extent of sexual violence and abuse shocked many feminist activists. The newfound knowledge about the experiences of abused and raped women made them aware that some women were so oppressed that they were unable to rebel or to extricate themselves from an abusive relationship. Thus, according to Bjerck, the task became to show solidarity with these women so that they could shed their role as victims. In 1983, Bjerck acknowledged that it was possible that the women's liberation movement overstated the extent of sexual violence and abuse in the face of such "new and frightening knowledge." Still, one could not ignore the fact that abuse occurred: "If the women's liberation movement did not address this issue, it would betray not only the victims of violence, but also the hope of women's liberation," Bjerck stated.[65]

Unlike the Norwegian feminists, the French MLF activists perceived women as victims right from the start. "Women, slave-bound, humiliated /Bought, sold, raped," goes a strophe of the MLF anthem from the early 1970s (see Chapter 2).[66] In the campaign against rape, the basic demand was to recognize raped women as victims and not as responsible for having provoked the rape. The responsibility for rape should be placed on the abuser. The aim was for victims to stop being victims, a goal that would be achieved through women's solidarity. This understanding of the relationship between victim and abuser was gradually adopted by Norwegian feminist activists. "Recognizing that women are oppressed—that women are actually victims—is a fundamental prerequisite for rebellion and solidarity," the feminist Liv Finstad argued in

---

[64] Bjerck, Birgit (1983): "Mannen som problem" [The Man as Problem], in B. Bjerck et al. (eds.): *Mannfolk! 13 innlegg om mannshat i kvinnebevegelsen* [Men! 13 Contributions on Man Hatred in the Women's Movement]. Oslo: Pax Forlag, pp. 17–18.

[65] Bjerck 1983, p. 18.

[66] "Hymne du MLF" [MLF Anthem], *Le Torchon Brûle* no. 3 [1972].

1983.[67] Offering "harsh descriptions of women's lives" was, according to Finstad, not the same as depriving women of the ability to revolt, but could, on the contrary, sow the seeds of revolt. For example, abused women could call crisis shelters and discover that their problems were not unique to them, but a shared condition that they could act against.

Critics of the women's movement did, however, claim that their focus on women as victims of abuse entailed seeing them as passive and lacking responsibility. But does passivity necessarily accompany the position as victim?[68] Being a victim can be associated with helplessness and paralysis, but when viewed as the relationship between an abuser and a victim, the victim position does not say anything about individual characteristics.[69] Sociologist Unn Conradi Andersen has shown how the victim position changes meaning depending on who is defined by others or is defining her/himself as a victim.[70] For resourceful people, the victim position can be attractive. Andersen uses the Norwegian debates on same-sex marriage in the 2000s as a case in point. One of the most vehement opponents of the new marriage law was the philosopher (and former New Feminist) Nina Karin Monsen, who, in the debates, had no trouble portraying herself as a victim of the "system" and the "gay-friendly" state. Defining oneself as a victim presupposes that there is a perpetrator. This victim positioning does not necessarily imply passivity, but it does serve to place the responsibility for the problem with someone else. The stigma attached to the position of abused women as victims can be explained as a manifestation of their lack of sufficient financial and social power to be in a position of being a victim in the "right," non-passive way.[71]

[67] Liv Finstad: "Kvinnen på en pidestall?" [The Woman on a Pedestal?], *Klassekampen*, 28 November 1983, p. 4.

[68] Korsvik 2014, pp. 11–43.

[69] Ericsson, Kjersti (1993): "Kvinner som handlende offer" [Women as Victims with Agency], *Nordisk tidsskrift for Kriminalvidenskab*, vol. 80, no. 2, pp. 76–85; Høigård, Cecilie (1993): "The Victim as Expert: Active and Captive," *Nordic Journal of Women's Studies (NORA)*, vol. 1, no. 1, pp. 51–64.

[70] Andersen, Unn Conradi (2013): "Offerposisjonens paradoks. Offentlig debatt om surrogati" [The Paradox of the Victim Position. Public Debate on Surrogacy], *Tidsskrift for samfunnsforskning* no. 1, pp. 31–62.

[71] For example, the perspective that the status of the victim automatically leads to passivity is prominent in Jessen, Liv (ed.) (2007): *Det ideelle offer. Tekster om prostitusjon* [The Ideal Victim. Texts on Prostitution]. Oslo: Koloritt forlag. The book highlights the

Another aspect of the criticism of the attention to women as victims, revolves around the portrayal of all men as abusers. Activists of the women's liberation movement in France, Norway, and elsewhere, have argued that all men are potential rapists. Claiming that rape is something any man is capable of is controversial but can be interpreted in several ways. It can be understood literally: that all men, without exception, can commit abuses, and that it is within the biological nature of men to be abusers. The statement can, however, be understood in a more indirect way: that abusers do not differ from other men in terms of social background, age, ethnicity, and so forth, and that there are features of the male role that make rape and other abuses possible. This alternative interpretation was widespread in the French and Norwegian women's liberation movements. As the revolutionary French feminists put it: "Although not all men rape women, all who rape women are men, and these men are 'manifestations of the patriarchal system.'" Although this interpretation is based on the fact that the role of men is socially constructed and thus susceptible to change, it also implies viewing men as a group and acknowledging the political significance of gender.[72] Hence, men as a group are expected to take responsibility for other men's sexual abuse, a mandate that can clearly be seen as unfair (Fig. 5.2).

British historian and feminist Sheila Rowbotham has argued that the increased awareness of men's sexual violence against women of the 1970s and 1980s was useful because it brought clarity to otherwise complex and contradictory social relationships and mechanisms of oppression.[73] The problem was that the attention also led many feminists to see heterosexuality as inherently controlling and violent, and to perceive all men as abusers, and thus as enemies. In Rowbotham's view, some feminists adopted a conservative pessimist vision of the aggressive male role as more or less predetermined in men from birth. In the United States, a tendency that the women's movement referred to as *cultural feminism*

---

victim position as a serious problem for prostitutes, which is seen as a counterpart to choices of action.

[72] The fact that women's gender-political organization causes men to be defined as a group of gender-political significance is a key point in Eduards, Maud (2002): *Förbjuden handling: om kvinnors organisering och feministisk teori* [Forbidden Action: About Women's Organizing and Feminist Theory]. Malmö: Liber.

[73] Rowbotham, Sheila (1990): *The Past Is Before Us: Feminism in Action Since the 1960s*. Harmondsworth: Penguin Books, p. 253.

Fig. 5.2 "THIS MAN IS A RAPIST THIS MAN IS A MAN." Poster from 1980. Who made the poster is not known, but it is signed "mouvement de libération des femmes," by then copyrighted by Psych et Po. Thus, the journal of Psych et Po, *Des femmes en mouvements hebdo,* warned that this was not a legitimate MLF poster. It claimed that the poster encouraged hatred against men and that it was motivated by a "sexist terrorist feminism" that would not stop rape. Facsimile from the article "Non au terrorisme sexiste!," *Des femmes en mouvements hebdo* no. 35, July 11, 1980

insisted that women's and men's sexuality is essentially different; whereas the former is gentle and loving, the latter is aggressive and violent.[74] This essentialist approach to gender and sexuality was less visible in the French and Norwegian feminist women's movements, which were largely influenced by Simone de Beauvoir's analysis of gender differences as socially constructed and thus changeable.[75] The political campaigns manifested a belief in the possibility of changing attitudes concerning violence and sexual exploitation of women. In both countries, the movements proposed concrete remedies, such as demanding that rape be taken seriously by the judiciary, increasing funding for crisis shelters for abused women, or enforcing laws against violent pornography.

The Limits of Freedom

In any discussion about pornography, the question of freedom is fundamental, whether in the form of sexual freedom or freedom of speech. The pornography debates in Norway in 1983 brought about interesting perspectives concerning freedom and tolerance for so-called "deviants," who, according to Tor Erling Staff, the lawyer for the "porn king" Leif Hagen, were in need of violent and child pornography to "relieve the pressure."[76] The term "deviant" is no longer in public use, but the debates over the dilemmas of freedom are still relevant: freedom for one can result in lack of freedom for others. Arguing against attorney Staff in 1983, lawyer and peace activist Fredrik S. Heffermehl articulated the dilemma in this way: "Freedom for someone to gorge themselves on depictions of sexual violence and rape means that others have to be in constant fear, stay indoors, or be abused."[77] Heffermehl argued that "free pornography and prostitution provide a climate in which women don't have freedom" because "they are held down in a constrained and oppressed position, without willpower and life goals of their own,

---

[74] Bronstein 2011, pp. 38–62 and 269–275.

[75] An important exception was Psych et Po, which distanced itself from this form of feminism and emphasized the inherent sexual differences between women and men (cf. Chapter 2). It is also highly possible that some feminists held a negative view of men's sexuality without writing about it in public.

[76] *Aftenposten*, 29 October 1983.

[77] Fredrik S. Heffermehl: "Enøyet frihetsbegrep hos Staff" [Staff's Narrow-Minded Concept of Freedom], *Aftenposten*, 2 November 1983.

as objects of use and pleasure for men." Since freedom of speech was not unrestricted in terms of defamation and attacks based on race, religion, and homosexuality, Heffermehl argued that it was "reasonable that women should also soon be protected from incitement to hatred, scorn, and abuse."

The feminist journalist of the liberal newspaper *Dagbladet*, Sissel Benneche Osvold, held that there is a tendency toward gender-specific views on pornography. While women more than men identify themselves with the victims or those depicted, many men take a more theoretical approach to pornography when referring to freedom of speech and the needs of the "deviants." Osvold asked, "Are we allowed to require such efforts by fellow human beings to meet the needs of the deviants? Are we allowed to sacrifice a number of women and children because we ideally pay homage to the principle of absolute freedom of speech?"[78] She declared a willingness to identify with the victims of pornography in her statement that "To speak their cause can't possibly be to restrict freedom of speech so that it impedes our obligation to fight against abuse of power against weak groups."

As a result of feminists' political mobilization against sexual exploitation and violence against women in the 1970s and 1980s, men—to a greater extent than before—made public statements of solidarity with the victims of sex abuse. One of them, Arne Wam, a journalist and later leader of the Norwegian Committee on the Role of Men (1986–1991), will provide the final thoughts for this study. His reflections during the porn debates of 1983 on society's tolerance for sexual exploitation are still thought-provoking:

> In order to protect human dignity in society, we sometimes must exercise intolerance toward those who want to work for less freedom and more inequality. In other words, it is perhaps a question of whether we, in our society, show too much tolerance for all the injustice that does not affect ourselves. Our ability to adapt to injustice is probably greater than our solidarity with the oppressed among us.[79]

[78] Sissel Benneche Osvold: "Pornoen har også ofre" [Porn Also Has Victims], *Dagbladet*, 2 November 1983.

[79] Arne Wam: "Om menn, sex og porno: Idealer, myter—og virkelighet" [About Men, Sex and Porn: Ideals, Myths—and Reality], *Arbeiderbladet*, 6 December 1983.

References

Literature

Aanesen, Ellen (1981): *Ikke send meg til en "kone", doktor! Fra tre års fengsel til selvbestemt abort* [Do Not Send Me to a "Wife" Doctor: From Three Years of Prison to Abortion on Demand]. Oslo: Oktober.

Ågotnes, Knut (1989): *Kvar i sin dal—?: komparasjon som metode i lokalhistoriske studiar: rapport frå HIFO-seminar 14–16 oktober 1988* [Everyone His Valley—? Comparison as Method in Local History: Report from HIFO Seminar 14–16 October 1988]. Trondheim: Tapir forlag.

Andersen, Unn Conradi (2013): "Offerposisjonens paradoks. Offentlig debatt om surrogati" [The Paradox of the Victim Position. Public Debate on Surrogacy], *Tidsskrift for samfunnsforskning*, no. 1, pp. 31–62.

Århelle, Tone (1981): *Pornografiens vilkår i Norge. En undersøkelse av domstolspraksis i Oslo 1953–78*. Institutt for offentlig retts skriftserie [Conditions of Pornography in Norway. An Investigation of Court Jurisdictions in Oslo 1953–78. Department of Public Law, University of Oslo]. Oslo: Universitetsforlaget.

Artières, Philippe (2008): "Pierre Overney, le militant ouvrier assassiné" [Pierre Overney, the Assassinated Worker Activist], in P. Artières and M. Zancarini-Fournel (eds.): *68. Une histoire collective (1962–1981)* [68. A Collective History]. Paris: Éditions La Découverte, pp. 550–551.

Association du Mouvement pour les luttes feminists [Association of the Movement for Feminist Struggles] (1981): *Chroniques d'une imposture. Du mouvement*

© The Editor(s) (if applicable) and The Author(s), under exclusive   269
license to Springer Nature Switzerland AG 2021
T. R. Korsvik, *Politicizing Rape and Pornography*,
Citizenship, Gender and Diversity,
https://doi.org/10.1007/978-3-030-55639-6

de libération des femmes à une marque commercial [Chronicles of a Deception: From the Women's Liberation Movement to a Commercial Brand]. Paris [author].

Bard, Christine (1999): "Les antiféminismes de la deuxième vague" [The Anti-Feminisms of the Second Wave], in C. Bard (ed.): *Un siècle d'antiféminisme* [A Century of Anti-feminism]. Paris: Fayard, pp. 301–328.

Bard, Christine (2012): *Le féminisme au-delà des idées reçues* [Feminism Beyond Preconceived Ideas]. Paris: Éditions Le Cavalier Bleu.

Beauvoir, Simone de (1977): "Préface," in A. de Pisan and A. Tristan: *Histoires du M.L.F.* Préface de Simone de Beauvoir [The History of M.L.F: Foreword by Simone de Beauvoir]. Paris: Calmann-Lévy.

Beckwith, Karen (2000): "Beyond Compare? Women's Movements in Comparative Perspective," *European Journal of Political Research*, 37, pp. 431–468.

Beckwith, Karen (2005): "The Comparative Politics of Women's Movements," *Perspectives on Politics*, vol. 3, no. 3. pp. 583–596.

Bergen Kvinnesaksforening [Bergen Association for Women's Rights] (2007): *Vi var med... Kvinnekamp i Bergen på 1970-tallet* [We Participated ... Women's Struggle in Bergen in the 1970s]. Bergen: Bodoni Forlag.

Bergman, Solveig (2002): *The Politics of Feminism: Autonomous Feminist Movements in Finland and West Germany from the 1960s to the 1980s.* Åbo: Åbo Akademi University Press.

Bernheim, Cathy, Liliane Kandel, Françoise Picq, and Nadia Ringart (eds.) (2009): *Mouvement de Libération des Femmes. Textes premiers* [The Feminist Movement: First Texts]. Paris: Stock.

Berven, Nina, and Per Selle (eds.) (2001): *Svekket kvinnemakt? De frivillige organisasjonene og velferdsstaten* [Impaired Woman's Power? The NGOs and the Welfare State]. Oslo: Gyldendal Akademisk.

Bjarnar, Ove (1995): *Veiviser til velferdssamfunnet. Norske Kvinners Sanitetsforening 1946–1996* [Showing the Way to the Welfare Society: Norwegian Women's Public Health Association 1946–1996]. Oslo: Norske Kvinners Sanitetsforening.

Bjerck, Birgit (1983): "Mannen som problem" [The Man as Problem], in B. Bjerck et al. (eds.): *Mannfolk! 13 innlegg om mannshat i kvinnebevegelsen* [Men! 13 Contributions on Man Hatred in the Women's Movement]. Oslo: Pax Forlag.

Bjørneboe, Jens (1966): "Istedenfor en forsvarstale" [Instead of a Defense Speech], in A. Nordhus et al. (eds.): *En tråd. Seks innlegg om pornografi* [A Thread. Six Posts About Pornography]. Oslo: Pax Forlag.

Blom, Ida (2005): "Brudd og kontinuitet. Fra 1950 mot årtusenskiftet" [Rupture and Continuity: From 1950 to the Turn of the Millennium], in I. Blom and S. Sogner (eds.): *Med kjønnsperspektiv på norsk historie* [Gender Perspective on Norwegian History]. Oslo: Cappelen Akademisk Forlag.

Bonnet, Marie-Josèphe (2012): *Histoire de l'émancipation des femmes* [History of Women's Emancipation]. Editions Ouest-France.

Bourseiller, Christophe (1996): *Les Maoïstes: la folle histoire des gardes rouges français* [The Maoists: The Crazy Story of the French Red Guards]. Paris: Plon.

Brantenberg, Gerd, et al. (eds.) (1976): *Forbrytelser mot kvinner. Internasjonalt tribunal i Brussel 4.–8. mars 1976* [Crimes Against Women: International Tribunal in Brussels 4–8 March 1976]. Oslo: Kvinnehuset, Tribunalgruppa.

Bronstein, Carolyn (2011): *Battling Pornography: The American Feminist Anti-pornography Movement, 1976–1986*. Cambridge: Cambridge University Press.

Bussemaker, Jet (2007): "Vocabularies of Citizenship Since the 1970s," in R. Lister et al. (eds.): *Gendering Citizenship in Western Europe*. Bristol: The Policy Press.

Chaperon, Sylvie (1995): "La radicalisation des mouvements féminins français de 1960 à 1970" [The Radicalization of the French Feminist Movements from 1960 to 1970], *Vingtième Siècle. Revue d'histoire*, vol. 48, no. 1, pp. 61–74.

Chaperon, Sylvie (2000): *Les années Beauvoir (1945–1970)* [The Years of Beauvoir (1945–1970)]. Paris: Fayard.

Choisir la cause des femmes (1976): *Viol. Le procès d'Aix* [Rape. The Process in Aix]. Paris: Gallimard.

Cixous, Hélène (1975): "Le rire de la Méduse," *L'Arc*, vol. 61, pp. 39–54. English: "The Laugh of the Medusa," *Signs*, vol. 1, no. 4 (Summer 1976), pp. 875–893.

Clayhills, Harriet (1980): "Kvinneforbund, Norsk" [Women's Federation, Norwegian], *PaxLeksikon*. Oslo: Pax Forlag.

Corbin, Alain, Jean-Jacques Courtine, and Georges Vigarello (eds.) (2006): *Histoire du corps* [History of the Body], vol. 2, *Les mutations du regard. Le XXe siècle* [The Mutations of the Gaze: The Twentieth Century]. Paris: Éditions du Seuil.

Dahlerup, Drude (1998): *Rødstrømperne. Den danske Rødstrømpebevægelses udvikling, nytænkning og gennemslag 1970–1985* [Red Stockings: The Danish Red-Stockings Movement's Development, Innovation and Impact, 1970–1985]. Copenhagen: Gyldendal.

Dahlerup, Drude, and Brita Gulli (1985): "Women's Organizations in the Nordic Countries: Lack of Force or Counterforce?," in E. Haavio-Mannila (ed.): *Unfinished Democracy: Women in Nordic Politics*. Oxford: Pergamon Press.

Dahlgren, Lars, and Bengt Starrin (2004): *Emotioner i vardagsliv & samhälle. En introduktion till emotionssosiologi* [Emotions in Everyday Life and Society: An Introduction to the Sociology of Emotions]. Malmö: Liber.

Danielsen, Hilde (ed.) (2013): *Da det personlige ble politisk. Den nye kvinne- og mannsbevegelsen på 1970-tallet* [When the Personal Became Political: The

New Women's and Men's Movement in the 1970s]. Oslo: Scandinavian Academic Press/Spartacus Forlag.

Davidsen, Silje, and Trine Rogg Korsvik (2006): "Hippielegen. Jan Greves psykedeliske kamp mot autoriteter" [The Hippie Doctor. Jan Greve's Psychedelic Struggle Against Authorities], in T.E. Førland and T.R. Korsvik (eds.): *1968. Opprør og motkultur på norsk* [1968. Rebellion and Counterculture in Norway]. Oslo: Pax Forlag.

Dreyfus, Michel (1995): *Histoire de la CGT. Cent ans de syndicalisme en France* [The History of CGT: One Hundred Years of Syndicalism in France]. Bruxelles: Éditions Complexe.

Duchen, Claire (1986): *Feminism in France: From May '68 to Mitterand*. London, Boston, and Henley: Routledge & Kegan Paul.

Duclert, Vincent (2008): "Le PSU, une rénovation politique manquée?" [PSU, a Missed Political Renovation?], in P. Artières and M. Zancarini-Fournel (eds.): *68. Une histoire collective (1962–1981)* [68. A Collective History]. Paris: Éditions La Découverte, pp. 152–157.

Dupont [Delphy]: "L'ennemi principal," "Libération des femmes, année zéro" [The Main Enemy, Liberation of Women, Year Zero], *Partisans* (Summer 1970). The article was translated into English in *Gender Issues*, no. 1 (1980).

Dworkin, Andrea (1981): *Pornography—Men Possessing Women*. London: The Women's Press.

Eduards, Maud (2002): *Förbjuden handling: om kvinnors organisering och feministisk teori* [Forbidden Action: About Women's Organizing and Feminist Theory]. Malmö: Liber.

Enger, Lill Kristin (2007): "Straffbar pornografi—Har jussen endret seg i takt med samfunnet?" [Criminal Pornography—Has Law Changed According to Societal Changes?], Master's thesis, Faculty of Law, University of Oslo.

Eyerman, Ron, and Andrew Jamison (1991): *Social Movements: A Cognitive Approach*. Cambridge: Polity Press.

Ezekiel, Judith (2002): "Le Women's Lib: Made in France," *European Journal of Women's Studies*, vol. 9, no. 3, pp. 345–361.

Ferree, Myra Marx, and Aili Mari Tripp (eds.) (2006): *Global Feminism: Transnational Women's Activism, Organizing, and Human Rights*. New York: New York University Press.

Ferree, Myra Marx, and Carol McClurg Mueller (2004): "Feminism and the Women's Movement: A Global Perspective," in D.A. Snow, S.A. Soule, and H. Kriesi (eds.): *The Blackwell Companion to Social Movements*. Malden, MA: Blackwell.

Ferree, Myra Marx, and David A. Merrill (2004): "Hot Movements, Cold Cognition," in J. Goodwin and J. Jasper (eds.): *Rethinking Social Movements: Structure, Meaning, and Emotion*. Lanham, MD: Rowman & Littlefield.

Finstad, Liv, Lita Fougner, and Vivi-Lill Holter (1981): "Oslo-prosjektet. Erfaringer fra to års forsøksarbeid blant barne- og ungdomsprostituerte i Oslo 1979–1981" [The Oslo Project. Experiences from Two Years of Experiential Work Among Child and Youth Prostitutes in Oslo 1979–1981]. Barnevernskontoret i Oslo [Oslo Child Protection Office], 28 September 1981.

Finstad, Liv, Lita Fougner, and Vivi-Lill Holter (1982): *Prostitusjon i Oslo* [Prostitution in Oslo]. Oslo: Pax Forlag.

Fjeld-Pedersen, J.J. (1976): *Hele verden på et sølvfat* [The Whole World on a Silver Platter]. Oslo: Zenith Forlag.

Flynn, Thomas (2012): "Jean-Paul Sartre," in E.N. Zalta (ed.): *The Stanford Encyclopedia of Philosophy*. http://plato.stanford.edu/archives/spr2012/entries/sartre/.

Førland, Tor Egil, and Trine Rogg Korsvik (eds.) (2006): *1968. Opprør og motkultur på norsk* [1968: Rebellion and Counterculture in Norway]. Oslo: Pax Forlag.

Førland, Tor Egil, and Trine Rogg Korsvik (2008): *Ekte sekstiåttere* [Real Sixty-Eighters]. Oslo: Gyldendal Akademisk.

Fouque, Antoinette, et al. (eds.) (2008): *Génération MLF 1968–2008* [The MLF Generation 1968–2008]. Paris: Des femmes—Antoinette Fouque.

Friedan, Betty (1981): *The Second Stage*. New York: Summit Books.

Furre, Berge (1991): *Vårt hundreår. Norsk historie 1905–1990* [Our Century: Norwegian History 1905–1990]. Oslo: Samlaget.

Gammelsrud, Terje: "Cupido—hvordan det begynte" [Cupido—How It Started], *Cupido*, 28 October 2014 (updated 2019), https://www.cupido.no/articles/3262.

Gamson, William A. (1992): "The Social Psychology of Political Action," in A. Morris and C. McClurg Mueller (eds.): *Frontiers in Social Movement Theory*. New Haven: Yale University Press.

Godbolt, James (2008): *Den norske vietnambevegelsen 1967–1973* [The Norwegian Vietnam Movement 1967–1973]. DPhil thesis, Faculty of Humanities, University of Oslo.

Goffman, Erving (1974): *Frame Analysis: An Essay on the Organization of Experience*. Cambridge: Harvard University Press.

Goodwin, Jeff, James M. Jasper, and Francesca Poletta (eds.) (2001): *Passionate Politics: Emotions and Social Movements*. Chicago: University of Chicago Press.

Goodwin, Jeff, and James Jasper (eds.) (2004): *Rethinking Social Movements: Structure, Meaning, and Emotion*. Lanham, MD: Rowman & Littlefield.

Goodwin, Jeff, James M. Jasper, and Francesca Poletta (2006): "Emotional Dimensions of Social Movements," in D.A. Snow et al. (eds.): *The Blackwell Companion to Social Movements*. Malden, MA: Blackwell.

Greenwald, Lisa (2019): *Daughters of 1968: Redefining French Feminism and the Women's Liberation Movement*. Lincoln, NE: University of Nebraska Press.

Gros, Frédéric (2008): "L'antipsychiatrie: la folie change de visage" [Antipsychiatry: Madness Changes Face], in P. Artières and M. Zancarini-Fournel (eds.): *68. Une histoire collective (1962–1981)* [68. A Collective History]. Paris: Éditions La Découverte, pp. 592–599.

Guadilla, Naty García (1981): *Libération des femmes: le M.L.F.* [Women's Liberation: The M.L.F.]. Paris: Presses Universitaires de France.

Gudevold, Rolf J. (1978): *Strømninger: mellom tradisjon og apokalypse: tidskritikk 1966–1978* [Currents: Between Tradition and Apocalypse: Time Criticism 1966–1978]. Oslo: Lanser Forlag.

Guisnel, Jean (2008): "Trois fois rien sur *Libération*" [Three Times Nothing on Liberation], in P. Artières and M. Zancarini-Fournel (eds.): *68. Une histoire collective (1962–1981)* [68. A Collective History]. Paris: Éditions La Découverte, pp. 688–692.

Gulbrandsen, Barbara, Lise Kari Holøs, and Anne Britt Bertelsen (1984): "Pornografi. Menns makt – kvinners avmakt? " [Pornography. Men's Power—Women's Powerlessness?], Term paper in journalism. Oslo: Norwegian School of Journalism.

Gulli, Brita M. (1979): "Flat organisering" [Flat Organization], *Pax Leksikon*. Oslo: Pax Forlag, pp. 352–356.

Gulli, Brita M. (2007): "Gjenerobring av kvinnekroppen" [Reclaiming the Female Body], Kvinnehistorie.no.

Haase-Dubosc, Danielle, et al. (2003): "An Introduction by the French Editors," in D. Haase-Dubosc et al. (eds.): *French Feminism: An Indian Anthology*. New Delhi: Sage.

Haavind, Hanne (1998): "Understanding Women in the Psychological Mode: The Challenge from the Experience of Nordic Women," in D. von der Fehr, A.G. Jónasdóttir, and B. Rosenbeck, *Is There a Nordic Feminism?* London and New York: Routledge.

Hagemann, Gro (2003): "Seksualmoral eller samfunnsmoral: stridende dirskurser i sedelighetsdebatten" [Sexual Morality or Social Morality: Conflicting Discourses in the Moral Debate], in G. Hagemann, *Feminisme og historieskriving. Inntrykk fra en reise* [Feminism and Historiography: Impressions from a Journey]. Oslo: Universitetsforlaget.

Hagemann, Gro (2004): "Norsk nyfeminisme—amerikansk import?" [Norwegian New Feminism—American Import?], *Nytt Norsk Tidsskrift*, nos. 3–4.

Halimi, Gisele (1978): "Le crime" [The Crime], in *Viol. Le procès d'Aix* [Rape: The Process in Aix]. Paris: Gallimard.

Halsaa, Beatrice (2007): "Det internasjonale kvinneåret 1975" [The International Women's Year 1975], Kvinnehistorie.no.

Halsaa, Beatrice (2013): "Muligheter for mobilisering: stat og kvinnebevegelse" [Opportunities for Mobilization: State and Women's Movement], in B. Bråten and C. Thun (eds.): *Krysningspunkter. Likestillingspolitikk i det flerkulturelle Norge* [Intersections. Gender Equality Policy in Multicultural Norway]. Oslo: Akademika forlag.

Haukaa, Runa (1982): *Bak slagordene. Den nye kvinnebevegelsen i Norge* [Behind the Slogans: The New Women's Movement in Norway]. Oslo: Pax Forlag.

Hellesund, Tone (2013): "Intimiteter i forandring—om hvordan den nye norske kvinnebevegelsen satte intimitet på dagsordenen" [Intimacy in Change—On How the New Norwegian Women's Movement Put Intimacy on the Agenda], in H. Danielsen (ed.): *Da det personlige ble politisk. Den nye kvinne- og manns-bevegelsen på 1970-tallet* [When the Personal Became Political: The New Women's and Men's Movement in the 1970s]. Oslo: Scandinavian Academic Press/Spartacus Forlag.

Hernes, Helga (1982): *Staten—kvinner ingen adgang?* [The State—Women No Access?]. Oslo: Universitetsforlaget.

Hernes, Helga Maria (1987): *Welfare State and Woman Power: Essays in State Feminism*. Oslo: Norwegian University Press.

Holmberg, Carin (1996): *Det kallas manshat. En bok om feminism* [It Is Called Man Hatred. A Book on Feminism]. Göteborg: Anamma Böcker AB.

Hompland, Andreas (2003): "Det feminiserte Norge" [The Feminized Norway], in T. Berg-Eriksen, A. Hompland, and E. Tjønneland (eds.): *Et lite land i verden. Norsk idéhistorie* [A Small Country in the World: Norwegian History of Ideas], vol. VI. Oslo: Aschehoug.

Høigård, Cecilie, and Liv Finstad (1986): *Bakgater. Om prostitusjon, penger og kjærlighet* [Backstreets: About Prostitution, Money and Love]. Oslo: Pax Forlag.

Isaksson, Emma (2007): *Kvinnokamp. Synen på underordning och motstånd i den nya kvinnorörelsen* [Women's Struggle; The View of Subordination and Resistance in the New Women's Movement]. Stockholm: Atlas.

Issorel, Irène (2000): "Le mouvement de libération des femmes vu par la presse nationale française 1970–1972" [The Women's Liberation Movement Seen by the French National Press 1970–1972]. Master's thesis in history, University of Toulouse-Le Mirail.

Jaggar, Alison M. (1983): *Feminist Politics and Human Nature*. Totowa, NJ: Rowman & Allanheld.

Jensen, Axel (1966): "Bølgen" [The Wave], in A. Nordhus et al. (eds.): *En tråd. Seks innlegg om pornografi* [A Thread. Six Posts About Pornography]. Oslo: Pax Forlag.

Jenson, Jane (1996): "Representations of Difference: The Varieties of French Feminism," in M. Threlfall (ed.): *Mapping the Women's Movement: Feminist Politics and Social Transformation in the North*. London: Verso.

Johnson, Jennifer A. (2011): "Mapping the Feminist Political Economy of the Online Commercial Pornography Industry: A Network Approach," *International Journal of Media and Cultural Politics*, vol. 7, no. 2.

Karlsen, Torill Enger (1991): "Anti-pornokampen i Norge gjennom 15 år (1974–1990)" [Anti-pornography Campaign in Norway Throughout 15 Years]. Published by the Women's Front of Norway.

Kjeldstadli, Knut (1988): "Nytten av å sammenlikne" [The Benefits of Comparing], *Tidsskrift for samfunnsforskning*, no. 5, pp. 435–448.

Klandermans, Bert (1997): *The Social Psychology of Protest*. Oxford: Blackwell.

Kocka, Jürgen (1996): "The Uses of Comparative History," in R. Björk and K. Molin (eds.): *Societies Made Up of History: Essays in Historiography, Intellectual History, Professionalisation, Historical Social Theory & Proto-Industrialisation*. Edsbank: Akademitryck.

Korsvik, Trine Rogg (2006): "Historien om Kvinnegruppa Ottar"[History of the Feminist Group Ottar], *Ottar*, nos. 2–3.

Korsvik, Trine Rogg (2008): "Sekstiåtter med rosa løpesedler. Intervju med Gerd Brantenberg" [Sixty-Eight-Year-Old with Pink Leaflets. Interview with Gerd Brantenberg], in T.E. Førland and T.R. Korsvik: *Ekte sekstiåttere* [Real Sixty-Eight-Year-Olds]. Oslo: Gyldendal Akademisk.

Korsvik, Trine Rogg (2010): "Kvinnekamp! Politiske spenninger i kvinnefrigjøringsbevegelsene i Norge og Frankrike i 1970-åra" [Women's Struggle! Political Tensions in the Women's Liberation Movements in Norway and France in the 1970s], in I. Helle, K. Kjeldstadli, and J. Sørvoll (eds.): *Historier om motstand* [Histories About Resistance]. Oslo: Abstrakt forlag.

Korsvik, Trine Rogg (2013): *"Pornografi er teori, voldtekt er praksis"*: *Kvinnekamp mot voldtekt og pornografi i Frankrike og Norge ca. 1970–1985* [Pornography Is the Theory, and Rape Is the Practice": Woman's Struggle Against Rape and Pornography in France and Norway approx. 1970–1985]. PhD thesis in history. Department of Archeology, Conservation and History, Faculty of Humanities, University of Oslo.

Korsvik, Trine Rogg (2014): "Fra offentlig skjøgevæsen til horekunder. Hundre års kollektiv mobilisering mot prostitusjon" [From Public Prostitution to Sex Buyers: One Hundred Years of Collective Mobilization Against Prostitution], *Materialisten. Tidsskrift for forskning, fagkritikk og teoretisk debatt*, no. 1–2, 2014, pp. 11–43.

Korsvik, Trine Rogg (2016): "Jentene på Holmenkolbanen. Pornokamp og 'AKP-bråk' i fagbevegelsen på 1970-tallet" [The Girls at the Holmenkollen Line: Porn Struggle and 'AKP Noise' in the Trade Union Movement in the 1970s], *Arbeiderhistorie 2016*, pp. 163–185.

Kraakman, Dorelies (1999): "Pornography in Western European Cultures," in Franz X. Eder, Gert Hekma, and Lesley A. Hall (eds.): *Sexual Cultures in Europe: Themes in Sexuality*. Manchester: Manchester University Press.

Kvam, Ragnar (ed.) (1966): *Norske sengehester. Ukyske noveller* [Norwegian Bedhorses. Unchaste Short Stories]. Oslo: Pax Forlag.

Lamont, Michèle, and Laurent Thévenot (2000): "Introduction: Toward a Renewed Comparative Cultural Sociology," in M. Lamont and L. Thévenot (eds.): *Rethinking Comparative Cultural Sociology: Repertoires of Evaluation in France and the United States*. Cambridge: Cambridge University Press.

Langfeldt, Thore (2005): *Erotikk og fundamentalisme. Fra Mesopotamia til Kvinnefronten* [Eroticism and Fundamentalism. From Mesopotamia to the Women's Front]. Oslo: Universitetsforlaget.

Larsen, IdaLou (1983): "Kjetterske tanker om samfunnets kvinnehat" [Heretical Thoughts on Society's Hate of Women], in B. Bjerck et al. (eds.): *Mannfolk! 13 innlegg om mannshat i kvinnekampen* [Menfolk! 13 Contributions About Man Hatred in the Women's Struggle]. Oslo: Pax Forlag.

Lasserre, Audrey (2010): "Les héritières. Les écrivaines d'aujourd'hui et les féminismes" [The Heiresses: Today's [Female] Writers and the Feminisms], www.revue-analyses.org, vol. 5, no. 3.

Laubier, Claire (ed.) (1990): *The Condition of Women in France 1945 to the Present: A Documentary Anthology*. London: Routledge.

Lederer, Laura (ed.) (1980): *Take Back the Night: Women on Pornography*. New York: William Morrow.

Liliequist, Jonas (1999): "Från niding till sprätt: En studie i det svenska oman-lighetsbegreppets historia från vikingtid til sent 1700-tal" [From Villain to Fop: A Study in the History of the Swedish Concept of Unmanliness from the Viking Age to the Late 18th Century], in Borggren, Anne-Marie (ed.): *Manligt och omanligt i ett historisk perspektiv* [Manly and Unmanly in Historical Perspective]. Stockholm: Forskningsrådsnämnden, report 99:4.

Lindtner, Synnøve Skarsbø (2013): "Over disk som varmt hvetebrød—Sirene og den norske populærfeminismen" [Over the Counter as Hot Wheat Bread—Sirene and Norwegian Popular Feminism], in H. Danielsen (ed.): *Da det personlige ble politisk. Den nye kvinne- og mannsbevegelsen på 1970-tallet* [When the Personal Became Political: The New Women's and Men's Movement in the 1970s]. Oslo: Scandinavian Academic Press/Spartacus Forlag.

Lindtner, Synnøve Skarsbø (2014): "Som en frisk vind gjennom stuen" – Kvinnebladet Sirene (1973–1983) og det utvidete politikkbegrepet ["A Spanking Breeze Through the Living Room"—The Feminist Magazine Sirene (1973–1983) and the Broadened Notion of Politics]. PhD thesis, University of Bergen.

Lindtner, Synnøve Skarsbø (2015): "Instead of Burning those Magazines, Maybe We Should Bring Them Home and Discuss Them with Our Husbands?," The

Feminist Magazine Sirene's Critiques of the Politics of the Norwegian Organized Women's Movement, *Ethnologia Scandinavica: A Journal for Nordic Ethnology*, pp. 158—171.

Long, Julia (2012): *Anti-porn: The Resurgence of Anti-pornography Feminism*. London: Zed Books.

Lønnå, Elisabeth (1996): *Stolthet og kvinnekamp. Norsk Kvinnesaksforenings historie fra 1913* [Pride and Women's Struggle: History of the Norwegian Association for Women's Rights 1913]. Oslo: Gyldendal Norsk Forlag.

Macey, David (1993): *The lives of Michel Foucault*. New York: Pantheon Books.

Maï (1975): "Un viol si ordinaire, un impérialisme si quotidien" [A Rape So Ordinary, an Imperialism so Everyday], *Les femmes s'entêtent* [Stubborn Women]. Paris: Éditions Gallimard, pp. 188–210.

Mazur, Amy G. (1996): *Gender Bias and the State: Symbolic Reform at Work in Fifth Republic France*. Pittsburgh: University of Pittsburgh Press.

McAdam, Doug, John D. McCarthy, and Mayer N. Zald (1996): *Comparative Perspectives on Social Movements: Political Opportunities, Mobilizing Structures, and Cultural Framings*. Cambridge: Cambridge University Press.

McAdam, Doug, Sidney Tarrow, and Charles Tilly (2001): *Dynamics of Contention*. Cambridge: Cambridge University Press.

Moksnes, Aslaug (1984): *Likestilling eller særstilling? Norsk Kvinnesaksforening 1884–1913* [Gender Equality or Unique Position? Norwegian Association for Women's Rights 1884–1913]. Oslo: Gyldendal.

Morgan, Robin (1977): "Theory and Practice: Pornography and Rape," *Going Too Far: The Personal Chronicle of a Feminist*. New York: Random House.

Mossuz-Lavau, Janine (1991): *Les lois de l'amour. Les politiques de la sexualité en France (1970–1990)* [The Laws of Love: The Politics of Sexuality in France (1970–1990)]. Paris: Éditions Payot.

Nordhus, Alf (1966): «Pornografiparagrafen», in A. Nordhus et al. (red.): *En tråd. Seks innlegg om pornografi*. Oslo: Pax Forlag.

Nordhus, Alf (1966): "Pornografiparagrafen" [The Pornography Clause], in A. Nordhus et al. (eds.): *En tråd. Seks innlegg om pornografi* [A Thread. Six Posts About Pornography]. Oslo: Pax Forlag.

Nørve, Siri (1978): "Bevisstgjøring" [Consciousness Raising], *Pax Leksikon*. Oslo: Pax Forlag, pp. 366–369.

Pavard, Bibia (2012): *Si je veux, quand je veux. Contraception et avortement dans la société française (1956–1979)* [If I Want, When I Want: Contraception and Abortion in French Society (1956–1979)]. Rennes: Presses Universitaires de Rennes.

Pennetier, Claude (2008): "PCF et CGT face à 68" [PCF and CGT Facing 68], in P. Artières and M. Zancarini-Fournel (eds.): *68. Une histoire collective (1962–1981)* [68. A Collective History]. Paris: Éditions La Découverte, pp. 336–347.

Picq, Françoise (1991): "A French Feminism," in Haase-Dubosc et al. (red.): *French Feminism: An Indian Anthology.* New Delhi: Sage.

Picq, Françoise (1993): *Libération des femmes. Les années mouvement* [Liberation of Women: The Movement Years]. Paris: Éditions du Seuil.

Picq, Françoise (2008): "Simone de Beauvoir et 'la querelle du féminisme'" [Simone de Beauvoir and "The Quarrel of Feminism"], *Les Temps Modernes,* vol. 647–648, no. 1, pp. 169–185.

Pisan, Annie de, and Anne Tristan [pseudonym for Annie Sugier and Anne Zelensky] (1977): *Histoires du M.L.F.* Préface de Simone de Beauvoir [Histories of the M.L.F: Foreword by Simone de Beauvoir]. Paris: Calmann-Lévy.

ProChoix, no. 46, 2008 [thematic issue]: "MLF le mythe des origines" [MLF the Myth of Origins], http://www.prochoix.org/pdf/Prochoix.46.interieur. pdf.

Rem, Tore (2010): *Født til frihet. En biografi om Jens Bjørneboe* [Born to Freedom: A Biography on Jens Bjørneboe]. Volume 2. Oslo: Cappelen Damm.

Remy, Monique (1990): *De l'utopie à l'intégration. Histoire des mouvements des femmes* [From Utopia to Integration: History of Women's Movements]. Paris: L'Harmattan.

Riot-Sarcey, Michèle (2002): *Histoire du féminisme* [The History of Feminism]. Paris: La Découverte.

Rodgers, Catherine (2000): "Elle et Elle: Antoinette Fouque et Simone de Beauvoir" [She and Her: Antoinette Fouque and Simone de Beauvoir], *MLN,* no. 4 (French Issue).

Rønning, Ole Martin (2005): "Kvinnekamp, imperialisme og monopolkapital. Kvinnefronten i Norge og ml-bevegelsen 1972–1982" [Women's Struggle, Imperialism and Monopoly Capital: The Women's Front in Norway and the Marxist-Leninist Movement 1972–1982], *Arbeiderhistorie,* Oslo: Arbeiderbevegelsens Arkiv og Bibliotek.

Rosen, Ruth (2000): *The World Split Open: How the Modern Women's Movements Changed America.* New York: Viking.

Roudinesco, Elisabeth (1990): *Jacques Lacan & Co: A History of Psychoanalysis in France, 1925–1985.* Chicago: University of Chicago Press.

Rowbotham, Sheila (1990): *The Past Is Before Us: Feminism in Action Since the 1960s.* Harmondsworth: Penguin Books.

Rowbotham, Sheila (1996): "Introduction: Mapping the Women's Movement," in M. Threlfall (ed.): *Mapping the Women's Movement: Feminist Politics and Social Transformation in the North.* London: Verso.

Rucht, Dieter (1996): "The Impact of National Contexts on Social Movement Structures: A Cross-Movement and Cross-National Comparison," in D. McAdam, J. McCarthy, and M.N. Zald (eds.): *Comparative Perspectives on*

Social Movements: Political Opportunities, Mobilizing Structures, and Cultural Framings. Cambridge: Cambridge University Press.

Russell, Diana E.H., and Nicole Van de Ven (1976): *Crimes Against Women: Proceedings of the International Tribunal*. Milbrae, California: Les Femmes.

Rustad, Unni (1983): "Porno er dop for redde menn" [Porn Is a Drug for Scared Men], in B. Bjerck et al. (eds.): *Mannfolk! 13 innlegg om mannshat i kvinnebevegelsen* [Menfolk! 13 Posts on Man Hatred in the Women's Movement]. Oslo: Pax Forlag.

Rustad, Unni (2007): "Kampen mot pornografi på 1970-tallet: Unni Rustad forteller" [The Struggle Against Pornography in the 1970s: Unni Rustad Relates], Kvinnehistorie.no.

Rustad, Unni (2010): "Spredte minner fra kampen mot porno" [Scattered Memories from the Struggle Against Porn], *Gnist Marxistisk tidsskrift*, no.1. https://marxisme.no/unni-rustad-2/.

Ryste, Marte (2003): "Kvinnekupp i Asker" [Women's Coup in Asker], Kvinnehistorie.no.

Schrumpf, Ellen (1984): *Abortsakens historie* [The History of the Abortion Campaigns]. Oslo: Tiden.

Siim, Birte (2000): *Gender and Citizenship: Politics and Agency in France, Britain, and Denmark*. Cambridge: Cambridge University Press.

Sineau, Mariette (2003 [1991]): "The MLF's Contribution to the Political Scene: An Unacknowledged Debt," in D. Haase-Dubosc et al. (eds.): *French Feminism: An Indian Anthology*. New Delhi: Sage.

Skjeie, Hege (2013): "Hva var statsfeminisme?" [What Was State Feminism?], in B. Bråten and C. Thun (eds.): *Krysningspunkter. Likestillingspolitikk i det flerkulturelle Norge* [Intersections: Gender Equality Policy in Multicultural Norway]. Oslo: Akademika Forlag.

Snow, David A., and Robert Benford (1988): "Ideology, Frame Resonance, and Participant Mobilization," in B. Klandermans, H. Kriesi, and S. Tarrow (eds.): *From Structure to Action: Comparing Social Movement Research Across Cultures*, in *International Social Movement Research*, vol. 1 (1988). Greenwich: JAI Press.

Sohn, Anne-Marie (2006): "Le corps sexué" [The Sexed Body], in A. Corbin, J. Courtine, and G. Vigarello (eds.): *Histoire du corps. Les mutations du regard. Le XXe siècle* [History of the Body. The Mutations of the Gaze. The Twentieth Century]. Volume 3. Paris: Éditions du Seuil.

Steinem, Gloria (1980): "Erotica and Pornography: A Clear and Present Difference," in L. Lederer (ed.): *Take Back the Night: Women on Pornography*. New York: William Morrow.

Stø, Ane, and Asta Håland (2013): "A Grassroots Story," in T.R. Korsvik and A. Stø (eds.): *The Nordic Model*. Feminist Group Ottar, pp. 15–29.

Storti, Martine (2010): *Je suis une femme, pourquoi pas vous? 1974–1979. Quand je racontais le mouvement des femmes dans Libération* [I Am a Woman, Why Not You? 1974–1979: When I Told About the Women's Liberation Movement]. Paris: Éditions Michel de Maule.

Tarrow, Sidney (1998): *Power in Movement: Social Movements and Contentious Politics.* Cambridge: Cambridge University Press.

Taylor, Verta (1995): "Watching for Vibes: Bringing Emotions into the Study of Feminist Organizations," in M. Marx Ferree and P.Y. Martin (eds.): *Feminist Organizations: Harvest of the New Women's Movement.* Philadelphia, PA: Temple University Press.

Tessem, Liv Berit and Kjetil Wiedswang (1984): *Pornorge. Krigere og kremmere på pornomarkedet i 30 år* [PorNorway. Warriors and Peddlers on the Porn Market for 30 Years]. Oslo: Universitetsforlaget.

Tilly, Charles (2004): *Social Movements 1798–2004.* Boulder: Paradigm Publishers.

Touraine, Alain (1968): *Le mouvement de mai: ou le communisme utopique* [The May Movement: Or the Utopian Communism]. Paris: Editions du Seuil.

Vigarello, Georges (1998): *Histoire du viol. XVIe–XXe siècle.* Paris: Éditions du Seuil [A History of Rape: Sexual Violence in France from the 16th to the 20th Century]. Oxford, Polity Press, 2001.

Volder, Bente, Adelheid Hommelvoll, Helen Vogt, Ulf Pettersen, Frøydis Eidheim, Unni Rustad, Marianne Sætre, and Elisabeth Bjørk (1982): *Porno* [Porn]. 2nd edition. Oslo: Friundervisningen Forlag.

Wærness, Kari (1995): "Epilog" [Epilogue], in O. Bjarnar (1995): *Veiviser til velferdssamfunnet. Norske Kvinners Sanitetsforening 1946–1996* [Showing the Way to the Welfare Society: Norwegian Women's Public Health Association 1946–1996]. Oslo: Norske Kvinners Sanitetsforening.

Welzer-Lang, Daniel (1988): *Le viol au masculin* [Masculine Rape]. Paris: Editions L'Harmattan.

Wiig, Birgit (1984): *Kvinner selv* [Women Themselves]. Oslo: Cappelen.

Zancarini-Fournel, Michelle (2004): *Le siècle des féminismes* [The Century of Feminisms]. Paris: L'Atelier.

Zancarini-Fournel, Michelle (2005): *Histoire des femmes en France: XIXe–XXe siècles* [The History of Women in France: XIXth–XXth Centuries]. Rennes: Presses Universitaires de Rennes.

Zancarini-Fournel, Michelle (2008a): "Le champ des possibles" [The Field of Possibilities], in P. Artières and M. Zancarini-Fournel (eds.): *68. Une histoire collective (1962–1981)* [68: A Collective History (1962–1981)]. Paris: Éditions La Découverte.

Zancarini-Fournel, Michelle (2008b): "L'épicentre" [The Epicenter], in P. Artières and M. Zancarini-Fournel (eds.): *68. Une histoire collective (1962–1981)* [68. A Collective History (1962–1981)]. Paris: Éditions La Découverte.

Zancarini-Fournel, Michelle (2008c): "Changer le monde et changer sa vie" [Change the World and Change Your Life], in P. Artières and M. Zancarini-Fournel (eds.): *68. Une histoire collective (1962–1981)* [68. A Collective History (1962–1981)]. Paris: Éditions La Découverte.

Zancarini-Fournel, Michelle (2008d): «Le début de la fin», in P. Artières and M. Zancarini-Fournel (eds.): *68. Une histoire collective (1962–1981)* [68. A Collective History (1962–1981)]. Paris: Éditions La Découverte.

Magazines and Newspapers

Magazines and newspapers of the women's liberation movement:
France:
Cahiers du féminisme (published by the Trotskyist party *Ligue communiste révolutionnaire*, LCR [The Revolutionary Communist League] 1977–1998).

Des femmes en mouvements – mensuel / Des femmes en mouvements hebdo (published by Psych et Po/MLF 1978–1982).

Elles voient rouge (published by feminists in the French Communist Party PCF 1979–1982).

Femmes travailleuses en lutte (published by Femmes en Lutte (Women in Struggle) 1975–1978).

F magazine (independent, 1978–1982).

Histoires d'elles (independent, 1976–1980).

L'Information des femmes (published by independent class struggle feminists 1975–1977).

La revue d'en face (published by the feminist publishing house Édition Tierce1977–1983).

Le Quotidien des femmes (published by Psych et Po 1974–1976).

Le Temps des femmes (continuation of *L'Information des femmes* 1978–1982).

Le Torchon Brûle (independent 1971–1973).

Les Nouvelles Féministes (published by Ligue du droit des femmes, LDF (League for Women's Rights) and edited by Simone de Beauvoir 1974–1977).

Les Pétroleuses (published by Pétroleuses 1974–76).

Sorcières (independent 1976–1982).

Norway:
Feministen (internal journal published by Nyfeministene [the New Feminists] 1973–?).

KjerringRåd (independent 1975–1986).

Kvinnefront (published by Kvinnefronten [the Women's Front] 1975–1982).

Kvinnejournalen (published by Kvinnefronten [the Women's Front] 1982–2004 when it changed into the feminist journal *Fett* 2004 to date).

Kvinnens årbok 1974 (1973), *Kvinnens årbok 1975* (1974), *Kvinnens årbok 1976* (1975); *Kvinnens årbok 1977* (1976) (yearbooks of the women's liberation movement published by Pax Forlag).

Lavendelexpressen (published by Lesbisk bevegelse [Lesbian Movement] 1975–1982).

Kvinnenes eget verk, Oslofeministene okt. 1976. En presentasjon [The Women's Own Creations, Oslo Feminists, Oct. 1976. A Presentation].

Oslofeministen (internal journal published by the Oslo chapter of the New Feminists, years of publishing unknown).

Sirene (independent 1973–1983).

Vi er mange (internal journal published by the Women's Front 1972 to date).

Other newspapers and magazines:
France:
Le Figaro, Le Monde, Le Nouvel Observateur, L'Humanité, Libération.
Norway:
Aftenposten, Arbeiderbladet, Dagbladet, Klassekampen, Kontrast, Nationen, Ny Tid, Røde Fane, Universitas, VG, Vårt Land.

FILM/TV

Debout! Une historie du Mouvement de Libération des femmes (1970–1980) [Get Up! A History of the Women's Liberation Movement (1970–1980)] (1999) documentary by Carole Roussopoulos.

Jag är nyfiken—en film i gult [I Am Curious (Yellow)] (1967) and Jag är nyfiken—en film i blått [I Am Curious (Blue)] (1968) directed by Vilgot Sjöman.

Kampen mot porno [The Struggle Against Porn] (1983) documentary by Ellen Aanesen, Norwegian Broadcasting Corporation (NRK), broadcast 5 October, 1983.

RADIO

"Sexreiser til Thailand. Intervju med en av deltakerne" [Sex Tours to Thailand. Interview with One of the Participants]. Ukeslutt, radio program, the Norwegian Broadcasting Corporation, 2 December 1977.

"Er det forskjell på erotikk og pornografi? Intervju med May Jacobsen og Solveig Skaare fra Kvinejournalen" [Is There a Difference Between Erotica and Pornography? Interview with May Jacobsen and Solveig Skaare from the Kvinnejournalen]. The Norwegian Broadcasting Corporation NRK's radio show Ukeslutt, 11 June 1983.

ARCHIVES

Arbeiderbevegelsens arkiv og bibliotek (The Norwegian Labour Movement Archives and Library) (ABA):
Archive of Fellesaksjonen mot pornografi og prostitusjon (FA) [the Joint Action Against Pornography and Prostitution] (1981–1997) (AAB/ARK-2582).
Archive of Kvinnefronten i Norge [the Women's Front in Norway] (1972–2001) (AAB/ARK-1584).
Archive of Inge Ås:
Uncollated unsorted material About the New Feminists (Nyfeministene), the Women's House in Oslo (Kvinnehuset) and Lesbian Movement (Lesbisk Bevegelse), including the journals *Feministen*, *LavendelExpressen* and *Oslofeministen*.
Archive of Ellen Aanesen:
Clips archive about the anti-porn struggle and recording of the TV documentary "Kampen mot porno" (1983).

Index

© The Editor(s) (if applicable) and The Author(s), under exclusive license to Springer Nature Switzerland AG 2021
T. R. Korsvik, *Politicizing Rape and Pornography*, Citizenship, Gender and Diversity, https://doi.org/10.1007/978-3-030-55639-6

Printed by Printforce, the Netherlands